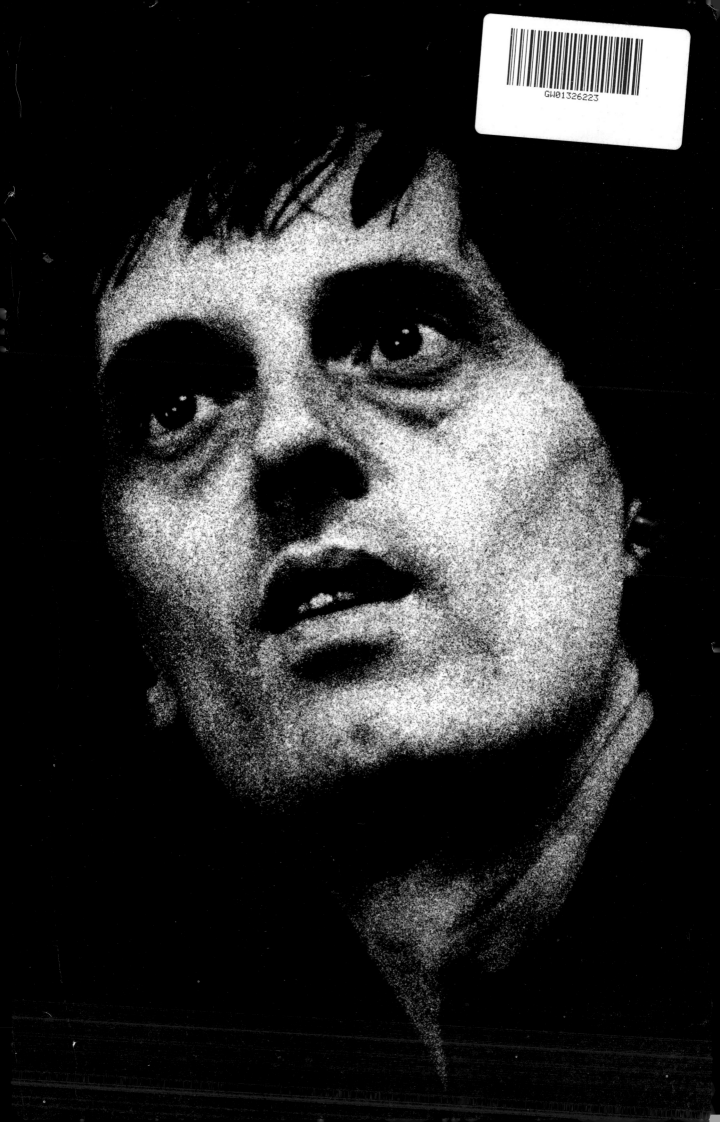

ART OF DARKNESS
THE CINEMA OF DARIO ARGENTO

First edition published by FAB Press, December 2000
This revised edition first published October 2001

3 5 7 9 10 8 6 4 2

FAB Press
Courtyard House
Mill Lane
Godalming
Surrey
GU7 1EY
England, U.K.

www.fabpress.com

edited by
Chris Gallant

A CIP catalogue record for this book is available from the British Library.

hardback:
ISBN 1 903254 07 8
paperback:
ISBN 1 903254 14 0

ART OF DARKNESS

the cinema of Dario Argento

edited by
Chris Gallant

ART OF DARKNESS

the cinema of Dario Argento

edited by
Chris Gallant

Cover designed by
Harvey Fenton

cover illustrations:
Suspiria (front)
Phenomena (back)
Inferno (inside front),
Tenebrae (inside back)

edited by
Chris Gallant

designed by
Stephen Thrower
Harvey Fenton

reviews
Chris Barber
Matthew Coniam
Roberto Curti
Robert Daniel
Mitch Davis
Chris Gallant
Julian Grainger
Mike Lebbing
Adrian Luther-Smith
Gary Needham
Kim Newman
Stephen Thrower

filmography
Julian Grainger

A **FAB PRESS** PUBLICATION

edited by
Chris Gallant

ART OF DARKNESS
the cinema of Dario Argento

primo tempo · chapters by Chris Gallant

secondo tempo · reviews

in più · reference by Julian Grainger

Introduction

by Chris Gallant

There are those who argue vehemently against taking an analytical, exploratory approach to the films of Argento. After all, why not simply allow oneself to be intrigued by their bizarrely convoluted narratives, be exhilarated by their surreal ultra-violence, or just gaze at the colourful eye-candy? One might argue that their surface-suggestive obsession with the aesthetic indicates that this on its own is enough. Those who expound Film Theory are open to accusations of missing the point. Theory is so often developed at the expense of fact, perhaps giving these films a resonance beyond their true value. So too can theorists be accused of intellectual snobbery, each opinion presuming its own cast-in-stone status as definitive, amongst the plethora of alternative accounts already on offer. So are we right in thinking that there is something beyond the films' seductive, multi-coloured surfaces that is worth considering? Or is it wallpaper?

Perhaps more than anything else, what seems to invite analysis is the placement of this body of work on an overlap between European art cinema and a genre labeled 'Exploitation'. These films disrupt what is so often perceived as an inflexible divide between the artistic and the commercial, high art and low art, forcing a surprisingly easy cohesion between the two. Preconceptions tied to Genre are thus swept aside. While the works of his American contemporaries only occasionally move the odd startled critic to bestow the complement of "thinking man's horror film" (and to many, this in itself is a contradiction in terms), Argento's films frequently win kudos through their fastidious attention to art direction and cinematography. Although inevitably aiming for commercial appeal, they seem also to target a cineliterate audience, one sensitive to context and convention.

The stylistic/narrational techniques of art cinema invite scrutiny, a premise which will form the backbone of this volume. Argento's cinema can hardly be accused of facilitating passivity in its audience. The films are full of over-determined signifiers, references which demand that these constructs be read against different contexts: in interviews, Argento himself frequently directs his audiences' attention towards the nature of the films' allusions, liberally dropping in references to painting, literature and psycho-analysis.

Of course, the problems of analysis are considerable. The director rarely explains himself to those who seek to lay bare the internal workings of his cinema, preferring to drop hints and leave them guessing: he told one writer " *I really don't like to expose too much of what's behind my films* "[1] - perhaps the very reason why his interviews so invariably leave the reader unenlightened. It is therefore tempting to come up with tidy, linear subtextual analyses and cogent, overarching interpretations - when the filmmaker himself won't comment, nothing can be proved or disproved and you can be as clever and inventive as you like. Instead, I would argue, what exists beyond the surface of the text is chaotic and anything but linear. If you're looking for a subtext, you're likely to find a rich, semi-coherent soup of dead ends, half-developed notions, tangents and digressions.

It is this appealing absence of order that I have tried to express through my own essays, which form the first part of this book, developing a series of ideas raised through the director's work, attempting to avoid neat conclusions and contrived explanations. I have also tried to steer clear of the strictly Freudian readings which the films so often encourage, simply because they represent an area already extensively covered by other writers. Instead, I hope that by considering a variety of rather different theoretical approaches, I have managed to touch on some new ground.

facing page:
Eleonora Giorgi sets out in pursuit of
forbidden knowledge in **Inferno**.

Dario Argento and daughter Asia
in the Ufizzi Gallery, filming
The Stendhal Syndrome.

The development of this project has been a long and often problematic process. In my collaboration with publisher Harvey Fenton, our 'brief' passed through any number of different incarnations. Early on, it became clear that the book would be structured as a celebration and exploration of Argento's directorial works, with his films as producer being afforded less space. *Art of Darkness* was conceived essentially as a study of authorship in his work, and while it is often rumoured that his creative and intellectual input into films such as **The Wax Mask** and **Demons 2** is substantial, I would argue that his contribution in such cases amounts to a more impersonal, finance-focused variety of box-office fodder. At a certain point it was decided that this volume would benefit from a film-by-film analysis of Argento's career, to which end we invited a number of 'guest' writers to each contribute an essay on their favourite work from the Argento *oeuvre*. With the scope of analysis thus expanded, the project took on an entirely different character.

I am of course indebted to those who agreed to lend their support, since *Art of Darkness* can now be considered a showcase for some of the most incisive commentary on Dario Argento that has emerged over recent years. There is now inevitably a diversity of perspective, which the book previously lacked. It gives me great pleasure to include in the list of authors such widely-read and acclaimed writers as Kim Newman, alongside commentators both new and familiar from all veins of genre criticism. The collaboration between Stephen Thrower and Chris Barber is typically excellent, and dwarfs every other study of **Tenebrae** I have ever read, while Mitch Davis casts his filmmaker's eye over **Inferno**, exploring its aesthetic with an enthusiasm unmatched by any other writer. Each voice represented within these pages is unique, their individual merits too numerous to list.

In addition to the writers who took up our challenge and added this new dimension with their ideas and their devotion to Argento's output, there are numerous others who deserve credit for their assistance, support and hard work. Julian Grainger in particular deserves a vote of thanks for his exhaustive, meticulously researched filmography. The guide to video releases has been updated by Nick Dawe of the Dark Dreams website (www.darkdreams.org). Adrian Luther-Smith provided invaluable proof-reading and sub-editing, as did Harvey Fenton of FAB Press, who also played a large part in mapping the final structure of the finished work and carried out all the pre-press chores. Special thanks in particular go to Stephen Thrower, who not only wrote for the volume, and sub-edited the text, but also designed most of the book itself. I must also thank those who contributed stills and posters to this beautifully illustrated volume: Bill Bennett, Mitch Davis, Kenneth Eriksen, Harvey Fenton, Adrian Luther-Smith, David Miller, Marc Morris, Salvatore Pazzi, Stephen Thrower, The Associates, Tartan Video, Salvation Films, Fox Video, Medusa (Paolo Pagetta) and Opera Film (Carla Alonzo and Dario Argento) all provided images contained herein. Above all, special credit must go to Alan Jones, who donated the largest proportion of illustrations. At the eleventh hour, Alan provided what must surely be the most extensive collection anywhere in the world of photographs and artwork relating to the cult of Argento. In fact, not only did Alan provide the stills - he provided the cult. His devotion to the Argento cause introduced this unique filmography to English-language audiences in the first place. He can thus be considered responsible in a broader sense for cultivating the enthusiasm which has given rise to *Art of Darkness* and all other critical reactions to this unequalled body of work.

From what began as a relatively minute expression of opinion has resulted a collaboration which exceeds any expectations I originally harboured. You can expect from *Art of Darkness* a vast diversity of vision, and a unique exploration of works which scour the darkness through an art-form which is born from light. Enjoy.

1.   McDonagh, Maitland: *Broken Mirrors, Broken Minds: The Dark Dreams Of Dario Argento* (Sun Tavern Fields, London 1991), p.245.

Threatening Glances

Voyeurism, eye-violation and the camera: from Peeping Tom to Opera

Peeping Tom opens with a shot of an archery target, beginning with a zoom out from its centre, as an arrow is fired into the bullseye. The words "A Michael Powell Production" are displayed in front of the image and we cut to an extreme closeup of a closed eye, which opens and stares straight at us. Juxtaposed in this way, the two images suggest a notion of threatened spectatorship similar to that of Buñuel's slashed eyeball in **Un Chien Andalou**. But Powell's concept is a rather more complex one, and closer examination of the film's opening reveals that here the string of associations runs further than just simply a variation on the popular theme of "eye-violation".

Peeping Tom: Sadism and Reflexivity

In fact, eye-violation (in a metaphorical sense) is only part of **Peeping Tom**'s compli-cated series of ideas related to looking and being looked at. The arrow piercing the target suggests a number of themes before the narrative has even begun. First of all, it is the symbol Powell has chosen as his authorial stamp. The emblem is similar to the one used on the collaborations between Powell and Pressburger, and so functions not only as an emblem for this particular film, but as a reminder of Powell's directorial involvement and constant presence. The image links Michael Powell the director with the thematic content of **Peeping Tom**[1] (Powell also reappears at various points in the film, both as a vendor of pornography and as Mark's psychoanalyst father), and so prepares us for an examination of *cinema* and voyeurism, rather than a discourse confined solely to the voyeuristic behaviour of characters within the film. The zoom could be taken to serve a similar purpose. This technique was soon to fall from favour, considered overly artificial, clumsily cinematic. Throughout the film, Powell prefers to use tracking shots, but here the zoom might serve to lay an emphasis upon technique, and thus artificiality.

The firing of the arrow suggests more ideas. The arrow is phallic, like the murder weapon in the film. It penetrates in the sense that it both pierces the target/skin and represents sexual penetration. Powell was clearly aware of this popular association: shortly before putting **Peeping Tom** into production, the director was involved with preparations for an aborted project on Freud,[2] hence this film's general overload of Freudian symbolism. The firing of the arrow also connects with the continuous theme centred around shooting/firing/projecting. Mark projects and shoots his films. The camera's gaze is aimed at, and penetrates, his victims. Towards the end of the film, Mark breaks a window and aims his camera at the police, providing a replacement, as Jean-Paul Torok points out, for the more conventional machine gun: *"One shoots with one's eyes and also, more effectively, with that substitute for the eyes, the camera,"* Torok wrote of the film.[3]

So, in the first (extra-diegetic) shot, we have already been presented with notions of eye-violation, authorship, film spectatorship, penetration and projection. The second shot, the opening of the eye, expands on this. The widening of the eye suggests fear and it stares straight at the camera, straight at us. This suggests both our reflection in the screen, with our own fear staring back at us, and the reflexivity which Powell repeatedly emphasises throughout the film. The eye is looking at us/the camera. It is watching us watching it watching us, an infinite series of reflections of the gaze.

To whom does the eye belong? Is it Mark's or is it that of a victim? Either way, it acts as a precursor to the film's reflexive commentary on voyeurism. Mark's victims watch

opposite:
Enzo Sciotti's promotional artwork
for Argento's **Opera**.

The man with the movie camera:
Carl Boehm, above, and right with Pamela
Green, in Michael Powell's **Peeping Tom**.

themselves (in a mirror) and they also watch him watching them (the lens of the camera protrudes through a hole in the mirror). We also watch Mark, observing him at his most intimate moments of sexual/sadistic/artistic experience and he looks back at us, at times pointing his camera in our direction.

The image of the eye threatens the spectator in more ways than one. Powell presents us with a metaphorical representation of an arrow being plunged into an eyeball. We associate the bullseye of the target with the eye in the second shot, warning us that what we are about to see will shock and horrify us, the violence will assault our eyes, our gaze will be violated. Also, by having the eye stare directly at us, he challenges our position as passive observers, voyeurs. We are no longer anonymous onlookers, sitting in the dark auditorium, looking in on the action of the film unobserved. The film is looking back at us - we are the object of its gaze. It scrutinises us every bit as much as we scrutinise it. It objectifies us. We are thus drawn into the action of the film and implicated. We are both the victim and the sadistic voyeur, the psychopath who impales/rapes his victims using his camera/our screen.

Spectatorial uncertainty

Little attention has been paid to the enormous influence that **Peeping Tom** exerted over the Italian horror film. Many critics have located the genesis of the giallo[4] in **Evil Eye** (1962) and **Blood And Black Lace** (1964), two films by Mario Bava. But while **Evil Eye** exhibits the hallmarks of Hitchcock's influence, the gruesome and baroque **Blood And Black Lace** bears striking similarities to **Peeping Tom**, in terms of both directors' use of camera movement, colour, lighting and basic story structure. While Bava was less interested in voyeurism and the disruption of passive spectatorship than dressing up his *grand guignol* masterpiece with eccentric decor, the theme of eye-violation found a place in the Italian horror tradition in no small way. Directors such as Lucio Fulci have based their careers around popping out people's eyes in films like **The Beyond** and **Zombie Flesh Eaters**. But it is in Argento's **Opera** that the legacy of **Peeping Tom**'s influence is to be found at its most complex and ingenious.

Although perhaps it takes something of a leap of imagination to suggest that **Opera** can be read as a response to Powell's film, I would assert that both **Peeping Tom**'s visual style and its themes of spectator/screen relations became absorbed by Italian horror film

Rising star Betty (Cristina Marsillach) and her agent Mira (Daria Nicolodi) prepare to confront an unwelcome visitor in **Opera**.

culture, and that drawing comparisons between the two films may illuminate the contents of both, the connections between them being considerably more than tenuous. However, Argento extensively problematises the issues of voyeurism, exhibitionism and sadism, rendering them even more ambiguous than in Powell's seminal masterwork, as I shall argue in due course.

Opera, of course, is not the first of Argento's films to explore issues of voyeurism and the sadistic gaze. As far back as **The Bird With The Crystal Plumage**, psychopathic subjective shots became a staple element of his work. Initially using hand-held photography and tracking shots, and later steadycam, Argento has frequently forced us to see through the eyes of his murderers, a technique later popularised by John Carpenter's **Halloween**. **The Bird With The Crystal Plumage** set a precedent: we are given an androgynous figure (almost invariably dressed in a black hat, all-concealing coat, black gloves), whose optical point of view is represented through prowling camerawork, but whose identity remains concealed. **The Cat O' Nine Tails** delivered an unsettling variation on the same formula. The killer-POV shots are suddenly and unnervingly interrupted by closeups of the murderer's eye. Like the staring eye in the second shot of **Peeping Tom**, it looks directly at us. This injects a note of ambiguity into the relationship between spectator and spectacle. We occupy the position of the killer, seeing what he sees, but aware at the same time that we are not him, for we too are being watched.

Deep Red offers a similar, but far more startling instance of threatened spectatorship: as one of the soon-to-be victims searches the interior of her dingy home, a disembodied eye stares out from the shadowy depths of an open closet. There is no face, not even the merest suggestion of human form, just the eye, which looks to one side, as though taking in its surroundings, then stares directly into the camera, fixing us with its penetrating gaze.

This surreal moment is representative of the voyeuristic excess with which **Deep Red** is imbued. The camera rarely remains static, intrusively moving about the sets, emblematic of our own voyeuristic pleasure and at the same time relentlessly disorientating. The spectatorial uncertainty here comes from our frequent inability to find our bearings in the diegetic space. A typical example of this can be seen in the opening of a sequence in Marc's apartment. The scene begins with an extraordinarily convoluted external shot: we see an unidentified part of a building and a portion of a large sign, but instead of simply cutting to the interior, the camera suddenly zooms out, through a gap between two pillars, simultaneously leaping up to the first floor of an entirely different area of the building (or perhaps even a different building altogether) and we then cut to a closeup of an open window. The sudden shift in location is momentarily confusing. Which building, and which apartment are we supposed to be looking at? Instead of giving us an easy entry into the following sequence, Argento temporarily frustrates our attempt to orientate ourselves. The pleasure associated with cinematic voyeurism is turned to displeasure, as we are made aware of our voyeuristic engagement with the film, and our complete lack of control over the image compounds our discomfort.

In **Suspiria**, dislocated point of view shots are thrown in with disquieting regularity. Silently we approach the swimming pool to look down on imperilled heroines Sara and Suzy from a high balcony, and we spy on them through the gap between parted sheets in a cavernous dormitory (ironically, Sara's ghastly fate involves having nails driven through her eyes, her punishment for seeing too much). Adding to the sense of unease is the fact

that we are never presented with a figure to whom these subjective shots may be assigned, and we are often left uncertain as to whether what we are watching is the literal representation of a character's visual field, or just another eerie but unmotivated tracking shot.

Opera: exhibitionism and scopophilia

In **Opera**,[5] the killer's optical point of view is represented by elegant steadycam photography. From the perspective of the anonymous psychopath, we skulk in the corridors of the beautiful Milan opera house, we watch Betty perform on stage through a pair of opera glasses, and we sink into a disturbing reminiscence of a past crime. Even when not bombarding us with subjective shots, signalling the killer's presence, the camera prowls ceaselessly, unacknowledged by the characters, constantly reminding us of our status as voyeurs.

Julia (Suzy Kendall) looks on as a maniac strikes in **The Bird With the Crystal Plumage**.

In certain instances we are implicated even more directly. At one point we approach Betty's apartment from the outside, the camera leaping up from ground level to the third or fourth floor, and we peep in through her bedroom window, spying her silhouette against the lace curtains. A moment later, inside the apartment, Marc draws Betty's attention to the unwelcome presence of a voyeur, who has been watching her from the street through binoculars. The killer has been caught looking, drawing attention to the fact that we too have just been peeking through her windows.

Recalling the central motif of **The Cat O' Nine Tails**, staring eyes return our gaze in startling closeup. Indeed, the very first image of the film is that of a raven's eye, occupying the entire screen, which both scrutinises us and reflects the rows of seats in the auditorium of the opera house. In a later scene, we assume Betty's position as she walks down a flight of steps on the stage during a performance. Looking down from her vantage point, we see Macbeth before us and, behind him, the faces of the entire audience, all gazing in our direction. Accustomed to playing the part of the passive spectator, we suddenly find ourselves occupying the position of the object of our scopophilic desires. We have become the spectacle on the receiving end of the audience's gaze, disrupting our comfortable one-way relationship with the screen.

To make the spectator aware of his position as a voyeur induces an inevitable distanciation between audience and spectacle. To a degree, the illusion of reality must fall. But the diegetic world of this film is close to disruption all the time. Argento foregrounds its cinematic, inherently artificial qualities. The purpose of continuity editing is to preserve the illusion of reality and mask the spectator's lack of control over what he is seeing,[6] but Argento works towards the opposite objective, cutting to impossible angles, at one point positioning his camera in the plug-hole of a basin, then placing it inside the killer's head to give us a closeup view of his palpitating brain, and later hanging it from the ceiling of Betty's apartment, so that we can look down upon the actors below, the frame gradually rotating. Even literal point of view shots can be manipulated to lay bare their artificiality: when the killer first enters the opera house, we glide down the corridors with him, only to see the film suddenly speed up and we dissolve from this subjective shot to the next. To introduce both a change in film speed and a dissolve during a point of view shot is highly unconventional, a departure from the illusion of natural vision.

While **Peeping Tom** suggests eye-violation purely through metaphor, Argento is nowhere near as euphemistic. In **Opera**, eyes are prodded with needles until they bleed, gouged out, shot at close range and eaten by birds, each atrocity delivered in graphic closeup. As Linda Ruth Williams observes, *"The most resonant image of the film is that of its heroine Betty as she is forced to witness a series of murders after a row of needles is strapped to her lower lids so that she must look if she is to avoid impaling her eyes by blinking. Her eyes bleed a little, but the real violence comes from the fact that she cannot close them."*[7] Williams also identifies the death of Mira, shot when she spies the killer through the peephole of a door, as a key moment in Argento's ongoing assault on the eye: *"from the moment Mira kneels down to keyhole level (again, in Betty's sight) and we see with her through the keyhole that the killer is there with a gun, the vulnerability of her eye is signalled. The keyhole is an opening for the killer, not her, even though she is the one who looks. First we see her seeing in profile, then we cut to the irised image through the keyhole, only to see a hand turning the gun until the barrel points towards us. In the space of a second we look with her into the eye of the gun, see the white flash of the bullet's release, and watch the oblique side view of it spinning to its destination."*[8]

As Williams points out, the eye *"is the supreme organ of violation not just because of what it does [it looks] but because of what it is: grotesquely penetrable, soft, liable to cry, bleed, respond with discharge, exquisitely sensitive to light and touch."*[9] Argento tirelessly emphasises and re-emphasises the vulnerability of the eye: when Santini attacks Marc in Betty's dressing room, for a moment he presses the barrel of his gun into Marc's eye; Betty's eyes cloud over and become useless when she anoints them with eye drops; and it is the loss of an eye that brings the killer's quest for love to an end - *"How can you love me, a monster?"* he groans, forlornly rubbing the empty, dripping socket.

Like the piercing of the target which opens **Peeping Tom**, the on-screen eye mutilation in **Opera** serves as a metaphor for the violated gaze of the audience, and consequently Argento launches a series of assaults on the camera, our 'eye' in the film. Part of Mira's murder is photographed from her point of view, placing us in her position as the gun is fired just in front of her eye. Similarly, when Giulia knocks the killer unconscious with a heavy iron, she attacks the camera, blocking out our vision at the moment of impact. The climactic attack on Santini also places us on the receiving end of violence - when the birds swoop down upon him in the auditorium of the opera house, the camera is positioned in his seat, looking up as the ravens descend - in fact we cut between two points of view, Santini's and that of the attacking birds, allowing us to alternate between the perspectives of both perpetrator and victim.

facing page:
Don't look now: Cristina Marsillach is the reluctant audience in **Opera**.

Love "haunted by the spectre of AIDS."
The classic giallo killer's gloves sheathed
in prophylactic, in **Opera**.

This frantic shifting between the points of view of violator and violated is the core of **Opera**'s complex commentary on the ambiguity of looking and being looked at. Whilst in **Peeping Tom** we alternate between objectifying on-screen characters from Mark's point of view, and being objectified by Mark's camera or the staring eye, **Opera** complicates matters, placing a greater emphasis upon the ambivalence of the gaze. Murder, in **Peeping Tom**, is a scenario which unfolds between three parties: Mark, Mark's victim and the audience. In **Opera**, Argento widens this circle to include Betty, the captive audience, our diegetic stand-in.

Consider the arrangement of gazes during the two key scenes of Betty's violation (the murders of Stefan and Giulia): the killer looks at/objectifies Betty; the killer looks at the victims; and Betty looks at the victims. We, of course, assume all three perspectives at certain times. But to what extent is Betty's point of view aligned with that of the killer? She objectifies the victims just as he does, so how far removed from his sadistic gaze is her own? Argento seems to draw only a thin line between her optical point of view and his. In fact, their perspectives coincide increasingly as the film progresses: in a dream, Betty remembers having witnessed the murder of a female victim in a stone chamber at the top of a spiral staircase, this sequence being almost identical to the killer's recollection of the same incident earlier in the film. Indeed, the flashbacks are so similar that certain shots are common to both, the very same footage being used to represent both the killer's optical point of view and Betty's. The killer's aim in all this is to coax her into taking pleasure in the murders, an ambition which he seems to at least partially fulfil - whether or not she really has any sadistic inclinations worth arousing is left unstated (Maitland McDonagh has argued that she does[10]), but he does succeed in forcing her to assume a perspective which virtually matches his own.

Leon Hunt has argued that the spectator (predominantly through Betty) *"is placed as the object of sadistic instruction"*.[11] One must bear in mind, however, that in the film's hierarchy of looks, Betty's point of view is highly privileged. This is, to a certain extent, at odds with the repeated violation of her eyes. Her gaze is violated, but her point of view is constantly being forced into alignment with the sadistic gaze of the killer. This parallels the most ambiguous dimension of the relationship between audience and screen: our gaze may be violated, but at the same time we derive a salacious pleasure from the very things which violate us.

Consider also the film's commentary on exhibitionism. In discussing **Peeping Tom**, Parveen Adams wrote: *"It is in general a supplementary feature of any perversion to incite a spectator, as if the aura of the perversion is made up of a consumption of vision, which demands that a spectator restore the visual energy that is exhausted in the scene. 'Look at me,' says any representation of perversion in a structure of fascination."*[12] It is using this argument that Adams claims that **Peeping Tom**'s Mark may be read as an exhibitionist. Acts of exhibitionism demand visual attention, an assertion which certainly applies to the murders of Stefan and Giulia in **Opera** - the murderer performs the killings as though on a stage (the room in which Stefan dies, we are told, *"looks like a museum"*, although 'theatre' might be more apt). Like macabre pieces of performance art, these exhibitionist slayings unequivocally scream 'look at me.'

The anonymous psychopath is not the only exhibitionist in this narrative, however: Argento goes to enormous lengths to highlight the exhibitionist position occupied by Betty. On stage, she performs in front of huge audiences, TV cameras trained upon her, and throughout the murder scenes she is similarly on display. When the killer ties her to a pillar and later imprisons her in a glass case, she assumes the positions of both audience and spectacle, forced to watch, but at the same time clearly there to be looked at. If the

The camera as hyper-sophisticated murder
apparatus: Carl Boehm and Anna Massey in
Powell's **Peeping Tom**.

An eye for an eye: Inspector Santini (Urbano Barberini) takes his revenge in **Opera**.

bodily mutilation inflicted by the killer can be argued to be an exhibitionist perversion, then we must also remember that the threat of Betty's self-inflicted mutilation (the needles) represents a second, similar consumption of "visual energy" - the powerful and horrifying image of Betty's tortured eyes is both symbolic of our own spectatorial gaze, and the site of a gruesome spectacle which we cannot help but look at.

The sadistic gaze

There is another important dimension to the interpretation of the gaze in **Peeping Tom**, and one which is equally relevant to **Opera**. E. Ann Kaplan has accused Powell's film of misogyny, claiming that it formed part of a trend of patriarchal horror films which attempted to *"eliminate woman's threat, first by dominating her through the controlling power of the gaze; second by fetishising her; and finally through murder."*[13] While it seems almost risible to identify Mark's actions in **Peeping Tom**'s narrative as a reflection of Powell's character, it is also hardly surprising that the film has provoked such a strong reaction. Kaplan seems to be hinting that domination by the camera parallels sexual domination, a metaphor which is barely disguised in this film. The camera is a stand-in for the eye, and in **Peeping Tom** it penetrates the women it films with a bayonet attached to the tripod. The invading stare of the camera/the eye is hence representative of rape.

Mark's voyeurism is frequently associated with impotence. He can penetrate his victims only with a phallic blade (his first victim is a prostitute, skewered while she undresses in front of him). After being embarrassed in front of Helen, when her friends laugh at him as he peeps in through her window, he rushes upstairs to examine his murder documentary - after humiliation in front of a woman to whom he is attracted, he must reassert his power over the feminine by re-experiencing the moment of penetration.

Like **Peeping Tom**, **Opera** suggests a parallel between the gaze and sexual penetration. The look, the phallus and the phallic blade are all metaphors for each other, and all perform a similar function. This is most clearly articulated in a scene in which the killer replays Betty's stage performance on a video monitor. As he watches, he zooms in on a part of the image, and scrapes his dagger across the surface. The monitor, like the cinema screen or Mark's camera in **Peeping Tom** is a metaphorical eye. Here the visual apparatus is most definitely one-way - Marco, Mara Cecova and the killer all watch Betty on television screens, unseen by her. The screen in this instance is a very concrete representation of the killer's gaze. He traces a line across the glass with the knife, cuing us in to the parallel between his penetrative blade and penetrating stare.

But the television screen is, of course, impenetrable. There is a layer of thick glass between the sharp steel point and the glowing pixels which make up the representation of Betty's body. The blade slides impotently across the glazed surface of the image, prefiguring the killer's consistent failure to consummate his desire for Betty, his inability to impale her on his phallic knife.

above:
Helen (Anna Massey) learns the meaning of fear in **Peeping Tom**.

below:
Betty plays the dangerous game of looking in **Opera**.

The image we are offered in this scene is replicated when we later see Betty imprisoned in a glass case. The display cabinet is reminiscent of the television screen, and similarly serves to place a transparent barrier between the murderer and the object of his desire. He can, of course, open the case, which he does, but penetration - either with the phallus or the blade - is still impossible, now hindered by barriers which are intangible, but no less insuperable: his impotence with her. Instead he holds the point of a pair of scissors against her crotch, removing them after barely touching her. *"I can take you whenever and wherever I want,"* he gloats, but his threat is a rather hollow one. Although Betty later comments that the experience was *"worse than being raped"* (in the Italian version, at any rate), the killer consistently demonstrates his inability to 'take her' in any sexual sense.

The pair of scissors is one he has only just used to murder Giulia, an act which seems to have greater significance as a show of his sexual potency than as an effort to retrieve that pesky bracelet. The killing is metaphorical of oral rape - he inserts the point of the closed pair of scissors into her mouth. Similarly, he establishes his sexual superiority over his rivals Stefan and Marco, repeatedly stabbing them both, which is again suggestive of sexual aggression. After watching him dispatch Marco, Betty tells him: *"I wanted you to win."* Her choice of words implies a strong element of competition, sexual rivalry between Marco and the killer. Nevertheless, Betty herself remains entirely unattainable, like her mother (*"She wouldn't let me touch her,"* the murderer recalls).

This suggests a connection with what might be considered an interesting footnote to **Opera**'s commentary on the look. The unfulfillable sexual desire, one could argue, has a place in what Argento has claimed is an underpinning AIDS allegory: *"In **Opera** love is haunted by the spectre of AIDS; in fact, nobody loves in this film... Betty doesn't want and can't have sexual relations, and relations between people are generally cold; people are distant with each other. This is surely the personification of the AIDS nightmare."*[14] In **Opera**, the 'coldness of relations' becomes something of a fetish all of its own. Betty's unattainability becomes part of the killer's masochistic role-play and he separates them with barriers, both metaphorical (the screen of the TV monitor) and literal (the glass cabinet). The generic black gloves are this time encased in an extra layer of thin plastic, suggesting a fear of tactility. The ending sees Betty retreating into isolation altogether, the film's commentary on separation reaching its natural conclusion. As Santini is unceremoniously carted off by hordes of armed police, Betty wanders off into a meadow. Through a voiceover, we are told that she wants to *"escape from everyone"*, believing herself to be so much more in touch with nature than she is with the rest of civilisation.

It stands as one of the most intricate ironies of this film that penetration becomes inadequate or unattainable, the game of sexual cat and mouse reaching its conclusion in the alienatory landscape of the closing scene. But in **Opera**, the gaze and the threat of sexual penetration are inexorably linked, drawing spectator and diegesis together into a pattern of constantly shifting, unstable relationships. The central discourse on the ambivalence of the gaze eschews causality and logic and remains devoid of any structuring linearity. All threads are drawn together in the film on the level of its imagery, finding their apotheosis in the unforgettable image of the tortured eyes of its heroine.

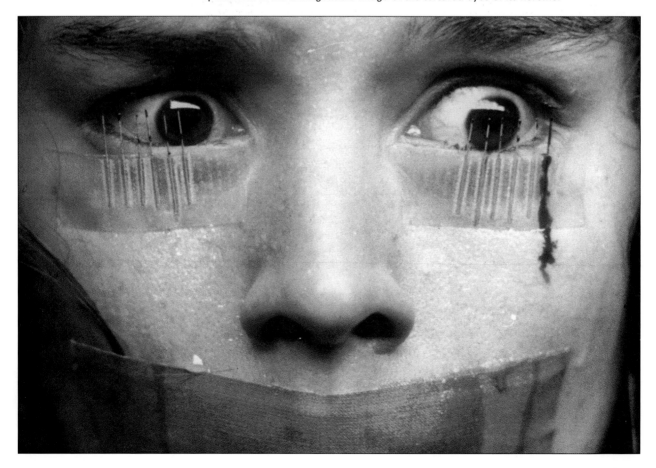

Notes

1.   **Peeping Tom** tells the story of Mark, a psychopath who documents the death throes of women with a film camera while he impales them on the pointed leg of his tripod. In a pre-credits sequence, we see him murdering a London prostitute, and then watching the snuff footage of her death. Mark shares his house with a number of lodgers, including the young Helen Stephens and her blind mother. Helen's sympathy is aroused by Mark's apparent shyness, and the two begin a tentative romance. As Helen learns more of Mark's background, we discover that the root of his obsessive voyeurism lies in his childhood: his father, an eminent psychologist, studied him throughout his formative years, spying on him mercilessly with a camera, using him as a guinea pig upon which to perform his experiments into behavioural responses to fear. Meanwhile, Mark continues to add to his murder "documentary", one night luring film stand-in Viv to the studio where they both work, stabbing her in the throat and once again using his camera to capture his victim's dying expression of fear. As he views the footage of his latest exploit, he is interrupted by Mrs Stephens. Suspicious of Mark, and concerned for the safety of her daughter, she has found her way into his darkroom and secret cinema. Unable to bring himself to kill her, Mark leads her to the door, promising her that he will never attempt to photograph Helen. His search for the image of the ultimate incarnation of fear, that of death staring itself in the face, now becomes more desperate. Apparently on an impulse, he murders Millie, a model he often uses through his part-time job as a small-time pornographer. He then returns home where he finds that Helen has stumbled across his macabre documentary. He confesses to the killings, showing her how he used a concave mirror in order to force his victims to watch their own expressions of fear as they expired. As the police storm the building, he impales himself on the spear-like tripod, staring into the mirror, finally able to see the reflection of fear with his own eyes.

2.   Wollen, Peter, "Dying For Art", Sight & Sound, vol.4 n.2, December 1994, p.120

3.   Torok, Jean-Paul: "Look At The Sea: Peeping Tom", Powell, Pressburger And The Others, edited by Ian Christie (British Film Institute, London 1978), p.60

4.   *Giallo*, which translates literally as "yellow" is the Italian term for the whodunit thriller, derived from the yellow covers of detective novels, rather like the French *serie noir*. In the Italian language, the word may just as easily refer to an Agatha Christie novel as to an Argento thriller, and applies to whodunit detective fiction in a broad sense. In the vocabulary of English-speaking audiences, its application tends to be restricted to the Italian whodunit-thriller film (one wouldn't refer to an Agatha Christie novel as an example of the "giallo" in English). The genre as it tends to be categorized by English-speaking audiences has its own conventions and clichés: the visual enigma, which may be solved through the gradual exploration of memory; anxiety over gender confusion; the murder sequence as an elaborate and artistic tableau, and so on. The 'giallo film' draws heavily upon the tradition of Agatha Christie's fiction, hard-boiled American detective novels and film noir. **Blood And Black Lace** is one of the genre's earliest examples, the tale of a series of gruesome murders in a fashion house. Bava's film and **Peeping Tom** must share some of the responsibility for ushering in and popularising the plot that revolves around the murders of a series of young women, with its overtones of misogyny and sexual aggression.

5.   **Opera**'s synopsis runs like an updated adaptation of Gaston Leroux's classic *The Phantom of the Opera*. When Mara Cecova, the star of an avant-garde production of Verdi's *Macbeth*, is injured in an accident, her young understudy, Betty, is given the coveted role of Lady Macbeth. In spite of her initial sense of foreboding, she is an instant success, shooting to overnight stardom. However, an anonymous opera buff finds his way into the opera house on the opening night, watching Betty's performance from an empty box, then impaling a meddlesome stagehand on a coat-hook. Later that night, he overpowers Betty, ties her to a pillar and forces her to watch the murder of her boyfriend, Stefan, taping a row of needles beneath each of her eyes, in case she should try to close them. Disturbed by half-hidden childhood recollections of the same hooded fiend, Betty chooses not to go to the police, confiding instead in Marco, her director. The following day, as Inspector Alan Santini questions the opera house staff about Stefan's murder, and probes an apparently connected attack on the troubled production's pet ravens, Betty telephones her agent, the motherly Mira, for advice. Later that day, the killer strikes again, this time capturing Betty in the opera house and forcing her to witness the murder of wardrobe mistress Giulia, who has stumbled across and swallowed an incriminating bracelet. Betty hurries home, where Inspector Santini promises her a permanent guard. Mira arrives, but is shot through the eye as the killer attempts to gain entry into the apartment. Betty escapes through a ventilation shaft and runs back to the opera house, where Marco reveals that he has conceived a plan to trap the killer. The following night, Betty takes to the stage again as Lady Macbeth, but her performance is interrupted when Marco unleashes a flock of vengeful ravens into the audience. Recognising the face of their enemy, the birds swoop down upon him, gouging out one of his eyes. The murderer, who is revealed to be Santini, evades capture and subsequently pounces upon Betty as she recovers in her dressing room. Dragging her to a far-flung quarter of the building, he reveals the motive behind his persecution of her: he was once her mother's lover, cruelly murdering helpless young women at her behest, tying her up and staging the killings in front of her. But when she became increasingly greedy for sado-sexual thrills, he killed her too, and now his desire has been rekindled by her reincarnation: her daughter. Blindfolding Betty and tying her to a chair, Santini sets fire to the room and stages his own death in front of her. Betty, however, breaks free and escapes from the blaze to be comforted by Marco. The two leave the country to recuperate in the Alps, but Santini turns up yet again, stabbing Marco before finally being dragged away by the police. Betty wanders off into the meadow to seek solace in nature. There she finds an ugly lizard trapped in the grass and releases it, telling it to "Go free."

6.   Dayan, Daniel: "The Tutor Code Of Classical Cinema", Film Quarterly, v.28 n.1, Fall 1974, pp.22-31. In his account of the writings of Jean-Pierre Oudart, Dayan asserts that the shot/reverse-shot structure, which characterises continuity editing, is put in place to dissipate the threat of the deconstruction of the representation system governing images. Dayan argues that the frequent breaks in the series of views which make up a cinematic sequence raise the question "Who is watching this?" Since systems for producing ideological messages must operate in a covert way, the message must be made to conceal ideology, making itself appear complete and coherent. When we see a shot, our identification with the visual field is disrupted when we perceive its cinematic, constructed nature. We are aware, according to Dayan, that the visual field is being seen by a figure whose presence we are not allowed to see (described by Oudart as "the absent one"), and that this figure is occupying a space, the opposite field to the one we are seeing, which is also being concealed from us. This incongruity is smoothed over by the employment of a second shot, the reverse shot, which reveals a character who may be presented as the owner of the glance which corresponds to the visual field seen in the first shot. This masks the presence (or rather, non-presence) of the "absent one" with a fictional character. Whether or not you buy Dayan's argument in its entirety (and here I am presenting a somewhat pruned version), all arguments regarding continuity editing are underpinned by the same principle: that the continuity system is designed to reduce any sense of distance between spectator and diegesis, endorsing the illusion of reality and the suspension of disbelief.

7.   Williams, Linda Ruth: "An Eye For An Eye", Sight & Sound, v.4 n.4, April 1994, p.16

8.   Williams, Linda Ruth: "An Eye For An Eye", Sight & Sound, v.4 n.4, April 1994, p.16

9.   Williams, Linda Ruth: "An Eye For An Eye", Sight & Sound, v.4 n.4, April 1994, p.16

10.   McDonagh, Maitland: Broken Mirrors, Broken Minds: The Dark Dreams Of Dario Argento (Sun Tavern Fields, London 1991), p.207

11.   Hunt, Leon: "A (Sadistic) Night At The Opera: Notes On The Italian Horror Film", The Velvet Light Trap, n.30, Fall 1992, p.73

12.   Adams, Parveen: "Father, Can't You See I'm Filming?", Supposing The Subject, edited by Joan Copjec (Verson, London 1994), p.185

13.   Kaplan, E. Ann, Women And Film (Methuen & Co, London 1983), p.73

14.   Palmerini, Luca and Mistretta, Gaetano: Spaghetti Nightmares (M&P edizioni, Italy 1996), p.14

In the Mouth of the Architect

Inferno, alchemy and the postmodern Gothic

To be strictly accurate, it would be true to say that 'Gothic', as a literary tradition, began in 1764 with Walpole's *The Castle of Otranto* and was ushered out in the mid 1820s.[1] It is hard to be so specific though, when Gothic is a cultural form which trades primarily on cliché and reappropriation, and has remained very much alive through not only literature, but across film, fashion, architecture and painting. The term derives, of course, from the medieval castles and cathedrals, with their pointed turrets and gargoyles, but ultimately its influence is pan-cultural, unconstrained by time or medium. Victor Sage and Allan Lloyd Smith's *Modern Gothic*, for example, traces its manifestation in everything from David Lynch's **Blue Velvet** to Madonna's bra - it's a versatile form and the possibilities of its application are, it seems, unlimited.

Towards A Definition of the Gothic

Definitions of the Gothic however, remain vague and non-specific. It's a commonly used term, but outside of its most orthodox usage (the literary movement and architecture), its actual meaning is rarely considered. It could be a coded set of iconography, a series of motifs, a narrative formula. The spinoffs of Gothic are so immensely varied that accuracy seems altogether impossible: we talk about 'Gothic horror', the 'Gothic melodrama', and its sartorial application, which ties fashion to the music of the 1980s. Any hope of finding a single unifying factor shared by all its forms has been lost through its continued reinvention. Iconography often seems to be the key, but there are no hard and fast rules. The term 'Gothic' has become something of a catch-all and few concrete criteria exist for its invocation.

Perhaps one of the reasons that it is so difficult to anchor is that it rarely refers to any particular historical period. The imposing features of medieval architecture are only a starting point. Gothic is something which plunders iconography from across history indiscriminately. As Sage and Lloyd Smith put it, *"The Old Gothic [as exemplified by Robert Louis Stevenson's* The Body Snatchers*] doesn't stand still as a point of reference: even in the eighteenth century, it was itself an anarchic, popular and indeed 'camp' recycling of the past."* [2] The literature of the Gothic period 'proper' includes the stories of Bram Stoker and Ann Radcliffe, Jane Austen's *Northanger Abbey* and Mary Shelley's *Frankenstein*, frequently tales which occupy a self-consciously contrived diegetic world characterised by an atmosphere and aesthetic of 'pastness'. The iconography, cultural conventions and cultural antitheses of the Gothic combine to place it in a mythologised age, a never-never land of incongruent historical detail. Time is set free from the rigid order which history imposes upon it, conjuring up a fairytale sense of timelessness by disrupting time's very nature.

The purpose of all this is debatable. It has been suggested that the Gothic places an emphasis upon the aesthetic and superficial in order to encourage readers and audiences to *"deduce for themselves complex inner psychological movements"*, or that the Gothic text is a *"hysterical text"* which presents us with symptoms but veils causes and explanations. Angela Carter has observed that *"Its characters and events are exaggerated beyond reality, to become symbols, ideas, passions... Style will tend to be ornate, unnatural - and thus operate against the perennial human desire to believe the word as fact... [The Gothic] retains a singular moral function, that of provoking unease"*,[4] while Laura Mulvey draws her version of the psychology of the hysterical text from Freud, by asserting that *"the*

Aesthetics of decay: Rose Elliot (Irene Miracle) explores the hidden recesses of Mater Tenebrarum's lair.

insistent pressure of a repressed past on the conscious mind may be displaced onto imagery of ruins or the archaic." [5]

I shall explore further the notion of the Gothic as code or hysterical symptom, but my principal aim in sketching the background arguments surrounding this mode is to attempt to orientate one particular of its descendants - the Gothic horror film. Peter Hutchings has observed that 'horror' is frequently identified as *"a vulgarised, exploitative version of Gothic"* [6] and that 'Gothic horror' cinema is often perceived as a genre or sub-genre which draws on the iconography of medievalism and feudalism (Roger Corman's Poe films, for instance, or the Argento/Soavi collaboration **The Church**). Hutchings extends his argument to the slasher films of the 70s and 80s, with their emphasis upon the consequences of a repressed, hidden or forgotten past (the hit-and-run accident in **I Know What You Did Last Summer**, to cite a recent example) and the transformation of the familiar, domestic environment into a dark, alien space concealing imagined terrors, vengeful assailants or the threat of unfamiliar sexuality. I shall confine myself to the former, however, the horror film which ransacks the catalogue of historical aesthetics, exemplified by Argento's **Inferno** and **Suspiria**.

In the interiors of **Inferno**, gaudy, garish art deco collides with an aesthetic of decay and the decrepit. The maze of cobweb-choked secret passages, the dilapidated underwater ballroom and the derelict basement of the haunted apartment block are all hallmarks of the Gothic. And the dungeon-like cellar beneath the library, with its blazing fires, bubbling cauldrons and ogre-like alchemist-in-residence, is a vision of camp, fantasy medievalism. The costumes tend to be either old-fashioned or timelessly conservative and the sets are littered with tokens of an eclectic and non-specific past: the dusty, ancient volumes which fill the library, for example, or the assortment of antiques and old world trash which is crammed into Kazanian's shop. While taxis, telephones and the incongruous presence of a hotdog salesman serve to anchor us to the late twentieth century, the majority of the film's interiors are decked out with an iconography of the archaic.

The exaggeration of the ornate and baroque, referred to earlier, is a pronounced component of **Inferno**'s style, verging almost on the Expressionist tradition of mirroring psychology through aesthetics. But in **Inferno** and **Suspiria**, colour, shape, music and movement do more than simply articulate the anxieties of their characters - they substitute character psychology altogether. The people that inhabit these worlds are ciphers, their two-dimensionality flaunted unrestrainedly, while their physical environment is psychologised in the extreme. The aesthetic of **Suspiria** and particularly **Inferno** is one of quasi-motivated hysteria and heightened contrivance.

The Church, made around a decade later and directed by Michele Soavi, presents a far more specific invocation of the past. It eschews the historical vagueness of **Suspiria** and **Inferno** in favour of far more concrete and motivated references to the Middle Ages. It opens with the massacre of a small village by a band of 'Teutonic Knights', and then switches to the present day, spinning a story of heresy and demonic possession around the cathedral built over the ancient mass grave. The Gothicism of **The Church** is tied to the architecture of the cathedral, Gothic in a strictly accurate sense.

The Deconstructional Gothic

In *Image-Music-Text*, Roland Barthes made his famous distinction between 'work' and 'text', a distinction upon which he was to elaborate further in *S/Z*. The 'work', he argued, is a physical artifact, a book for example, not to be confused with the 'text', which is a *"methodological field"* [7] in which we see the blending of voices, influences and writings. The text can be broken down into further categories: the 'readerly' text is that which excludes any form of interaction with those who consume it, encouraging readerly passivity, while the 'writerly' text (constituting Barthes' definition of the 'modernist') is that which encourages participation. In Robert Stam's words, the modernist text *"stimulates and provokes an active reader sensitive to contradiction and heterogeneity, aware of the work of the text. It transforms its consumer into a producer, foregrounding the process of its own construction and promoting the infinite play of signification."* [8]

It is, however, important to note that Barthes revised his view of the apparent polarity of the two categories in *S/Z*, suggesting that the readerly text might become the writerly, depending upon the reader's relationship with it. The key to the modernist is analysis - in analysing a text, we engage with it, rendering Barthes' distinction between the two categories less a question of authorial intention and more one of the reader's input.

The Gothic, of course, is rich in the hallmarks of the writerly. Spectacle and visual ornamentation are two of its most salient, and most derivative constituent parts. Never original, they are closely tied with what Barthes has termed the 'already-written', the infinite body of material (films, novels, stories, paintings) upon which this text may draw.[9] To recognise familiar elements of the Gothic (the old dark house, secret passages, archaic ruins) is to be aware that we have seen them all before, in a whole plethora of contexts. But the invocation of the 'already-written' here serves a specific purpose - the complexity and plurality of the Gothic hinges largely upon its culturally determined antitheses, in particular the oppositions associated with ancient and modern, giving rise to uncertainty and indeterminacy.

Allan Lloyd Smith has argued that indeterminacy may be read as a reaction against classicism and the Enlightenment. The Gothic encourages the interaction of its audience, frustrating our attempts to find answers by posing enigmas but not solving them and by alienating us from the backdrop against which the narrative unfolds. The environment inhabited by the characters of **Inferno** is one of fragmentation, instability and partial orders, a diegetic world based upon the antitheses of the modern and the archaic. It is a world in which neither its own characters nor its audience can orientate themselves effectively.

Italian locandina for Michele Soavi's
The Church.

"The second key is hidden in the cellar..."
Irene Miracle in **Inferno**.

as above, so below: Two guises of the "Mother of Darkness": Leigh McCloskey and Veronica Lazar in **Inferno**.

Christian zealots on the rampage in the opening scene of Michele Soavi's **The Church**.

As the malevolent contagion spreads, the occupants of the demon-infested Church devise increasingly inventive means of escape.

Inferno carries resonances of the crisis of knowledge which dominated the close of the eighteenth century, the obsession with epistemology which gave birth to the Gothic form. What we know, what we think we know and ontological questions of the nature of being are repeatedly problematised as our surroundings become unfamiliar or illusory. Allan Lloyd Smith has identified paranoia over technology as crucial to this epistemological crisis and the consequent rise of the Gothic:[10] it flourished as the world stood on the threshold of technological upheaval - industrialisation and the birth of capitalism. The result, he argues, was a form imbued with uncertainty, for industrialisation *"opens the possibility of what exceeds our understanding; the system running itself, for itself; and hence generates anti-humanism, plots beyond comprehension."* [11] It is this, the *"aesthetic of anxiety and perplexity"*, which ties the Gothic to the Postmodern in their mutual obsession with the impossibility of knowing and the fruitless search for answers in the wake of a complete loss of control over our environment.

In **Inferno**, this epistomological and ontological crisis is sublimated onto a complex stream of dark theology. Like the film's 'period' iconography, its 'religion' is unconcerned with unity and continuity, and the mythology of the Three Mothers is founded on an arbitrary mishmash of literary and theological sources. It draws heavily on the opium-inspired fantasies of Thomas De Quincey (specifically, his essay *Levana and Our Ladies of Sorrow*), pays lip-service to Gnosticism, combines elements of Giordano Bruno's writings with Trinitarianism and drops references to Fulcanelli, tying it all together in a web of popular superstition and half-accurate theology.

Alchemy is integral to the narrative, given supremacy over all its other mythological and religious influences. The houses of the Three Mothers (of which there is one in New York, one in Rome and one in Freiburg - retrospectively knitting **Suspiria** into this subsequent narrative) were, we are told, designed and built by *"an architect and highly respected alchemist by the name of Varelli."* The houses in Rome and New York are crammed with alchemical symbolism, all of which is confusing and opaque, hinting at holding a place in a larger, meaningful cosmic pattern. Broadly, this symbolism can be divided into four categories: the symbolism of colour (the unmotivated hues of the light, the interior walls of the house), cosmic/natural symbols (the moon, the eclipse, the waves in Mark's dream), apparently incidental iconographic symbols (the staring eye in Rose's necklace, the snake design in her key ring, the breaking of glass prior to each death) which may be accidental but which seem to relate to the fourth category, symbols which are identified as alchemical in nature and origin, built into the mansions as part of a premed-itated code.

Inferno's obsession with surface encourages these symbols to be foregrounded, for us to take note of their existence, suggesting concealed meaning. For example, the profusion of lizard imagery calls to mind the mythological significance of such signs as the winged serpents to be seen in architectural design and painting: there are lizards represented in the mosaics which surround the door to the house in Rome; they are also engraved in the masonry of the block in New York; there is an abrupt, extra-diegetic glimpse of a lizard preying on a moth; Rose steps on a lizard in the chamber where she is about to die. The connections are there to be made, but ultimately the pattern is indecipherable.

above:
Evan (Tomas Arana) reaps the wages of sin in **The Church**.

facing page:
Sara (Eleonora Giorgi) embarks on a quest to solve an alchemical riddle in a library of the damned (top) and takes a taxi ride into hell (bottom) in **Inferno**.

New York nightmare: Central Park takes on an eerie new aesthetic in **Inferno**.

In view of this confusion of iconography, it is necessary to turn to the sources which inspired it, not necessarily in order to break the code, but instead to explain its invention and its placement in the film, on both diegetic and non-diegetic levels.

Making Myths

Alchemy is both theology and science, its two elements of the material and the mystical articulated in what was a popular maxim amongst its practitioners: *"Pray theosophically, and work psycho-chemically."* [12] Its introduction into Europe by the Arabians, however, coincided with the spread of witchcraft, leading many to regard alchemy as a form of magic (*"Alchemy is a demonic science,"* sneers a religious leader in **The Church**). In **Inferno**, the narrative this time manages to show some degree of fidelity to historical fact - the 'magic' is elemental, natural magic. The supernatural is manifested through fire and water, astrology. Its most obvious point of reference is Fulcanelli, who is paralleled in the character of Varelli. Like Varelli, he was a modern alchemist who disappeared under mysterious circumstances, leaving behind a manuscript about alchemy and architecture. His true identity has never been revealed, the secret behind his pseudonym lost forever, his only legacy being a strange book full of indecipherable commentaries on a number of Gothic buildings.

Fulcanelli's *The Mystery of the Cathedrals* is a bizarre, vexing work, hinting at some obscure logic, comprehensively laying down complex theories on the elemental and theological significance behind the symbolism to be found in such buildings as the Cathedral of Notre Dame. Fulcanelli reads the signs one by one, deconstructing the 'language' of architecture in minute detail, but ultimately the exercise is frustrating - full of process but apparently devoid of meaning. In one section he mentions the "language of colours",[13] tying it to the stained glass windows of the cathedrals. *"The colour black,"* he writes, *"was given to Saturn. In spagyric art he is the hieroglyph for lead; in astrology, a maleficent planet; in hermeticism, the black dragon or Philosophers' Lead; in magic, the black Hen, etc... This is the symbolical colour of the shades and the Cimmerian darkness, the colour of Satan, to whom black roses were offered. It is also the colour of primitive Chaos, in which the seeds of all things are confused and mixed."* [14]

In **Inferno**, black is the colour of the Three Mothers and their agents. They wear black robes and gloves. It is a very simple symbology: black is the colour of darkness, the colour of the unknown and unknowable, while the victims of Mater Tenebrarum are frequently dressed in white. Red, on the other hand, is *"the hue of the fire of the sages"* [15] and, according to Fulcanelli, *"shows exaltation, predominance of spirit over matter, sovereignty, power and apostleship."* [16] Red is the colour of the interior of Mater Tenebrarum's house, the colour of its walls and stained glass. It is also the colour of blood and fire: as she laments the destruction of her mansion, the Mother of Darkness hints at the purifying, renewing effect of fire. In a speech imbued with the principles of Gnosticism, she tells Mark: *"Your journey has come to an end. Everything around you will become dark and someone will take your hand. You'll be pleased, not unhappy. You'll*

Mark (Leigh McCloskey) sets out on an esoteric paper chase in **Inferno**.

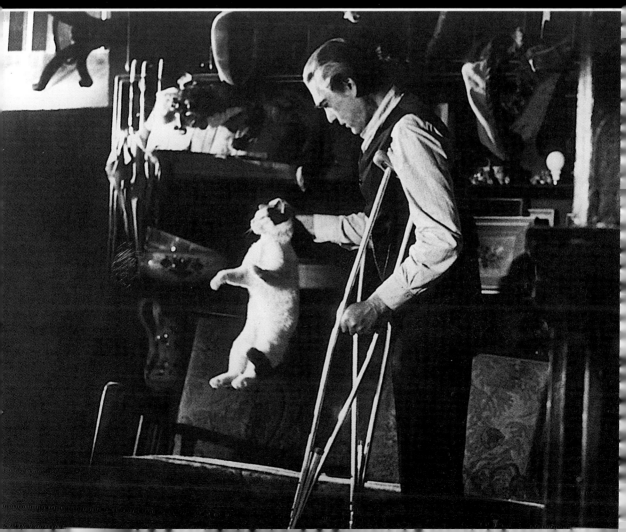

Kazanian (Sacha Pitoeff) disposes of another of Mater Tenebrarum's familiars in a feline-infested quarter of New York.

Sara (Eleonora Giorgi) incurs the alchemist's
wrath in the cellars of the cursed library.

*enjoy moments of incredible brightness... Now we have to hurry because we still have to
pass through a number of strange phases in your change. You were looking for me, just
like your sister. This is what you wanted."* Her 'explanation' hints at the evil of material
creation: the Gnostics believed that certain individuals contain sparks of divinity and are
thus destined for salvation, to be released from the bondage of matter and return to their
celestial origins.

   The Church, however, presents us with a slightly different slant on the Fulcanelli story:
Evan, having read Fulcanelli's book, is convinced that he can unearth the secret behind the
cathedral in which he is working as a librarian, believing that buried beneath the imposing
structure is *"the key to some unknown science we've lost all trace of, something that
could turn the finder into a superman, a god."* His ambition echoes the writings of influential Hermeticist Giordano Bruno, whose quest for divine knowledge resulted from the
Renaissance obsession with Man as Miracle who, in the words of Frances Yates, *"is divine
in origin and can become divine again."* [17]   Bruno's belief in elemental magic, celestial
magic and supercelestial or religious magic brings him closer to Fulcanelli. The three
aspects of his work, according to Yates, may correspond with the three worlds of the
Cabalists, although Cabalism was only secondary to his ideas - primarily he was
concerned with Egyptianism and Hermeticism. The Egyptian language is made up of
sacred letters, symbols derived from nature. The quest for divine knowledge, one might
conclude, is a quest through language.

Searching For The Key

   What Fulcanelli, Bruno, Evan and Mark all share is their seemingly fruitless quest for
knowledge. As Lisa puts it in **The Church**, quoting Fulcanelli, *"The Gothic cathedrals are
part of a cosmic design, but the meaning of this design is beyond our knowledge."* Like
Inferno, **The Church** is full of puzzles, the fact that they are concealed planting the
misleading suggestion that they represent meanings beyond the surface: a wall crumbles
away to reveal a parchment carrying an obscure, Bruno-like design; a torn page from an
ancient volume has to be pieced together like a jigsaw in order to reveal a painting which
in turn points to the burial spot of the secret behind the cathedral. Layers of suggestive-
ness are placed one behind another, but meaning never seems to materialise.

   In **Inferno**, as in **The Church**, it is the alchemist's knowledge which becomes the
narrative's central enigma. The riddles which punctuate the film are first presented to us
through Varelli's book, which presents a series of pointers, purporting to lead the reader
to the truth behind the mansion's secret, but enlightenment escapes us at every turn: the
portrait in the cellar, which should reveal the face of Mater Tenebrarum, turns out to be
impossible to see; the secret passages which are concealed *"under the soles of your*

shoes" just make up a never-ending maze; and the disgusting smell which permeates the area all around is never adequately explained. Each character engages with the search for knowledge, picking up on the three pointers outlined in Varelli's book, described as the three keys. Rose instigates the search by reading the book. This leads her to the cellar where she must retrieve her door-key from an underwater room, her search for the key bringing, instead of answers, a confrontation with a rotting corpse - a symbol of the breakdown of orders, dissolution, insufficiency and chaos. Sara subsequently sets out on a hunt for the truth in a library - the key must be hidden in a book, which is, rather frustratingly, printed in Latin. Once again, solutions to the enigma are not forthcoming - Sara dies in the chaos which breaks out in her apartment, while 'Va Pensiero' plays on the turntable, a piece which she and Mark listened to earlier in the day, following it on a printed score. Again the emphasis is placed upon the reading of a language, a code made up of symbols. Mark picks up the trail at Sara's apartment and is led to Rome by a torn fragment of his sister's letter, a line of text which, in itself, means nothing. Argento emphasises the readability of signs endlessly: Rose is a poetess, immersed in language, while Mark and Sara read sheet music in their occupation as music students. Kazanian is one of the few to draw attention to the utter futility of the characters' concern with language, snapping *"What's that, a riddle? I'm not good at riddles."* Towards the end of the film, Mark attempts to follow the signs etched into the exterior of the building (lizards again), but like all of **Inferno**'s alchemical symbolism, the designs form a part of a language which is ultimately non-functional.

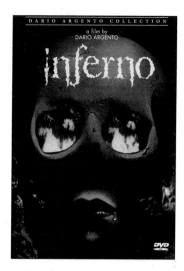

Cover artwork for American DVD release.

In their introduction to *Modern Gothic*, Lloyd Smith and Sage claim that *"the Gothic is not merely a literary convention or a set of motifs: it is a language, often an anti-historicising language."* [18] In **Inferno**, the language of Gothic is fleshed out, given layers, but refuses to convey any semblance of meaning. This brings the Gothic close to the postmodern concern with information overload - *"boundless signs without referents"*,[19] signs which are, but stand for nothing. Rosemary Jackson has argued that the fantastic (and, for our purposes, the Gothic) problematises *"vision (eye) and language (I) as reliable constituents of reality"* and that it *"plays upon difficulties of interpreting events/things as objects or as images, thus disorientating the reader's categorisation of the 'real' to such an extent that reason and reality appear as arbitrary shifting constructs."* [20] In **Inferno**, there is just such a confusion between image and object, suggesting a slippage between sign and referent: a puddle in the cellar turns out to be the portal to a subterranean world; one of the interior walls of an apartment is revealed to be a delicate sheet of fabric when it is torn in half by a corpse; Mater Tenebrarum's very physicality is rendered ambiguous when she appears to be one moment solid and real, then a reflection in a mirror, then perhaps a form which exists within the world of the mirror itself.

Rose (Irene Miracle) delivers herself into the hands of one of Mater Tenebrarum's henchmen in **Inferno**.

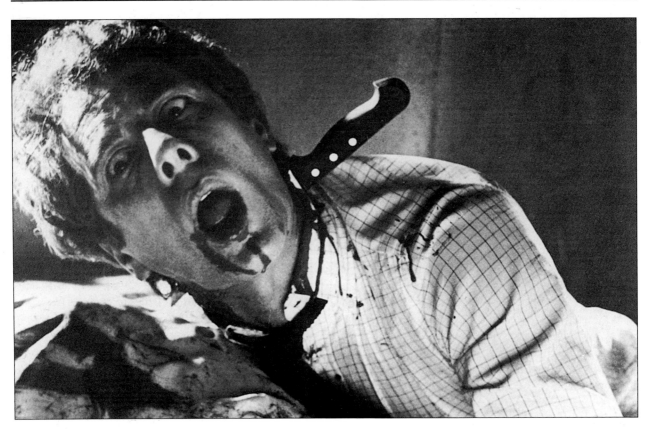

Gabriele Lavia pays dearly for his fleeting involvement in the mysterious New York house of Mater Tenebrarum, in **Inferno**.

The uneasy shift between image and object is central to the transference from connotation to uncertainty. Things do not always conform to their physical appearance and words and symbols make up a language which does not convey anything that it purports to. It is empty, devoid of answers. The narrative's central enigma must be insoluble - at its core lies the characters' search for forbidden knowledge as they attempt to orientate themselves in their illusory, disorientating surroundings, following language and codes, trying to grasp meanings which essentially don't exist. The Gothic, as discussed earlier, has frequently addressed unanswerable questions of epistemology and ontology, sublimating them onto the cloak and dagger antics of its characters. Here it articulates these concerns through the very meaninglessness of signs. In themselves the signs are, of course, arbitrary: in **Suspiria**, the key to the activities within the school is represented by a blue iris, once again an arbitrary sign - not even a real iris, but a painted one, displaced once again from its 'referent' through a mirror. In both **Inferno** and **The Church**, the key concern is the impossible search for answers to the unknowable. In **The Church**, language and its inoperability is once again central to the characters' inability to reach a satisfactory end-point in their quest. The secret, which Evan believes will explain the existence of the cathedral and its significance in a larger cosmic plan, is never revealed. Its nature is never discussed, its implications barely hinted at - it is just 'a secret' and never becomes anything more than that. The characters are lead towards it as they decipher faded designs, piece together coded maps and read the cryptic inscriptions carved into the stone, but ultimately, the pivotal piece of knowledge, their 'lost arc', remains undiscovered and the language of alchemical symbolism with which they surround themselves fails to bring enlightenment. The secret, whatever it is, must remain buried within the corpse of its creator, at the literal origin of language - the only conclusion, a highly ironic one, to the film's linguistic riddle: the secret is hidden in the architect's mouth.

Notes

1. Sage, Victor/Lloyd Smith, Allan: Modern Gothic (Manchester University Press, Manchester, 1996), p.6
2. Sage, Victor/Lloyd Smith, Allan: Modern Gothic (Manchester University Press, Manchester, 1996), p.1
3. Sage, Victor/Lloyd Smith, Allan: Modern Gothic (Manchester University Press, Manchester, 1996), p.9
4. Sage, Victor/Lloyd Smith, Allan: Modern Gothic (Manchester University Press, Manchester, 1996), p.145
5. Sage, Victor/Lloyd Smith, Allan: Modern Gothic (Manchester University Press, Manchester, 1996), p.39
6. Sage, Victor/Lloyd Smith, Allan: Modern Gothic (Manchester University Press, Manchester, 1996), p.89
7. Barthes, Roland (82): Image-Music-Text (Fontana, London, 1982), p.157
8. Stam, Robert: New Vocabularies in Film Semiotics (Routledge, London, 1992), p.192
9. Barthes, Roland (74): S/Z (Jonathan Cope Ltd, London, 1974), p.20
10. Sage, Victor/Lloyd Smith, Allan: Modern Gothic (Manchester University Press, Manchester, 1996), p.16
11. Sage, Victor/Lloyd Smith, Allan: Modern Gothic (Manchester University Press, Manchester, 1996), p.16
12. Ahmed, Rollo: The Black Art (Senate, London, 1994), p.129
13. Fulcanelli: Le Mystere des Cathedrales (Brotherhood of Life, New Mexico, 1991), p.84
14. Fulcanelli: Le Mystere des Cathedrales (Brotherhood of Life, New Mexico, 1991), p.85
15. Ahmed, Rollo: The Black Art (Senate, London, 1994), p.129
16. Fulcanelli: Le Mystere des Cathedrales (Brotherhood of Life, New Mexico, 1991), p.16
17. Yates, Frances: Giordano Bruno and the Hermetic Tradition (The University of Chicago Press, Chicago, 1991), p.266
18. Sage, Victor/Lloyd Smith, Allan: Modern Gothic (Manchester University Press, Manchester, 1996), p.1
19. Sage, Victor/Lloyd Smith, Allan: Modern Gothic (Manchester University Press, Manchester, 1996), p.16
20. Sage, Victor/Lloyd Smith, Allan: Modern Gothic (Manchester University Press, Manchester, 1996), p.146

opposite:
Spanish poster for
The Bird With the Crystal Plumage.

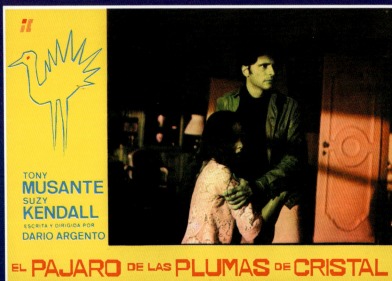

TONY
MUSANTE
SUZY
KENDALL
ESCRITA Y DIRIGIDA POR
DARIO ARGENTO

EL **PAJARO** DE LAS **PLUMAS** DE **CRISTAL**

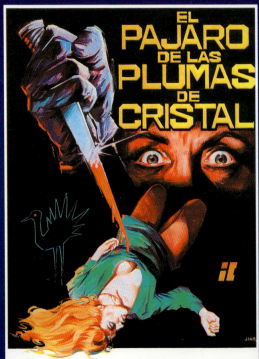

EL
PAJARO
DE LAS
PLUMAS
DE
CRISTAL

TONY
MUSANTE · **KENDALL** · **SALERNO** · **RENZI** Y **ADORF**
ESCRITA Y DIRIGIDA POR **DARIO ARGENTO**

top: Suitably grotesque promotional artwork for **The Bird With the Crystal Plumage**.

above: A shot from the denouement features on a Spanish lobby sheet for the film.

right: Lurid artwork for the Spanish release of **The Bird With the Crystal Plumage**.

above: All in your mind: Suzy Kendall at the mercy of a psychopath in **The Bird With the Crystal Plumage**.

right: Poster for film's 1972 American re-release, when it was retitled as **The Phantom of Terror**.

below: A collage of images on one of the original Italian lobby sheets for Argento's directorial debut.

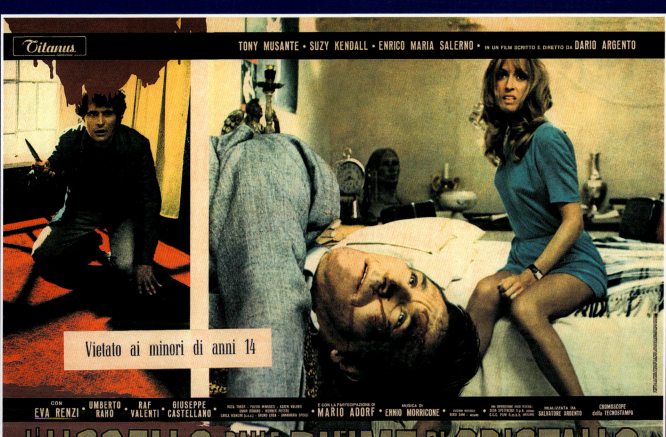

Titanus TONY MUSANTE • SUZY KENDALL • ENRICO MARIA SALERNO • IN UN FILM SCRITTO E DIRETTO DA **DARIO ARGENTO**

L'UCCELLO DALLE PIUME DI CRISTALLO

CON **EVA RENZI** • **UMBERTO RAHO** • **RAF VALENTI** • **GIUSEPPE CASTELLANO** • ROSA TOROS • FULVIO MINGOZZI • KAREN VALENTI • E CON LA PARTECIPAZIONE DI **MARIO ADORF** • MUSICA DI **ENNIO MORRICONE** • REALIZZATA DA **SALVATORE ARGENTO** • CROMOSCOPE della TECNOSTAMPA

opposite top: Alone in the dark, Julia (Suzy Kendall) struggles to keep a serial killer at bay in **The Bird With the Crystal Plumage**.
opposite bottom: Italian fotobusta (lobby sheet) for **The Bird With the Crystal Plumage**.

this page top: The original British theatrical poster for **The Bird With the Crystal Plumage**, and three Italian fotobuste.
below: Fotobusta for **The Cat O' Nine Tails**.

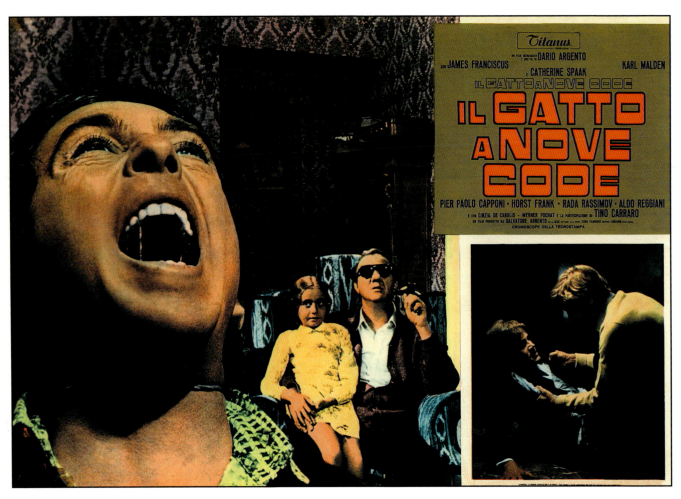

this page: Bizarrely juxtaposed images adorn the lobby sheets for **The Cat O' Nine Tails**.

opposite: Startling, grotesque artwork on an Italian poster for **The Cat O' Nine Tails**.

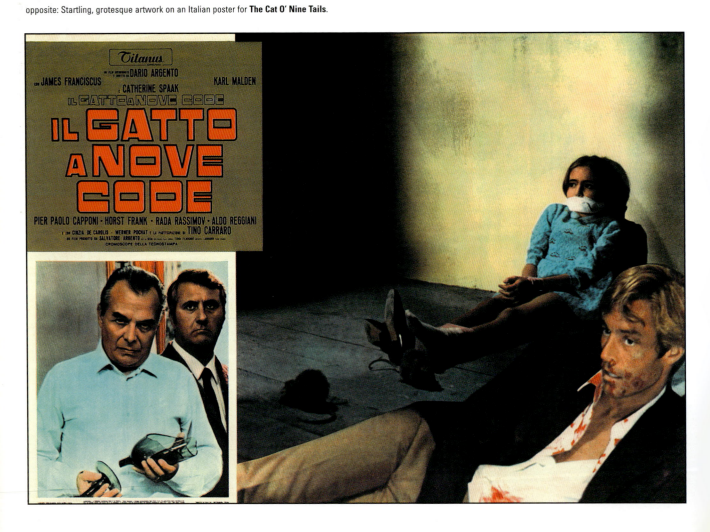

UN FILM SCENEGGIATO E DIRETTO DA **DARIO ARGENTO**
CON **JAMES FRANCISCUS** **KARL MALDEN**
E **CATHERINE SPAAK**
IL GATTO A NOVE CODE

IL GATTO
A NOVE CODE

PIER PAOLO CAPPONI • **HORST FRANK** • **RADA RASSIMOV** • **ALDO REGGIANI**

E CON **CINZIA DE CAROLIS** • **WERNER POCHAT** E LA PARTECIPAZIONE DI **TINO CARRARO**

CROMOSCOPE DELLA TECNOSTAMPA

FROM THE MASTERS OF TENSION WHO GAVE YOU
"THE BIRD WITH THE CRYSTAL PLUMAGE"
—THE PICTURE THAT OUT-PSYCHOED 'PSYCHO'!

"CAT O'Nine Tails"

It's nine times more suspenseful!

NATIONAL GENERAL PICTURES PRESENTS
A FILM WRITTEN AND DIRECTED BY DARIO ARGENTO
STARRING JAMES FRANCISCUS · KARL MALDEN
AND CATHERINE SPAAK
CAT O'NINE TAILS'' · Produced by Salvatore Argento For Seda
Technicolor® Techniscope® A National General Pictures Release

GP ALL AGES ADMITTED
Parental Guidance Suggested

un film de
DARIO ARGENTO **Quatre mouches de velours gris**

avec MICHAEL BRANDON · MIMSY FARMER
et JEAN-PIERRE MARIELLE
ALDO BUFILANDI · CALISTO CALISTI · MARISA FABBRI · ORESTE LIONELLO
FABRIZIO MORONI · STEFANO SATTA FLORES · COSTANZA SPADA
et avec FRANCINE RACETTE
et avec BUD SPENCER

Musique originale de ENNIO MORRICONE · Un film produit par SALVATORE ARGENTO
pour SEDA SPETTACOLI-Rome et UNIVERSAL PROD. FRANCE-Paris · TECHNICOLOR-TECHNISCOPE
DISTRIBUE PAR CINEMA INTERNATIONAL CORPORATION

DARIO ARGENTO

PROFONDO ROSSO

RIZZOLI FILM e SALVATORE ARGENTO presentano un film di DARIO ARGENTO con DAVID HEMMINGS DARIA NICOLODI in

PROFONDO ROSSO

con GABRIELE LAVIA · MACHA MERIL · EROS PAGNI · GIULIANA CALANDRA · e con la piccola NICOLETTA ELMI · e con GLAUCO MAURI
e con la partecipazione di CLARA CALAMAI · soggetto e sceneggiatura di DARIO ARGENTO e BERNARDINO ZAPPONI · musica di GIORGIO GASLINI
produttore esecutivo CLAUDIO ARGENTO · un film prodotto dalla SEDA Spettacoli s.r.l. · regia di DARIO ARGENTO · colore lux di LUCIANO VITTORI

opposite: A moment of childhood trauma, frozen in time beneath the plaster of **Deep Red**'s house of horrors

this page: Fotobuste for **Deep Red**

DARIO ARGENTO

PROFONDO ROSSO

RIZZOLI FILM e SALVATORE ARGENTO presentano un film di DARIO ARGENTO con DAVID HEMMINGS DARIA NICOLODI in

PROFONDO ROSSO

con GABRIELE LAVIA · MACHA MERIL · EROS PAGNI · GIULIANA CALANDRA · e con la piccola NICOLETTA ELMI · e con GLAUCO MAURI

opposite top: Deranged Marta seeks to bury the secrets from her past in **Deep Red**.
opposite bottom: Reluctant eyewitness Marc Daly lifts the body of Helga from a cradle of broken glass.

above: David Hemmings as Marc Daly.
right: The American poster for **Deep Red**.
below: Amanda Righetti (Giuliana Calandra) is scalded to death in her bath.
bottom: **Deep Red**'s pivotal childhood nightmare.

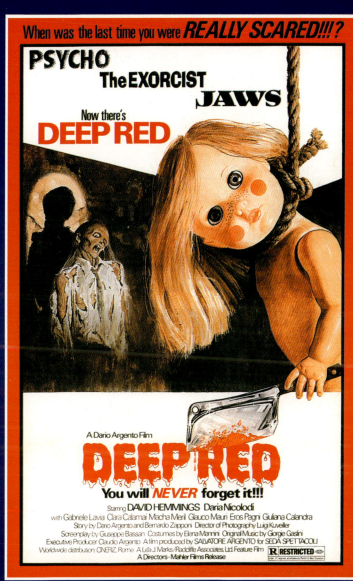

Above: This striking promotional artwork forms the basis of the Italian poster for **Deep Red**.

Below: The ghost of Christmas past comes back to haunt the characters of **Deep Red**.

un film de
Dario Argento

ROJO OSCURO

David Hemmings • Daria Nicolodi • Macha Meril

color

The Phantom's Bride

Hysteria, abjection and corporeality: the Gothic heroine from page to screen

Historically, the Gothic is a gendered mode. Critical debate surrounding Gothic litera-ture has tended to recognise a gender-defined distinction between such works as *The Monk* by Matthew Lewis, and the novels of Ann Radcliffe or Angela Carter. Over the late eighteenth and early nineteenth century, Radcliffe's work was frequently to be seen in women's journals - darkly romantic escapist fiction for bored middleclass wives. I have already discussed some of the structural and linguistic questions raised by this mode in connection with **Inferno**, but one issue which perhaps draws Argento's output closest to the Gothic novel is that of gender. Analytical responses to Gothic literature tend to identify three recurrent character types: the virtuous heroine, the male paranoiac and the sexual woman. In the course of this essay, I shall focus particularly on the first, to discuss her evolution through a number of key films and attempt to shed some light on her centrality to Argento's essentially Gothic narratives.

Hysteria, abjection and the 'Voice of the Author'

As Argento's first incarnation of the Gothic heroine, **Suspiria**'s Suzy Banyon perfectly fits the stereotype of the wide-eyed innocent of Ann Radcliffe's novels, thrust unprepared into a disturbing and overwhelming adult environment. The students at Freiburg's renowned Tanzakademie seem to have been relegated to the position of children, with the witches, their teachers, occupying the position of threatening parental figures, an impres-sion heightened through design: the sets were constructed so as to dwarf the actresses, with characters swallowed up by vast elevator doors, or reaching up to grasp doorhandles which have been placed unnaturally high.

A note of sexual repression is detectable in **Suspiria**'s principal setting, and its heroine's virtue presents us with a kind of tension as it is pitted against the darker powers of corrupt authoritarianism. Readings of the Gothic heroine frequently identify her as a hysteric, whose body becomes a site of nervous inscription. This calls to mind a scene in which Suzy, on her entry into her sinister new home, collapses during a practice session and begins to haemorrhage from the nose and mouth. While the school doctor presents us with an entirely logical explanation, focusing on the physical, the film clearly implies supernatural causes. But the notion of physical symptoms arising from psychiatric unrest is the subject of much of the discussion centring on the Gothic heroine, whose sexual repression finds its mode of inscription on her unsocialised body. In her discussion of Female Gothic, Ros Ballaster comments: *"If, in feminist psychoanalytic literary theory, the Freudian 'hysteric' emerges as a proto-feminist (writer), struggling to bring into expres-sion through displaced bodily (or textual) signs her experience of the denial of female agency in a patriarchal culture, then it is the Gothic heroine who most powerfully and explicitly 'represents' this hysterical condition to the feminist reader."*[1]

Ballaster's argument hinges on what she identifies as a common misreading of the feminine Gothic, asserting that in fact sexual repression is no more than a smokescreen, the real terror of the text emerging from woman's exclusion from politico-material power. In Ann Radcliffe's novels, the Gothic heroine frequently misinterprets disturbances in her environment as supernatural, this being more acceptable than the reality of exploitation by men. **Suspiria**'s narrative excludes this possibility, however, through marginalising its male characters and instead presenting us with a number of powerful and terrifying maternal figures (although I shall argue that the notion of masculine control is not

opposite:
Incarnations of Asia: the director's
daughter stars as Christine in
The Phantom of the Opera.

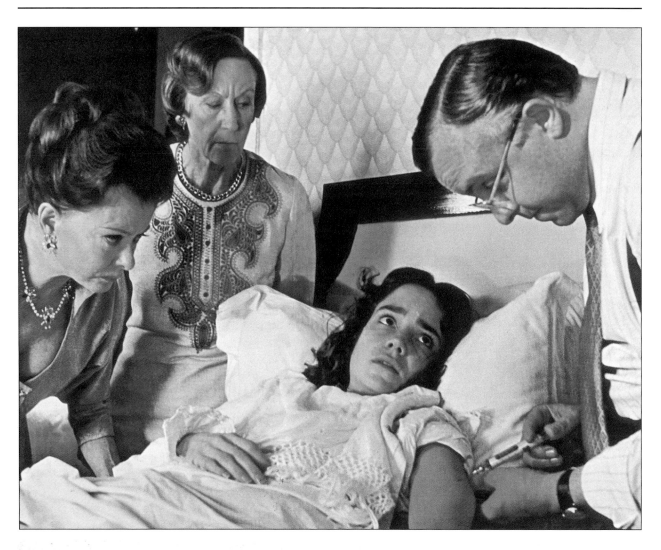

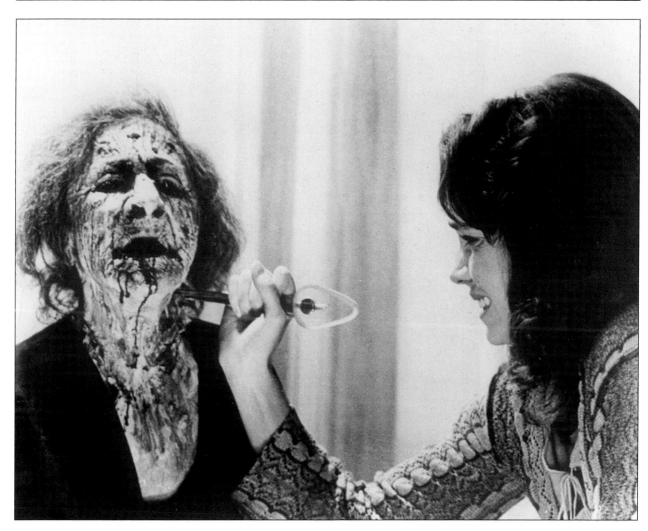

altogether eradicated from this and other narratives). Susanne Becker has suggested that, in the figure of the classic Gothic heroine, there is a duality, a division between the superficial romantic love story and the desire for female community, linking the attendant horror with female sexuality.[2] Barbara Creed comments on **Suspiria**'s representation of female sexuality as a site of abjection in *The Monstrous-Feminine*, observing, *"The witch is an abject figure who dwells with abject things: in* **Suspiria***, the mother/witches are associated with maggots, in* **Inferno** *with rats. Each one lives in a house where she hides her 'filthy secrets' in dark secret places which suggest the 'evil womb' of the abject mother.* **Suspiria** *and* **Inferno***, as well as* **Black Sunday***, reinforce the stereotypical image of the witch as a malevolent, destructive, monstrous figure whose constant aim is the destruction of the symbolic order."*[3]

Motherhood, as Creed suggests, lies at the very core of **Suspiria**'s representation of woman as a monster and it is the quest for the maternal which provides Suzy's trajectory towards her encounter with Helena Markos. Markos finally makes her ghastly appearance in the film's final scenes, as a grotesquely wizened old hag who cackles maniacally as the terrified Suzy cowers in the corner of her bedroom. **Suspiria**'s 'abject mother' is, in a sense, a variation on the deranged castrators Monica (**The Bird With The Crystal Plumage**), Nina (**Four Flies On Grey Velvet**) and Marta (**Deep Red**), all four characters bearing strong similarities to the Gothic novel's most oft-quoted representation of female as Other, the deranged, unsocialised madwoman, the 'sexual woman' of Gothic fiction: *"In the deep shade, at the farther end of the room, a figure ran backwards and forwards: what it was, whether beast or human being, one could not, at first sight tell: it grovelled, seemingly, on all fours: it snatched and growled like some strange wild animal: but it was covered with clothing, and a quantity of dark, grizzled hair, wild as a mane, hid its head and face."*[4]

The *"strange wild animal"* is Bertha Mason-Rochester, the 'madwoman in the attic' of Charlotte Brontë's *Jane Eyre*. Susanne Becker's analysis of Bertha focuses on the controlling power of the male gaze, observing that *"The figure of Bertha Mason has thus become a prototype of the sexual woman in the feminine Gothic: affirmative femininity turned into the monstrous - or, in narratological terms, into a voiceless textual object, controlled by the male gaze. This imprisoned position of the sexual woman figure has become one of the most powerful horrors that shape feminine Gothic texts."*[5]

Argento's account of the sexual woman is something of a variation on this. Monica, Nina and Marta are all invited down from their respective attics: told from a male perspective, the 'most powerful horror' is derived from the initial absence of any masculine control, a control which the male onlooker seeks to establish, this in itself becoming an exercise constantly problematised by the structures of male narcissism. Becker draws attention to Bertha's imprisonment and her voicelessness. More threatening still,

above:
Suzy (Jessica Harper) comes face to face with "The Black Queen", in **Suspiria**.
and
Mimsy Farmer as Nina, deranged wife of the befuddled male lead in **Four Flies on Grey Velvet**.

opposite top:
Suzy Banyon (Jessica Harper) finds herself in the company of witches in **Suspiria**.

opposite bottom:
Monica Ranieri, another of Argento's deranged castrators, in **The Bird With the Crystal Plumage**.

above:
An agent of the Black Queen emerges from the darkness to terrify imperilled heroine Suzy Banyon (Jessica Harper) in **Suspiria**.

facing page:
Lady of the flies: Jennifer Connelly in **Phenomena**.

Argento's madwomen are free to roam the streets in search of victims and, far from voiceless, are especially articulate in their lunacy.

Even in **Suspiria**, where men are for the most part excluded from the diegetic world, the narrative is introduced via a male narrator, the film's opening lines spoken by Argento himself over the credits. The device is put in place, I think, to mark the text with the director's authorial stamp, to cue us in to exactly whose perspective we are seeing this through. The literal 'voice of the author' reemerges in **Phenomena** (commenting on Jennifer's arrival at the school) and again in **Opera** (observing that Betty's recurrent nightmare might in fact be a memory of lived reality).[6] In all three instances, Argento's voiceover serves no purpose in facilitating the telling of the story. It rarely does anything but reiterate that which we already know (that Jennifer is arriving at her new school), that which we are about to find out (that Suzy has come to Freiburg to study ballet) or that which is coded but easily deducible (that Betty's dream is a memory and not entirely imagined).

Argento has, throughout his career, had occasion to make use of such personal 'appearances': he also gave brief introductions to two series of short TV films, more or less following the blueprint of *Alfred Hitchcock Presents*: *The Door To Darkness* and *The Nightmares of Dario Argento* (included in the gameshow *Giallo*). Aside from the inherent vanity of such an exercise, these utterances by the author's voice have performed the function of consolidating Argento's position as a public figure, branding his product, whilst also encouraging an awareness of his identity and control beyond the fiction.

This highlights what is the essential instability of the films' attempted construction of female fantasy. The notion of female subjectivity becomes unsustainable - what we are seeing may be a narrative told predominantly through female characters, but the structures of voyeurism and fetishism, as well as the controlling voice of a storyteller, are inevitably defined as masculine. In all three films, the heroine with whose point of view we are invited to identify is rarely released from the objectifying gaze, the eroticising gaze of the masculine spectator. The films' terms of address suggest female subjectivity whilst placing it in an implicitly phallocentric context. The hysteric of the Argento films (like her literary ancestor) is one product of their collision: in **Suspiria** and **Phenomena**, the implied frigidity of the setting (the Tanzakademie and the Richard Wagner School) seems to induce masochistic fantasies and sexual/supernatural nightmares.

above:
Argento directs Jennifer Connelly
on the set of **Phenomena**.

right:
Jennifer Corvino (Jennifer Connelly)
discovers one of the better kept secrets
of motherhood in **Phenomena**.

Sleepwalking and corporeality

It wasn't until ten years later that Jennifer Corvino provided a variation on the same character in **Phenomena**. Like Suzy, Jennifer is immediately placed in a traditionally Gothic context: she is a young girl who has travelled from her home far away to a strange new country (this time the aptly-named 'Swiss Transylvania') to join an all-girl school presided over by a cruel, authoritarian headmistress and her polite but unusually twitchy deputy Frau Bruckner.

Phenomena employs the notion of the double as integral to the heroine's interaction with her disorientating new environment, an important characteristic of her essential duality. Jennifer is doubled in at least two characters, first through Ella, associated with violence and the primitive, with animalistic passions and untamed instincts (the film frequently aligns Jennifer with animals) and then with Frau Bruckner's son, her male equivalent in her quest for the maternal.

Once again, the mother's sexuality is presented to us as a source of horror. Frau Bruckner's rape by (or seduction of) a psychiatric patient in a hospital has produced a disgustingly deformed infant, himself a necrophiliac who wallows in abject things. Frau Bruckner, who at first appears to be no more than a mild-mannered do-gooder, is eventually revealed to be a tyrannical parental figure. She invites the trusting heroine into her home, only to set about beating her, poisoning her and leaving her to drown in a slimy soup of putrefying body parts. The Bruckner child, as Jennifer's double, represents abject sexuality in opposition to Jennifer's innocence: entomologist John McGregor observes that as a necrophile, he delights in surrounding himself with decomposing flesh - in an early scene we see him making off with the decapitated corpse of a fourteen year-old Danish tourist.

Like Franco's reading of Sara in **Suspiria**, Jennifer is perceived as a hysteric by those who surround her - after catching her sleepwalking, her headmistress insists that she be subjected to a brainscan and demands to know if she has any history of epilepsy or drug abuse. This time, however, there is no implication that her body is genuinely exhibiting the marks of repression or female disempowerment, and instead the film seems to be presenting us with a virtual withdrawal from the corporeal. This brings to mind Helen Stoddart's observations on Isak Dinesen's *Seven Gothic Tales*, which encourage a similar rereading/rewriting of the Gothic heroine. Stoddart argues that relations between women and narration are *"expressed positively through* Seven Gothic Tales *in the form of certain recurrent themes - weightlessness, mutability, fakery, transience, superficiality, role-playing and the deliberate and imaginative denial of the categories of the real and realism in favour of the dreamed and fantastic."[7]*

It would not do to lay too much emphasis upon Stoddart's reading of Dinesen, the connection with Argento being fairly tenuous. There is, however, some value in Stoddart's comments on the 'weightlessness' which seems to be a common characteristic of

Dinesen's female characters, and her observation that this *"distance from the body"* represents a deliberate rereading of the Gothic heroine, a radical shift from the hysteric who has, necessarily, a *"relationship of immediacy to her body"*.[8]

The uncanniness associated with Jennifer is linked to her ability to communicate telepathically with the insect world, thus placing an emphasis upon her mind as opposed to her physical body. Her withdrawal from the body as a site of signification, her "weight-lessness" as Stoddart would have it, is reiterated by a scene in which she sleepwalks her way through the derelict building on her first night at the school and then again prior to her roommate's murder. Her body seems to follow her wandering mind, her obscure perspective represented through a series of bleached-out point of view shots. In a sequence deleted from **Phenomena**'s final cut, but shown in Michele Soavi's documentary **Dario Argento's World of Horror**, Jennifer literally defies the laws of gravity, levitating above the heads of her classmates, a scene which again suggests a shift away from the corporeal and the persistent fascination with woman's physicality.

School sages force Jennifer to undergo a brain scan in an attempt to 'explain' her problematic femininity in **Phenomena**.

Feminine dependency and the "cult of invalidism"

After a slew of critical reactions to Argento's work which laid their emphasis upon the psychoanalytic, **Trauma** made almost camp use of its Freudian foundations. Aura's relationship with Adriana is open to all manner of Freudian readings, but most striking in the context of this debate is its articulation of the recurrent theme of the Gothic heroine's quest for the maternal. Susanne Becker's argument, alluded to previously, hinges on her assertion that the story of the Gothic heroine's hunger for romantic love is pure surface: *"As early as in* The Mysteries [of Udolpho], *the female subject is constructed as 'competent subject' in the sense of a Greimasian actant not by romantic love for the hero, but by her quest for the mother. This quest develops in a parallel plot to the surface romance, and comes to question that surface's primacy as well as its (patriarchal) ideology."*[9] The Gothic heroine is, then, a divided subject, whose drama is derived from being perpetually torn between the two.

Aura's relationship with her mother is, we are told, deeply unstable (Becker has also pointed out that the security of the mother-daughter bond has traditionally been called into question, its sanctity undermined) and the film's finale sees Aura struggling to shut out her mother's overwhelming influence as she fends her off from within her refuge in the cellar, the 'womb' of her mother's house.

Xavier Mendik's discussion of the placement of John Everett Millais' *Ophelia* in **Trauma** sets the film's mother-daughter relationship against the context of post-Freudian feminist psychoanalysis and draws attention to other fundamental aspects of the Argento heroine.

Mendik's argument hinges upon a scene close to the end of the film, in which David, wandering the streets after the apparent suicide of Aura, happens to glance at a painting in the window of a gallery. The painting is a reproduction of Millais' *Ophelia*, and as he looks at it he glimpses a young woman, whom he momentarily mistakes for Aura,

below:
Jennifer Corvino and Frau Bruckner (Daria Nicolodi) deep in "the Swiss Transylvania" of **Phenomena**.

next two pages:
The virginal heroine (Asia Argento, left) and the monstrous matriarch (Piper Laurie, right) present the two Gothic visions of the feminine in **Trauma**.

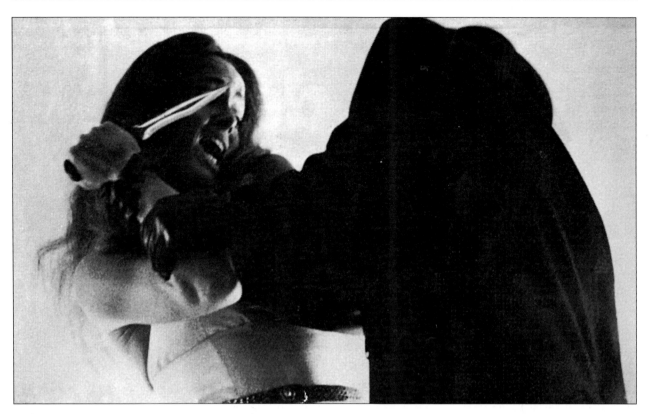

Deadlier than the male: 'femme castratrice'
Monica Ranieri (Eva Renzi, above) turns
swooning victim (opposite top) in
The Bird With the Crystal Plumage.

reflected in the window. Mendik observes that the image is "split", with Ophelia (a representation of woman as passive, submissive and unstable) sharing the frame with a figure which appears to be Aura (but, significantly, isn't).[10]

For Mendik, what is pivotal in this scene is the primacy of the masculine gaze: the Argento male, as exemplified in **Trauma** by David, is another key figure which recognisably belongs to the world of the Gothic. As Todd French has observed, *"Far from being indefatigable macho avengers who are every bit a match for Argento's ubiquitous black-gloved assassins, his artists/sleuths are paranoid, alienated seekers."*[11] The 'alienated seeker' finds his counterpart in Gothic literature through the figure of the male paranoiac, that indispensable cornerstone of the Radcliffe tradition, whose project is the ramifications of phallocentricity and patriarchal structures. Argento's 'heroes' frequently refuse to recognise female characters as anything but passive ciphers, victims by very nature of their femininity. Sam Dalmas makes this mistake in **The Bird With the Crystal Plumage**, when he witnesses a struggle between a man and a woman in an art gallery. The man, dressed from head to toe in black, is assumed to be the aggressor and the woman is his helpless victim, whom Dalmas must rescue. The image is a trick, however, and it isn't until the very end of the film that our hero's gender-related preconceptions are swept aside by the realisation that it was in fact the woman holding the knife.

Deep Red follows a similar track, once again using the reversal of gender roles as a pivotal turning point in the narrative. Marc Daly has frequent disputes with feminist girlfriend Gianna, and even resorts to arm-wrestling in his efforts to prove that men are superior to women (he loses, of course). His anxiety, his 'nervousness' as Gianna puts it, is fuelled by the fragility of his male narcissism. His investigation into a murder he has witnessed (and again the psychopath in the gender-concealing raincoat is taken to be a man) tests his assumptions repeatedly: his friend Carlo is discovered to be a homosexual, whose androgynous lover is a clear source of disquiet to Daly; the sweet little girl whose father holds the key to the killer's former home turns out to be a petty sadist; and when caught off guard in the derelict mansion, it is he who must be rescued by Gianna, and not the other way around. The ending entirely demolishes his perception of the carefully laid 'rules' of gender (the killer is revealed to be a woman) and he is left staring at his reflection in a pool of blood, a cruelly ironic visual pun on his now shattered narcissism.

According to Mendik, David's understanding of Aura's femininity articulates exactly these concerns. He notes that David's perception of Aura hinges on her vulnerability, the inherent weakness of woman and her mental instability. In an early scene, he saves her from suicide when he finds her perched on the edge of a high bridge, and *"The revelation of her anorexia is used by David to consolidate his position of womanhood."*[12] Millais' *Ophelia* is a perfect reflection of these preconceptions. According to Bram Dijkstra, it forms part of a trend in nineteenth century art and literature dubbed 'the cult of invalidism'. Dijkstra writes: *"Throughout the second half of the nineteenth century, parents, sisters, daughters, and loving friends were kept busy on canvases everywhere, anxiously nursing wan, hollow-eyed beauties who were on the verge of death. For many a Victorian husband his wife's physical weakness came to be evidence to the world and to God of her physical and mental purity - that precious commodity which would ultimately secure him spiritual succour from the world of sordid business affairs and rescue his soul from perdition. Late nineteenth-century painters were eager to oblige his sense of virtue with affecting images of feminine weakness bearing such titles as "A Shadow", "A Lull", "Anxiety", "The Dying Mother", "In Excelsis" and so on."*[13]

'The cult of invalidism' manifested itself in the paintings of Millais, Waterhouse and Rossetti, as well as in the literature and poetry of Poe and Baudelaire, alongside numerous other popular nineteenth century writers and artists. Self-starvation became fashionable amongst middle-class wives and so the cult of invalidism became a widespread killer amongst wealthy married women, as well as big business in the art world. *The Lady of Shalott*, who in Tennyson's poem becomes sickly, consumptive and eventually dies from unrequited love, was committed to canvas over and over again by nineteenth century painters, most famously by Waterhouse and William Holman Hunt. Pale, consumptive beauties from literature, poetry, myth and legend were rediscovered and redesigned to cash in on the trend.

Dijkstra continues by observing that *"even Tennyson's heroines had to yield in popularity to Shakespeare's Ophelia, the later nineteenth-century's all-time favourite example of the love-crazed self-sacrificial woman who most perfectly demonstrated her devotion to her man by descending into madness, who surrounded herself with flowers to show her equivalence to them, and who in the end committed herself to a watery grave, thereby fulfilling the nineteenth-century male's fondest fantasies of feminine dependency."*[14] Arthur Hughes painted her gazing absently into the brook, having knotted reeds into her hair, versions by Ernest Hébert and Georg Richard Falkenberg lay an emphasis upon her hollow, haunted, staring eyes, and Waterhouse depicted her in varying states of mental degeneration.

Millais' *Ophelia*, however, is the most appropriate choice as an icon of its generation. The most famous of all the Ophelias, it even has the dubious distinction of having caused the death of its model (in circumstances which bear a striking resemblance to Poe's story *The Oval Portrait*, Elizabeth Siddal contracted a serious illness when she posed in a bath of cold water for the duration of the winter, instigating a series of maladies which eventually killed her ten years later). But in **Trauma**, the image conceals an entirely different story. Aura's apparent death in the lake is a red herring (water, in Argento's cinema, has frequently been called upon to symbolise the womb, and Aura's note, *"I've gone to join my mother"*, mockingly points us in the right direction whilst encouraging us to leap to the wrong conclusion at the same time). Mendik cites Aura's dream, in which her father leers at her, rubbing his hands as she lies in bed, as *"yet another misleading visual 'fragment' that has to be reread."* He continues, *"As Freud himself concluded, such fantasies often 'concealed' the spectre of a dominant maternal figure, who continues to exert a powerful influence in the daughter's later life."*[15]

Mendik's essay makes no mention of the one startling 'fragment' which truly seems to validate his whole argument: within the pivotal image, behind the reproduction of *Ophelia*, are several other paintings, one of which appears to be a representation of either Salome or Herodias, handling the severed head of John the Baptist (this second canvas is partly obscured and difficult to see, but the style is typical of Aubrey Beardsley). In *Idols Of Perversity*, Dijkstra comments extensively on the representations of the

Marc Daly (David Hemmings), the "alienated seeker" of **Deep Red**, follows the gender signposts.

Jennifer is depicted as a more spiritual than corporeal heroine in **Phenomena**.

Salome story which are to be found amongst nineteenth century art, an alternative to the image of femininity conveyed through the cult of invalidism, which this time sought to portray woman as a predatory, aggressive headhunter: *"Flaubert's virginal Salome is a blind tool of her calculating mother, who had made certain that her daughter would grow up to be an innocent lure in service of her power-hungry parent."*[16] Mendik comments on the casting of Piper Laurie as the head-hunting matriarch Adriana, associating it with the concept of the *"pre-Oedipal mother"*, the infant's primary love object who *"retains an influence as a threatening figure"*, arguing that her presence may be a reference to her similar role in Brian De Palma's **Carrie** (interestingly, Mendik also suggests a connection between the attempted suicide of Aura and that of the ambivalent character of Madeleine in Hitchcock's **Vertigo** - Kim Novak was Argento's original choice for the role of Adriana).

According to Barbara Creed, the figure of the castrating mother is a recurrent one in the modern horror film. She refers to the pre-credits sequence in **Deep Red** as a kind of 'primal scene', a representation of the mother as threatening and deranged, whose son is subsequently plagued by a fear of women (hence, according to the Freudian logic of the film, his homosexuality)[17]. Her discussion centres around **Psycho**, through which she identifies a particular set of coded iconography which should cue us in to the presence of the castrating mother: *"Once we become aware of the prevalence of the image of woman as castrator in the horror film, we can more easily recognise the signs of her presence - cruel appraising eyes, knives, water, blood, the 'haunted' house."*[18] All of these elements are evident in **Deep Red** and **Trauma** in some shape or form, as they are in **Carrie**, which Creed discusses at some length, and which Xavier Mendik has suggested is one of **Trauma**'s closer relatives. Creed asserts that *"The mother-child relationship in **Carrie**, as in **Psycho**, is depicted as abnormal and perverse. Carrie [like Aura] desires independence and yearns to lead her own life, yet is unable to break away from her mother's dominating influence."*[19]

Gendered perspectives and Gothic spaces

The portrait we assemble of the Gothic heroine through **Suspiria**, **Phenomena** and **Trauma** is, therefore, one of an evolving character, but one who consistently embodies key thematic concerns: her immediacy to / distance from her body and her unstable relationship with the maternal, which represents female sexuality as threatening, even abject. **The Phantom of the Opera**'s Christine is, then, something of a departure. One element of Gaston Leroux's novel which is conspicuously absent here is that of the mother figure, Mamma Valerius. There is no maternal presence, abject or otherwise, and the love story between Christine and The Phantom is certainly more than a mere surface for darker passions, taking priority over all other narrative elements.

What is articulated most strikingly here is the primacy of the male gaze and its centrality to readings of Christine. As Susanne Becker has pointed out in her account of *Jane Eyre*'s Bertha Mason-Rochester, the representation of woman, in the Gothic novel, traditionally depends upon who is doing the looking.[20] By allowing the love story a position of supremacy within the narrative, Argento lends Christine's character a greater degree of complexity: in Leroux's novel, her naivety is central to her involvement with Erik, whom she has never seen and innocently believes to be an angel. Her sexuality is left unexplored, whilst Argento's film has her willing to be seduced by The Phantom amongst the dilapidated finery of his subterranean home. A sense of ambiguity is injected into her character and, at least in the eyes of male onlookers, she is perceived as morally suspect: the ratcatcher denounces her as *"The Phantom's whore"*, and both Raoul and The Phantom picture her in visualised fantasies posing lasciviously before them, reconstructing her as temptress.

But Christine is unable to choose between her two suitors, a dilemma which becomes central to the narrative's dramatic construct and which serves to focus another fundamental duality which here is cited as central to the character of the Gothic heroine. She herself articulates this when, as she stares at her reflection in a mirror (her 'double'), she observes *"I, who know nothing about love, have fallen in love with two men,"* and again later when she warns Raoul of a *"darkness"* which exists within her, a darkness which appears to be linked with her new awareness of her sexuality, which the passionate, unsocialised Phantom has awakened in her.

In another of the film's Gothic motifs, the narrative structure emphasises doubling through the characters of Raoul and The Phantom. While Raoul is the product and reflection of order and social convention, The Phantom is entirely emblematic of the rejection of such norms. In Argento's adaptation he has no name, marking his exclusion from the world of the civilised; he lights the way to sexual indulgence and the amoral; he lives underground in the catacombs, murders his visitors using his teeth and from the very beginning of the film he is linked with the abject through his association with rats and corpses. This conflict between the world of the civilised and that of the dark and chaotic becomes pivotal as the finale approaches. Having been carried unconscious into the caves by The Phantom, Christine awakes and attacks him, screaming to Raoul for help. A moment later she seems to change her mind once again, begging to be forgiven and entreating him to escape with her from Raoul and the pursuing authorities. She never willingly makes a choice between them. Like Anna in **The Stendhal Syndrome**, she becomes a victim of masculine control - inevitably, the diegetic world is phallocentrically organised. While in **Suspiria**, **Phenomena** and **Trauma**, the heroine's predicament is rooted in the mother's terrifying sexuality, Christine's position at the centre of what resembles a masculinist plot brings her closer to the literary heroines of the Radcliffe tradition.

facing page:
Gothic spaces: The Phantom of the Opera (Julian Sands) at home in the catacombs.

Julian Sands bears his teeth as The Phantom (with Nadia Rinaldi).

Christine Daée (Asia Argento) prepares for a rendezvous with an amorous killer in **The Phantom of the Opera**.

Argento's **The Phantom of the Opera**, perhaps more so than Leroux's novel, assumes a compatibility between female desire and victimisation/masochism. Although Christine is never placed in danger in quite the same way as Betty in **Opera** or Suzy in **Suspiria**, the voyeuristic, fetishistic gaze through which she is objectified is quite explicitly defined as masculine. The Opera House too is complicit in her victimisation: like the Tanzakademie in **Suspiria** or Adriana's house in **Trauma**, it is full of secret places, divisions, spaces which mark an opposition between that which is known and that which is unknown, the horror frequently related to gender-defined societal spaces. In **Suspiria**, **Deep Red**, **Inferno** and **Trauma**, the 'haunted' house or family home is strongly associated with the feminine, more specifically with the evil influence of the maternal, while here the building is identified as a male domain, belonging to The Phantom. Recalling the implications of the author's voice in **Suspiria** and **Phenomena**, this once again places the narrative squarely and unambiguously in the sphere of masculine control.

Jessica Harper as Suzy Banyon in **Suspiria**.

Notes

1.   Ballaster, Ros: "Wild nights and buried letters: the Gothic 'unconscious' of feminist criticism" in Modern Gothic, edited by Victor Sage and Allan Lloyd Smith (Manchester University Press, Manchester, 1996), p.60
2.   Becker, Susanne: "Postmodern feminine horror fictions" in Modern Gothic, edited by Victor Sage and Allan Lloyd Smith (Manchester University Press, Manchester, 1996), p.76
3.   Creed, Barbara: The Monstrous Feminine (Routledge, London, 1993), pp.76-77
4.   Brontë, Charlotte: Jane Eyre (Penguin, London, 1966), p.321
5.   Becker, Susanne: "Postmodern feminine horror fictions" in Modern Gothic, edited by Victor Sage and Allan Lloyd Smith (Manchester University Press, Manchester, 1996), p.72
6.   In all three instances, the point is lost in English language translations: in **Suspiria** and **Phenomena**, Argento's voice is replaced by that of American narrators while in **Opera**, the voiceover is spoken in the first person by Betty.
7.   Helen Stoddart: "Isak Dinesen and the fiction of Gothic gravity" in Modern Gothic, edited by Victor Sage and Allan Lloyd Smith (Manchester University Press, Manchester, 1996), p. 84
8.   Helen Stoddart: "Isak Dinesen and the fiction of Gothic gravity" in Modern Gothic, edited by Victor Sage and Allan Lloyd Smith (Manchester University Press, Manchester, 1996), p. 85
9.   Becker, Susanne: "Postmodern feminine horror fictions" in Modern Gothic, edited by Victor Sage and Allan Lloyd Smith (Manchester University Press, Manchester, 1996), p.76
10.   Mendik, Xavier: "Upon the Eyelids of Ophelia: The Sexual 'Fragment' of Trauma" in Necronomicon, n.7, p.21
11.   French, Todd: "Dario Argento: Myth and Murder" in The Deep Red Horror Handbook, edited by Chas Balun (FantaCo Books, New York, 1989), p.11
12.   Mendik, Xavier: "Upon the Eyelids of Ophelia: The Sexual 'Fragment' of Trauma" in Necronomicon, n.7, p.21
13.   Dijkstra, Bram: Idols of Perversity (Oxford University Press, New York 1986) p.25
14.   Dijkstra, Bram: Idols of Perversity (Oxford University Press, New York 1986) p.42
15.   Mendik, Xavier: "Upon the Eyelids of Ophelia: The Sexual 'Fragment' of Trauma" in Necronomicon, n.7, p.21
16.   Dijkstra, Bram: Idols of Perversity (Oxford University Press, New York 1986) p.381
17.   Creed, Barbara: The Monstrous Feminine (Routledge, London 1993) p.140
18.   Creed, Barbara: The Monstrous Feminine (Routledge, London 1993) p.140
19.   Creed, Barbara: The Monstrous Feminine (Routledge, London 1993) p.78
20.   Becker, Susanne: "Postmodern feminine horror fictions" in Modern Gothic, edited by Victor Sage and Allan Lloyd Smith (Manchester University Press, Manchester, 1996), p.72

The Art of Allusion

Painting, murder and the 'plan tableau'

Accusations of misogynist characterisations, sloppy scripting and narrative incoherence have surrounded Argento's output since the beginning of his career. The one criticism most often levelled at his visual style, however, seems to concern its utter exuberance and supremacy over narrative causality. Referring to **The Cat O'Nine Tails**, one reviewer wrote: *"This vomitous offering comes from the Italian writer/director who made his debut with **The Bird With the Crystal Plumage**, an equally badly dubbed flashy-stylish murder mystery that had some popularity last summer among famished thriller nuts."*[1] The implication here, expanded upon by countless other film critics, is that the film's "flashy-stylish" extravagance counts only as a device put in place to distract attention from the perceived weaknesses of the distinctly un-Hollywood approach to storytelling. For many, the aesthetic fussiness of many of the Argento films is little more than superficial flourish, artistic gloss, particularly in the likes of **Inferno**, a film which, although full of painterly touches, is bound to cause endless frustration to anyone searching for a conventionally structured narrative. 'Painterly' is a particularly apt term for the aesthetic sensibilities of Argento's cinema, a body of work across which aesthetics operate on a number of different levels. The director has commented recently on how the work of Georges de la Tour influenced his style of composition and lighting in **The Phantom of the Opera**,[2] while in an article in *Cahiers du Cinéma*, Jean-Francois Rauger observes that detectable in his style are the distinctive hallmarks of an extremely broad range of painters and movements, *"from Caravaggio (**Trauma**) to hyperrealism (**Deep Red**) and the surrealists (**Suspiria**)."*[3] It is therefore interesting to consider how and why his films appropriate painting, and to examine what implications this might have on a larger scale.

The Cinema of Painting

To form a better understanding of exactly what relationship exists between painting and the Argento films, it is worth considering the history of the polemics surrounding the cinema of painting, ideas which have been developed primarily by French film theorists since as early as 1919. Fernand Léger and Marcel Gromaire both put forward ideas on painting and how this might be developed through the relatively modern art form of film. Léger asserted that *"Thanks to the screen, the prejudice against 'things larger than life' no longer exists."*[4] He suggested that the future of cinema as painting might lie in the photography of objects or parts of objects, shot in closeup, an attention to detail which recalls the painting of still life. This, he maintained, carried heavier emotional weight: a closeup of a moving stage door makes a more powerful image than a shot of the character who is moving it. To this end, he suggested, the subject should be removed, which along with literature and sentimentality, he argued, brings the cinema too close to theatre. *"True cinema involves the image of the object"* he declared.[5] Léger's ideas do in some senses prefigure the use of the closeup in modern film, but don't quite cover the aesthetic qualities of Argento's painterly cinema. Films such as **Inferno** and **Opera** make use not only of the "image of the object", but also of the accumulation of detail on a grand scale.

Marcel Gromaire put forward some interesting ideas on the potential future of the painterly cinema in 1919. Before going into specifics, Gromaire advances some ideas which help to define his concept of film as an art form. He writes that *"The cinematic composer should respond to the changing plastic forms of [a] spectacle; whereas the*

opposite:
Art becomes a vessel for schizophrenic
fantasies in **The Stendhal Syndrome**.

Now you are here among us: Suzy Banyon is welcomed into the fold in **Suspiria**.

painter synthesises the continuous movement into stable form."[6] The primary difference between cinema and painting, then, has to do with movement. The reference to "plastic forms" brings the cinema closer to sculpture, while the element of change adds a further dimension. He writes that the cinema *"is an essentially modern art because it is mobile and restless,"* again stressing the animation not shared by sculpture and painting, perhaps bringing film closer to theatre, an art form with which the cinema of painting has done its best to avoid comparison. It is also interesting to note that Gromaire identifies *"the director, the actors and the landscape"* as the artistic lifeblood of the cinema.[7] Writers, he asserts, must tailor their screenplays for these three factors: *"One must proceed by using them as the basis of the imagined form; the film must be conceived expressly for them. One must not merely adapt a literary work for the cinema."* Gromaire's sympathies clearly lie with those works in which narrative is entirely subordinated to the aesthetic.

The similarities and differences between the cinema and other art forms, and the way in which painting helps to shape these, constitute an argument which is crucial in defining this area as a polemic. The art form which most immediately springs to mind when one is looking for close relatives of the cinema is photography. The notion of a cinema of painting helps to distract from this preconception, lending it a 'high art' status. Ginette Vincendeau has described the heritage cinema, which has close links with the cinema of painting, as having *"gained currency on account of the films' opulent recreation of the past and use of canonical literature... To this genre also belong such films as **Jean de Florette**, **Howard's End**, **Cyrano de Bergerac** and **Babette's Feast**... targeting a middle-class and 'middlebrow' audience. Being among the few European films to penetrate the world market, they increasingly define European/French cinema as an international luxury product with high audience appeal."*[8] Vincendeau's term "international luxury product" gives some clue as to a possible reason for the reappropriation of painting in the Argento films. Unlike his American counterparts, Argento strives to win kudos as a serious art film director. Although his films find favour with teenage audiences and slasher movie fans, audiences little different from those of their US equivalents, they aim also to present their audiences with a high quality product, a slice of highbrow art for the global media market.

In the opening chapter of his fascinating study of painting and cinema, *Décadrages*, Pascal Bonitzer refers to André Bazin as having written that there are two sorts of cinéaste: those who believe in reality and those who believe in the image.[9] This, he argues, is a typically French distinction. He claims that such a dichotomy does not exist in the American cinema, where the two go together: *"it's the American dream,"* he concludes, of which *"hyperrealism is the result."* This distinction has been explored in the polemics expounded between Marcelin Plynet, Jean Mitry and others, as to whether the camera is a *"purely ideological apparatus"* which produces a perspective code derived from the Quattrocento, or if it is an apparatus which simply *"mechanically reproduces natural vision.*"[10] Argento too has come close to voicing this distinction, having once[11] claimed to be a follower of Pasolini's poetic approach to filmmaking, as opposed to the simple rendering of an objective vision of reality.

Suspiria could hardly be said to present us with objective and entirely faithful representations of the real. Its aesthetic is heavily stylised, in terms of camera movement, decor, colour, perspective and composition. The grandiose *mise en scène* is more aligned with what Bazin and Bonitzer refer to as *"believing in the image"*. It comes as no surprise that it is this kind of representation, the belief in the image, that Bonitzer argues is the basis for the cinema of painting.

I have suggested that the painterly cinema frequently defines itself in terms of its similarities to and differences from other art forms, but perhaps an equally central issue is how it defines itself in terms of other branches of its own. The appropriation of painting sets it apart from theatre, and its subject matter draws it slightly closer to literature (upon which Argento's films draw heavily, from Agatha Christie and Sir Arthur Conan Doyle, to Thomas De Quincey and Gaston Leroux), but primarily it draws these diverse artistic references into a relationship with the American cinema. Argento's films, for all that they are painterly in ways that American horror films more frequently aren't, have a great deal in common with American cinema. Films like **Opera**, **Inferno** and **The Stendhal Syndrome** aim for impressive production values, and like their American counterparts they exploit sex and violence, depicting rape, torture and murder in elaborately composed tableaux. The painterly aesthetic contributes to the expensive and artistic pitch of the films, with the intention of selling them to audiences as a higher quality equivalent with greater artistic and cultural value.

Pure, fairytale primaries: Jessica Harper and Stefania Cassini in **Suspiria**.

The notion of a 'painterly cinema' as an international luxury product can be applied to the work of numerous directors, from Bertolucci to Greenaway and Rivette. Argento's visual style serves for far more than just simply a signpost of high-brow respectability. In an article entitled *"Aesthetics of Ambiguity"*, Patricia Moir has argued that his use of colour, composition and movement combine to lend his films *"a maddening tone of ambiguity,"* which ultimately transports the viewer *"into a new and uncertain space."*[12] Elaborating on this, she writes: *"The palette is always meticulously controlled; in the case of **Suspiria**, for example, the colour was manipulated to achieve sequences of pure, fairytale primaries. **Tenebrae**'s icy modernism, balanced with the precision of a Mondrian canvas, is punctuated with startling slashes of red, which disrupt and reorganise the composition, transforming the intellectual calm into emotional brutality."*

Moir's observation that changes in colour parallel the similar transitions between rational/calm and uncertainty, distress or violence is spectacularly evident in **Suspiria**. The famous opening scene, depicting Suzy's departure from the world of the rational into that of the bizarre is marked with a sudden change in colour scheme: a momentary glare of red gives way to the muted, dull colours of the interior of the airport, until the glass doors

A new and uncertain space: a chaotic canvas of convergent lines, shapes and primary colours in a scene from **Suspiria**.

Shades of darkness: Sara (Eleonora Giorgi)
takes a step into the unknown in **Inferno**.

open and Suzy is delivered, unnerved and disorientated, into the multicoloured
nightmare landscape of Freiburg. Paradoxically, darkness, in the worlds of **Suspiria** and
Inferno, is where the colour of light dictates the tone of anxiety and unease. Scenes in
daylight present us with an environment of logic and security: it is in the bright, stable,
almost too quiet world of the rational that Suzy is allowed the comfort of a psychiatric
explanation from Franco (*"Bad luck isn't brought by broken mirrors, but by broken
minds"*), but the lustreless, pastel-coloured equilibrium is drastically altered as darkness
brings an outpouring of anguish, horror and the supernatural. The gaudy decor of
Suspiria's dance academy, which seems almost cheerful if not exactly subtle in the light
of early morning, is transformed into a ghastly canvas of intense reds and greens as
night approaches.

The *"Plan-tableau"*

Bonitzer asserts that *"The creation of shots is what draws the cinéaste closer to
painting, the cinema of painting."*[13] Composing a shot, then, may be conceived in the
same way as composing a painting. What Bonitzer is referring to, primarily, is the *plan-
tableau*, the shot which resembles a painting. *"The function of the plan-tableau is interac-
tive,"* we are told. *"Ambivalence, discourse in two voices, the unstable mixing of the high
(painting) and the low (cinema), of movement (the shot) and of stasis (the painting)."* The
conjunction of movement and stasis is an idea upon which Bonitzer expands, telling us
*"The plan-tableau is extra-narrative in function, which is why it has been employed by
those cinéastes who privilege mise en scène and the plastic over the scenario and
narrative progression, like Godard and Pasolini."*[14] It is worth dwelling upon this point. In
his article *"L'Epée devant les yeux"*, Hubert Damisch writes *"the reference to painting is
always ambiguous in the cinema. When one sees the appearance in a film of an element
connoted as pictoral, a stasis is produced."*[15] This stasis, he concludes, has the effect of
producing a sense of limbo, the suspension of the narrative.

To what end, then, is this stasis brought into play? One can see the point that Bonitzer
and Damisch are both making, that the *plan-tableau* usually involves a moment of inanima-
tion, both in terms of on-screen movement and narrative progression, and sets the spectator
back from the film temporarily - all the better to take notice of the film's painterly aesthetic,
and therefore to appreciate its status as high-art cinema. A second reason that a stasis may
be desirable is that in creating a distance between audience and spectacle, it causes the
illusion of reality to fall: a crack is created in the surface of the fiction, a gap through which
meaning may be conveyed. Bonitzer suggests that the *plan-tableau* draws attention to its
own presence, demanding that the audience spot a reference and thus decipher a coded
idea: *"the plan-tableau always implies therefore, not only a cultural acknowledgement on
the part of the public, but also a call for reading, for decoding."*[16] Bonitzer argues his case
using a shot from Rohmer's **La Marquise d'O** which resembles Goya's *The Nightmare*. It is
at this point that the appropriation of painting becomes most literal in the films of Argento.
Like Rohmer, he invokes specific works of art, both through placing paintings on the set, and
through emulating well-known images through composition. References to an actual work
frequently forge a connection between the film and the connotations or cultural context of
the painting, demanding to be read, rather than merely to be looked at.

In *The Black Cat* segment of **Two Evil Eyes**, Madeleine Potter as Annabel comes close
to the ideal of femininity represented through Pre-Raffaelite art, and in fact bears a striking
resemblance to Elizabeth Siddal, the 'Ophelia' of John Everett Millais' famous painting.
The reference to *Ophelia* is made directly when Annabel, having been murdered by her
lover, is left to sink into a bath of diluted blood, the image composition roughly mimicking
that of the Millais painting. The implications of this illuminate Argento's approach to the
Poe text, bearing on the representation of women both in horror fiction in general and in
this film in particular.[17]

above:
Anna reconstructs herself in the image of Botticelli's Venus in **The Stendhal Syndrome**.

left:
Pre-Raffaelite art in motion: Elizabeth Siddal lookalike Madeleine Potter as Annabel in *The Black Cat* segment of **Two Evil Eyes**.

Ophelia reappears in **Trauma**, this time as a print placed in a gallery window. Instead of recreating the image through composition, as a *plan-tableau*, Argento instead makes a more direct reference, actually showing us the painting, inviting us to read it against a certain context. The print is seen by David as he passes in the street, and he immediately associates it with the memory of Aura, his teenaged lover whom he believes has drowned herself in a lake. Once again, *Ophelia* acts as a reference to the nineteenth century obsession with inscribing the female body with notions of submission and passivity, a debate on which I have expanded elsewhere in this volume.[18]

While **Trauma** presents us with a covert reference to an ideological trend through a painted image, **The Stendhal Syndrome** takes these ideas associated with reference and representation far more literally. Graziella Magherini's book *La Sindrome di Stendhal* offered the director fertile ground for a more extensive exploration of the referential possibilities of famous works of art. Magherini's account covers the observations she made while at the psychiatric department of the Santa Maria Nuova hospital, regarding an unusual condition which causes patients to undergo a variety of forms of emotional disturbance when confronted with powerful works of art.

According to Freudian psychoanalyst Magherini, finding the correct reading of the image which has brought on the attack, and associating this with the patient's own mental history, is crucial if one is to divine the reason for its extraordinary effect. Amongst the many cases she outlines, that of Franz, a Bavarian tourist is a perfect example: whilst exploring the Uffizi Gallery in Florence, Franz became bewildered and began to suffer some sort of visual impairment, the exact nature of which he found difficult to define. It was when he caught sight of Caravaggio's *The Young Bacchus*, however, that Franz was forced to leave the room, overcome by the bombardment of sensations. Magherini's explanation focuses on the patient's repressed homosexuality, claiming that it was the homoerotic associations of Caravaggio's painting which caused him such distress.[19]

Mal D'art

Magherini's observations suggest the basis of the formula which Argento has incorporated into his film, sketching Anna's psychiatric background, which unfolds gradually as we see the effect that the various paintings invoke. The film opens with a number of scenes which bombard us with powerful works of art, each piece carrying a thinly veiled significance. Argento's complex web of references begins with the opening credits sequence, which juxtaposes a series of images of men, women, water and death, spanning history, from Bruegel's *Dulle Griet* to Warhol's Marilyn Monroe prints.

We open on a view of Florence as Anna hurries through the crowded streets. Various statues including Dante and David, all patriarchal icons of masculine superiority, tower above her. Upon entering the Uffizi, she spies Paolo Uccello's *The Battle of San Romano* and stops to stare, unsettled by something in the image. The canvas is overwhelmingly crammed with detail, with associations directed towards threatening machismo and phallic superiority. Argento's closeups emphasise its iconography of menacing sexuality, the sharp phallic pikes and penetrating arrows. The soundtrack becomes filled with the echoes of aggressive male voices, raised in cries and shouts.

Disturbed, Anna turns away and steps into a different room. There she finds herself momentarily transfixed by Botticelli's *The Birth Of Venus*. Botticelli's Venus is a faintly ambiguous representation of woman. Here we see her standing upright, stronger than the delicate, swooning Venuses that came later, like that of Alexandre Cabanel, and yet she appears to be swaying in the wind, laying an emphasis upon her fragility. To the left, we see Zephyrus blowing a breeze at her, as he hovers in the air with Zephyritis, his female counterpart, clinging to him for support.

From this tableau of passive femininity, Anna passes to a more complex image, Botticelli's *Primavera*, a work which has perplexed historians with its elusive hints at concealed meaning for more than a century. Although less well known than *The Birth of Venus*, *Primavera* is an infinitely more controversial work. Since it was first put on public display in 1853, the image has become regarded as an insoluble enigma. As to when, why and for whom it was painted, we can only guess, and readings can only ever be subjective. From left to right, the painting is commonly believed to depict Mercury, stirring the ether with a wand; The Three Graces; Venus, with Cupid hovering above her; Primavera, the goddess of Spring; the nymph Chloris (who at that moment is being transformed into Flora), and Zephyr on the far right. Theories surrounding the painting have ranged from ideas related to birth and regeneration to Jungian notions of the search for the anima and simple allegories borrowed from mythological texts focusing on love.

But, as Magherini has striven to demonstrate, the 'Stendhal Syndrome' hinges on the subjective - that is, not the plethora of theories offered by art historians, but the associations the image suggests to those affected by it. In this case, it has to be the film's representation of the work which leads us to an interpretation. As with all the paintings shown in this sequence, Argento introduces the *Primavera* by taking in the entire canvas on a wide-shot, then cutting to closeups of those details which, we infer, hold some special significance. The first closeup is a long pan, which takes in one of the Three Graces, then Venus, then Primavera, three representations of woman in Botticelli's court of Venus. Each of them is pregnant, and each one presents us with an entirely unthreatening and unthreatened image of the feminine. It is when we cut to Chloris and Zephyr, however, that something disturbing enters the image. He appears to be swooping down to catch hold of her, and as he does so, flowers sprout from her mouth. According to Magherini, *"The nymph is being seduced by Zephyr. The rose in the mouth represents the actual moment of deflowering... [This part] is about Botticelli's adolescence."* She goes on to suggest that the seduction of Zephyr is a detail which expresses sexual anxiety - a simultaneous need for and fear of love.[20] Regardless of whether or not Magherini's attempt at psychoanalysing Botticelli himself is an entirely successful one, the moment of deflowering depicted in the tableau is a clear cause of anxiety for Anna, who perceives it as an allegory for predatory male sexuality on the one hand, and female vulnerability on the other.

Confronted with Caravaggio's shield of Medusa, Anna's anxiety significantly deepens. In stark contrast with Uccello's depiction of aggressive male sexuality, and Botticelli's visions of passive femininity, Caravaggio's shield represents female sexuality as abject and threatening. Unlike the decapitated heads of Medusa traditionally painted on the shields of warriors, Caravaggio's is alive, her mouth wide open and screaming. According to Freud, Medusa's head represents a source of male fears through its relation to castration anxieties: *"To decapitate = to castrate. The terror of Medusa is thus a terror of castration that is linked to the sight of something. Numerous analyses have made us familiar with the occasion for this: it occurs when a boy who has hitherto been unwilling to believe the threat of castration, catches sight of the female genitals, probably those of an adult, surrounded by hair, and essentially those of the mother... The hair upon Medusa's head is frequently represented in works of art in the form of snakes, and these once again are derived from the castration complex."*[21]

Barbara Creed, however, suggests that the head of Medusa represents not so much the castration of the female genitals, but the threat that they actually castrate, the 'vagina dentata', the devouring/castrating female genitals: *"Representations of the snake coiled in a circle, its tail/phallus in its mouth/vagina is a ubiquitous symbol of bisexuality found in*

below and opposite:
Mad about art: Anna Manni (Asia Argento)
suffers the ill effects of powerful paintings
in **The Stendhal Syndrome**.

Unity and identity slip away in the wake of Anna's violation in **The Stendhal Syndrome**.

all cultures. Freud isolates the phallic and ignores the vaginal significance of the snake as a sexual symbol... Freud's interpretation masks the active, terrifying aspects of the female genitals - the fact that they might castrate. The Medusa's entire visage is alive with images of toothed vaginas, poised and waiting to strike."[22]

Finally, Anna glances up to see Bruegel's *Landscape With The Fall Of Icarus* on the other side of the room. Here we see no obvious references to female sexuality, and the image is a relatively opaque one, although it is photographed in the same way as the other paintings, a sort of visual code which suggests that it holds equal significance - Argento first takes in the entire canvas on a wide, then cuts to a detail in closeup. The fact that it is the only image to have been deliberately drafted in from elsewhere (*The Fall of Icarus* hangs in Brussels, not Florence) suggests that there is a definite reason for its being there. The myth itself is commonly taken to be little more than an allegory for the danger one faces through rising above one's station (Icarus tries to fly but his wax wings melt from the heat of the sun and he plunges into the ocean).

What the painting provides us with is the image of the sea, a huge, overwhelming expanse of water, which engulfs and devours Icarus. Anna passes out, slipping into an hallucination in which she identifies with the male figure of Icarus, and dives into the water. There she is confronted by a large fish with a human face, which she kisses before she returns to the surface. Like Aura in **Trauma**, her association with the water could be taken to represent the pervasive influence of the absent mother. She returns to the womb (like Rose in the underwater ballroom of **Inferno**) and finds an image of fragmentation and confusion - the fish bears a strong resemblance to the creatures we can see in the paintings of Bosch, and other paintings by Bruegel, many of which hold similar connotations. Bosch's paintings, full of images of animals with human features (or vice-versa) may be interpreted as schizophrenic visions of dismantled bodies. Like the infant who has failed to pass through Lacan's 'mirror phase', these bodies represent disunity of (and confusion over) the human body, and the fragmentation of identity.

It is of passing interest to note that Bosch was the original inspiration behind **The Stendhal Syndrome**, forming the backbone of early drafts. The female protagonist, originally to have been played by Bridget Fonda, was to have undergone an attack of the mysterious condition at an exhibition in Arizona. In 1993, Argento described the project to Alan Jones: *"She'll view a Bosch painting and become like the painter himself. She'll dress like him, wear this enormous scarf, become self-destructive, mutilate her face and start thinking of herself as a monster. Through her self-discovery, she skirts madness and* *turns assassin after seeing one particular landscape.*"[23]   Clearly, this would have been a very different film had the original premise been retained, the only hint of Bosch remaining in the final version being the surreal, slightly Lovecraftian fish.

An attack of amnesia causes Anna to return to her hotel, where she reestablishes the tenuous grasp on her identity through entering another painting, this time Rembrandt's *The Nightwatch*. The image recalls *The Battle of San Romano* through its depiction of a group of men, assembled in a conspiratorial huddle, situating Anna in a heavily male-dominated and male-oriented environment. If the opening scenes of the film present us with Anna's crisis point, the remainder unfolds in two directions, charting the onward disintegration of her identity, and working backwards into the past to bring to light the roots of her confusion. Her relationship with her family is deeply unstable, we are told, the absence of her mother and the anxiety over her position in the now all-male household providing the seeds for her uncertainties over gender. The need for a maternal figure is hinted at when (in a scene deleted from English language versions) she establishes a bond with Marie's mother (played, in an ironic piece of casting, by **Inferno**'s Mother of Darkness Veronica Lazar). Anna's history is left only vaguely defined, however. There is even a suggestion that the anxieties now threatening to overwhelm her were already in place in early childhood, and intensified through her mother's death. In a flashback, she recalls her earliest brush with the unnerving power of art, when, in the company of her mother, she visited the local Etruscan Museum and fainted before a piece of sculpture representing a man and a woman.

The film's final image sees the invocation of the *plan-tableau* in the sense in which Pascal Bonitzer originally defined it: the shot that resembles a painting. Anna is lifted from the ground by a group of police colleagues, who carry her through the street as the closing credits role. The composition of the shot and the placement of the figures is strongly suggestive of Pietistic art, the most celebrated example of which is Caravaggio's *The Entombment of Christ*. Commissioned for one of the chapels in the church of Santa Maria in Vallicella, it depicts Christ being carried by his disciples and the Marys from the cross to his tomb. Like Raphael's version, the inspiration for its distinctive composition can be traced back to early Greco-Roman reliefs showing the hero being carried from the battlefield. The hanging right arm of Christ in both versions is intended to evoke pathos, although Caravaggio's painting is undeniably the darkest of all the works belonging to the genre of the Pietà.

The closing shot from **The Stendhal Syndrome** is pietistic only in a generic sense. If Argento intended to refer to one particular work, Caravaggio's for example, he could have mimicked the composition more precisely. Instead, he seems to be referring to the entire genre. The composition of the image is emblematic - it may not be an exact replication of any one painting, but the positioning of the figures is so distinctive that the reference to pietistic art is clear. In *The Entombment of Christ*, we have a man (generally limp, vulnerable, passive and broken) being carried by a group of his former companions. In most versions, the disciples are predominantly women, all lamenting and comforting him. It is an image imbued with an overwhelming sense of male masochism.

In Argento's film, Anna occupies the position typically reserved for the tortured body of the male, and she is surrounded by her male companions. Anna's body is limp and broken - in certain details the image diverges from The Entombment, but the overall composition is the same. Her face is sorrowful and resigned, her companions comfort her in vain, and her arm, instead of hanging limp by her side, is draped across her. This ending sees the undermining of values based on her perception of masculinity (after she is raped by Alfredo, she rejects the socially constructed attributes of femininity and assimilates male traits). In some senses echoing the closing moments of **Deep Red**, the armour of machismo which she has assumed in the mid third of the narrative, which resurfaces at the end, is cruelly and violently shattered.

The Bosch-inspired underwater fantasy of
The Stendhal Syndrome.

Notes

1. McDonagh, Maitland: Broken Mirrors, Broken Minds: The Dark Dreams of Dario Argento (Sun Tavern Fields, London 1991) p.69
2. Jones, Alan: "Dario Argento's The Phantom of the Opera" in Shivers, n.54, June 1998, p.37
3. Rauger, Jean-Francois: "Dario Argento Decrypté" in Cahiers du Cinéma, n.493, p.8
4. Abel, Richard: French Film Theory and Criticism vol.1 (Princeton University Press, Princeton 1988) p.372
5. Abel, Richard: French Film Theory and Criticism vol.1 (Princeton University Press, Princeton 1988) p.373
6. Abel, Richard: French Film Theory and Criticism vol.1 (Princeton University Press, Princeton 1988) p.174
7. Abel, Richard: French Film Theory and Criticism vol.1 (Princeton University Press, Princeton 1988) p.175
8. Vincendeau, Ginette: "Unsettling Memories" in Sight & Sound, vol.5 n.7, July 1995, p.30
9. Bonitzer, Pascal: Décadrages (Cahiers du Cinema/Editions de l'Etoile, Paris 1987) p.11
10. Bonitzer, Pascal: Décadrages (Cahiers du Cinema/Editions de l'Etoile, Paris 1987) p.23-13
11. during an interview at London's National Film Theatre
12. Moir, Patricia: "Aesthetics of Ambiguity" in Cinefantastique, vol.27 n.8, April 1996, p.18
13. Bonitzer, Pascal: Décadrages (Cahiers du Cinema/Editions de l'Etoile, Paris 1987) p.30
14. Bonitzer, Pascal: Décadrages (Cahiers du Cinema/Editions de l'Etoile, Paris 1987) p.31
15. Damisch, Hubert: "L'Epée devant les yeux" (publisher/date unknown), p.32
16. Bonitzer, Pascal: Décadrages (Cahiers du Cinema/Editions de l'Etoile, Paris 1987) p.33
17. To expand upon the issue of the representation of women in Edgar Allan Poe's literature would be unnecessarily repetitive, since the same ground is covered in my discussion of Poe's influence in a separate essay. It is, however, of passing interest to note that Argento is not the only horror film maker to have displayed a fascination with Ophelia: Wes Craven constructs a similar image in **The Last House On The Left**, a film which provides a rather different account of the subjugation of women.
18. See Chapter 3: The Phantom's Bride
19. Magherini, Graziella: La Sindrome di Stendhal (Ponte Alle Grazie, Florence, 1995) p.66-67
20. Of Graziella Magherini was interviewed on a documentary entitled "Botticelli's Primavera: Myths or Fingerprints?", commissioned for Channel 4. Her comments on the painting are taken from that programme.
21. Creed, Barbara: The Monstrous Feminine (Routledge, London 1993) p.111
22. Creed, Barbara: The Monstrous Feminine (Routledge, London 1993) p.111
23. Jones, Alan: "Sunday in the Park With Dario" in Shivers, n.0, August 1993

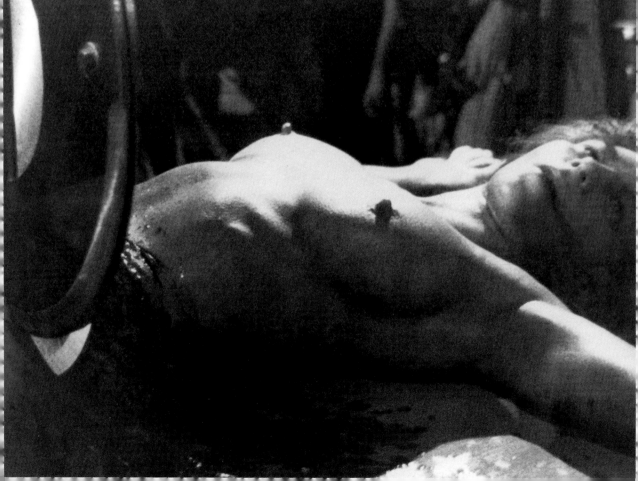

Quoting the Raven

Philosophies of composition and the female corpse as objet d'art: the influence of Edgar Allan Poe

One of the most daunting factors involved in adapting Edgar Allan Poe for the screen has to be the sheer volume of previous adaptations. Poe's most popular tales (*The Fall of the House of Usher*, *The Pit and the Pendulum*, *The Masque of the Red Death* and particularly *The Black Cat*) have been committed to celluloid numerous times, embodying a broad variety of cinematic visions. Few of these screen versions really ring true though, rarely managing to convey the sense of unease and anxiety embodied in the original Poe texts. Feature-length versions tend to flesh out the bare bones of the author's stories with generic cliché, or entirely substitute the original plots with new narratives based around hackneyed formulae. Rarely do they come close to capturing the disturbing qualities of the writings of their creator, inevitably rupturing the finely balanced economy of Poe's narrative style.

Argento's version of *The Black Cat*,[1] then, is something of a departure from the rather innocuous costume dramas of Roger Corman, Charles Band and others. Argento chose to set his film in contemporary Pittsburgh, drawing together references which span the entire body of the author's work, from *Berenicë* and *The Pit and the Pendulum*, to *The Fall of the House of Usher*. Ultimately, the adaptation comes as something of a disappointment, however. For a director who claims to be so heavily influenced by Poe, Argento's exploration of the notions embodied in the original texts falls short of comprehensive, instead amounting to little more than a tribute to his mentor's work. In an introduction to a collection of Poe's tales, Argento wrote: *"When I began to make films, I recognised that my themes had some affinity with events told by Poe in his stories; his hallucinatory worlds, his bloody visions. I asked myself: Have I opened my Pandora's box? Would I be invaded by my mad and perverse characters? Can a mind exist in peace that takes its inspiration from hell?... In my solitary moments when some frightening idea strikes me and I think: 'With this I will make a film,' Poe's handsome and intense face watches me, warns me to pay heed, be careful."*[2] Hyperbole aside, the question of Poe's influence over the Argento canon is worth exploring, particularly when one considers the polemics which surround his writings. Through the translations of Baudelaire, Poe's poems and short stories received a new lease of life and a fresh critical perspective in Europe, a perspective which tended to recognise the foundations of modernism and postmodernism in his style, and has paved the way for all contemporary readings of his work.

Self-Reflexive Fictions

Poe's style seems to consciously strive to make us aware of its constructed nature: his short stories are most often told in the first person, consistently employing stylistic devices which prevent us from sinking into the fiction, constantly reminding us that these are not direct experiences, that they are *written*. They are full of extensive, seemingly rambling ruminations on the storyteller's state of mind, and frequently present us with long passages of tangential description which set us back from the diegetic world. Consider, for example, the following passage from *The Black Cat*: *"And then came, as if to my final and irrevocable overthrow, the spirit of PERVERSENESS. Of this spirit philosophy takes no account. Phrenology finds no place for it among its organs. Yet I am not more sure that my soul lives, than I am that perverseness is one of the primitive impulses of the human heart — one of the indivisible primary faculties, or sentiments, which give direction to the character of man. Who has not, a hundred times, found himself commit-*

Tenebrae: accusations of misogyny.

ting a vile or a silly action, for no other reason than because he knows he should not? Have we not a perpetual inclination, in the teeth of our best judgment, to violate that which is Law, merely because we understand it to be such? This spirit of perverseness, I say, came to my final overthrow."[3] Here Poe halts the progression of the narrative to enter into a wordy discussion on perversity. He describes it, qualifies it, develops it as the basis of a divergent debate. His writing rarely confines itself to relating events, motivating them, conveying impressions and sensations. Instead, the unfolding of the narrative frequently grinds to a halt, while he analyses its content at some length, bringing us back to an awareness of the events he is relating as forming part of a text, a text which provides a running commentary on its own significance, thus drawing attention to its own process of articulation.

In addition to this, there are regular references to textuality, reading and writing. An obsession with the written word emerges time and again as a characteristic of the neurosis of the Poe male. The central character in *Berenicë*, for example, suffers from a form of monomania, a *"nervous intensity of interest"* which brings him *"To muse for long unwearied hours, with my attention riveted to some frivolous device upon the margin or in the typography of a book."*[4] The narrator of this particular story is entirely submerged in language. Indeed, the drama of his self-analysis and vain attempts at defining and 'explaining' femininity is played out against the backdrop of his library. *"In that chamber was I born."* he tells us. *"Thus awaking, as it were, from the long night of what seemed, but was not, nonentity, at once into the very regions of fairy land - into a palace of imagination - into the wild dominions of monastic thought and erudition."*[5] From the protagonist in *Berenicë* to the narrator of *The Raven*, who ponders *"weak and weary, Over many a quaint and curious volume of forgotten lore,"*[6] Poe's characters seem more often than not to be immersed in literature whenever anything untoward is about to happen. A number of essays and short stories take this theme further still: *X-ing a Paragrab*, for example, is entirely constructed around self-referential jokes concerning representations of the text.

This is an area of common ground between Argento and Poe. Argento's films are typically set against the backdrop of the art world, and are frequently filled with references to literature and storytelling. **Tenebrae** takes this self-reflexivity more literally than most, predating **Scream** with a deviously clever whodunit plot which repeatedly comments on its own construction. 'Tenebrae' refers to the title of the best-selling novel of protagonist Peter Neal, who visits Rome on a publicity tour and becomes embroiled in the mystery surrounding a series of 'real life' murders. The characters spend the duration of the film analysing their own fictional world, discussing everything from narrative construction and literary influences to the representation of women. Their commentary is loaded with irony: feminist critic Tilda attacks Neal with accusations of misogyny, barking, *"Tenebrae is a sexist novel. Why do you despise women so much? Women as victims, ciphers. The male heroes with their hairy macho bullshit. How can you say it isn't?"* When Neal tries to

A reference to Poe's *Berenicë*, and a nod to the terrifying 'vagina dentata' in **Two Evil Eyes**.

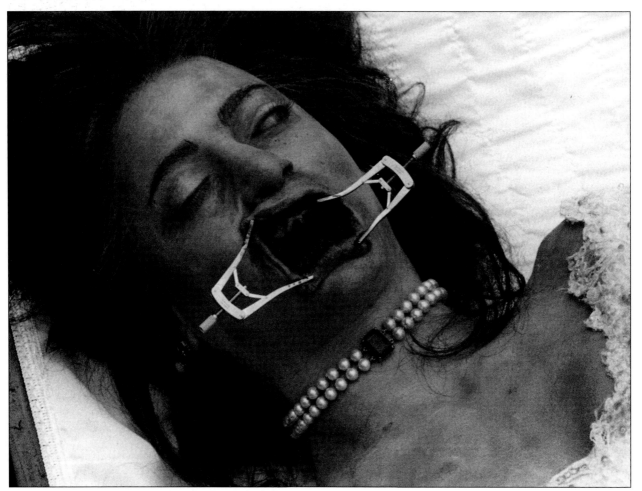

The author (Anthony Franciosa, right) and his critic (John Steiner, left) discuss the ethics of perverted fiction in **Tenebrae**.

placate her by telling her that he supported the Equal Rights Amendment, she retorts, *"So explain the books."* Had he continued, Neal might have pointed out that his female characters are representations, there to be read, as indeed Tilda is herself. She is commenting on the polemics underpinning her own representation in the fiction, and her own death scene - shortly afterwards she is dispatched by a misogynous maniac with a razor, who whispers, *"Pervert. Filthy, slimy pervert!"* before slashing her throat. All the masculine insecurity she has only just been criticising is invested in her murder.

Later Neal confides in Inspector Giermani, *"I've made charts, I've tried building a plot the same way you have. I've tried to figure it out. But I just have this hunch that something is missing, a tiny piece of the jigsaw. Somebody who should be dead is alive, or somebody who should be alive is already dead."* He is dropping hints, not only amusing himself by flaunting the solution to the mystery in front of Giermani, but also acknowledging an awareness of the structure of the scripted narrative of which he is a constituent element. The twist Neal is referring to, the pivotal identity switch, is pure Agatha Christie. In fact, the film cites its own influences when Giermani tells us, *"I read all those books - Agatha Christie, Mickey Spillane, Rex Stout, Ed McBain."* At another point he implores Neal not to reveal the identity of his latest whodunit's villain, since he'd like to save the revelation until the end of the story. Naturally, Neal wouldn't dream of it, and it isn't until the final scenes of the film that he is unmasked as **Tenebrae**'s killer, upon which he confides that planning and carrying out the murders was *"like writing a book."*

Less explicit examples can be found in other works: **Opera**, for example, contains a sub-plot revolving around the relationship between the killer and the imperilled heroine's mother, which mirrors the production of Verdi's *Macbeth* which we see enacted on stage at various points in the film. Rod Usher's book "Metropolitan Horrors" in **The Black Cat** is

A gap in the fiction: a moment of narrative stasis gives way to grisly ultraviolence in a scene from **Tenebrae**.

a collection of grisly real-life death scenes, reflecting Argento's penchant for aestheticised tableaux based around inventive murders. When Rod follows his girlfriend's cat around the house, we assume his point of view as he frames it between his fingers in a series of imaginary portraits, mimicking the framing apparatus of Argento's camera. Later this is repeated when he strangles the unfortunate feline to provide a cover image for his book, and we witness the killing through the viewfinder of his SLR, recalling similar scenes in **Tenebrae**, in which blood-spattered 'models' are photographed for posterity by their killer.

The Materiality of Language

Argento's fascination with the self-reflexive text, and the dynamics of its surface-obsessed construction bring us back to Poe, and most particularly to his 1846 essay *The Philosophy of Composition*, in which he deconstructs *The Raven* as part of an introspective and highly controversial study on the process of creative writing. Kenneth Silverman has identified *The Philosophy of Composition* as a crucial point in Poe's career, arguing it as the basis of contemporary literary theory: *"In the essay he wholly devaluated inspiration and empathy in art, and correspondingly emphasised technique and artistic detachment. His determined separation of the man who suffers and the artist who creates has long been recognised as a preliminary manifesto of literary modernism and postmodernism... In his essay Poe dramatised the making of a depersonalised art indifferent to political and moral considerations, its subject being its own dynamic inner relationships."*[7]

The Philosophy of Composition draws attention to Poe's use of the "refrain", the repetition of a phrase or word to produce an artistic effect, in his words, an *"artistic piquancy which might serve me as a key-note in the construction of the poem."*[8] Theories of modernism interpret this as a model of self-referentiality in his linguistic system - repetition draws attention to structure and the process of articulation. A reading of the poem creates an awareness in the reader that the repetition of the word 'Nevermore' is such a "key-note", and this in turn draws attention to its constructed nature. Roman Jakobson famously expounded ideas on "the poetic function", in association with the Russian formalist poets. The poetic function lays an emphasis upon the tangibility of signs, widening the gap between words and objects. Like Poe, the Russian formalist poets were concerned with the materiality of language, representing a radical shift in emphasis from signified to signifier.

When applied to cinema, the poetic function has most often been associated with Russian montage, which iterates the shot as a cellular unit. Argento has exemplified this in his favoured technique of cutting to the rhythm of his music scores, with sections of the score sometimes composed even before shooting has begun. But his style is self-reflexive in a far broader sense. Style, and the materiality of style, are emphasised through cutting to impossible points of view, exaggerated contrivance in decor and camera movement, sudden jarring cuts to apparently peripheral detail, all of which serve to set us back from the fictional world, the signified, and contemplate instead the process of articulation, the signifier. Again, **Tenebrae** furnishes us with a perfect illustration of this, in the scene where Tilda arrives home to confront her unfaithful lover. They argue, after which Tilda retreats to the living room to sulk. So far, all the action in the scene has been confined to the interior of the house, but suddenly we cut to an external view as Tilda looks out through a window. The camera ascends to the upper floor of the building, and then the roof, leaving Tilda behind. Without cutting, it crawls over the top of the house, finally sinking towards the ground on the other side, where we glimpse the killer in the act of breaking in. This highly contrived and unconventional shot seems to serve no definite purpose. It is entirely extra-narrative, playing no part in the fiction. In fact it disrupts narrative progression, interrupting the story at a critical point purely in order to allow us to admire this frivolous piece of cinematic virtuosity. Its purpose is to draw attention to the process of signification: the presence of the camera, and its involvement in producing either progression or stasis.

To return to Poe and his use of the refrain, however, it is important to note that he stresses variation as essential to its deployment. *"I determined to produce continuously novel effects,"* he writes, *"by the variation of the application of the refrain - the refrain itself remaining, for the most part, unvaried."*[9] Narratively, **Inferno** makes extensive use of such a device, using this system of repetition and variation to draw attention to the structured nature of narrative. The entire film is constructed out of a number of separate narrative strands, all related, running parallel and partly interwoven, which begin and end at different points, but follow an almost identical pattern. This comes close to a mode of filmmaking which David Bordwell has called 'parametric narration', a narrational system which bears strong resemblances to Poe's poetic system. Bordwell has defined parametric narration as

Feline fixation: Kazanian (Sacha Pitoeff) dodges the cats in his antique shop in **Inferno**.

Arterial Artifice:
Shoplifting violent fiction has unforeseen consequences for this victim in **Tenebrae** (played by Ania Pieroni, Mater Lachrymarum in **Inferno**).

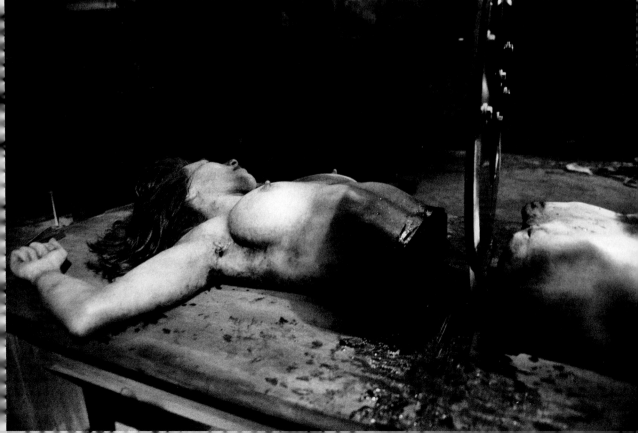

a method through which style and narrative operate on two distinct tracks, with style setting its own pattern, rather than following the demands of a narrative.[10] The Alain Robbe-Grillet and Alain Resnais film **Last Year at Marienbad** is a perfect example: a central narrative thread (a man and a woman meet in a hotel and argue over an affair which they may or may not have had the previous year) is thrown into disarray by its total subordination to the film's stylistic conceits. Sacha Pitoeff's unfathomable game becomes a recurrent motif, mirroring the similar non-progression of narrative, and becoming more of a play on shapes than on theme (Pitoeff's presence in **Inferno** suggests a possible reference).

Bordwell's theory places its emphasis upon style as the guiding principal underpinning narration, while Richard Kwietniowski's analysis of Chantal Ackerman's **Toute une nuit** identifies the scene as *"replacing the shot as a cellular entity, returning the spectator to new space, new protagonists, new little story."*[11] Like **Inferno**, Ackerman's film repeats the basic narrative unit, taking it through a series of variations, none of which (in contradiction with the argument offered by Bordwell) is wholly reliant upon style. In **Inferno**, the paradigmatic narrative structure follows its own set of rhythmic principles, creating its own visual/narrative 'rhymes'. The basis of the "cellular entity" here, rather than the shot or the scene, is a mini-narrative: each character's search for forbidden knowledge, ultimately leading to a confrontation with death. Recalling the matchstick game in **Last Year at Marienbad**, these narrative strands are each marked with recurrent motifs - the breaking of glass (a crystal door handle, an ashtray, an ornamental statuette) and the cutting or pricking of each victim's hand.

Exquisite Corpses

But the arena in which *The Philosophy of Composition* has provoked the most discussion is in the representation of women. In a passage which has since made the essay infamous, Poe writes: *"I asked myself - 'Of all melancholy topics, what, according to the universal understanding of mankind, is the most melancholy?' Death - was the obvious reply. 'And when,' I said, 'is this most melancholy of topics most poetical?... When it most closely allies itself to Beauty: the death, then, of a beautiful woman is, unquestionably, the most poetical topic in the world.'"*[12]

In **Inferno**, woman is presented as an artistic construct - we first hear of the Three Mothers through a book, and first glimpse Mater Tenebrarum as a painting, hidden in the waterlogged chamber beneath the cellar (recalling Poe's tale *The Oval Portrait*, in which the artist's wife only truly exists in the world of the storyteller as a painting, a representation). Similarly, the character of Anna in **The Stendhal Syndrome** finds herself inescapably immersed in artistic representation, eventually becoming part of the artworks she creates by covering herself in paint. Ultimately she is driven to perceive herself as a construct of femininity, and she strives to reconstruct her identity as a result. Poe's claim that *"the death of a beautiful woman is, unquestionably, the most poetical topic in the world"* has provoked extensive discussion, and Elizabeth Bronfen has provided an expansive semiotic analysis of the statement, observing that to suggest that it merely represents Poe's attempt to denigrate women is to ignore the *"multiplicity of themes"* condensed in the image of the dead woman,[13] and that in order to properly address this issue, one must entirely separate notions of *"lived reality"* from *"aesthetic depiction"*.

Her argument helps to situate the image of the female corpse in a structure of death and male desire, and has significant bearing on similar representations to be found in the films of Argento. Poe's statement is contradictory, she suggests, since woman is traditionally associated with life, unity and nourishing nature. Her death, on the other hand, brings an end to procreation. The words "beautiful", "poetical" and "death" also create a conflicting and uneasy combination, since death is a *"decomposition of forms, the breaking of aesthetic unity."*[14] Beauty, according to Bronfen, is invoked to mask the inevitability of human decomposition. Bronfen's argument most readily calls to mind the paintings of J.W. Waterhouse, Toby Rosenthal and John Everett Millais who, far from representing the corpse as abject, 'immortalised' women on the canvas, beautifying death through art. The wafer-thin models of the Pre-Raphaelites are intended to embody purity, wholeness and physical perfection, blocking out notions of insufficiency and disintegration. It is important to place Poe's works within this artistic, literary and social context. The representation of women in his writings may be regarded as an exemplar of or criticism against (Bronfen argues the latter) romanticised images of death through the beautiful corpse.

In **The Black Cat** Argento forges a connection between the character of Annabel and Millais' *Ophelia*, when she is left to sink into a bath of blood, elegantly composed in a *tableau vivant* which recalls Millais' famous painting. The image provides an implicit reference to the nineteenth century obsession with idyllic depictions of death in the form of graceful, beautiful female corpses. The elements of literary representation, painterly representation and *"the death of a beautiful woman"* are thus combined, indexing a specific artistic context. Argento adds an additional layer, however, when the finale of the film sees a layer of shelves of books torn away (again, a possible reference to the representation of the text) to reveal the abject, now rotting corpse, which has been hidden behind a wall and, until now, concealed within the fiction. The invocation of the icon of the beautiful corpse therefore ultimately reveals what it is designed to disprove: that it veils the inevitability of decay, decomposition and the dissolution of identity.

In the works of both Argento and Poe, the male characters' engagement with this image serves to underline its duplicity, its dual significance as both an object of desire and a symbol for death. It is a monolithic characteristic of Poe's (masculine) storytellers which seems to have found its way into the psyche of the beleaguered Argento male: **Tenebrae**, **Opera** and **The Black Cat** all reflect this desire to repress images of decay and abjection

opposite top:
The camera stops to peer in through the windows of a soon-to-be victim's house as it journeys over the rooftops in **Tenebrae**.

opposite bottom:
Argento weaves in a reference to *The Pit and the Pendulum* in an early scene from **The Black Cat**, taking it to a shocking conclusion only ever threatened in the original text.

A flirtatious shoplifter (Ania Pieroni) steps into a literary minefield in a scene from **Tenebrae**.

through the deaths of beautiful women, while their male protagonists follow the tug of an irresistible trajectory towards certain doom through their creative acts of destruction.

The uncanniness of the not-quite-dead-enough woman becomes a source of absolute loathing in the Poe stories. In *Berenicë*, the narrator's bride-to-be shows all the signs of physical decomposition as she sinks into a debilitating malady associated with epilepsy, but the narrator's main concern is for her teeth: while the rest of her body has shrunken away, her teeth remain unaffected (*"not a speck upon their surface, not a shade on their enamel"*[15]). Berenicë's teeth are thus the only sign of youth and vitality which remains, the only things which prevent her from occupying her proper place in death as a decayed corpse. What seems to horrify so often, in characters such as Berenicë, Ligeia and Morella, is the female's apparent predisposition towards hovering noncommittally between life and death.

Inferno articulates this in explicit terms, exploring woman's equivalence to death first by presenting us with images of the deaths of beautiful women, then by personifying death in the form of the Three Mothers. As Varelli remarks in the film's opening scene, the Mothers are *"incapable of creating life"* - they are instead associated with plague, rats, death and the smell of decay. While exploring the basement of Mater Tenebrarum's home, Rose discovers an underwater room, the 'womb' of the building (the house is elsewhere described as an analogue of the living body), but it yields only death in the form of a rotting corpse. As Elizabeth Bronfen observes, through creating life, woman condemns man to the one certainty of his existence - death,[16] and within Mater Tenebrarum's unhealthy sphere of influence, womb equates with tomb. The film's finale brings us the revelation that the witches represent Death itself in human form: *"Men call us by a single name... They call us Death!"* shrieks the Mother of Darkness, as she bursts through a mirror, suddenly transformed into a grinning skull in a black cloak. The summoning up of Death in its traditional (and less than convincing) Grim Reaper garb brings us back to the beginning: the observation that woman's equivalence to death is part of a representation, a symbol. Moments before, Mater Tenebrarum appears as an image in a mirror, replacing Mark's reflection, suggesting that ultimately she is a part of him, inseparable from him because his existence is finite.

Mark escapes from **Inferno**'s blazing tower block physically unscathed, but like all the male protagonists of Argento's cinema and Poe's literature, his attempt to understand and define the feminine, to tame it by explaining it, inevitably ends in disillusionment. Whether psychopaths or sleuths, Argento's male heroes invariably attempt to define their masculinity against feminine passivity. When Tilda criticises the gender politics of Peter Neal's pulpy bestseller in **Tenebrae**, the argument she proffers is a perfectly justified one. Later we learn that Neal's empathy for her killer is rooted in an obscure and painful memory of having been assaulted by a young woman on a beach. Her beauty is imbued with shades of disquieting ambiguity (she was played by a transsexual), and her red

left and above:
On the set of **Inferno**, Argento
directs Sacha Pitoeff, known for
his role in Alain Resnais' enigmatic
Last Year At Marienbad.

stiletto shoes take on threatening, phallic connotations when she rapes Neal by forcing one of the pointed heels into his screaming mouth. It is a memory that will return to plague him for the rest of his life - at one point he stands alone in a hotel bathroom, crying out in torment. He is condemned to follow a fruitless quest to erase the notion of his inadequacy, first by killing the girl from the beach, penetrating her repeatedly and fatally with a blade. He steals the offending high-heels and later presents them to his ex-wife, Jane, so that she may be wearing them when she dies. He must reassert his sexual superiority over the female, cutting off Jane's arm, severing her from the gun she holds in her hand (a self-conscious castration metaphor if ever there was one) before burying his axe in her chest. Jane serves as the sacrificial icon in the ritual reenactment of the death of Neal's tormentor, enabled to replace her by donning the red shoes.

Stealing the shoes can't erase their implications, but removing them represents an attempt at obliterating their owner's threatening sexuality, like the character in *Berenicë*, who feels a strange compulsion to extract his lover's teeth: they are sharp, threatening (reminding us of Barbara Creed's account of the vagina dentata, discussed elsewhere in this book). Berenicë's smile is loaded with all the horror of aggressive feminine sexuality. Incidentally, Argento makes an explicit reference to this in the cemetery scene of **The Black Cat** - perhaps this explains why Rod Usher can gaze upon so many mutilated female corpses without flinching, but can't bear to look into the box which contains the girl's teeth. Peter Neal's odyssey, like that of Mark in **Inferno**, or Sam in **The Bird With the Crystal Plumage**, concludes with the reaffirmation of his fears. Anne, his ally and lover (and Jane's replacement) penetrates him with a lethal, gleaming shard of steel, bringing his nightmare to life. Almost all of Poe's 'heroes' follow the same trajectory to a similar end point - woman triumphs over death and the natural. The gender politics of both are suspect, but these representations are there to be read. The female body is treated as much as a display of the tangibility of signs as is the surface of the text. Corpse and corpus thus occupy parallel positions in this self-reflexive, infinitely self-referential play on signification.

Notes

1. **The Black Cat** is Argento's entry in **Two Evil Eyes**, a portmanteau project incorporating two sub feature-length Poe adaptations, the other being George A. Romero's **The Facts in the Case of Mr Valdemar**.
2. McDonagh, Maitland: Broken Mirrors, Broken Minds: The Dark Dreams of Dario Argento (Sun Tavern Fields, London 1991) p. 214
3. Poe, Edgar Allan: The Unabridged Edgar Allan Poe (Running Press, USA, 1983) p.839
4. Poe, Edgar Allan: The Unabridged Edgar Allan Poe (Running Press, USA, 1983) p.157
5. Poe, Edgar Allan: The Unabridged Edgar Allan Poe (Running Press, USA, 1983) p.156
6. Poe, Edgar Allan: The Unabridged Edgar Allan Poe (Running Press, USA, 1983) p.1043
7. Silverman, Kenneth: Edgar A. Poe: A Mournful and Never-Ending Remembrance (Weidenfeld and Nicolson, London, 1992) p.295-296
8. Poe, Edgar Allan: The Unabridged Edgar Allan Poe (Running Press, USA, 1983) p.1083
9. Poe, Edgar Allan: The Unabridged Edgar Allan Poe (Running Press, USA, 1983) p.1083
10. Bordwell, David: Narration in Çthe Fiction Film (University of Wisconsin Press, USA, 1985) p.275
11. Kwietniowski, Richard: "Separations: Chantal Akerman's News From Home and Toute une nuit" in Movie, n.34-5, Winter 1990, p.114
12. Poe, Edgar Allan: The Unabridged Edgar Allan Poe (Running Press, USA, 1983) p.1084
13. Bronfen, Elizabeth: Over Her Dead Body (Manchester University Press, UK, 1992) p.60
14. Bronfen, Elizabeth: Over Her Dead Body (Manchester University Press, UK, 1992) p.60
15. Poe, Edgar Allan: The Unabridged Edgar Allan Poe (Running Press, USA, 1983) p.100
16. Bronfen, Elizabeth: Over Her Dead Body (Manchester University Press, UK, 1992) p.67

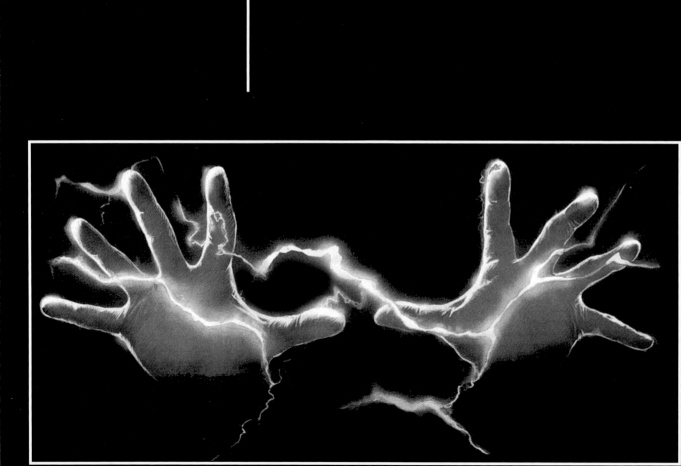

THE FILMS OF
DARIO ARGENTO
reviews

 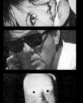

The Bird With the Crystal Plumage

Gary Needham

ITALY/WEST GERMANY

1970

Walking home late one night, Sam Dalmas, an American writer living in Rome, witnesses an assault in an art gallery upon a woman, Monica Ranieri. Rushing to her aid, he is trapped in the space between a double set of glass doors, unable to save her until a passer-by notices him and calls the police. Monica Ranieri, the gallery owner's wife, is only wounded in the assault. Dalmas is questioned by the police who confiscate his passport until the crime is solved. The police believe the assault is linked to a spate of serial murders sweeping Rome. But Dalmas finds he's unable to shake the feeling that he's overlooked something important. Obsessed with what he witnessed at the gallery he begins his own investigation, parallel with that of Inspector Morrisini. Dalmas' investigation leads him to an antique dealer who bought a disturbing painting from the killer's first victim the same day she was murdered. This leads Dalmas to the artist who originally painted the picture, which was based on a real life incident of violent sexual assault on a young girl. The killer, aware of Dalmas and his girlfriend Julia's investigations, attempts to murder Julia. The young couple also receive a threatening phone call from the killer, which is recorded by the police, the analysis of which reveals a strange screeching noise in the background. The noise comes from a rare bird with 'crystal' plumage, the only one in a Roman zoo. The zoo where the bird is caged is close to the Ranieris' flat. Dalmas and the inspector head over to confront Alberto Ranieri, only to have him leap suicidally out of the window. His last words are a confession to the serial murders in Rome. Meanwhile, Julia has disappeared from the scene. Dalmas goes looking for her and finds himself retracing his steps back to the gallery. What he finds there is the original print of the painting and the dead body of his friend Carlo. The killer reveals herself to be Monica Ranieri. What Dalmas had witnessed that first night at the gallery was Monica assaulting her husband but getting injured in the process. Dalmas becomes trapped under a falling piece of art in the exhibition space and Monica is ready to kill him when the police arrive in time to knock her unconscious and save Dalmas. It is finally revealed that Monica Ranieri's husband had been covering for her since her exposure to the painting had unlocked the unresolved repression of her childhood assault and triggered a murderous psychosis, as she transferred her identity onto her childhood assailant.

Throughout the western hemisphere, the late sixties was a pivotal time for politics, economics, and art. The counterculture which spread through most of the US shook the American film industry into a state of crisis and fragmentation, while across Europe the student revolts of May '68 left the young generation with a radical new sense of political awareness. Many films of the period were equally radical, as political upheavals were reflected in filmmakers' style. Young directors with a heightened perception of cinema as an art form began to surface, bringing with them a desire to transgress the boundaries and conventions of the older generation of filmmakers. Two directors with truly modern visions, both in form and content, were introduced to the public in the late sixties; Dario Argento and Bernardo Bertolucci refigured Italian cinema with fresh approaches to their craft. Both were born in Rome and became good friends in the sixties, working together on the screenplay for Sergio Leone's **Once Upon a Time in the West**. Argento, a former film critic for the Italian newspaper *Paese sera*, and Bertolucci, a student of the C.S.C (Centro Sperimentale del Cinema), are linked by a third and highly influential figure, triple Oscar-winning cinematographer Vittorio Storaro. While Argento is truly a master of his art, **The Bird With the Crystal Plumage**'s aesthetic and psychological effect is in part due also to Storaro's cold modernist approach to framing, tone, and depth. His extremely

top:
Sam Dalmas (Tony Musante) becomes
trapped between the doors of an art gallery.

above:
Dalmas climbs into the grotty bohemia
of the artist's lair.

influential cinematographic style can also be seen in Bertolucci's **Il conformista** / **The Conformist** (1970) and **La strategia del ragno** / **The Spider's Stratagem** (1970) and in Luigi Bazzoni's *giallo* **Giornata nera per l'ariete** / **The Fifth Cord** (1971).

With his first feature, Argento made a distinctive mark in a period of prolific genre output for Italian cinema. The *giallo* (mystery thriller) was already an extremely popular genre thanks to the efforts of Mario Bava and journeyman directors such as Umberto Lenzi, who directed three *gialli* starring Carroll Baker during this period. Coming from a family background in photography and cinema, himself a critic and screenwriter, Argento brought his knowledge of film history and technique to a genre overly imbued with convention and indebted to its US counterpart. The director uses **Bird**'s thriller scenario to explore the tension between gender and genre. The execution of this tension is carefully orchestrated around several sequences that are underscored with ambiguity, alienation, and a detailed attention to masculinity as a conventional construct.

The narrative - reworked from Fredric Brown's novel *The Screaming Mimi* - is almost arbitrary to the visual dynamic of the film. A surgical precision seems to guide every pan and tilt of the camera, which remains fluid and cold. In several sequences, rapid editing between high angled long shots and nervously framed close-ups is used to increase suspense and the viewer's sense of claustrophobia. The famous 'art gallery sequence', which provides the film's initial narrative drive, perfectly illustrates the key themes and devices.

The relationship between gender and genre is perhaps the most significant, if not the most complex, of themes running through Argento's work. Although there has been much recent interest in questions of femininity and the female body in Argento's films, the representation of masculinity has not been sufficiently addressed. In order to explore how such issues relate to **Bird** it is necessary to summarise some of the theoretical groundwork already undertaken in this area. Representations of masculinity in the 20th century have hinged upon the physicality of the male body as an agent of action, doing, and progress. In cinema, and other cultural forms, the male body is central to the production of its meaning as a cultural construct; masculinity is generally thought to be something that emanates from the male body and is located at the surface. Mainstream filmmakers seem to be obsessed by representing male bodies as spectacles of muscular excess (Arnold Schwarzenegger, the *peplum*), as agents of action and control through 'legitimate' violence (John Wayne, the **Die Hard** series) or as displaced erotics via violence (Martin Scorsese's films) or comedy (**The Full Monty**). The female body in such works is often positioned in an inferior relation to the male body, both scientifically and culturally, as a passive object of patriarchal discourse. Masculinity is a construction that can be read as concealing insecurities, anxieties, and a fear of femininity; elements which, to make a rather clichéd statement, throw it into crisis. It must be made clear at this point that we are talking about constructions that essentially do not reflect 'real life', although the ideological effects have serious implications beyond the cinematic apparatus. In order to conceal vulnerability and exert authority, the performance of masculinity attempts to sustain, with its body and the many meanings it produces, ideas on the nature of what it means to be 'masculine'. It almost passes without detection, in the same way, for example, that constructions of whiteness conceal it as a marked racial category. I am drawn to Argento because he plays with the polarities of gender, sexuality, and generic convention in a most critically engaging and stylish manner. The weight of meaning and the core premise of several Argento films revolve around the visual or aural fragmentation of an event not yet understood. These events are often the nexus for a crisis in the protagonist's identity and control of their gender position. Sam Dalmas (and later, Marc Daly in **Deep Red**) reveal an inability to fulfil a trajectory of 'good' detection, which also reveals a more fundamental instability at the level of their identity.

In the worlds of cinematic and literary detection, the central investigative agent is the perfect role model of Cartesian subjectivity ordered by rationality and logic in the presence of the absurd and the perverse. However, in Argento's work, detection doesn't function in such an ordered and rational way, for his universe is entrenched in the irrational and the ambiguous. Argento's agents of detection are subjected to their environments, unlike the classical detectives who subject environments to their investigation. Sam Dalmas and Julia, foreigners abroad, become physically and mentally trapped by the puzzle that they fail to solve; victims of a hostile environment. In **The Bird With the Crystal Plumage** power relations are reversed, representations of violence are intricate and explicit, and the logic of comprehension and common sense is often disregarded. It is the powerlessness of Sam Dalmas and the hidden psychosis of Monica Ranieri which is the focus. Tension is elaborated between identity and agency, and the male body's treatment is framed by important stylistic devices that foreground alienation, helplessness and instability.

What Sam Dalmas witnesses in the gallery at the start of the film is the source of his doubt and confusion, providing the premise for his investigation parallel with that of Inspector Morrisini. We are given a clear contrast very early on between two models of masculinity. Sam Dalmas is already a stranger to his situation as an American in Rome. Transient, and confused at the incident in the gallery, he begins an illegitimate investigation in pursuit of Monica Ranieri's assailant. Inspector Morrisini, on the other hand, is the classic Cartesian detective. Being on the side of the law, he is rational, puts his trust in science and subjects his environment to lawful investigative agency. Argento offers us two men with different constructions of masculinity but with the same goal to catch the killer. It could even be argued that Dalmas is on the side of the feminine with his explicitly marked emotions and investigative pursuits outside of the law, in other words, outside the 'Symbolic'. For Dalmas, the enigma lies not in the usual avenues of detection but instead in the narrative of a vicious painting and his troubled (mis)perception of events in the art gallery. His investigation involves his emotionally dependent girlfriend Julia and tenuous 'interviews' with criminals and eccentric artists. Inspector Morrisini on the other hand is

above: Urban paranoia... a hitman strikes and Sam finds himself hunted down on the streets of Rome.

below: Sam Dalmas (Tony Musante) watches helplessly as the disruptive gender politics unfold before his eyes.

EAGLE FILMS present

The Gallery Murders.
cromoscope

SUZY KENDALL · TONY MUSANTE · EVA RENZI

top:
Inspector Morrosini (Enrico Maria Salerno),
Monica Ranieri (Eva Renzi) and Sam Dalmas
(Tony Musante) confront the prime suspect.

above:
Dalmas interrogates a comedy criminal
as he investigates a series of brutal
murders in Rome.

opposite top:
Julia falls victim to the gender chaos of
The Bird With the Crystal Plumage.

opposite bottom:
Sam Dalmas comes face to face with
yet another red herring.

surrounded by technologies of science to aid his investigation. It is not that the technologies are completely futile, or ridiculous, but rather that his masculine assumptions lead him to fixate on a male gendered killer. Morrisini equates femininity with passivity, which is also the key to Dalmas' misrecognition in the gallery. This is the point that I wish to emphasise the most for it is central to the way the film refigures the genre. Female killers were quite common in cinema by the sixties but this is not the point I am making. The opposition of an active and aggressive feminine with a passive and helpless masculine is used to undermine assumptions that we place onto the thriller as a genre. We become wrapped up in Morrisini's 'male sex maniac on the loose' theory as much as we are horrified, retrospectively, that Monica Ranieri could have conducted savage sexual assaults on her victims. Yet the possibility is there that the killer is female. The film works towards disguising this fact, playing on our social and ideological assumptions of gender. Argento would push the codes of feminine madness to new extremes across the following two decades.

Argento's *mise-en-scène* is an explicit language system and it's in the space-object relations of **The Bird With the Crystal Plumage** that a large proportion of the film's meanings are invested. Dalmas, trapped between the glass doors of the gallery, is emasculated, denied the possibility of coming to the aid of Monica Ranieri, and unable to be heard by a passer-by who probably finds him a more distressing sight than the wounded woman. The *mise-en-scène* enunciates the theme of entrapment, alienation, and the fragility of Dalmas' masculinity. Returning to the gallery at the end of the film Dalmas becomes trapped once again, this time under a magnificent and lethally spiked piece of art that pins him to the ground. If masculinity is tied to the male body then these scenes clearly offer us an image of it as immobilised and pathetic.

above:
Immobilized and pathetic... Sam Dalmas
at Monica Ranieri's mercy.

right:
French poster.

TONY MUSANTE
SUZY KENDALL
ENRICO MARIA SALERNO
dans un film écrit et réalisé par
DARIO ARGENTO

**l'oiseau
au
plumage
de
cristal**

avec
EVA RENZI - UMBERTO RAHO
RAF VALENTI - GIUSEPPE CASTELLANO
et avec la participation de
MARIO ADORF
musique de ENNIO MORRICONE
produit par SALVATORE ARGENTO
COULEUR
UNE COPRODUCTION ITALO-ALLEMANDE
SEDA SPETTACOLI S.P.A (ROME)
C.C.C. FILM G.M.B.H. (BERLIN)
distribué par LES ARTISTES ASSOCIÉS

INTERDIT AUX MOINS DE 13 ANS

In mainstream cinema masculinity is also characterised by themes of victory and defeat and a movement towards order and control. These characteristics are inverted, as **Bird** doesn't offer images of men in control but rather images that foreground their powerlessness. Argento repeatedly offers a counter-paradigm to mainstream notions of masculinity. Gender identities in Argento's films are never fixed. Dalmas' masculinity is constantly unstable and through his detective pursuits he hopes to attain mastery and control over the situation, only to ultimately lose it. Argento transgresses the thriller/*giallo* format by articulating the dynamic possibilities of gender and genre, thus underscoring the fragility of masculinity and femininity as normalised and fixed constructions.

Argento draws his influences - and he is keen to discuss this in interviews - from Fritz Lang and Russian Formalism. Although I cannot readily read any explicit references to early Soviet cinema through his films, apart from montage, the use of Expressionism is quite distinct throughout his career. In **Bird**, the expressionism is more subtle than that of say, Film Noir, but the foggy streets of Rome are far closer to Fritz Lang's **M** than any Italian gothic antecedents. Because of our initial gender assumptions we don't know that Monica Ranieri is psychotic but the raw and craggy art that furnishes her gallery is a physical embodiment of her psychic discontent. Did she choose the art subconsciously? Expressionism is after all an art form which aims to convey human emotion in the physical world. The relationship between her disturbed mind and her 'bizarre' art comes to a climax when a sculpture collapses upon Sam Dalmas and pins him to the gallery floor. Art is a key mechanism in Monica Ranieri's psychosis in that it not only reflects her mind but also triggers its murderous discontent. When she discovers the painting, which recalls her assault as a young girl, it twists her beyond control as she transfers her identity onto her assailant. The director begs us to psychoanalyse his character's motivation and madness through his implicit reference to lay Freudian/Lacanian concepts. Argento's first killer already marks a deviant sexuality. The *giallo* trademark costume of shiny black mac and hat makes a shift from mere disguise to sheer fetish. Knives are not just matter-of-fact murder weapons but carefully kept objects in soft red casing to be admired and selected for their aesthetic as well as their murderous potential. The world of the killer becomes a universe of symbolism and sexual curiosity in the hands of Argento.

Jack The Ripper with a twist:

top:
Bird's androgynous maniac claims another victim.

middle:
Julia and Sam run for their lives.

bottom:
Sam enters the home of a psychopath.

top:
Suzy Kendall strikes a pose as Julia,
the emotionally dependent lover of
Sam Dalmas.

above:
Danish video cover.

opposite:
Remember **Psycho**?
An infestation of strap-lines dominates
a theatrical poster for **The Bird With
the Crystal Plumage**.

The most distinguished feature of Argento's textuality is its radically different organisation of screen space. Many elements contribute to this but, in terms of a depiction of object-relations, the key changes are those produced by the widespread introduction of zoom and telephoto lenses. In fact Argento pushes these technologies further as he penetrates the mouth of a screaming victim with an endoscopic style camera as if to take the spectator as close to the horror of death as possible. The 'zooming' of Argento's camera is not there to support point of view but instead provides a radical disturbance of the mind's perception. He uses this previously conventional camera lens as a matter of aesthetic choice and not conventional necessity. Zooms that once covered movement in space now rob the space of movement. Such choices show that Argento is less concerned with achieving the transparency sought by mainstream cinema; instead he foregrounds technical means to explore the possibilities of film as an artistic medium. Importantly, Argento isn't looking to displace the thriller genre. What he does is to effect a revision that brings to the fore complex political arguments through film style, hence the tension between gender and genre.

A distinctive feature of **The Bird With the Crystal Plumage** is the score by Ennio Morricone, incorporating vocals by Edda dell'Orso. The soundtrack brings out the suspense in the modern and often quite flat visual space that Argento has constructed. Around this time in film's technological history the soundtrack underwent some redefinition. Enhanced recording equipment meant that film-makers could explore the possibilities of sound and create less 'directional', more 'atmospheric' sound design. The range and style of Edda dell'Orso's incredible voice underscores the tension and suspense in an extraordinary performance of her talent. The only other *giallo* I can think of in which her talents for conveying suspense are used to great effect is Aldo Lado's **La corta notte di bambole di vetro / The Short Night of the Glass Dolls** (1971). She vocalises the desperation of Monica Ranieri crawling across the gallery floor with gasps and intoned breaths, and underscores the suspense with a series of 'lalalalalalal' vocals interspersed with the vibrant chimes, puncturing brass shrills and deep plucking bass of Morricone's orchestration. The music commands audience attention and focuses their emotions on the tone of the scene. Morricone produced some of his best scores around this time and Edda dell'Orso was certainly at the peak of her career. This successful collaboration between Morricone and Argento was carried on through **The Cat O'Nine Tails** (1971) and **Four Flies on Grey Velvet** (1972) but unfortunately their recent alliances on **The Stendhal Syndrome** (1996) and **The Phantom of the Opera** (1999) are merely routine and undistinguished.

The points I have stressed concern what I would argue are the fundamental foundations on which Argento has built his career. The use of camera and music in accordance with generic revision and film technology and the socio-political context in which the film was made should be considered relative to each other. **The Bird With the Crystal Plumage** is perhaps the most important of Argento's films because it lays bare his obsessions and his pursuit of transgression; qualities that have marked him out as genius, madman, and auteur.

WARNER BROS.
presente

JAMES FRANCISUS • KARL MALDEN
CATHERINE SPAAK

LE CHAT A
NEUF QUEUES

Un Film de
DARIO ARGENTO   WB   EASTMANCOLOR

The Cat O'Nine Tails

Mike Lebbing

ITALY/WEST GERMANY
FRANCE

1971

This second part of the 'Animal Trilogy' has for some time been considered the weakest film in its director's *oeuvre*, but now that **The Phantom of the Opera** has left Argentophiles around the globe flabbergasted, **The Cat O'Nine Tails** probably no longer occupies the lowest ranking. Although it could be argued that **Cat** is not typical of Argento's otherwise spectacular output, it is nevertheless an engaging work, and certainly rises above the glut of routine *gialli* which emerged from the industry at the time. (In spite of the protestations of Argento fans, **Cat** was a commercial success, beating box-office big boys like Sergio Leone's **Duck You Sucker!** and Vittorio De Sica's terrific, Oscar-winning **The Garden of the Finzi-Continis**.) The film boasts a solid cast, with Karl Malden as blind Franco Arno and James Franciscus as news reporter Carlo Giordani providing two powerful leading performances. The screenplay is sufficiently entertaining and well paced to maintain interest throughout and Enrico Menczer's cinematography, while seldom flamboyant, is often striking and made all the more effective thanks to Franco Fratticelli's expert cutting. And on closer inspection, through the haze of what otherwise seems like a rather functional plot, some off-beat elements and a sense of ambiguity begin to surface.

At the time when **Cat** was released in Italy, cinemas were being flooded with a deluge of *giallo* pictures, most of them failing to amount to anything more than violent escapism. A handful of directors, like the young Sergio Martino, had an unmistakable talent for revitalising the clichés by complimenting their wild screenplays with stylish widescreen photography. But even these proved ultimately shallow and unrewarding. Only the great Mario Bava and the underrated Duccio Tessari (whose 1971 *giallo* **Una Farfalla con le ali insanguinate** / **The Bloodstained Butterfly** provides us with a masterpiece which can at least hold a candle to the best of Argento's *gialli*) were able to twist and bend the rules of the genre to attain any great degree of artistic success. But Dario Argento was taking the genre even further. He was creating something of a cinematic universe of his own, even if **Cat** falls short of developing the creative potential that had been suggested through **The Bird With the Crystal Plumage** and would later blossom so wonderfully with **Four Flies on Grey Velvet**.

The Cat O'Nine Tails' greatest asset lies in the way it effectively thwarts the audience's expectations around the killer's identity. Argento imbues his picture with a pervasive sense of his villain's omnipresence, as though he is always there, just outside the frame. He murders without leaving clues, while Malden and Franciscus are always just one step behind. For added intensity, there is an abundance of shots from the point of view of the murderer, intercut with extreme close-ups of his blood red tinted retina. Consequently the viewer becomes restless, probing the screen for snippets of information, the senses pitched like those of blind Franco Arno, with Ennio Morricone's nerve-jangling score adding to the discomfort. Perhaps this would appear to play into the hands of Argento's detractors, who would claim that he is merely a competent technician, complying with convention. But, even in **The Cat O'Nine Tails**, there's plenty more beyond the surface than meets the viewer's eye.

The duality between the stalker and his prey has been one of Argento's concerns since his debut film, and of course **Cat** is no exception. Malden's character is developed effectively over the opening few scenes. It seems that he has a natural curiosity, leading him to eavesdrop on a conversation between blackmailer Dr Calabresi and the man who will soon be responsible for his murder. Arno is blind, a cruel irony given the film's obsessive preoccupation with the visual. But he sees things in his mind, he hears things,

facing page:
Hero and villain battle it
out on the rooftops.

Carlo Giordani (James Franciscus), Lori (Cinzia de Carolis) and Franco Arno (Karl Malden) are the unlikely sleuths in **The Cat O'Nine Tails**.

Blind ex-journalist Franco Arno (Karl Malden) puts his puzzle-solving powers to the test in the hunt for a killer.

and somehow he seems to know more than anybody else. (The notion of blind people 'knowing more' and thus becoming marked as potential opponents and likely victims would again be explored in **Suspiria** and later **Demons**.) There is an air of ambiguity about Arno, his apparent 'second sight' lending him a sense of menace.

When Giordani observes that there's *"something fishy"* about genetic engineer Casoni (Aldo Reggiani), Arno's only response, a pointedly ambiguous one, is *"Isn't there something fishy in all our lives?"* At the same time, the bond with his young niece Lori (Cinzia De Carolis) is tinged with sentimentality, coming across as heartfelt and sincere. This sense of ambiguity subtly permeates the whole film, but Argento cranks up the tension with less reserve during the climatic roof-top finale. The killer is unmasked as Dr Casoni, one of the film's least carefully developed characters, as though the director wishes to express his contempt for the thriller format as a mere formal guideline. After Giordani has failed to apprehend Casoni, Arno appears as though from thin air. The policeman is helpless and relegated to watching from a distance, but the blind man proves to be powerful enough to dispose of the young Casoni by throwing him into an elevator shaft, devastated by his boast that he has just murdered Lori. But the boast turns out to be a lie - we hear Lori calling Arno by his pet name, 'Cookie', in the film's closing moments - he has killed Casoni for nothing.

Another interesting paradox lies in the contrast between the film's focus on the warmth of its characters, embodied by Franciscus, Malden and De Carolis and its visual coldness, exemplified by the mild Technicolor hues, sombre art direction and gritty violence. The scenes between Malden and De Carolis (the brilliant child actress who also appeared in Giorgio Ferroni's **Night of the Devils**) display a tenderness and appealing *naïveté* that Argento appears to have lost touch with since the early seventies, capturing the audience's unequivocal sympathy for the unlikely pair. Humour manages to creep into even the most suspenseful of sequences - when Arno and Giordani wander through a cemetery at night, searching for Bianca Merusi's tomb, Argento frames the two men just behind a gravestone which carries the inscription 'Di Dario'!

The violence, however, is often highly realistic and at times difficult to watch. The majority of the victims are garrotted, the demise of Giordani's photographer friend Righetto (Vittorio Congia) representing the most horrific of all the killings. After having wrung the life out of him, the killer carves two nicks in the dead man's face. (A later scene, in which Giordani is shaved at the barber's shop, combines his horror at the death of his friend with comic relief; the effect is puzzling.) We are only a few minutes into the film when Argento delivers one of the most memorable set pieces with the brilliantly edited demise of Calabresi, crushed to death when he is thrown in the path of an oncoming train. Together with the climactic plunge down the elevator shaft, it's the only truly over-the-top

this page from top:
Investigative reporter Carlo Giordani (James Franciscus) finds himself immersed in the weird science of the Terzi Institute.

Giordani lies wounded as a scientist with corrupt chromosomes sets out on a killing spree.

Advertisement for the British release.

The blind leading the blind: Franco and Lori venture deeper into an increasingly convoluted plot.

Franco gains the upper hand at the denouement of **The Cat O' Nine Tails**.

WARNER BROS.
présente

JAMES FRANCISUS • KARL MALDEN
CATHERINE SPAAK

LE CHAT A
NEUF QUEUES

Un Film de
DARIO ARGENTO   EASTMANCOLOR

INTERDIT
MOINS DE 18

Anna Terzi (Catherine Spaak), daughter of the incestuous scientist.

Carlo Giordani (James Franciscus) and Franco Arno (Karl Malden) are held to account for their meddling by a ruthless psychopath.

top:
Murderous Dr Casoni (Aldo Reggiani) comes
to grief atop the roof of the Terzi Institute.

above:
A private view: Giordani (James Franciscus)
and Arno (Karl Malden) share observations
on the Institute killings.

sequence in an otherwise more subtle film, but it's still strong enough to induce a sense of nausea. The prolonged, drawn-out killing of Rada Rassimov's character is also fairly tough stuff: saliva dribbles from her mouth as she is strangled, her head beaten against the floor. All this is nothing in comparison with the carnage of **Suspiria** or **Tenebrae**, but in **Cat**'s closed, naturalistic environment, the scenes are harrowingly sadistic. It would be reasonable to observe, however, that these set pieces are nowhere near as stylized as those on offer in Argento's other work, inspired perhaps by the sweaty violence of spaghetti westerns, a logical progression when one considers where Argento's career in screenwriting began, and his oft-quoted assertion that *"Sergio Leone is my true mentor."*

Perhaps the most striking theme to surface in **Cat** is the way in which the Terzi Institute of Genetic Research becomes the centre of suspicion, twisted relationships and wickedness. Throughout the film the building is also called upon to yield essential information needed in order to 'solve the puzzle', supplying the nine clues of the film's title. All five of the principal suspects work there, the theft of the all-important genetic formula and the first killing take place there, and the climactic rooftop chase takes on some strange symbolic significance, as if some divine intervention has infiltrated the very core of evil. In some of his following films, notably **Deep Red**, **Suspiria** and **Inferno**, the invocation of buildings as places of wisdom, evil and fascination for the unknown would become a recurrent theme. In **Cat** the idea is explored for the first time, although perhaps without some of the mystique which surrounds the 'evil dwellings' of later works. But here the Terzi Institute provides some of the most interesting and controversial material of the narrative. On breaking into Terzi's house with the help of weirdo 'Gigi The Loser' (Ugo Fangareggi), Giordani discovers documents which reveal that Anna (Catherine Spaak) is not in fact Terzi's real daughter, but adopted. The mystery becomes darker as Terzi's diary hints at the possibility of an incestuous relationship between the two, articulating his thinly disguised lust with such utterances as *"I adore her"* and *"I often ask myself if these are the sentiments a father normally feels for his daughter."* (The father and daughter show an uncanny woodenness in the scenes in which they appear together, as though they share some dark secret or taboo.)

Argento said of the premiere of **The Cat O'Nine Tails**: *"I was so depressed. I found it too American, too easy for my taste."* It is true to say that it lacks the sheer energy, visual flamboyance and heavily layered subtext which would characterise his later work. But 'American' is a relative concept - no American director would ever have made this film in quite the way that Argento did. As it stands, **The Cat O'Nine Tails** is a solid, entertaining thriller, a tale well executed, which provides plenty of reasons for a critical reappraisal.

(The Argento quotes are from the September 1996 issue of *Sight And Sound*, which featured a 'Private View' of **The Cat O'Nine Tails**.)

Four Flies on Grey Velvet

Kim Newman

ITALY/FRANCE

1971

The last of the loose trilogy of nominally animal-themed *gialli* that established its director's reputation, **Four Flies on Grey Velvet** is prefaced by the legend - still fairly unusual in 1971 - 'a film by Dario Argento'. Clearly, we're in the presence of a creator who has a sense of his fictional universe and of his place above it. **Deep Red** returns to the whodunit mode of these early pictures, but it can more profitably be seen as the beginning of the next chapter in Argento's development. **Four Flies**, therefore, has to stand as the summation of a mode already developed by **The Bird With the Crystal Plumage** and **The Cat O'Nine Tails**. If it remains one of Argento's less-known movies, it may be because it is the most difficult to see in anything like a decent print.

It is, because of its strangely neutral protagonist, one of Argento's chilliest films and perhaps the hardest to get a grip on. We can't really like Roberto Tobias (Michael Brandon), who casually seduces his wife's adoring cousin (Francine Racette) and is targeted for persecution because he reminds the killer of her sadistic father. But, more even than the heroes of the earlier films, he is an Argento lookalike - especially when he slips under the bathwater and pretends to be drowning - and it's open to question whether the director intended his hero to come off as the self-absorbed, whinily neurotic git Brandon can't help but make him. We learn at the end that Roberto's own wife Nina (Mimsy Farmer) has been systematically tearing his life apart (*"I want so badly to see you die slowly, painfully"*) on the flimsiest of motives (*"the killer's a homicidal paranoid,"* explains the script helpfully, *"cases like that commit the most horrendous crimes for what appear to be insignificant reasons"*), but it's hard to feel the victim is being treated unfairly. If anything, thanks to Farmer's sincere explosion of insanity after she is revealed as the killer, we take her part. The film brushes off the saving of the hero's life to concentrate on the slow-motion decapitation of its villainess in a car accident.

Like its predecessors, **Four Flies** begins in style. The credits sequence is almost a pop video in itself, as rock drummer Roberto is seen during a session, playing frenzied rhythms for a very strange-sounding band while being pestered by a persistent fly (which winds up squashed by the final cymbal clash). Roeg-like flashbacks indicate Roberto realises a man in dark glasses glimpsed at the studio has been following him for some time, but cuts of a beating, valentine-shaped red heart introduce spots of throbbing quiet amid the pounding rock. Ennio Morricone's score prefigures the use of dreadful heavy metal in 1980s Argento, but there is at least a sense of irony in that we can take it that Roberto's group actually are pretentious rubbish. When Roberto apologises for his *"bad scene"*, a fellow musician tells him *"we're so far out, who's gonna notice?"* There are so many gimmick shots (one from inside a guitar) in this kaleidoscope of images that it's a relief to get into the film proper, which begins with Roberto confronting his mystery man (Calisto Calisti) in a deserted theatre and semi-accidentally stabbing him as a spotlight is turned on the crime and a figure in a disturbing child mask snaps a roll of photographs of the killing.

Later, we learn that Calisti's death has been faked, but Roberto never finds this out. Another movie hero might feel guilty about the killing, but Roberto just doesn't want to be caught. Before he learns who is behind the crimes against him, a bunch of secondary characters have to get killed in set-piece scenes: a blackmailing maid is slashed in the park, a gay private eye is stabbed in the chest with a hypo of glowing blue poison and the cousin is knifed in the dark. In a bit of pseudoscientific nonsense (recapped in **Wild Wild West**), the last victim's extracted eyeball captures the image she saw as she died, four flies (presumably on grey velvet). Roberto is such a glum lead, the film has to work hard on the

facing page:
The psycho in the smiley mask initiates a trail of mayhem in **Four Flies on Grey Velvet**.

Tormented Nina Tobias (Mimsy Farmer) loses her head as she makes a bid for escape in the film's closing scene.

Roberto Tobias struggles with a throwaway suspect.

The gay Private Investigator hits on the solution to his final case

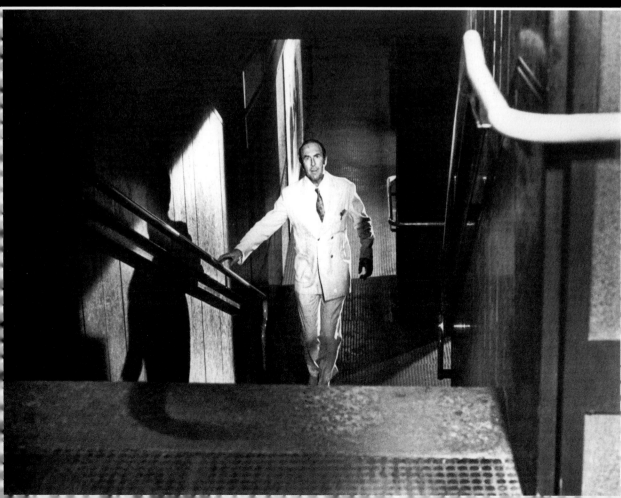

The stark geometry of a darkened street sets the tone of unease in **Four Flies on Grey Velvet**.

Michael Brandon as insipid, neurotic 'hero' Roberto Tobias

from top:
Roberto Tobias (Michael Brandon) stumbles into a nightmarish game of blackmail and paranoia.

Tobias hits on the answer to the riddle of the four flies.

Roberto Tobias (Michael Brandon) becomes a reluctant criminal when he stabs Carlo Marosi (Calisto Calisti) in the not-quite deserted theatre.

supporting characters: **The Bird With the Crystal Plumage** used everything from Fredric Brown's novel *The Screaming Mimi* except the philosophical drop-out named God (for Godfrey), but he turns up here in the hulking shape of Bud Spencer [Carlo Pedersoli] and demands to be called 'God Almighty'; and Jean-Pierre Marielle's balding, swishy PI is a step forward from the gay stereotype Werner Peters in **Bird**, at least solving the case (after a string of reported failures) before he dies. Still, we keep coming back to the drummer, who suffers a series of precognitive dreams of an execution which seems to be the opening of **The Face of Fu Manchu** staged in the style of **Last Year at Marienbad** and might well derive from the visions of decapitation found in Fellini's **Toby Dammit**.

Though commentators have more than noted Argento's debts to Mario Bava and Alfred Hitchcock, he actually draws far more often on Michaelangelo Antonioni.* The slo-mo finale as Farmer's car ploughs into a truck, detaching her startled head Jayne Mansfield-style, is staged in the manner of the final explosion in **Zabriskie Point**, to the extent of using the same camera gadget (**Tenebrae** borrows similarly from **The Passenger**) to get the effect. Also Antonioniesque is the milieu of shallow, supposedly creative, affluent Romans - some early 70s fashions and hairstyles are of Jason King-esque proportions - who affect such an unshockable *ennui* that any of them might be the killer. As always, there's a mix of contempt for the requirements of the whodunit (the clues are deliberately unfathomable - when Roberto notices his wife's giveaway fly-in-lucite pendant it's the first we have seen of it and he doesn't seem to have noticed the thing before either) along with a bare-faced cheek that might pass for satire (the asylum functionary who admits *"I would definitely describe it as an extreme case of homicidal mania"* but is nevertheless convinced his ex-patient is entirely cured). Like Raymond Chandler, Argento tends to let his misogyny scupper his mystery: his killers are usually the most powerful women in the stories.

Though not as extreme as **Tenebrae**, in which the apparent hero/directorial stand-in turns out to be the mad killer, **Four Flies on Grey Velvet** is among the most cynical and cruel of Argento's *oeuvre*. None of the characters amounts to much, and we observe their struggling against fate much as Roberto views the buzzing fly under the credits, prolonging the agonies only to set up a satisfying squashing.

*It may be that giallo obsessives who track down each last Umberto Lenzi movie haven't bothered to see all that many Antonioni movies.

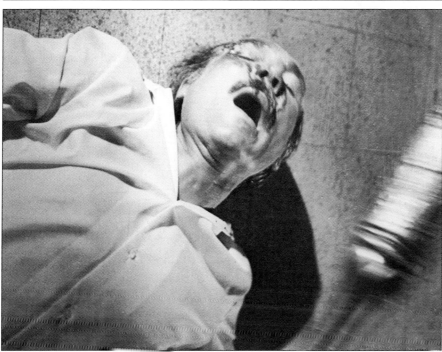

top:
Roberto Tobias (Michael Brandon) sets
upon his beleagured postman.

middle:
The bleached-out decapitation fantasy.

bottom:
Dead again: fraudulent murder victim Carlo
Marosi (Calisto Calisti) meets a more
permanent end.

Le cinque giornate
aka 'The Five Days of Milan'

Chris Gallant

ITALY

1973

The opening shot of **Le cinque giornate**[1] is of a cannon, the credits displayed against the static image until the camera finally arcs around it, the director's name superimposed over the enormous barrel, which appears to be aimed directly at us. It becomes an emblem, the first of many, for the film's provocative ultra-violence. The brutality of **Le cinque giornate** is frequently more harsh, more abrasive and impersonal than the intimacy of murder, that which exists between Argento's killers and their victims. By far the least well known and least celebrated entry in the director's filmography, this blood-drenched period drama is most frequently referred to as Argento's 'film for Italy.' The narrative takes as its premise a five-day uprising against occupying Austrian authorities, using it as a vehicle for the adventures of convicted thief Cainazzo, who escapes from jail onto the streets of Milan, only to become embroiled in a bloody and ultimately pointless revolution.

The opening scene, in which Cainazzo kills a prison rat and tosses it into the mouth of a sleeping fellow convict sets the tone for this bizarre, but often flawed political comedy. Upon his escape, Cainazzo finds a companion in Romolo, a baker whose shop is razed to the ground in the surrounding disorder, and together they stumble aimlessly and ineptly from one scuffle to another, alienated by patriots and occupying enemy alike. The background of a city in turmoil presents an abundance of opportunities for quirky, raucous humour. On his escape from the closed, safe environment of the prison, Cainazzo is plunged, head first, into a realm of chaos. Initially he is markedly a-political, his standing as an outlaw obliging him to side with whichever group can help him to retain his freedom, although gradually his adventures lead him to a greater understanding of the difficulties of patriotism, his naivety allowing him an insight which extends beyond that of the mob or the presiding politicians, aristocrats and priests.

Although **Le cinque giornate** represents a radical, if temporary, change of direction, certain characters are familiar: the busty countess is the ultimate incarnation of the sadomasochistic, thrill-seeking whore. She stands on the sidelines of a gun battle, laughing and cooing with delight, later seducing the gang of blood-crazed mutineers in the darkness of her mansion. Similarly, the dented machismo of earlier Argento heroes returns through the characters of Cainazzo and Romolo, their masculinist identity becoming the focus of much of the comedy. All too often they are seen running away from battle, in one scene they are intimidated by the countess' camp lackey and later they throw up their hands in horror when faced with the task of playing midwife to a woman in labour. But while the perceived inadequacies of Sam Dalmas and Roberto Tobias became part of a cynical commentary which undermined their standing as 'heroes', here it provides the saving grace for the two men, who retain a degree of honour and solidarity while the surrounding rabble becomes corrupted by anger. While Cainazzo does his best to conform with the vengeful patriots, the horrific consequences of their struggle repeatedly confound him, providing a constant source of discomfort and guilt. With ill-concealed glee, they vent their hatred on the occupying Austrians, while the disturbing set pieces - a crying baby crawls from its dead mother's arms, a young woman screams with grief at the sight of a row of hanging corpses - provide an awareness of their barbarity. Cainazzo wanders amidst the brutality and destruction, alienated and dismayed. His ultimate disillusionment arises from the death of Romolo, who is gunned down by a firing squad after he tries to prevent the rape of a young Austrian woman. Cainazzo continues to be swept up in the fever of revolution, forced to suffer his own hypocrisy as he comes to understand the futility of the struggle - the revolution has served only to elevate another corrupt social elite and the 'people' of Milan are no better off than they were in the first place.

opposite:
A 'film for Italy':
Blood-crazed patriots prepare for battle
and Cainazzo (Adriano Celentano) looks
on as chaos breaks out.

top:
The Countess (Marilu Tolo) discovers
the eroticism of violence.

above:
French video cover.

The visual style of **Le cinque giornate** is more exuberant, more outrageously experi-mental than even that of **The Bird With the Crystal Plumage** or **Four Flies on Grey Velvet**, paving the way for the insane sensory experience which would emerge from the visuals of **Deep Red** - the two films share the same director of photography, Luigi Kuveiller, and art director, Giuseppe Bassan. The profusion of tracking shots is close to the relentless prowling of the camera in Argento's next delirious thriller, the period setting providing adequate justification for baroque art direction. With the repeated invocation of Peckinpah's trademark slow-motion violence, the style is utterly frenetic, excessive in virtually every sense, almost exhausting to watch.

In purely commercial terms, **Le cinque giornate** was a bold, if unsuccessful move. It seems inevitable that a slapstick political comedy would fail to appeal to an audience which associated the Argento 'brand' with sophisticated psychological thrillers. Although the director seems to derive enormous enjoyment from experimenting with the politics and cinematic conventions of the genre, it is easy to see that he is far from comfortable with his material, a script originally written with comedy director Nanni Loy in mind. Perhaps he should have followed his original plan and hired a director with a greater affinity for the genre to helm the project, but the result is not entirely unrewarding. For all that **Le cinque giornate** is frequently passed over as a mere footnote to an otherwise spectacular career, it is a curious, one-of-a-kind piece, which occupies a unique position within its director's filmography.

Notes

1.   **Le cinque giornate** translates literally as "The Five Days". Although most often referred to in English-language texts as either **The Five Days of Milan** or, less commonly, **Five Days in Milan**, the film has never been released in any English-speaking territory, which raises doubts over the validity of either of the English variations on the title. The sources consulted here (Julian Granger, researcher, and Nick Alexander, who has produced English-language versions of many of the Argento films) confirm that, to the best of their knowledge, no English dubbed or subtitled version has ever been produced. **The Five Days of Milan** was listed in an edition of Variety as a provisional title while the film was in production, although in the absence of any reliable evidence that the title was ever used, arguably it constitutes little more than an oft-repeated myth.

you're getting closer...

and closer...

to the most unnatural
kind of death!

Deep Red

Julian Grainger

ITALY

1975

The 1970s was Dario Argento's best decade and **Deep Red** is his crowning achievement during that period. The film is stylish, visually stunning in its use of colour, composition and framing, contains a terrific score that meshes exquisitely with the images and is perhaps Argento's most humorous and playful work. It also contains two of the best performances (from David Hemmings and Daria Nicolodi) to be found in any of his films. But it is also the director's contrary take on the *gialli*, the thrillers that made him a household name in Italy. He packs just about every cliché from the genre into two short hours and sends up the whole lot in what can be seen as just about the final word on the subject.

Argento develops a series of strategies in the film relating to his use of camera movement, the positioning of the camera in relation to what the audience sees and to the music. And then he breaks these strategies. This is an extraordinarily contradictory film that can prove a tad frustrating until you realize that contradiction was precisely what Argento was after. He didn't want anything that was "formal - too precise". This also applies not just to the way the film was shot but also to the plot: an audience expecting a by-the-numbers investigation into a series of mysterious murders (the staple of the *giallo*) were in for a bit of a surprise. The film is chock full of ideas and theories, clues as to the killer's motivation, red herrings and pointless asides. Try really hard to work out who's guilty in this one and all you'll get is a headache.

The film's opening scenes are quite extraordinary: under the credits plays the remarkable Goblin-performed score. First the actors', then the writers' names appear - but then these credits are interrupted. The Goblin music fades and we can hear a voice singing a childish tune. The picture fades in to show - from floor level - a 'fifties-style living room with a Christmas tree. Just as the eye traverses the picture to take in the back wall and what appears to be the shadows of two figures engaged in a terrible struggle, the sickly-sweet music is interrupted by a horrendous scream. The shadow that has been making a series of stabbing movements appears to complete its grisly work and suddenly a bloodied knife is dropped on the floor, right in front of the camera so as to startle the audience. There is a new lyrical phrase to the music and two feet walk up to the knife. From the shoes and socks it is clear they belong to a child. The picture fades....

Cinema audiences often talk over the opening credits - especially in Italy - but this sequence really grabs the attention. There is a rapid music cross-fade back to the Goblin score as the rest of the credits unroll. With the appearance of Argento's name as 'regia' (director); it is significant that once again music abruptly stops.

Next we see David Hemmings rehearsing with his jazz band but soon he stops them playing, interrupting the music in mid-flow. He admonishes his colleagues:

> *"It's precise - too formal"*.

One of Argento's strategies is already becoming clear: he is constantly interrupting what is on-screen, as if saying to the audience: 'Don't get carried away. Keep your distance. Be vigilant.'

It's an intriguing way to start a film. Usually the director is only too desperate to draw the audience into his world, to make them 'suspend disbelief' and become emotionally wrapped up in the story being told. Argento does the opposite; he is going to be playing an elaborate game and he wants us to keep our wits about us.

facing page:
Amanda Righetti (Giuliana Calandra)
hears a song from the grave.

Seasonal jollity is brought to a shocking end
in **Deep Red**'s Freudian 'primal scene'.

Gianna Brezzi (Daria Nicolodi) attends a
conference on parapsychology.

Having urged us to stay vigilant, Argento now starts developing his thesis. It is not to
damn **Deep Red** to describe it as An Essay in Perception; it functions beautifully as a classy
slice of entertainment but there's a lot more going on besides. First and foremost this is a
film about looking and, crucially, about seeing. It's an obvious statement but everything
we see in the cinema is mediated by the camera, that imperfect, clunky stand-in for the
human eye. And the way scenes are filmed, where the camera is placed and so-on, is
crucial in the way it places us, the audience, in relation to what is happening on-screen.
How we are supposed to relate to what is happening, what we are supposed to feel and
think, depends on how the camera is used.

The next scene is at a conference being held on the subject of parapsychology. The
camera behaves like it is a person, 'walking' into the building, through an anteroom and
past a hat check guy and a ticket attendant. It's weird but these two people don't seem to
be aware that anyone is walking past them - they don't even look up. At the moment we
are the subject, the 'I' of the camera but we don't know who we are. We have only our
expectations and prejudices to rely upon. We can look out at the world, we can interact
with it, but until we look in a mirror we won't even know what sex we are - and Argento
isn't letting on. We aren't looking at someone entering the conference, we are that person.
To draw our attention to this specifically, Argento has curtains leading into the conference
hall proper violently pulled open as 'we' pass through them.

We then get the first of many shots throughout the film demonstrating a strong visual
perspective: we look down the aisle at the conference speakers. The film is peppered with
such shots: there are the grave-lined walkways at the cemetery, the corridors of the
school, shots through the many rooms that make up Amanda Righetti's apartment and of
course - crucially - the painting-lined hallway in Helga Ulmann's apartment. Perspective
shots present an exaggerated sense of the distance between the subject (the camera, us)
and the object in any given shot. In drawing our attention to this, Argento is again saying
to us, 'maintain your perspective, keep your distance'. He is also playing a visual trick on
the audience: this type of shot naturally draws the eye down the lines of perspective to
what we expect to be the object of the shot - the back of the apartment, the end of the
hallway and so-on. In **Deep Red** everything of significance is happening halfway along the
line of sight. Could it be that our attention is being deliberately mis-directed?

The conference is concerned with the apparent ability of all living things to communicate by telepathy - from the animal kingdom through to people - but, says academic Mario
Bardi: *"we lose telepathy as we learn to communicate verbally"* (a point Argento
humorously comments upon by showing an old man tapping irritably at his malfunc-
tioning hearing aid, suggesting that the spoken word is at best a rather flawed method of
communication). Argento seems to be pointing out the difference between looking and
seeing, hearing and listening. Marc Daly is a musician who looks without seeing (he looks
right at the murderer in the flat but doesn't see her) and hears without listening (both
Gianna and Carlo tell Marc that he must know the murderer's identity but he doesn't
understand what they mean until much later in the film).

Just as we are getting into the flow of conference verbiage, psychic Helga Ulmann lets
out a piercing shriek as she perceives someone in the audience who she knows has killed
before and will kill again. The presence of Helga contradicts Bardi's statement. She is a

telepath who has maintained her psychic ability despite learning to speak. She can 'see' without using her eyes. The irony is that it doesn't help her at all - while she knows that someone in the audience is a killer, she can't properly identify them and she can't see that she will be the next victim. In fact her telepathic powers lead straight to her death since her detection of the murderer makes her a target. Like most of the characters in **Deep Red**, she can see something but, crucially, she can't see enough. And this is central to Argento's thesis; that we are forced to make decisions based on imperfect information because at best we are likely to get only a glimpse or a detail of the whole picture. What she does do, without knowing the meaning of what she is saying, is to mention *"child's music"* and *"the villa"*, making sure the audience connect the killer she is talking about to the murder they watched during the film's opening credits. This is the first point in the film where Argento explicitly signals to us that we are going to have a privileged position, that we are going to be shown more than the characters in the film and thus know more than they do.

"It's always a maniac and they never catch them!" Amanda Righetti (Giuliana Calandra) suffers a horrible death in **Deep Red**.

Once again we are treated to the camera's point-of-view as it rises from its seat and (with some trouble) leaves the hall with the conference still in full swing. Helga's outburst has made the killer uncomfortable enough to leave in case they are identified.

The penny drops.

Helga is referring to us - it is we who are this terrible killer whose appalling presence she can detect *"like a blade entering my flesh"* (which of course it will). And if we can see through the eyes of a killer, we also see the eye of the killer as it spies on its victim. These murders are not opportunistic or crimes of passion, these are planned in advance, premeditated. Furthermore spying often implies not just curiosity but also, in anonymity, desire. The killer does a hell of a lot of creeping about and spying in this film and most of it precedes a murder. Could it be a form of foreplay? The extraordinary brutal stabbings and slashings leave gaping slits in the victims and later on, Carlo will toast the departed Helga as a *"raped virgin"*. Murder as sex, spying as foreplay. In **Deep Red**, the act of watching is far from neutral.

In case we doubt Helga's words about how terrible the killer is, we are taken into a rest room where we see a tap turned on and the camera follows the water as it pours into the sink, round the basin and down the plug hole. Argento is making a deliberate reference to **Psycho** as, in the aftermath of Janet Leigh's murder in the shower, Hitchcock follows a mixture of blood and water as it drains away. In case you think this reference is a little obscure, it's worth remembering that the shot from the Hitchcock film begins with a huge close-up of Leigh's (dead) eye, and moments later in **Deep Red** we will be treated to the killer applying black eye shadow in another huge close-up of an eye. Argento wants us to be in no doubt that we are dealing with a psychopath.

In just a few minutes Argento has established the three main visual strategies within the film: the first is the most prosaic, the usual place the audience finds itself, watching unobtrusively while standing outside of the action. The second is a little more unusual: we will be fed information that the characters within the film are not, placing us in a privileged position regarding the unfolding story. The third is more unusual still: at certain moments we will be shown the world of the film through the eyes of a particularly sick killer, thus implicating us directly in the subsequent murders. That's quite a heady mix and we are going to be challenged to solve a crime while absorbing information from three, conflicting points of view. Tough call.

So what about the plot? **Deep Red** looks on first glance to be a classic *giallo*: a series of murders is being committed and we expect that the plot will be advanced by the central protagonist(s) getting ever closer to solving the mystery - drawing us through a variety of possible outcomes before arriving at the right one. Traditionally there was the upper class

Marc Daly (David Hemmings) digs deep in the house of the screaming child.

top:
Gianna's investigations lead her to a
deserted school where she is stabbed
by a shadowy assailant.

above:
Comedy relief / battle of the sexes.
Marc's dignity is bruised by a drive
in Gianna's car.

sleuth, Agatha Christie's Hercule Poirot/Miss Marple or Conan-Doyle's Sherlock Holmes, whose powers of deduction verged on the supernatural. The audience was seldom expected (or even allowed) to keep up with the plot as it unfolded, rather to watch with passive admiration as the brilliant sleuth set about solving the crime. These sleuths were clearly not on the same plane as us and they seldom deigned to interact emotionally (or, God forbid, romantically) with the other characters they encountered. Miss Marple was, after all, a Miss.

Film noir introduced the cinema to another type of investigator altogether; the down-at-heel private eye who was often operating on the fringes of the law and who maintained a somewhat ambivalent relationship with the cops. These guys (and they were almost always men) were far more your average Joe, an Everyman-type more likely to wear sturdy walking shoes than have a chauffeur on call. And unlike their predecessors who maintained a professional, discreet distance, they also had an eye for the ladies and a penchant for falling for the gangster's moll. They would usually get their man but this was usually through a combination of luck, inspiration and sheer dogged determination.

It was on television that the police procedural genre flourished; a world-weary cop assigned to a difficult case, this guy had his instincts and twenty years of experience to help him achieve his collar. Like the private eye he was a regular, hard-working man who had sacrificed a personal life to the demands of his job.

Argento drew on the German brand of murder-mystery (or *krimi*), usually based on the works of Edgar Wallace and hugely popular in the 1950s and 1960s. In Wallace's novels the hero was usually a Scotland Yard detective but the cases he was called upon to solve often had something of the bizarre or exotic about them. Both **The Cat O'Nine Tails** and **The Bird With the Crystal Plumage** were sold in Germany as based on novels by Edgar Wallace's son Bryan. The Italian *giallo* mixed the *krimi* with the police procedural and added a twist of its own; an almost fetishistic attention to the murderer and the killings he (and sometimes she) perpetrated. Momentarily **Deep Red** looks as if it will contain a significant plot strand relating to the police's investigation of these murders through its introduction of Eros Pagni as Police Inspector Calcabrini (who receives fairly prominent billing). Not a bit of it: Argento portrays the police as cretins to a man. Towards the end of the scene in Helga's apartment, journalist Gianna Brezzi (Daria Nicolodi) is introduced. She arrives at the scene of the crime very quickly, apparently having discovered that a murder had been committed almost as soon as the police. She then proceeds to humiliate them by turning out to know far more about poor Helga than they do, obliging them to ask her for details of the victim's background.

Furthermore Argento chooses to lampoon the police through the curious medium of food (an Italian tradition going back at least as far as the comic buffoons of the *commedia dell'arte*): we first see Calcabrini stuffing his face with a sandwich while trying, unsuccessfully, to remember the word 'violin'. He has six men working in Helga's apartment and with the exception of barely glimpsed token C.S.C. actor Lorenzo Piani dusting for fingerprints, almost all the other actors playing police officers have been deliberately cast because they are overweight! There is the ageing, rotund and seemingly half-blind police photographer (played by Dante Fioretti), round-faced, moustached and terminally useless Salvatore Puntillo who can just about manage to offer Hemmings a cup of coffee, pudgy Piero Vida has his mouth so full of food he can only gesture helplessly at Puntillo, and in the background taking notes is Vittorio Fanfoni, so heavyset that the phrase 'missing link' springs to mind. Only crinkly-faced Fulvio Mingozzi (an Argento good-luck charm to be found in every film from **The Bird With the Crystal Plumage** through **Phenomena**) defies the fat-policeman paradigm and he's the cop who has the thankless task of dragging Hemmings down to police headquarters to fill in reams of paperwork - in other words he's just another hopeless bureaucrat. And in case we hadn't quite got the message, the next time we see Calcabrini he is possessed with impotent fury because he can't even get the cola machine to dispense any cans. It is almost as if Argento is suggesting that the police's overwhelming need to take in food renders them useless in seeing what is going on around and outside of them (this from a director who has long been a walking advertisement for the dangers of self-starvation). And that's about the extent of the police's involvement. Neither Calcabrini or his men come up with anything of significance in the investigation and are quietly dropped from the plot of **Deep Red**.

So with no Poirot, Sam Spade or Sgt. Joe Friday on hand to solve the mystery of Helga's violent demise, Argento gives us instead two slightly less likely protagonists: a music teacher Marc Daly (David Hemmings) who is an inadvertent witness (wrong place, wrong time) to the first murder, and the ambitious and clever journalist Gianna Brezzi, who is on the lookout for a scoop. These two characters are well-drawn; in fact the famously actor-blind Argento elicits fine performances of considerable subtlety from his two leads. Hemmings manages brilliantly to convey a man feeling his way through a mystery whose components have nothing to do with his usual experience of the world, while Nicolodi makes a triumph of her intelligent, independent and resourceful journalist. Nevertheless this looks like fairly traditional stuff: their enquiries (working both apart and together) providing the main method for drawing the audience through the plot, moving the narrative forward as they gradually get closer to discovering the identity of Helga's murderer. But rather than just have the audience slavishly (and passively) follow their investigation, Argento deliberately challenges us to get there first, providing motivation by giving us little extra titbits of information his characters don't possess and allowing us to feel superior in the possession of greater knowledge.

The supplying of additional information to the audience is achieved in a bizarre and unusual way: a given scene will start as one would expect, the camera focusing on a particular character going about his or her business while we, the unnoticed observer, stand back and watch. But then the camera will break off to go exploring 'by itself' - not motivated by the actions of a character but explicitly controlled by the hand of the filmmaker. At one point early on in the film we see Helga Ulmann talking on the telephone in her luxurious and expensive apartment. We listen to her chattering away for a few

Danish video cover.

left:
Amanda Righetti (Giulia Calandra) contemplates the eerie symbology of
Deep Red.

Dario Argento sets up **Deep Red**'s horrific final act.

Argento directs Macha Meril as she listens to the tortured voices in her head

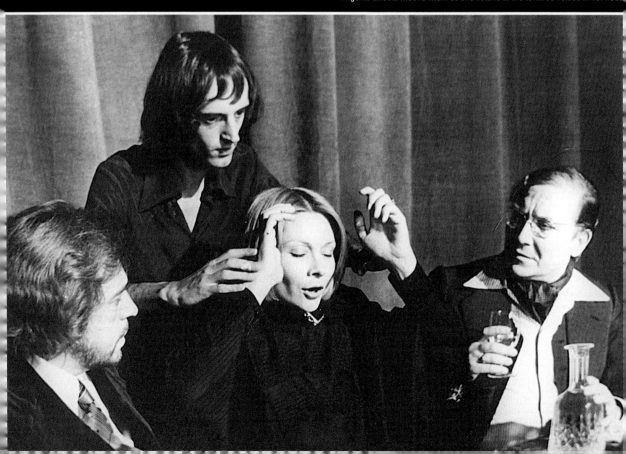

DARIO ARGENTO

PROFONDO ROSSO

RIZZOLI FILM e SALVATORE ARGENTO presentano un film di DARIO ARGENTO con DAVID HEMMINGS · DARIA NICOLODI in

PROFONDO ROSSO

con GABRIELE LAVIA · MACHA MERIL · EROS PAGNI · GIULIANA CALANDRA · e con la piccola NICOLETTA ELMI · e con GLAUCO MAURI
e con la partecipazione di CLARA CALAMAI — soggetto e sceneggiatura di DARIO ARGENTO e BERNARDINO ZAPPONI — musica di GIORGIO GASLINI
produttore esecutivo CLAUDIO ARGENTO — un film prodotto dalla SEDA spettacoli s.p.a. — regia di DARIO ARGENTO — colore Lv di LUCIANO VITTORI

Marta pays the price for a lifetime of lunacy in the film's final scene.

moments... and then the camera sets off on its own! First it checks out the rest of the room she is in and then moves round to reveal an adjacent corridor lined with paintings. Later on in the film the camera follows Hemmings and his friend, jazz pianist Carlo (Gabriele Lavia), along the street as we listen to their conversation. But after a while the camera slows, lets them walk out of shot, then pops round the corner into someone's house to watch some television. And of course it just happens to be showing a news bulletin about reports that a witness (Marc) saw Helga's murderer fleeing the scene of the crime. These moments are a startling break with normal cinematic conventions, however the information they impart is not necessarily reliable: while in the first case the audience is shown the corridor that will be so important to the resolution of the film's plot and the revelation of the killer's identity (even if its significance is as yet obscure), the second makes the deliberately misleading suggestion that Marc stands to be next victim.

This is a little strange if you think about it: challenge your audience to work out a fiendishly difficult whodunit and then spend almost the entire film feeding them completely misleading red herrings.

It isn't just the stylistic elements that are misleading; this also applies to substantial elements of the plot and the dialogue. Having established Brezzi/Nicolodi as extremely bright, Argento has her say to Marc/Hemmings: *"You saw everything. You're the super eyewitness"*. Brezzi is here acting almost like a Greek chorus: she couldn't possibly know what Hemmings has seen, so these lines only make sense if you realize that Argento is talking directly to the audience.

There are other occasions when the dialogue gives the impression that Argento is speaking, none too subtly, to the audience rather it being in the service of the plot or characters. Witness this exchange between Marc and Carlo outside in the street:

Carlo: *"Maybe you don't realize the importance of what you saw"*
Marc: *"Sometimes what you really see and what you imagine get mixed in your memory like a cocktail... and you can't distinguish the flavours any more."*

The metaphor itself is hopelessly 'mixed' but the overall point is clear enough: Marc may have seen more than he thinks he did - and therefore so might we. As Calcabrini walks Marc down the painting-lined hall in Helga's apartment he says: *"Strange pictures, eh?"* How nice, Argento is giving us yet another retrospective clue. And that's the point, even if these can be recognised as clues, all three conversations occur after Marc has inadvertently seen the murderer. It is already too late to pay extra close attention to what he (and we) saw in Helga's flat and even if we could see that scene again, the vital details are so obscure as to be virtually impossible to comprehend. If you go back to that scene on your tape or DVD, you'll discover that Calamai is indeed reflected in the mirror - but you almost certainly won't see her without using your 'still frame' facility (obviously this was an option not available to 1975 cinema-goers, unless they wanted to pay their money

Marc and Gianna pool resources to unveil the murderer - but are they on the right track?

and go back in for repeated viewings). Calamai's face appears in the mirror with three other ghostly faces apparently reflected from another of the paintings, for a mere ten frames, less than half a second. The whole of the mirror is visible but for a single frame and to make matters worse, the camera is moving, this dolly shot making it very difficult to focus on the relevant part of the screen in time to take in the vital details. (Ironically the mirror is positioned at the edge of the frame so those viewers watching the film in a pan-and-scanned version would have even less chance of spotting this pivotal moment). Quite simply the audience could not possibly be expected to see Calamai and thus solve the puzzle - and anyway we haven't been introduced to her character at this point, we have no idea who she is. Argento tacitly acknowledges this when, at the film's climax when Calamai is finally revealed in the mirror, Argento does something we couldn't possibly have done, he zooms in to a close-up on Calamai's face.

None of this is accidental. Argento's great joke in **Deep Red** is that actually he couldn't give a damn who did it. It is a murder mystery in which the revelation of who committed the murder is of no importance. The audience are not supposed to solve the film's (apparently) central conundrum. Who cares that it is Clara Calamai's character (Carlo's mother) who is guilty, rather than Carlo or indeed Professor Giordani (or even a schizo-phrenic Marc Daly)? Argento isn't really interested in the whys and wherefores, in fact he doesn't seem interested in the plot content of the film full stop. What does seem to get him all fired up is playing around with the form of the murder mystery, providing a little lecture on the pleasures of looking through the movie camera and hopefully drawing his audience in to enjoy the experience with him.

Which is why almost nothing is what it seems. Red herrings are piled on top of red herrings, real clues confused with false leads until we are forced to sit back and disengage from the whole whodunit scenario. If the puzzle was there to be satisfactorily and easily solved, the audience would get it and then just as likely give up on the film. What would be the fun in that?

Argento tries to fit as much into **Deep Red** as he can, so overloading the content that he comes dangerously close to pastiche. The conversation between Gabriele Lavia and Hemmings in which the former accuses Marc of being *bourgeois* (because he can play music for art's sake) while he, Carlo, must play music just to survive is never taken anywhere. It is a tantalizing idea to add class conflict to the general *mélange* but it is one Argento chooses not to develop. It is also another red herring since Carlo's mother may be a psychopath but she was also once a famous actress and doesn't appear to be short of a bob or two. Carlo seems to suffer more from wealthy indolence than grinding poverty.

Another example is the sequence, back in the rest-room at the psychic conference, where the killer is revealed putting on zip-up black leather gloves. By 1975 this was a *giallo* cliché: the ritualistic adornment of leather, with its connotations of fetishism and sex, suggesting that the killer isn't just a psychopathic murderer but kinky with it. The purpose of this scene is to provide extra information for later on, once Carlo is the main suspect. But with the revelation that it is his mother who is the murderer, you realize that Argento

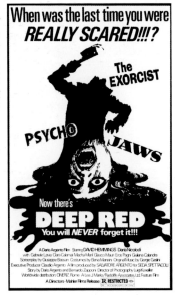

top:
A shocking act of violence meted out to
Professor Giordani (Glauco Mauri).

above:
American admat.

facing page:
Stylish artwork for the Japanese release of
Deep Red (billed as 'Suspiria 2').

is just having us on. Similarly the strange ritual whereby the killer applies eye shadow is
meant to conjure up intimations of some kind of 'sexual perversion' whereas the true
reason is rather prosaic; it allows the killer to look at other people through, say, a small
hole without the pink flesh around the eye being visible.

And all the stuff about corrupted childhoods falls into the same category: just so much
window-dressing. Argento presents the classic nurture/nature debate through the characters of the young Carlo (Iacopo Mariani), who represents childhood innocence corrupted
by the horrors of his environment, and of the caretaker's daughter, little Olga Rodi
(Nicoletta Elmi), representing a child simply, inherently evil. These two strands are
developed throughout the film: in the case of Carlo we first see him picking up the knife
just used to murder his father and staring at the bloodied blade in wonder. Then there is
the childish singing that the murderer uses to get 'in the mood' before a killing and the
detailed examination of tiny items that the camera indulges in several times in the film.
They are silly knick-knacks; little plastic animals, dolls and so-on that any child might
collect ...except there are also knives.

We are first aware of little Olga when her father (burly actor Furio Meniconi) belts her
across the face for no apparent reason. We assume she, like the little boy, has been
brutalised by yet another uncaring parent. We reappraise our opinions when we see what
Olga's father can see, that dear little Olga has left a lizard in the dust, writhing in agony with
a pin jammed through it's middle. Later he will say of Olga that *"she is macabre"*. This is
significant because we now have an example not of childhood innocence corrupted by the
actions of others, but of a child who seems to be inherently 'simply evil'. But of course this
is all so much hot air once the killer is revealed to be Carlo's mother Martha, whose
background we don't know anything about. All we know is that she is mad and has already
spent some time locked away. Argento is playing games - this is all one big wind up.

In one or two instances this seems infuriating rather than clever. Argento's apparent
need to chuck in everything he can think of into his film, to play as many games as
possible with the audience, runs the risk of backfiring. As noted above, Argento works
rigorously in the film's opening scenes to establish a series of shots from the killer's point-
of-view. But he ruins this system with the inclusion of a seemingly random shot - taken
from high up in one of the boxes - which doesn't make visual sense in terms of where the
camera has been placed. It's as if the magnificent visual stylist simply can't resist the
inclusion of a stunning, master shot of the conference hall from on high, even if it weakens
the surrounding material.

But there are few flaws in **Deep Red**. Most of what seems baffling about the film offers
itself up on closer inspection and there is undoubtedly much more to discover about this
ingenious, brutal, sarcastic and brilliant film. See it as often as you can, you won't be
disappointed.

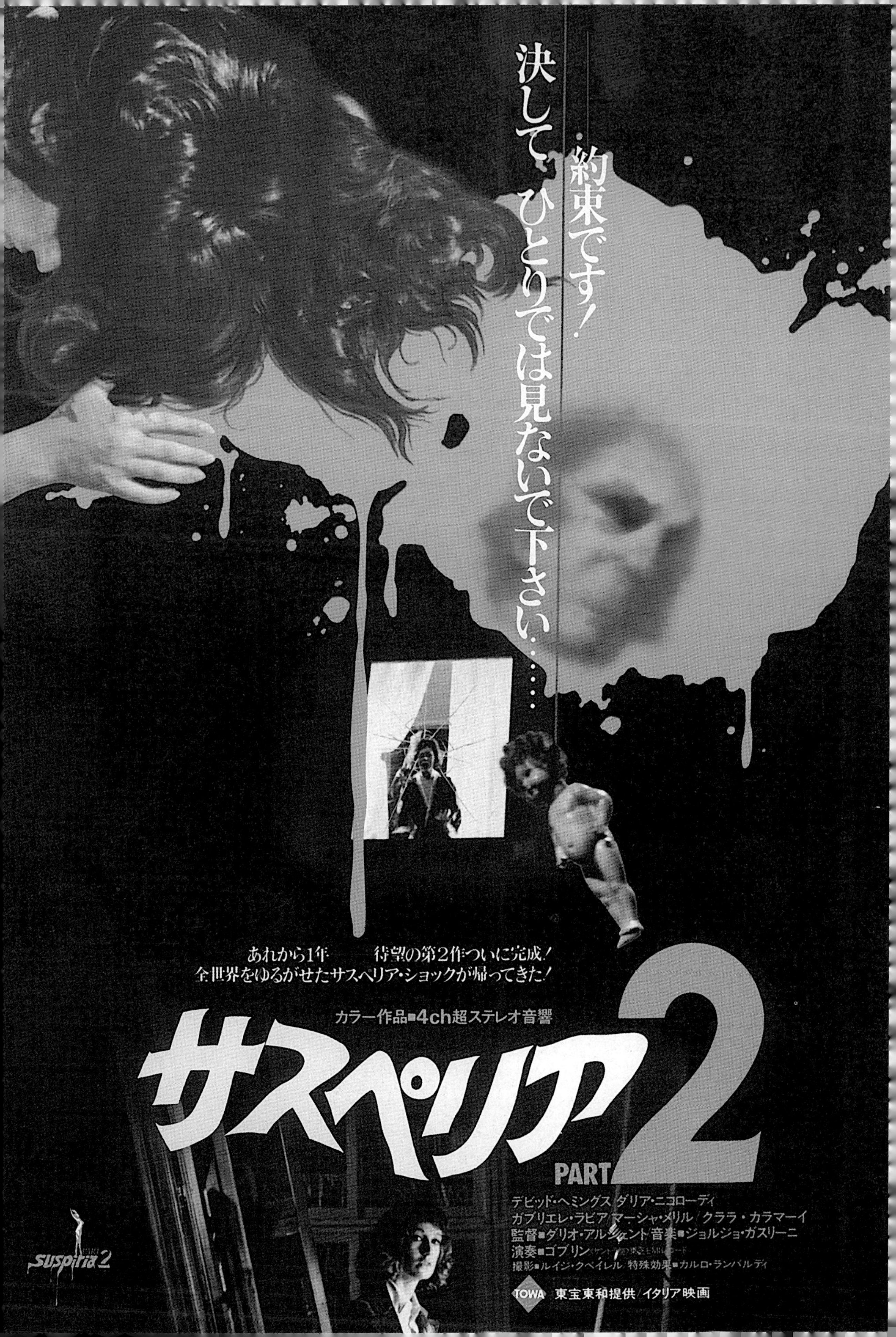

決して ひとりでは見ないで下さい……

約束です！

あれから1年　　待望の第2作ついに完成！
全世界をゆるがせたサスペリア・ショックが帰ってきた！

カラー作品■4ch超ステレオ音響

サスペリア2
PART

デビッド・ヘミングス　ダリア・ニコローディ
ガブリエレ・ラビア／マーシャ・メリル／クララ・カラマーイ
監督■ダリオ・アルジェント 音楽■ジョルジョ・ガスリーニ
演奏■ゴブリン（サウンドトラックはキネマ・レコード）
撮影■ルイジ・クベイレル 特殊効果■カルロ・ランバルディ

suspiria 2

TOWA　東宝東和提供／イタリア映画

The SOUND of fear..
You'll experience it
when you see ~

Suspiria x

Suspiria

Stephen Thrower

ITALY

1977

"*Anyone who applies himself, from his early youth, to the practise of graphic techniques may well reach a stage at which he begins to hold as his highest ideal the complete mastery of his craft. Excellence of craftsmanship takes up all his time and so completely absorbs his thoughts that he will even make his choice of subject subordinate to his desire to explore some particular facet of technique...*

I myself passed many years in this state of self-delusion. But then there came a moment when it seemed as though scales fell from my eyes. I discovered that technical mastery was no longer my sole aim, for I became gripped by another desire, the existence of which I had never suspected. Ideas came into my mind quite unrelated to graphic art, notions which so fascinated me that I longed to communicate them to other people. This could not be achieved through words, for these thoughts were not literary ones, but mental images that can only be made comprehensible to others by presenting them as visual images..." Max Escher (foreword to *The Graphic Work*, Taschen)

After the success of **Deep Red** in 1975, Argento considered for a while adapting the work of H.P. Lovecraft, an American writer whose stories of cosmic terror were frequently interlinked by an elaborate self-contained mythology. Among the themes Lovecraft obsessively proposed was a pantheon of awesomely powerful ancient beings, whose practise of the black arts had banished them to an outer darkness, from which they continually strove to return; occasionally succeeding to cause madness, mutation and havoc in Man and the material world. Perhaps because it required too great a devotion to another artist's inventions, Argento decided against working from Lovecraft, but he didn't entirely abandon the train of thought. Still drawn to the uncanny, he turned instead to his partner Daria Nicolodi's stories of her grandmother's experiences at a finishing school with occult connections.

The result was **Suspiria**. It was a totally new experience, and even the mainstream critics had to admit it: "*a deliberately overblown bit of Gothic ghoulishness that makes other tales of terror look anaemic*" opined Alexander Walker. Thunderous in volume, grotesque and yet beautiful, and soaked in outrageous washes of pure primary colour, it's an unforgettable piece of cinema. Telling a story of the supernatural, of witches and malefic influence, it shows Argento shaking free from the threads of logic and reason altogether, and unconditionally embracing the mystical beliefs of Nicolodi, herself a practitioner of witchcraft. Casting the young Jessica Harper, fresh from roles for Brian De Palma (**Phantom of the Paradise**) and Woody Allen (**Love and Death**), Argento fashioned a thrilling, violent fairy-tale that cemented his reputation, once and for all, as a film-maker out to overwhelm audiences with a dizzying excess of sensation. The simple story tells of the experience of Suzy Banyon, a pretty young dance student who enrols at a sinister Bavarian Dance Academy and discovers that the staff are actually a secret coven of witches, under the reign of the terrifyingly powerful 'Black Queen', Helena Markos.

Challenge to genre conventions

Suspiria was a sizeable international hit and launched Argento into the front ranks of the horror genre; remarkable, considering that it strays wildly from horror movie convention, and is sublimely unconcerned with the logical constraints of narrative cinema. When the film was conceived in 1976, the main structural paradigm for the horror genre was

opposite:
Poster design for the UK theatrical
release of **Suspiria**.

Straight into the heart of the storm:
Suzy Banyon (Jessica Harper) arrives in
Freiburg in the opening scene of **Suspiria**.

typified by the work of Stephen King, whose first two novels, *Carrie* and *Salem's Lot*, were published in 1974 and '75 respectively. King chose a style that was to ingratiate his work to millions of readers around the world (influenced by such effective best-sellers as Ira Levin's *Rosemary's Baby* and William Peter Blatty's *The Exorcist*), where supernatural intrusions into the lives of ordinary characters are embedded in a dense network of contemporary, rationalist social detail. By drawing finely observed backgrounds, populated by characters recognisable to the average reader as 'normal' and 'realistic', such stories can smuggle in elements of the macabre without breaking the spell and bouncing the sceptical reader out of the fiction.

William Friedkin's film of *The Exorcist* showed how this literary technique could be exploited in the cinema. Thoroughly (if not ploddingly) grounded in secular Hollywood 'realism', early seventies style, the film's gradual encroachment of supernatural horror takes its time, in order to flatter the reservations of pedants or sceptics. (Argento's regard for this cornerstone of mainstream horror can perhaps be inferred from an absurd exchange between two students in **Suspiria**: *"Maybe there's a hex on the place"* - *"Let's call in the exorcist and have a purge!"*). The same principle was still holding true ten years later; **Poltergeist**, a Steven Spielberg production that feels like it's based on an imaginary King novel, scored with audiences by likewise soft-pedalling the scares in the first hour. On the other hand, Stanley Kubrick's commercially successful screen version of King's third novel **The Shining** was frequently slated by critics who complained that Jack Nicholson's portrayal of family-man turned axe-murderer Jack Torrance neglected the novel's slow, gradual shift from man to monster. The clash of perspectives is striking: Kubrick's films have rarely concerned themselves with the 'normal' lives of 'ordinary people', unless (as in **2001**, with its bored astronauts) there's an irony to be relished. His fascination with Jack's encroaching madness precluded wasting screen time on a 'regular guy' backstory. As noted, the technique of grounding the fantastic in everyday detail certainly pays commercial dividends: for the daring, though, there are other ways to engage an audience, as Dario Argento, like Kubrick, was able to show.

Suspiria drops its audience straight into the heart of a storm, literally and figuratively, a maelstrom of sound and visual excess. The opening sequence, designed by Argento with the utmost confidence, transports us effortlessly into a violent, hyperkinetic new world, with only the briefest of 'once upon a time...' preludes. The first image we see is of the film's young heroine, ballet student Suzy Banyon, walking through a busy airport terminal and exiting through a set of automatic doors, portals which spring apart with a hydraulic hiss, exposing her to the demonic elements of wind, rain and darkness (and if you don't think darkness counts as an element, just go and watch the film!). In television and mainstream cinema, locations such as airports are mere groundings for supposedly realistic drama, unremarkable of themselves. Not so for Argento, who immediately seeks to incorporate heightened details of the real world (the hydraulic door mechanism, the storm drains), subjecting them to intense scrutiny, and discovering in these brute material objects not mundanity but wonder and menace. (Also implicit is the phenomenon of air travel; Suzy has just completed a trans-Atlantic flight, an everyday marvel that we casually - and trustingly - accept as normal). In a film whose themes number magic, witchcraft and the supernatural, this immediate transformation of the mundane refuses an easy contrast between normality and the occult, instead mobilising one of the film's key principles, the observation that *"Magic is everywhere"*. The attention paid to the airport doors thus marks the onset of the film's barrage of stylistic excess, and also alerts the viewer to the importance of portals, thresholds between worlds. Argento makes maximum use of the transition between different locations (the breath-taking sequence depicting a taxi's night-time journey), between interior and exterior (blind Daniel's walk from the noisy bierkellar to the imposing Munich square where he's killed) or just from room to room, always heightening our awareness of the threshold experience of crossing from one to another. He demonstrates a supersensitive visual awareness and creates moment after moment of tension and beauty from the spatial relationships between figure and environment. It is this preoccupation with spatial design that makes Argento one of the only directors of horror cinema to show an intelligent awareness of Antonioni's work; **L'avventura**, **Il deserto rosso**, **L'eclisse**, **Blow Up** and **The Passenger** would seem to have made their impression on various of Argento's films.

The importance of music

Suspiria incorporates music as a key element, in conjunction with colour, and in a more general way Argento approaches the composition of his film as a musician would. In which case, one might say that **Suspiria** is his first instrumental work. The film circles around, occupying and replenishing a dynamic field of energy, 'saying' very little but holding the attention in thrall through a cascade of mantric visual riffs.

Music, of all the arts, is perhaps the most intangible, its effect most often likened to magic, to the casting of a spell. It seems to rise invisibly and possess the very air, penetrating deeper into the body than the visual arts and asserting a more definitively visceral impression. Metaphor aside, music literally touches the listener. Attempts to assess and theorize the properties of sound have driven many intellectuals into absurdity. There remains something stubbornly undecidable, ambiguous, elusive about music, a network of non-verbal connections to which few, if any, hold the entire set of keys. (It's interesting that mixed metaphors are also common in its discussion!) Dario Argento's use of music was inspired from the start; his earlier collaborations with Ennio Morricone are keenly imaginative in their use of music to suggest emotional irony and neurosis.

Argento's most celebrated musical relationship, with the Italian rock group Goblin, had begun with **Deep Red** the year before. For that film the band had provided propulsive, bass-led pieces, incorporating elements of Deep Purple-style organ riffing and other more progressive keyboard wig-outs, of the sort favoured by Rick Wakeman of Yes and Keith

You can run from it.
You can hide from it.
You can't escape from it !!
Suspiria

Dario Argento with Stefania Casini and crew on the set.

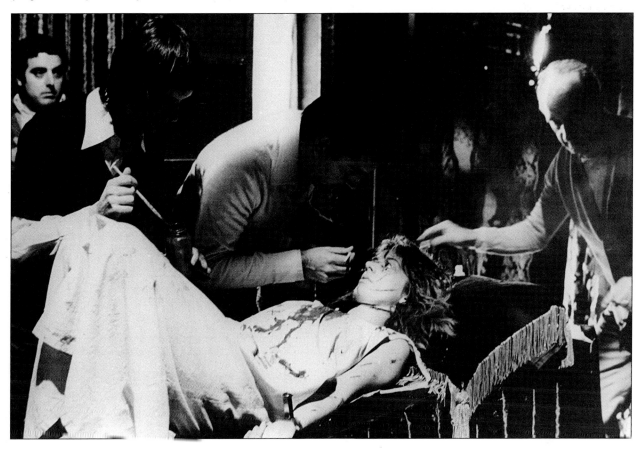

Suzy Banyon (Jessica Harper) grows suspicious of the 'special diet' recommended by the Academy's pet Doctor, Verdegast.

Emerson of Emerson, Lake & Palmer. The other element in the mix (noticeable mainly on the track *Death Dies*) was a strain of European jazz-rock, judiciously kept to the level of shading rather than full-on noodling. Argento greatly admired the grand excesses of British rock, particularly the progressive rock format as practised by such 1970s giants as Yes, ELP and King Crimson. Along with the elaborate and often collossally exaggerated song-forms favoured by these bands, he was drawn to the violence which would emerge from the theatricality of their live performances; especially ELP, whose Keith Emerson was wont to attack his keyboards with giant knives during the 'freak-out' sections of their act (and who went on to score Argento's next film, **Inferno**).

The music Argento was seeking for **Suspiria**, however, required Goblin (or 'The Goblins', as they are credited) to go even further out, in search of a total audio-visual delirium. In keeping with the fairytale elements of the story, the main theme resembles a tinkling music box or nursery rhyme tune, with undertones of Eastern European folk music, evoking a vague but powerful aura of the mysteries of the past in foreign lands. A simple rhythmic figure, the combination of a drum-beat and a deep, resonant synthesizer tone, adds excitement and threat, whilst a parched, mocking male voice wordlessly mimics the chiming melody. (There is actually quite a similarity here to the techniques used by Morricone on the soundtrack to **The Bird With the Crystal Plumage**, with its wordless, oversweet, mockingly spiteful female vocals.) As extra layers are added to the mix, including medieval instrumentation and more characteristically jazz-rockish synth lines, phased filtered chords emerge from the interweaving melody lines, creating a hallucinogenic sensation perfectly at one with Argento's visual hyper-awareness. Meanwhile, beneath the instrumentation a voice incants barely audible words, setting up the motif of obscured and occluded language that will continually impede characters' investigations into the secrets of the occult.

Another piece (called *Sighs* on the soundtrack album) grips the audience with a forward-cajoling syncopated bass guitar riff, leaning into timelessness via an implacable acoustic guitar oscillating between two tones. The notes of the bass-line constantly swoop in from beneath themselves, connoting both instability and determination. Traversing this cross-flux of seeking and danger, male voices arc like evil monks, rising in cavernous spaces impossibly lit by the stars. The hierarchical status of each new sound is shifted by the subsequent alteration in volume and syncopation (as the overdubbed sound elements slide out of synchronisation). Vortices of darkness curl around urgent organ chords, a black mass summoning elder spirits (with sexuality, as befits a tale of witchcraft, not far away). Here the influence is not so much progressive rock but the divergent experiments of German bands like Can and Faust. From Can comes the exploration of repetition as a form of change (to borrow a phrase from Brian Eno); from Faust the sense of cosmic mockery and irrational collision. Music this rich in association and mind-altering energies must take a significant part of the credit for the effectiveness of the whole.

Sara's death in the lethal chamber of wire.

The flawless melding of sound and image in the major set-pieces of **Suspiria** is probably the film's greatest innovation. Argento aims for a synaesthetic sensation, obsessively plastering light and sound into a malevolently pulsating whole. Alexander Walker, writing in the Evening Standard in 1977, described the film's *"fiendish stereo electronic-rock score which sounds as if 500 cats are having their tails tramped on in unison"*. The key phrase here is 'in unison' - whilst the free elements of the sound approach cacophony, the orchestrating focus never wavers. Such a powerful musical presence goes well beyond anything previously attempted in the horror genre and provides a definitive stamp to this period of the director's creativity. If anything signalled the sea-change in Argento's ability to bring off his particular brand of magic it was his decision (with **Phemomena**) to augment the horrors not with progressive rock, surprisingly well-suited due to its complexity and often dynamic use of counterpoint, but heavy metal, a rock music keen to project an impression of violence and forcefulness, but leeringly devoid of structural detail.

Style, excess and the 'set-piece'

Conventional wisdom on both the use of the film camera and the function of film music has it that the best examples efface themselves, remaining sufficiently restrained to avoid making the audience aware of their involvement. Directors like Sergio Leone and Jean-Luc Godard had deliberately ruptured this tradition with intrusive or grandiose camera-work, and with music used ironically, or snatched abruptly away, revealing its sly insinuation into our responses by its absence (a technique Argento uses to disorienting effect in the build-up to **Suspiria**'s 'room of wire' scene). But the main strategy employed in **Suspiria** is not the modernist fascination with disrupting the conventional modes of relation between audience and screen, but a baroque, decadent, epicurean relish for excess. Just as Ferreri's **La Grande Bouffe** exposes the dark side of the feast, so Argento's super-saturated visual pallette, his obsessional camera, greedy for images, and his use of quadrophonic sound (in the few cinemas equipped for it) strive to overwhelm with *too much* sensation. Rather than deconstruct the magic of cinema, Argento seeks insight through overload, a striving for epiphany through a kind of aesthetic debauchery, revealing his kinship with the French decadent poets and writers, Baudelaire, Rimbaud, Verlaine and Thomas De Quincey.

At times Argento's style can seem somehow 'vulgar' - I once played **Suspiria** to a film designer whose career spanned both the avant-garde and mainstream, and such was his response. I think it's true that Argento's visual sumptuousness betrays a certain vulgarity (as does the word 'sumptuous' itself, with its emphasis on costliness and its proximity to 'sump' or cesspool). However, Argento's aesthetic crimes are more interesting than mere 'good' taste, with its connotations of *bourgeois* complacency and the status-quo. Style is never just a given in Argento's work, it's something palpated in the (more-or-less) grubby hands of those who seek it, a beauty always at risk of looking tawdry, a poise on the brink of the pretentious. Argento's work shares a spirit with the music and lyrics of Bryan Ferry, not merely 'stylish' but about style, at first apparently staking all in a gambit of competitive elegance, where the price of a mis-step is humiliation, but actually more deeply concerned with the rupturing of the notion of style, to reveal, offset against their own lies, the hidden faces of those who cultivate it - here, the faces of cruelty and power. Wealth and social status provide a patina of style to characters in Argento's work, but it's never enough to protect them from the most appalling kind of death; instead it almost seems to act as a lure.

Sara (Stefania Casini) makes a bid for escape as the followers of Helena Markos close in.

Art design in Argento's films is frequently a matter of conflicting styles, rather than a picturesque appropriation of a single one (**Deep Red**, a film full of aesthetic schisms and conflicts, sets Art Nouveau and Art Deco at each other's throats). **Suspiria** is no exception; located mainly in the forbidding blood-hewn block of the Tanzakademie, it is simultaneously baroque and minimalist, flamboyant and restrictive. (As a locus of malign motherhood, the combination is apt). There is a tension here between two design impulses: the baroque (as in the golden serpentine balusters of the main staircase) with its tradition of excessive ornamentation, a celebration of beauty and wealth unto itself; and the Expressionist (for instance the misaligned geometrics of the windows seen in the main hall), with its idea of representing (unbalanced) interior states externally. The German location, and the presence of stylized, angular design, recall **The Cabinet of Dr Caligari** as a cinematic antecedent. The two styles are deployed ironically. Tyrannical Miss Tanner convenes ballet lessons in the 'Red Room' and 'Yellow Room': these oppressive primary-coloured spaces represent not artistic expression but the controlling aspect of the coven (and magick's aim to harness elemental forces). The feverish arabesques seen elsewhere in the Academy (principally in Madame Blanc's office) may parallel the dancers' aspirations of artistic freedom, but they also disguise the entrance to the coven's inner sanctum. They are there 'for show' (and the dancers doubly so), a facade of artistic revelation masking the secretive functions of the occult.

The film's most celebrated set-piece, in which Pat is murdered and her friend impaled by the wreckage of a falling window-frame, plays out in an apartment block of the most elaborate design, featuring a huge, primary-coloured glass ceiling, walls of geometric abstraction in coloured tiles, and a lift crowned, above its doors, by a glowing red pyramid whose angles are backlit to indicate ascent. Lavish isn't the word. Once in her friend's flat, Pat tries to relax and relate her traumatic experiences, but even here the design is scarcely more restrained, with Max Escher designs on the walls and gloss-painted mauves and whites agleam in the suffused indirect lighting. When Pat is left alone in a huge bathroom, and the horrors of the night reach out to invade this affluent sanctuary, the camera takes a position outside the window, hovering impossibly in the blackness to assume the viewpoint of a lurking, evil presence. The relative normality of the interior lighting is reconfigured in this shot as increasing, rather than soothing, Pat's insecurity. Seen from

Her fate already sealed, Pat awaits the minions of Helena Markos.

Les films *Jacques Leitienne* présentent
Un film de DARIO ARGENTO
Suspiria
INTERDIT AUX MOINS DE 18 ANS

Expelled pupil Pat (Eva Axen) pays the ultimate price for meddling in the affairs of The Black Queen.

Death in obscure interiors - Pat's demise at the half-way stage.

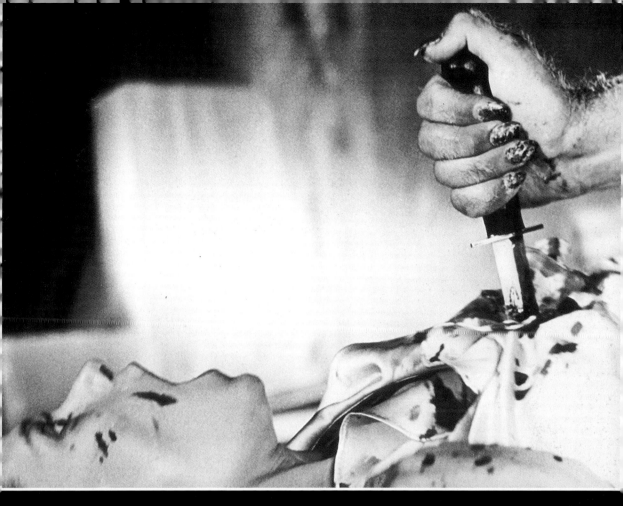

Two more moments of mayhem from the famed 'double murder scene' which opens **Suspiria**

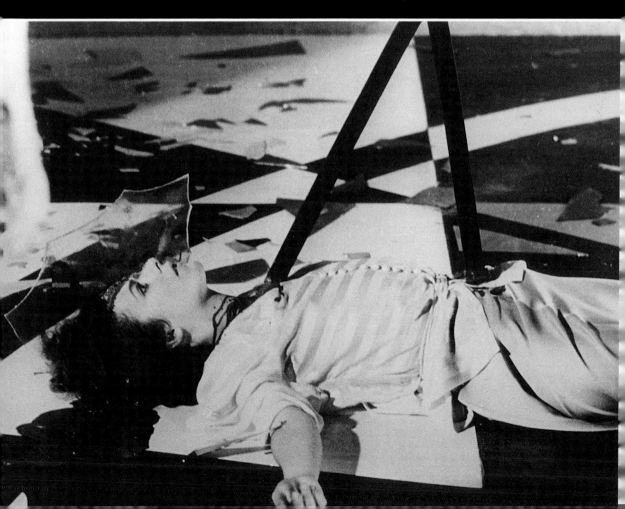

The ogre-like servants and their ward cast a spell over Suzy in the corridors of the dance academy.

outside, quaking in the illuminated window frame surrounded by threatening gloom, she is rendered more, not less, vulnerable. (The connotations of light are again complicated in another scene, when Suzy is made to fall mysteriously sick by one of the coven, a taciturn underling working as a maid, who deliberately reflects a sunbeam off a spike of ornamental glass into Suzy's face. And the fragility of light, at least of the man-made variety, is pointedly expressed in a marvellous shot later, when the camera rises to the ceiling to view a room through the clear glass of a lightbulb - the coil glows dully in tight foreground then cools as the switch is thrown, allowing Argento both a wonderful demonstration of lighting camerawork and the chance to show the simple, vulnerable 'magic' of a device that stands between Man and the dark).

Pat tries to see out of the window, and makes a futile attempt to illuminate the blackness beyond the glass by holding a lamp up to the pane; thus seeing even less of the exterior and more of her own frightened features reflected back at her. This is a beautiful way of showing how fear clouds our ability to see clearly. By clinging to the light, Pat learns nothing, gains nothing, except the reflection and doubling of her own fear, until a glimpse of a pair of cat-like eyes sets her flinching away (and even this revelation is something shown rather than discovered). When a hairy, wizened forearm then smashes through the glass and grabs Pat by the hair, Argento creates one of his most chilling images of terror. The hand clasps Pat's head and pulls her forward, and her grotesquely distorted, screaming face is crushed tight against the remaining windowpane. As her flesh squeaks against the cold glass, her breath condenses as mist on the pane, adding a shifting, blurring layer to her already distorted face, the skin of which is flattened and dragged out of shape. The image collides a powerful impression of physical and tactile subjectivity with a sense of the callous, material surface of the world of objects. When the glass shatters under the pressure and Pat's face breaks through, to be showered by the shards (another, more traumatic threshold experience), Argento's clear aim to terrorize his audience is seemingly achieved. But, like a lover possessed with the demon of an erotic rage, he goes further; as the monstrous figure, unseen except for its emaciated hairy arm and hand, drags Pat out of the window and into another obscurely connected interior space.

This transition is extremely disorientating, as Argento refuses to clarify the relationship between inside and outside. It seems we may be looking at a rooftop enclosure, bordered by metal gridding. We are left to surmise that it is reached via the balcony (we've had just the slightest hint of one, thanks to the washing hung on a clothes-line visible earlier on through the window). Whatever the spatial arrangements, we are given little time to ponder; the assailant proceeds to stab Pat in the breast and stomach as she backs away screaming. The stabbings are joltingly orchestrated, their viciousness swept up in an orgy of sound and image (Goblin's music in this sequence is a frenzy of howls and metallic drums, echoed and reverberated to the hilt). Again the location shifts, as Pat is swiftly trussed, noosed and then stabbed yet again, lying on the upper surface of the glass ceiling we saw from beneath earlier. In a shot of leering, delirious excess, we actually see her beating heart, exposed by the repeated slicing, and watch as it is pierced by one final

thrust of the blade. Gasping her last, she crashes through the glass ceiling to be released from the horror, shockingly hung by the neck from the roof. And still, even in death, Argento hasn't finished with her, or us... Pat's dangling body, dripping a Rorschach of blood onto the checkered tiles of the hall, is pressed into service for one more composition with the corpse of her unfortunate friend, artfully gored by falling metalwork nearby. The effect, with cathedral-detonating sounds from Goblin, is of the triumphal conclusion to some daemonic performance art spectacle; Rudolph Schwarzkogler meets Robert Wilson, pics by Helmut Newton. Argento has built his action to a sexual crescendo, with little in the way of ambiguity to distance the pungently aggressive violation. And yet, whilst the image of the beating heart of a screaming woman being penetrated by a knife borders on the pornographic, there's something alien and unerotic - and important - about the degree of theatricality that's been expended to get us there. It's in the tension between the erotic indulgence of sadism and its flamboyant exaggeration into artifice that Argento wields his distinctive sense of style.

top:
Dr Mandel (Udo Kier) explains away the darkness to ballerina Suzy Banyon (Jessica Harper).

above:
Night falls in the cursed dance academy.

The way we experience our lives is something narrative cinema disingenuously takes for granted. Life as a sequence of events progressing from problem to solution, with digressions allowed to incorporate conflicting trajectories (i.e. other people). More acute, phenomenologically-inclined film-makers like Nicolas Roeg have forged a counter-narrative cinema, where solutions are elusive or perverse if they exist at all, and where interjections occur just as powerfully on the planes of memory, myth and imagination. Within the inevitable constraints of film fiction more honestly aware of the irreality of cinema (i.e. not so much unreal as counter-real), Dario Argento's cinema consistently shows a predilection for the set-piece, that staged, artificial, self-consciously 'unrealistic' suspension of narrative's lies. **Suspiria** is made up of manically extended set-pieces. From the opening excursion to the rain-lashed Tanzakademie, the stunning double killing explored above, through the maggot-infestation sequence and the moving of the girls' dorm to the final discovery of the coven's secret, Argento disengages from the easy virtues of sequential storytelling and pitches his film as a series of terrifying, exhilarating events. This is highly appropriate to a story concerning witchcraft and the occult, where the rational passage of cause and effect is broken by unknown forces heedless of conventional causality ("I believe in ma-a-gick, why because it is so quick", as Arthur Lee put it on Love's *The Red Telephone*). We might see a similarity between the relationship of narrative and set-piece in film, and dialectics and aphorism in philosophy. The aim of dialectics is a rational, interlocking synthesis, whilst the aphorism exists in counter-rational isolation, a collaged juxtaposition, breaking up the notion of the possible mastery of a mode of enquiry. ("*Aphorisms, representing a knowledge broken, do invite men to inquire farther; whereas Methods, carrying the show of a total, do secure men, as if they were at farthest*" - Francis Bacon, *Advancement of Learning*, 1605). The impossibility of knowing, or at least an awareness of the slippery uncertainties we are forced to negotiate, characterises much of Argento's output, a concern which has driven many of his best films both before and after his foray into the occult.

above:
An infestation of maggots brings mayhem to
the corridors of the academy.

right:
Sisters Grim: Alida Valli, Joan Bennett and
a fellow coven-member gather on the stairs
to the main hall.

Class, power and the destructive feminine

Deep Red had its investigative lead drawn through his curiosity to 'The House of the Screaming Child', wherein he discovered a family horror that blurred the line between investigator and investigated. Although Hemmings' character is supposed to be merely following a lead, he has become obsessed; the film acts to conflate the hidden drama he uncovers with his own self-knowledge (and strives to blur the edges further, infecting the minds of viewers who may have taken Hemmings as a narrative identification figure). **Suspiria** takes the end of **Deep Red** as a cue and projects a world where the capricious, destructive feminine embodied by **Deep Red**'s maternal monster has gained total ascendancy. However, by pitting a girl against the powerful witches of the Tanzakademie, Argento seems to suggest that we should view the axis of tension not as one of male against female, but rather young against old, children against parents.

The search for a way of connecting with another level of existence leads many occultists into secretive, aristocratic, non-egalitarian beliefs. This throws into relief one of the schisms in Argento's sensibility, a fault-line around which a bruise of unease is discernible in his work - the issue of class. The culture of the dandy exemplified by Baudelaire has no truck with 'the common herd', will proudly proclaim its contempt for democracy, and prefers the notion of self-appointed Lords of the Spirit. Argento's previous films had shown a concern with establishing his awareness of class issues, suggesting a left-leaning sensibility. This creates incongruity with the aesthetic profligacy and decadence of his style (an incongruity he fleetingly addresses in **Deep Red**). In **Suspiria**, the issue of class is represented by dialogue emphasising money and wealth as motivating factors in black witchcraft, by the girls' rather tawdry obsession with financial matters, and by the way one of the young male dancers is the subject of snide gossip about his lack of financial means, in terms which make the insinuation simultaneously one of a lack of male potency:

> Olga: *"He's cute... except he doesn't have any, erm... and he never has enough money for room and board at school. that's why that bitch Tanner has got him under her thumb, she gives him a thousand and one errands to do."*

Whilst the exhilaration of abandoning rationality provides the updraft in **Suspiria**'s psychic weather, the downblast comes from suggestions about the conflict between masculinity, rationality and democracy on the one hand, and femininity, the irrational and aristocracy on the other. The all-female coven exploits and controls its more-or-less castrated male entourage (pretty-boy dogsbody Mark, blind 'pianist for hire' Daniel, Pavlos, the handyman who lost all his teeth in a bout of gingivitis that Miss Tanner seems suspiciously amused by, and 'little Albert', the effete blonde boy dressed up in an archaic manner stifling of any further development, like something from a Visconti film). Whilst male rationality comes in for plenty of stick in **Deep Red**, in **Suspiria** it is suggested that, for all the limitations and negative aspects of patriarchal dominance, we have the development of social order, democracy and even the socialist principles of equality to thank it for (in other words, a 'what have the Romans ever done for us?' argument). The feminine irrational, on the other hand, is depicted as disruptive of any move to establish equivalence through law and social structure (reminiscent of Jean Baudrillard's proposition that Evil is the principle of irreconcilability of opposites). The witches in **Suspiria** are resolutely out for themselves, as Dr Milius, the occult expert Suzy is introduced to, clarifies for us: *"Their goal is to accumulate great personal wealth, but this can only be achieved by injury to others. They can cause suffering, sickness, and even the death of those who, for whatever reason, have offended them."*

opposite top:
Suzy Banyon (Jessica Harper) prepares for
a confrontation with The Black Queen.

opposite bottom:
Wired: Sara (Stefania Casini) writhes in
torment, trapped in vicious coils of steel.

The collapse of the houses of Mater Suspiriorum and Mater Tenebrarum, at the ends of **Suspiria** and **Inferno** respectively, represents the collapse not only of their control over events (one reason for the practise of magick being the need to exert control over the vagaries of chance and others' wills) but the collapse too of their 'social standing'. The Tanzakademie is a school, the two infernal houses of **Inferno** are apartment blocks; in both films these secretive houses are also public buildings, suggesting the way that corruption and power reside beneath a masquerade of facelessness in modern society. In both they end up in flames, at the end of narratives where water has been a constant. This is a further pointer to the relationship between patriarchal and matriarchal power that Argento envisages. Because we exist currently under some kind of nominal patriarchy, most radical social commentators are drawn to an espousal of the Feminine. Argento's work has many angles of attack against the Masculine, for example its presumptive superiority, blinkeredness and lack of imagination. Unlike the more mercurial Feminine, the Masculine has a problem with ambivalence, is too concerned with definition. **Suspiria** gives no power at all to men (except for the authorial honesty/indulgence of a third party male narration at the beginning), and yet it pulls no punches in its depiction of Feminine evil. It would seem as if Argento found strength in his alliance with a female writer, freeing him to take on the more destructive qualities of womanhood, without the defensiveness that might otherwise be required to 'mitigate' his maleness. Meanwhile, balancing the scales, for the first time in Argento's *oeuvre* the figure of the principal seeker is female (in **Deep Red**, Gianna becomes an investigative ally but the story begins and concludes with Marc). Both Suzy and the failed seeker Sarah are young women, embodying a propulsive curiosity and dissatisfaction more generally the province of male characters.

Magic and the occult

Writers who approach the subject of magic when discussing **Suspiria** and its follow-up **Inferno** generally do so with a missionary gleam in their eye and an armful of psychoanalytical/sociological tracts, the better to banish the uncomfortable feeling that they've been suckered by a load of mystical mumbo-jumbo. Maitland McDonagh adopts this slightly nervous attitude with her book on Argento, expanded from her master's thesis. Its title is taken from an exchange between Suzy, who is concerned about the disappearance of Sarah, her only confidante at the Tanzakademie, and Sarah's psychiatrist Doctor Frank Mandel:

> Suzy: *"But what does it mean to be a witch?"*
> Frank Mandel: *"Well as a believer in the material world, and a psychiatrist to boot, I'm convinced that the current spread of belief in magic and the occult is part of mental illness. Bad luck isn't brought by broken mirrors, but by broken minds."*

Mandel then introduces Suzy to another professor, the elderly Dr Milius, telling her, *"He wrote a book called 'Paranoia or Magic?', and believe me it's the final word on the subject!"* McDonagh writes that the rational Mandel is *"backed up by his friend Dr Milius"*, and Mandel's remark about Milius' book seems to be suggesting as much, but the conversation about witches Milius then has with Suzy unequivocally asserts the legitimacy of magical belief and the power of the occult: *"They're malefic, negative and destructive. Their knowledge of the art of the occult gives them tremendous powers. They can change the course of events, and people's lives, but only to do harm..."*

It's interesting that whilst many are quick to recognise the gender issues so prominently distributed throughout Argento's *oeuvre*, few attempt to engage with the issue of magical belief on even vaguely respectful terms. The conviction stems from the experience of then the most important woman in Argento's creative and personal life, actress and writer Daria Nicolodi. Belief in magic is typically one of the 'weaknesses' attributed to 'susceptible' women by the bullying rationalists of white patriarchy. (**Inferno** refers to this prejudice when Kazanian the antique dealer says *"Women are usually the worst readers of such stuff... or the best, if you prefer."*) Nicolodi, who has described herself as a (white) witch, drew on her grandmother's accounts of her stay at a school which turned out to be a front for the study of black magic, a story passed on through the female branch of her family.

Those who have set about 'validating' the art of Dario Argento (or more honestly their love for it), in the face of what used to be critical ignorance or dismissal, have generally done so on the axis of gender studies and psychoanalysis. However **Suspiria** and **Inferno**, two of the director's most acclaimed films, embrace a weird, bastard mysticism, a fact that sits uncomfortably with the discursive fashions generally prevailing in film studies and criticism. Thus it becomes necessary, for some, to explain away this unfortunate dalliance with the occult. Stanley Kubrick, whose artistic seriousness is seldom questioned, was nevertheless attacked for **The Shining** because of the disconcerting scene where Jack Torrance is released from a locked storeroom by a ghost, the only point in the film where the supernatural cannot be explained away by reference to psychosis, hallucination, projection, hysteria etc. The fact that Kubrick, the intellectual, the great chess-master of cinema, should insist on supernatural agency at a key point in his narrative troubles his devout materialist disciples. In Argento's case, **Deep Red** had already set in motion the shift from psychology and madness to metaphysics and Evil: the story progresses as if subtly derailing from causality, as a series of coincidences lead to insights at the far reach of plausibility. Much has been made of the doubling motifs in **Deep Red**, and they certainly make themselves felt at a structural level. But the doublings exist within the fiction too, and offer the possibility of the fantastic within the diegesis. Point of view is not only fragmented and rendered impossible within **Deep Red**, it is also suggestive of a lurking, depersonalised malevolence.

Poster advertising the film's belated American video release.

opposite:
Beyond the broken mirror:
Pat expires amid the baroque decor
of her friend's apartment.

top:
Making waves: Sara (Stefania Casini) and
Suzy (Jessica Harper) seek to reveal the
heavily guarded secrets of Helena Markos.

above:
The butchered corpse of Sara becomes a
vessel for the forces of evil.

The sensual experience of **Suspiria** is in no way equivocal about the existence of spirits and occult energies. The music is rife with hag-like screeches and keening wails, the art design conspires at every turn to induce terror of the formless void behind appearances, a void traversed by blasts of noisome energy (or coils of meshing steel). The presence of a Max Escher design on the walls of a flat belonging to the friend doomed Pat visits on running away from the Tanzakademie (and the Escher-like staircases painted on the walls of Madame Blanc's study) suggest the limits of perception and its inability to resolve paradoxes - Escher's intricate, formally controlled yet preposterous images depict conjunctions of layers, intricate interlacing of realities, angular relations impossible in the real world but stubbornly evident, standing up to the closest scrutiny, on the page.

One of the strongest images Argento constructs to visualise occult forces occurs in the scene where Suzy and Sarah go swimming. The pool is daylit through windows, although the deep blue hue of the water and the beautiful old stonework of the building mean the atmosphere within is anything but mundane. As the girls slowly swim and talk in hushed tones, the overhead camera captures rings, concentric circles, ripples, radiating around them as they tread water - the effect is of lines of force, magnetic fields (or with deference to Mel Brooks' **High Anxiety**, a web). Their conversation concerns Sarah's fears and suspicions about events at the Academy and the circumstances of Pat's death. As they have the pool to themselves, they are obviously hoping to discuss their fears without being overheard, but the hovering camera, and the concentric radiation of the water, suggest that they are being watched - and heard - at a distance; unaware of the way their actions are emanating far beyond their control. The ripples spreading from the girls remind us of the presence of many other waves and fields undetectable to the naked eye; implicit is the idea that there may be occult lines of force which we have hardly the senses nor yet the technology to measure. Sure enough, after telling Suzy about the book of notes she'd kept about the Academy's occult activities, the next scene has her running to Suzy's room whispering in terror that the book has gone.

Art is secular magic (and directors like Kenneth Anger would drop the secular in that formula), but we never get a feeling from the few glimpses of lessons at the Academy that personal artistic expression is high among the priorities being inculcated in the pupils. The coven seems disinterested in the students both as artists and as potential coven-members, existing as a rigidly pre-ordained closed circle. Miss Tanner's teaching role amounts to bullying dancers through mechanical postures, and enforcing rote-learning through tirades about the history of dance. The rooms where young artists are being groomed for their future careers juxtapose youthful energy with oppressive single colour surrounds, creating the impression of caged birds. Argento offers little to suggest possible links between the Academy's two functions. One might speculate that the coven feeds off the creative energies of the dancers, but if the feeding were vampiristic there would be few graduates of international merit, and so little reputation with which to attract pupils.

Despite opening a door to appreciation of the notion of occult power, neither **Suspiria** nor **Inferno** engage with any specific hermetic writings in a concerted, didactic way (and **Suspiria** does witchcraft in general scant justice!). The approach is scattershot, with elements suggesting observance of ritual magic, study of fairytale structures, pilfering of popular culture variants, and giblets of decadent literature, brewed together to produce a

Frankenstein-monster fictional world. Shooting **Suspiria** in Germany, and especially Munich, acknowledges the oft-posited association between fascism and the occult, although, despite the mass of popular literature speculating on Hitler's occult beliefs, such ideas are not elaborated in the narrative. As already mentioned, Argento was interested in adapting the work of H.P. Lovecraft, a writer whose series of interlocking short stories implied a skein of factual back-up for its cosmic horrors. There are those who still believe that the 'Necronomicon' of the mad Arab Abdul Alhazred, referred to frequently in Lovecraft's tales, is an actual grimoire. Rather than exploring Lovecraft's cosmic horrors, Argento instead adopted some of his strategies, using an obscure Thomas De Quincey essay, which drew on the writer's morbid opium fantasies, as the kernel around which (to mix metaphors in an entirely Argentoish way) a web of other fantasies could be woven for **Inferno**.

Both **Suspiria** and **Inferno** evidence the mystic's mistrust of language. The script for **Suspiria** especially would fill maybe 50 of the 120-or-so pages considered the average for a screenplay. *"Wherever we have spoken openly we have (actually) said nothing. But where we have written something in code and in pictures we have concealed the truth"* attests the alchemical grimoire *Rosarium philosophorum*. Whenever the protagonists of Argento's supernatural tales try to figure out the mysteries they've stumbled into, they find language the most inadequate and obstructive of means, whereas the genuine breakthroughs are invariably conducted in silence. In **Suspiria**, Suzy Banyon experiences difficulty in negotiating language straight away, as a surly cab-driver alleges to find her pronunciation of a German address incomprehensible. (When he scornfully reads the address from a card Suzy thrusts at him, the difference in pronunciation is very slight). Later, she tries to elicit explanations from girls at the dance school but finds they prefer to indulge in bizarre word-play. Olga, the school vamp, says: *"Suzy... Sarah... I once heard that names that begin with the letter 'S'... are the names of sssssnakes...ssssss!!!"* Her one fragment of a clue revolves around a barely audible phrase, heard in a howling storm, shrieked by an hysterical girl soon to be murdered. The cryptic words relate to an image of a flower. The only girl to speak openly about her suspicions, Sarah, is slaughtered. One night, just before she embarks on her final journey, Sarah tries to explain her insight to Suzy; who's been drugged and can't take in the words. When Suzy finally remembers the night's whispered conversation her memory is jogged not by words but the sound of footsteps, and then on into numbers, the act of counting footsteps heard echoing through the halls of the Academy at night. The mystic believes that truth can be heard *"more freely, distinctly or clearly [...] with a silent speech or without speech in the illustrations of the mysteries, both in the riddles presented with figures and in words"* (C. Horlacher, *Kern und Stern*, 1707). Suzy (and Mark in **Inferno**) both advance on the route to knowledge in silence (although Suzy has her every move accompanied by the Goblins' raging score). Enough said?

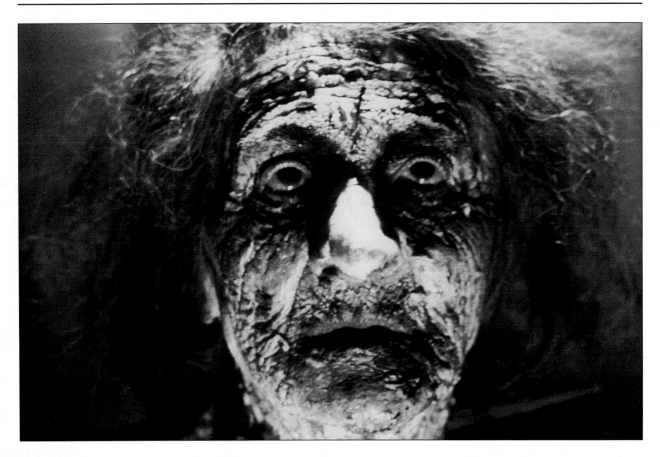

The ancient Helena Markos makes her ghastly appearance in the closing scenes of **Suspiria**.

Existential mysticism?

For those unhappy with unadulterated mysticism, there are other ways of seeing the film. **Suspiria** may deal with the paranormal, dabble in superstition, and rattle the bones of Gothic fairytale monsters for its manifest content, but as it is experienced in the round there's a powerful existential concern with presence in the film's construction. Characters are often stranded between the etiolated remants of the plot-line, elements or markers of which surface from the film's macabre psychedelia every now and again - establishing a synopsis is like navigating a course through a chain of tiny islands, an archipelago nearly lost in a rolling ocean. (Critics might counter that it's more as if the vertebrae of the plot are being stretched ever wider on the rack of Argento's stylistic bombast!) One watches with rapt attention as characters walk slowly and apprehensively down corridors flooded with colour and shadow. For long periods of time we are confronted with little but the walls and doorframes to gaze at, whilst the insistent camera and music cajole the adrenalin-marinated viewer into fanatical scrutiny of the screen. In Jean-Paul Sartre's *Nausea*, the protagonist reaches peaks of existential tension, oscillating between exhilaration and horror, whilst engaged in such apparently trivial pursuits as sitting in the park staring at a tree-trunk, or grasping the handle of a door. **Suspiria** amplifies the intensity of experience in a similarly ambiguous, double-edged way. There are times when the viewer is gripped by a feeling neither wholly pleasurable or discomfiting, where the tension-release pattern demanded by the horror genre has become so grossly attenuated that the structure is lost to virtual abstraction.

Ultimately, **Suspiria** is Argento's second first film, and the ideas tantalisingly initiated in its 98 or so minutes are yet to develop fully. **Inferno** picks up some of the same themes and precepts but takes them much, much further. One might say that, whereas **Suspiria** has wallpaper by Max Escher, **Inferno** is a Max Escher structure in film. The earlier idea of adapting H.P. Lovecraft was certainly no caprice on Argento's part, showing his awareness of the (unspeakable?) connections between existential and mystical viewpoints about the malleable nature of reality. The two opposing camps of magick and existentialism might disagree about the source of the blueprints, but that's just details. If science has failed in its bid to establish the pure form of matter, instead chasing its own hubristic tail down vista after vista of receding 'elementary' particles, what fate lies in store for the 'soft' sciences of psychology... and semiotics? Perhaps Dr Milius' book *Paranoia or Magic?* could tell us!

A search for the hidden way is part of the action of the film, part of what is required of the audience, and of course part of books like this. The hermetic tradition of magic draws its name from the same source as the practice of hermeneutics, or textual interpretation. Hermes was identified by the Greeks as the messenger of the gods, and became linked, through Greek colonists studying in Egypt, with the Egyptian Thoth, god of writing and magic; both were worshipped as the 'psychopompos', the soul's guide through the underworld. This symbolic aggregate of magic and writing may have provided the thread that Argento followed out of the supernatural labyrinth he'd been exploring. After **Suspiria** and **Inferno** he would take the subject of writing, and the interpretation of writing, as the basis for a very different nightmare, his stunning 1982 thriller **Tenebrae**.

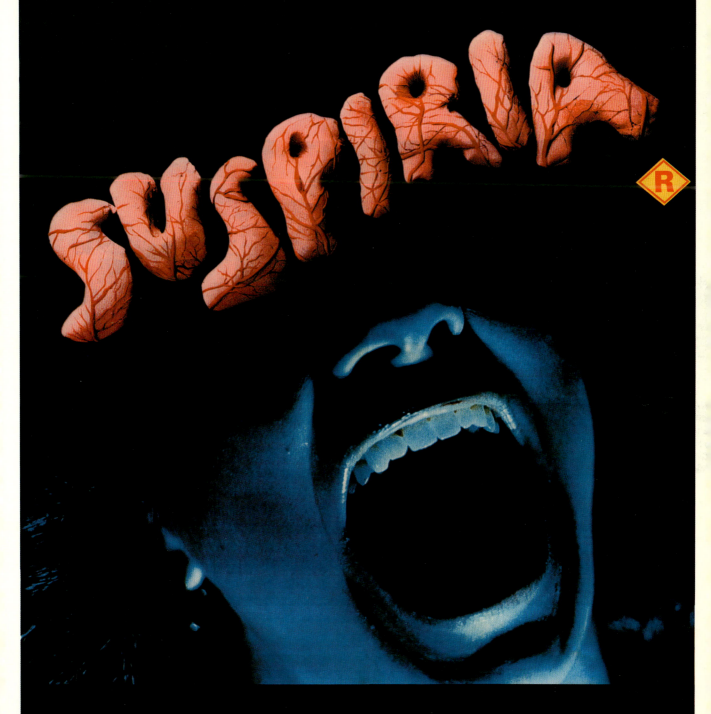

Witchcraft's
most Macabre Tale

SUSPIRIA

Once You've Seen It
You Will Never Again Feel Safe In The Dark

INTERNATIONAL CLASSICS INC.

© 1977 INTERNATIONAL CLASSICS INC.

The chaotic aftermath of Pat's murder in **Suspiria**.

As **Suspiria**'s coven collapses, the witches' house falls in a spectacular, supernatural storm.

The name of a snake: Suzy contemplates the malevolent influence of the feminine in **Suspiria**.

A bizarre publicity shot, showing Sara's death in a web of wire.

un film di DARIO ARGENTO
presenta
un film di DARIO ARGENTO
JESSICA HARPER STEFANIA CASINI

Suspiria

FLAVIO BUCCI MIGUEL BOSE
BARBARA MAGNOLFI SUSANNA JAVICOLI EVA AXEN
con ALIDA VALLI nel ruolo di Tanner e con JOAN BENNETT
direttore della fotografia LUCIANO TOVOLI
musiche dei GOBLIN con la collaborazione di DARIO ARGENTO
edizioni musicali BIXIO · CEMSA (Milano)
un film prodotto da CLAUDIO ARGENTO
per la SEDA Spettacoli S.p.A. (Roma)
distribuzione P.A.C. PRODUZIONI ATLAS CONSORZIATE
regia di DARIO ARGENTO
TECHNOVISION TECHNICOLOR

Suspiria
un film di DARIO ARGENTO

this page:

top: Italian lobby sheet for **Suspiria**.

left: Members of **Suspiria**'s teaching staff come together for a black mass.

above: Suzy (Jessica Harper) braves the rainstorm on her arrival in Germany.

opposite:

top left: Truly mortified: Madame Blanc (Joan Bennett) makes her apologies for an infestation of maggots.

top right: Colour dictates the tone of anxiety in a scene from **Suspiria**.

bottom: The meddlesome Pat comes to grief on a bed of stained glass.

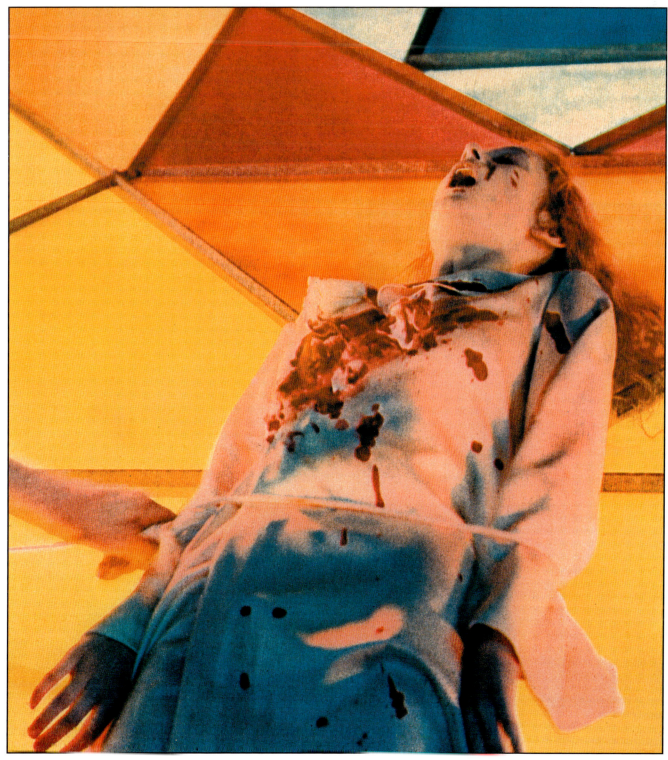

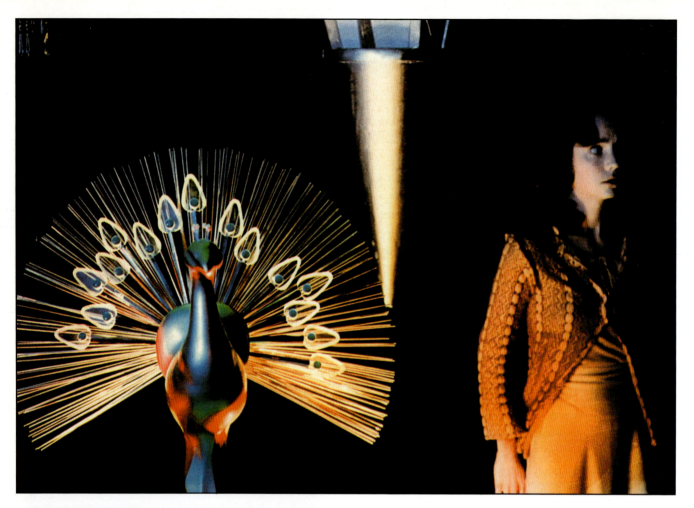

above: A bird with crystal plumage becomes Suzy's salvation in the closing scenes of **Suspiria**.

left: Suzy Banyon (Jessica Harper) is greeted by Miss Tanner (Alida Valli) on her first day at the academy.

bottom left: Dancers in the dark: extras congregate against the gaudy, garish art direction of **Suspiria**'s haunted academy.

below: Suzy takes aim in her climactic confrontation with The Black Queen.

opposite top: Japanese and French posters for **Suspiria**.

opposite bottom: Pat seeks sanctuary from the forces of darkness in **Suspiria**.

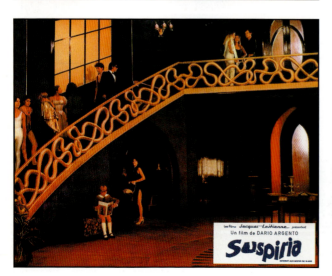

Italian lobby sheet.

Original UK threatrical poster.

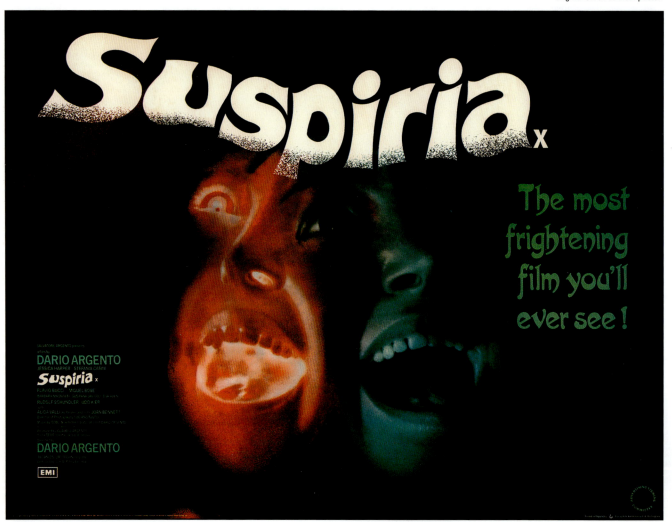

Daria Nicolodi as Elise in **Inferno**.

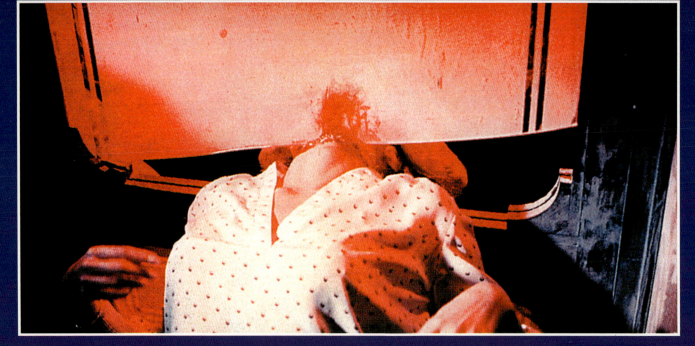

The full moon rises over **Inferno**'s cursed apartment block.

Irene Miracle discovers the secret in the cellar.

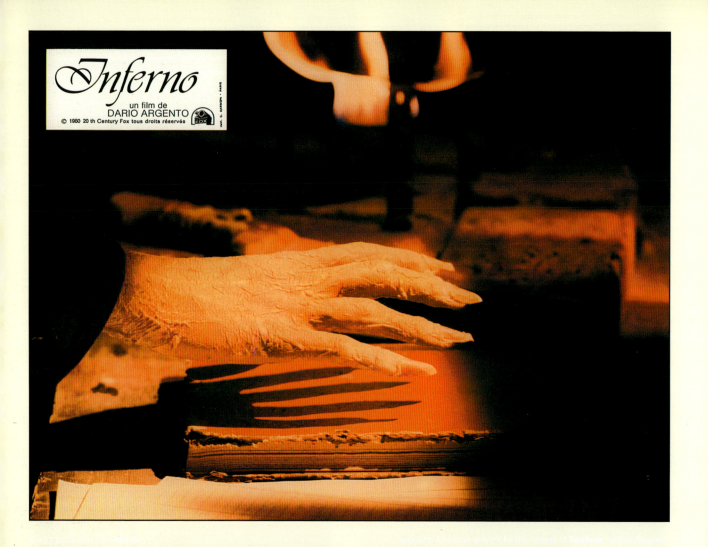

Inferno
un film de
DARIO ARGENTO
© 1980 20 th Century Fox tous droits réservés

FEUERTANZ DER ZOMBIES
© 1980 20 th Century Fox all rights reserved

Un film de DARIO ARGENTO
Inferno
LEIGH McCLOSKEY · ELEONORA GIORGI · VERONICA LAZAR
technicolor

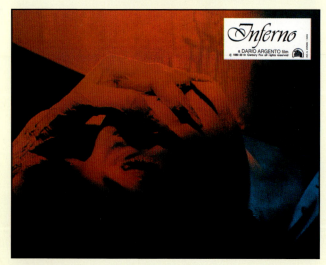

Inferno
a DARIO ARGENTO film
© 1980 20 th Century Fox all rights reserved

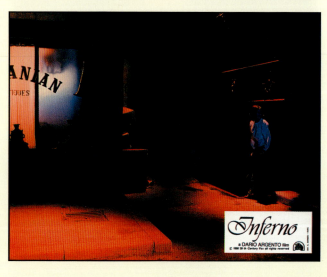

Inferno
a DARIO ARGENTO film
© 1980 20 th Century Fox all rights reserved

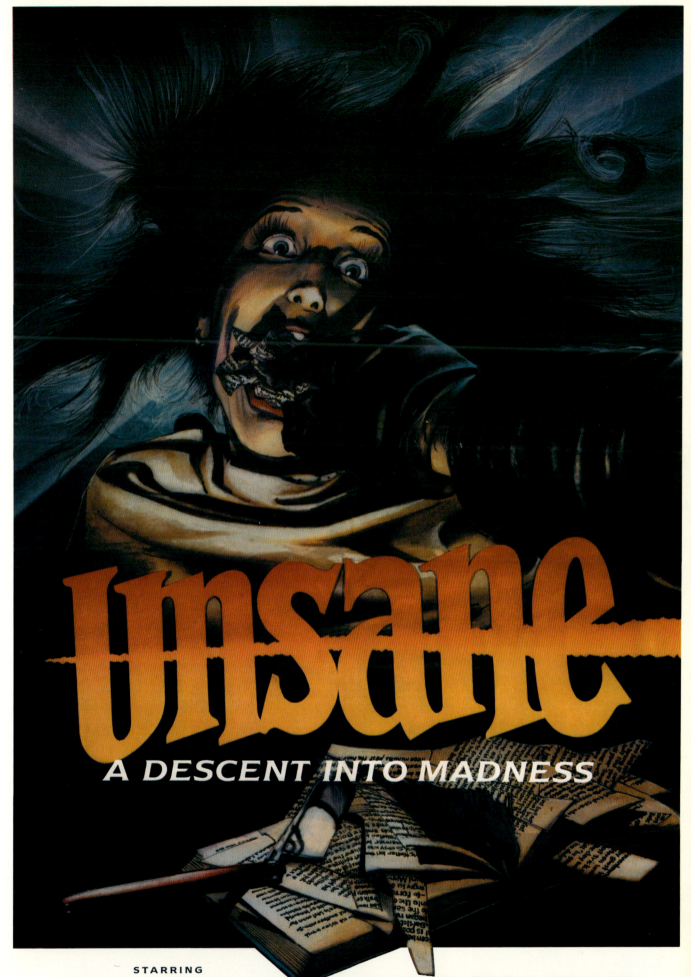

Unsane

A DESCENT INTO MADNESS

STARRING
ANTHONY FRANCIOSA   **JOHN SAXON**   **DARIA NICOLODI**
SCREENPLAY BY **GEORGE KEMP** EDITED BY **FRANK FRATICELLI** MUSIC BY **SIMONETTI**
PRODUCED BY **CLAUDIO ARGENTO**   DIRECTED BY **DARIO ARGENTO**
A **BEDFORD ENTERTAINMENT/FILM GALLERY RELEASE** IN TECHNICOLOR

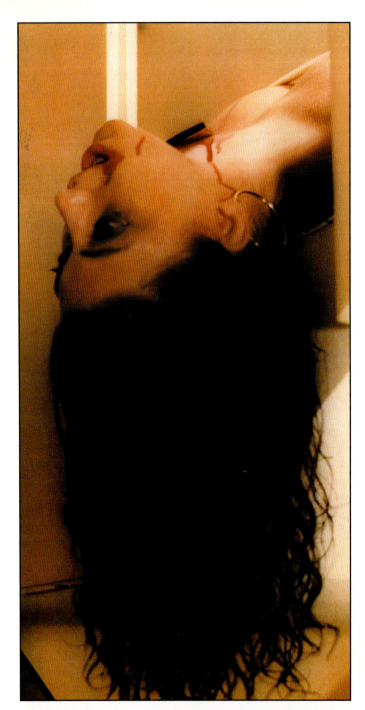

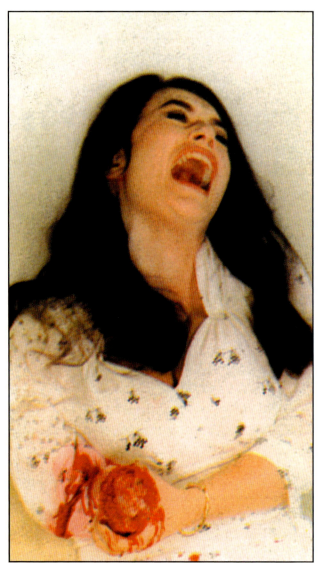

this page:
Mirella Banti, Veronica Lario and John Steiner each suffer the disturbing effects of violent fiction in **Tenebrae**.

opposite top:
Eating her words: an act of forced attrition in **Tenebrae**.

opposite bottom:
Nowhere to hide: Peter Neal's agent, Bulmer (John Saxon) is executed in broad daylight.

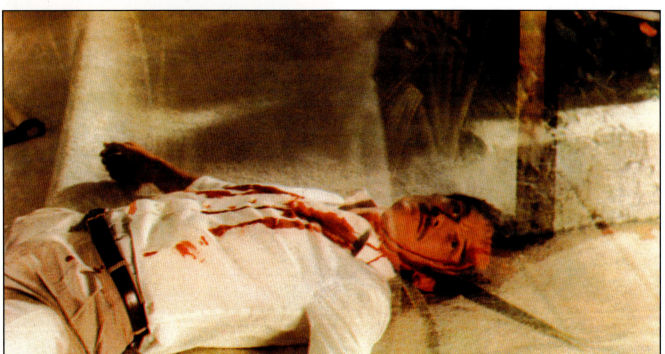

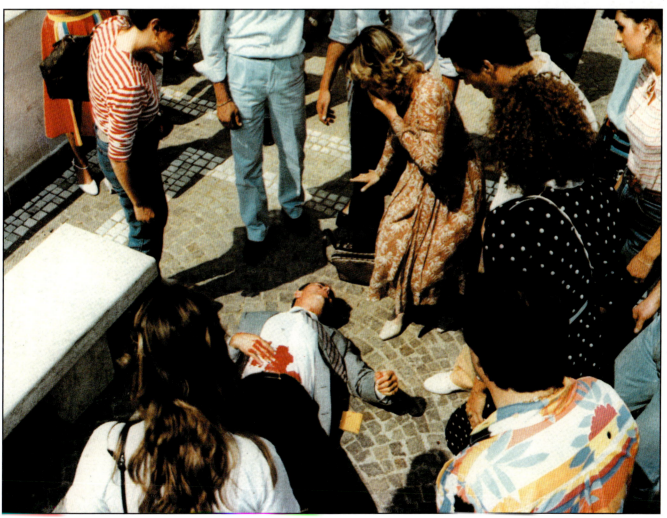

Inferno

Mitch Davis

ITALY

1980

Inferno is a special, entirely one-of-a-kind film whose power over me grows and grows with each awe-struck revisit. I first encountered Argento's irrationally overwhelming dream manifesto when I was around thirteen years old and at the time, I hated it or at the least, was confounded by what it was. I was definitely in awe of the film's colour crazy lighting, and the cruelty of its violence had a strong enough impact on me, but its defiant disregard for logic, linearity, or even the most basic principles of cinematic 'common sense' annoyed me beyond belief. Not because I felt challenged, but because at the time it struck me as carelessness. And the Keith Emerson score - a score that I now adore - drove me up the wall. I'll never forget the dumbfounded sense of pure what-the-fuck that tore through me when the taxi cab music came on. It all seemed so ridiculous, and for a multitude of reasons, **Inferno** just messed me up.

Two years later, I saw the film again, and this time my emotions flooded in ways that can barely be articulated. It was then that I recognized a brilliant, beautiful poetry at work. An incredible, fearless and terrifying sensibility that conformed to its own laws of nature. It was a sensibility of reciprocals and rhythms. Of music and magic, candy colours and cruelty. That night I realized the obvious - that the film worked as a liquid dream transcription, where the only 'real world' justifications for the events that transpired were simply because they happened to... Over the weeks that followed, I began to watch the film repeatedly, trying to decipher its diabolical power. I realized that Emerson's somber, almost campfire-tale-styled piano score, combined with the opening voice-over, key phrases of dialogue and the 'little girl lost' acting styles of the two female leads channelled the film's atmosphere into something much more particular than that of a mere nightmare - it was a child's nightmare. Everything about it seems to ooze with the sort of irrational suspicion and dread that makes early childhood so memorable and invigorating. There is a fear of elders (the three mothers themselves, the sickly older tenants of Rose's building), of pre-existing rules and, perhaps as a clue to the film's distinct aesthetics, of structure (also linking with the elders theme - note the eerie significance of Kazanian pointing out that *"our very lives are governed by dead people"*). There is also what would appear to be an apprehension of puberty, emphasised by the gorgeous (and apparently otherworldly) Ania Pieroni stroking her cat in class. It's interesting to note that the context here is within Mark's introductory scene - in a classroom, albeit university, in spite of being well into adulthood. There is also quite literally a fear of the dark, illustrated by the conspiratory realities at play whenever the lights go out. Add to this the sense of exploratory wonder in elements such as the pipes in the New York building interconnecting to allow tenants to have playful conversations through them. That Elise confesses *"it was our little secret"*, between her and her now-dead friend further drives the child nightmare atmosphere home. That their 'little secret' had, unbeknownst to them, been betrayed from the very beginning - by the building ITSELF - adds to it tenfold. Another childhood-incurring aspect is Elise's dependence on her manservant, who must literally carry her around and monitor her injection levels in order for her to survive. That he too betrays her trust compels the theme even further. The insert shots of hands severing the heads off paper dolls are also worth noting, and even then, these examples are only several of many. There are countless moments in the film that connect me to a sense of wonder and dread that I can only really associate with my childhood. In other words, it makes me feel like a frightened child, and as such, it is nothing short of exhilarating.

opposite:
Spanish poster for **Inferno**.

Alida Valli and Veronica Lazar as
inhabitants of the New York house of
Mater Tenebrarum.

In many ways, the film walks a tightrope between dream-logic and Fairy Tale. Take for instance the scene where Sara enters the cavernously massive library, looking for Varelli's book. She walks deep into the book-lined, blue-tinged catacombs, finally asks a decrepit caretaker where the book might be and discovers that it is in fact, directly behind her. This circumstance, in any other film would reek of narrative convenience (the library is MAMMOTH), but here, it only thickens the magical dream atmosphere of everything else around it. It is an event that would be as equally comfortable in a dream or Fairy Tale as it would be unlikely in conscious life - or straightforward narrative cinema. The opening voice-over intones the message that *"the three mothers are in fact wicked stepmothers, incapable of creating life"*, setting the liquefied Fairy Tale / Adult Child / Dream foundations for all that will follow. What fairy tale would be worth its weight in prose without a solid configuration of riddles? Both Mark and his sister will be faced with several - spoken (*"the second key is hidden in the cellar"*) and visual (the architectural maps). Other Fairy Tale trappings are incorporated along the way, from magic potions (*"heart medicine"*) to secret passageways and lairs that exist in places that are scientifically and geographically impossible.

Nature elements are also essential to **Inferno**'s transcendental horror, and the three basics can be found in abundance. For some reason, there appears to be a hierarchy to their ranking in importance to the story - water, then wind and lastly fire. The presence of wind is underlined when, at one point, the camera actually becomes this element and soars over the figures beneath it, as if about to crush them with its infinitely weightless weight. Above all, water imagery reigns supreme here, as a harbinger of both doom (the boiling cauldron in the library's basement, the rainstorm as Sara makes her life-altering decision in the taxi cab, Kazanian's central park murder) and healing (the natal atmosphere of the underwater ballroom, Mark's dream as he recovers from his heart attack). However you choose to decipher its presence, water is everywhere, running from walls, fountains and taps, falling from the sky and reflecting light in the film's countless puddles. Varying mountains of significance can be read into **Inferno**'s preoccupation with water imagery (Purity? Absorption? Corruption?), and it's inarguable that this element's significance is transformed with each new introduction, which is yet another explanation for the film's walloping subconscious impact. This is without a doubt Argento's ultimate cinematic Rorshach pattern, designed to be filtered through each individual's set of emotional baggage, with no two viewing experiences being quite alike. Set-pieces often occur under terms that can be read in a multitude of ways, and in places I wonder if Argento himself fully understands their reasons for being. Rounding out the workings of nature's arsenal is of course, the moon, ever-present, ever-full and easily as much a character as any of the actors. In fact, the moon is a silent witness - or accomplice - to each of the film's murders, be they indoors or out. By the time Kazanian meets his fate, he does so under nothing less than the hellish spotlight of a full lunar eclipse.

opposite:
Mater Lachrymarum, the Mother of Tears
(Ania Pieroni) materializes to the sound
of *Va Pensiero*.

Pushing the tenebrous Dream atmosphere even further is the film's use of reciprocals. For example, it is interesting to note that each of the film's key character murders (those who were actually in contact with the cursed book) are preceded by the ill fated figures' accidental breaking of an ornament; the mantelpiece in Sara's bedroom, the glass doorknob on Rose's bedroom door and the crystal statue that Kazanian frightens the cat into knocking over. The exception to this unspoken rule is the death of Varelli, but in a strange way, this would almost make sense. Presumably, the controversial and oft-censored death of the mouse needn't be applied to this abstract formula either, but it isn't without its own reciprocal, namely the butterfly seen earlier in the film, dying in the jaws of a lizard. That the butterfly is eaten to the score of Verdi while the mouse is later consumed with Emerson's Mater Tenebrarum symphonic-rock-opera shredding through the soundtrack might indicate something, or nothing at all. Another interesting reciprocal is the fact that both Rose and Sara return to their apartments on the night of their murders, soaking wet. Besides the fact that they both die on this same night, each in their apartments and on opposite sides of the ocean, their individual means of baptism aren't without their own poetic workings: Since Rose had actively researched the Mothers, it is fitting that she willingly descends into the surrealistically deep puddle for her contact with water, having been fatefully manipulated into searching for her keys (which is unbelievably ironic, seeing as she had only entered the cellar in search of the figurative 'second key' in the first place). Sara's involvement had been initiated by chance, having found Rose's letter to Mark, and reflecting this, it makes perfect sense that the water would rain down onto her in circumstances completely outside of her control. Kazanian too, is drenched in water before dying, and Elise is killed shortly after having taken a bath. Speaking of Kazanian, here's an interesting thread: the crutch-ridden book vendor drowns a bag full of cats, loses himself in glee and ends up falling into the river, where he is devoured by rats. Later we watch a mouse's death spasms as a cat chews into it. What's the connection between these images? Nothing solid, to be sure, but you've got to admit that there would appear to be a sort of otherworldly poetry to it all. And this is what **Inferno** is all about. It is an aria of seemingly disconnected yet oddly fused fragments of subconscious triggers and pure, atmospheric dread. There are moments in the film, where Emerson's music crescendos with camera movements and cuts, that get me emotional beyond expression, and this is achieved almost purely through abstraction. Very few films harness that sort of power (David Lynch's **Lost Highway** is the only recent example that comes to mind). Those that do are always going to divide their audiences like razor blades through shapeless foam, with elements of each opinion often bleeding over to 'the other side' after a certain period of time and thought.

opposite and below:
Rose Elliot (Irene Miracle) begins to uncover the secrets which lie within the house of the damned.

Underneath the soles of your shoes: Mark Elliot (Leigh McCloskey) solves the riddle beneath the floorboards.

Architect Varelli (Feodor Chaliapin), designer of the house of Mater Tenebrarum, now buried alive within his own creation.

Rose Elliot (Irene Miracle) descends deeper into the recesses of Mater Tenebrarum's labyrinthine home.

Irene Miracle emerges from the underwater ballroom set

Elise (Daria Nicolodi) falls victim to
the predatory cats in the attic of
Inferno's apartment block.

As could have been predicted, **Inferno** was greeted by a legion of baffled critics and even some irate fans upon its initial release - in those countries where it was fortunate enough to see theatrical light of day, Canada and the U.S. being criminally excluded due to a braindead shift of corporate powers at distributor Twentieth Century Fox. In the midst of the confusion, there were those who were almost religiously moved by it, and these were the people who went on record hailing it as the masterpiece that I feel it is. Surprisingly, many of those who adore **Suspiria** still have difficulty accepting much of **Inferno**. Granted, as a follow up it is even more free-form and dreamy than its predecessor, but this response has always puzzled me. I have an intense love for both films, but I definitely prefer the second one, finding it superior on every level that counts - narrative, technical and emotional.

I've already gone into the content, so let's talk about visuals. While it might not have benefited from the stunning - and now sadly, obsolete - three strip Technicolor dye transfer stock that **Suspiria** was shot on, I think it's inarguable that **Inferno**'s lighting schemes are equally, if not surpassingly, startling and creative, not to mention mind numbingly beautiful. **Inferno**'s cinematographer Romano Albani (who later lensed **Phenomena**) is every bit as innovative as **Suspiria**'s Luciano Tovoli. I would even go so far as to say that **Inferno** is one of the most beautifully lit films I've ever seen, with incredible configurations of deep blues, ambers and reds pulling painterly patterns across spectacular sets and locations in a manner which I've never seen replicated. One need look no further than the early establishing night shots of the New York hotel to see some of the most breathtaking coloured lighting ever burned into negative stock. I was fortunate to attend a rare 35mm screening several years ago and can distinctly recall a point where people were gasping at every cut, whenever a new series of colour patterns would appear. On a screen it is almost paralyzingly beautiful, and seeing it projected was without a doubt one of the strongest experiences I've ever had in a cinema. It is nothing short of breathtaking and totally, absolutely inspirational. Besides the more show-stopping lighting setpieces, there are countless subtle moments of creatively theatrical luminescence combining with clever staging that in some cases, only call attention to themselves upon repeat viewings. For one, it is fascinating to observe the many ways in which Argento incorporates the film's principal colour schemes of blue, red and amber into aspects of 'rational' light sources. For example, lightning flashes in deep red bursts, and the police car's lights at Sara's apartment flush Mark's face with deep blue hues - as do the lights of the fire trucks at the film's close (in yet another reciprocal). These richly saturated colours are first introduced in intensely supernatural atmospheres, but before long, they become ubiquitous, cleverly reinforcing **Suspiria**'s theme that *"magic is everywhere"*.

On the subject of light and staging, one particularly inspired moment occurs about an hour into the film, when Elise is sitting with Mark in his dead sister's apartment. The scene begins in a wide two-shot, with both characters sitting at either end of the screen, conversing. The room is nearly in blackness, furnishings barely discernible, with two glowing lights, one per character, each lighting from their immediate sides so that only they are lit against relative darkness. As Elise begins to speak about Sara's comments of Varelli, her light becomes a faint shade of blue. The camera cuts away as her voice continues on the soundtrack, to a low angle shot of an air shaft. The camera bobs lullingly

opposite top:
Dario Argento on the set of **Inferno**, setting up the murder of Sara (Eleonora Giorgi).

opposite bottom:
Mater Tenebrarum (Veronica Lazar) rants as her house burns.

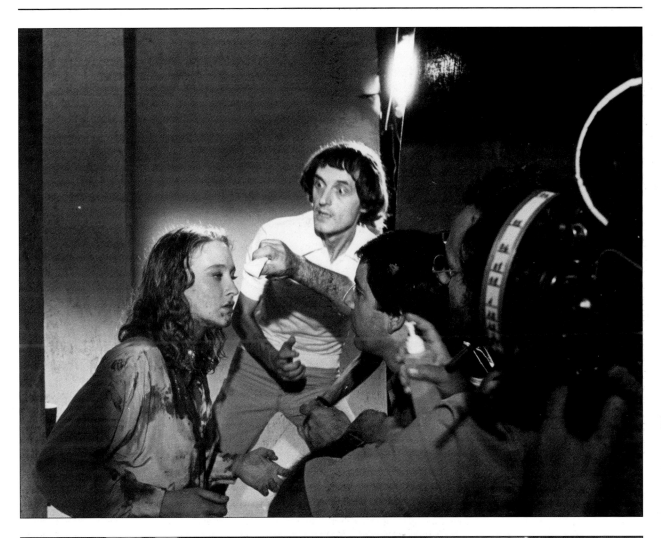

Mark finds his way into the secret hideaway
of the Mother of Darkness.

up and down as it approaches the shaft, seemingly having taken the form of her voice's
airwaves. A quick montage of pipes follow, and then laughter, at which point Argento cuts
back to a close-up of Elise, who has been startled by the laugh, and has stopped speaking
about the alchemist. The light on her is now the warm glow from before, but the entire
background of the shot is gelled a deeply saturated blue. When the camera cuts to a wide-
shot, we see that Mark is now standing outside in the hallway, gelled red. The time lapse
between this moment and the last that we saw of him sitting calmly is at best something
like thirty seconds. No explanation is given for this, and just in case the more attentive
viewers try rationalizing the gap by convincing themselves that Mark had quickly stepped
outside to investigate the laughter, Argento throws us this exchange:

> Elise: *"Did you hear that laugh?"*
> Mark: *"What laugh?"*

No further non-explanation necessary. By this point in the film, such elaborate
bendings of cinematic conventions barely register, and this alone is a testament to their
mind altering effectiveness. On the other hand, these sorts of devices sometimes confuse
viewers, and are misread as 'mistakes'. A phrase about breaking eggs to make omelettes
comes to mind, but I digress - and who would I be to talk anyway, having been a broken
egg myself back at thirteen? At the time of its release, Variety's critic actually claimed that
the film was *"full of clumsy shots that cannot be edited together"*!

Masterpiece? Out and out. Unforgettable? Absolutely. Flawless? Of course not. Like
the bulk of Italian horror's best entries, **Inferno** suffers from the sort of awkward post-
synch dubbing that only purists like us seem able to overlook. Just the same, most of the
'normals' seem to stop laughing pretty early on. Infinitely more distressing is the appearance of a ridiculously big boned, seemingly-elephant-sized, silly-looking-beyond-all-
fucking-belief skeleton at the film's conclusion. All the more frustrating, it makes its giggle-
inducing entry at a point so well built-up, so well conceived and so unbearably well staged
that it turns what would have been an ultimate, blood freezing punch line into one of the
sort I'm sure Argento wasn't looking for. And having it wave its arms around while it
throws a tantrum doesn't make matters any less hilarious. Still, whereas a flaw as severe
as the Goodyear Skeleton would be fatal in any other film, **Inferno** is drenched in such
utter and total brilliance that it's not so difficult to overlook - in spite of it pretty much
being the closing beat of the movie! Another bit that always rubbed me wrong was Elise's
murder, or rather, its subsequent explanation. I realize that Argento was building Alida
Valli's character up as a red herring to be suspected as New York's Mother, and her fiery
death definitely comes as an effective surprise, but then you're left with the possible
explanation that she killed Elise (I say this because it is implied that she is aware of what
happened to her - *"she won't be coming back"*) for her money. If this interpretation of
events is correct, then really, her means of dispatch is questionable to say the least. If
you're going to kill somebody, there must be easier ways than pelting your intended
victim with dozens and dozens of cats! Once again, something so preposterous would

Elise (Daria Nicolodi) seeks refuge
from the Mother of Darkness.

take away volumes from any other film, but **Inferno** is impervious to it, wearing its atmosphere like a bullet-proof vest. In fact, warts and all, not only is it my favourite Argento film, it's one of my favourite films PERIOD. It took me many years to reach this conclusion, and I made it having come from completely the reverse angle. To feel so strongly about a film that years ago I could barely stand is a fitting end to my journeys with a work as spectacularly and inexplicably poetic as this one. No exaggeration, while I might have seen films that were more perfected in their consistency, I have no qualms whatsoever in saying that I think **Inferno** is one of the greatest fucking movies ever made. Hidden beneath the soles of my shoes.

left:
Inferno makes its mark despite the blatant
artificiality of its skeletal 'punch-line'.

Tenebrae

Chris Barber & Stephen Thrower

ITALY

1982

What distinguishes **Tenebrae** from the plethora of psycho movies spawned during the 1970s and '80s is the sheer diversity, and often perversity, of ideological influences of which Argento is a function. The degree to which these textual constructs are consciously or unconsciously incorporated by him as 'director' becomes irrelevant, for the spectator is invited to join him in a cathartic exploration of these very antinomies: conscious/unconscious, subject/object, creativity/consumption, identification/alienation, reality/illusion. etc. Outside of the 'art circuit' such challenging engagement is almost unknown. (Another notable exception is Paul Verhoeven, director of **The Fourth Man**, **Robocop**, **Total Recall** and the fascinating but over-determined **Basic Instinct**). In Argento's case this is almost certainly due to his keeping production control within the family (Claudio and Salvatore Argento), minimising outside financial interference and commercial strait-jacketing.

Tenebrae, then, is a palimpsest, juxtaposing explicit and implicit dimensions; by layering a dazzling array of texts it demands an engagement in subjective interpretation, the contrast of alternative readings, different possibilities...

First there is the text. Before even the title sequence there's the page of an open book. In the background a fierce fire burns. Passion and fury, harbingers of death and destruction, rage to escape an enclosed fireplace; a vivid crackling is heard - danger threatens! A white page scarred by black words read aloud by a sinister voice - the subject is privy to the secret thoughts of a 'creative' mind. In extreme close-up, the text is revealed to our eyes, whilst the voice (of the reader?) meticulously relishes the sonorous script. But whilst the voice must progress in strict linearity, the visual text is exposed in a grouping of three typed lines, the camera's motion across them allowing us to scan both forwards and backwards at will, against or in anticipation of the flow of the voice-over. The words are contiguous, inviting the subject to read - and create - the text, although at no point is the entire passage completely visible. (Most written text can be scanned in this way - consider for example how hard it is not to read the last page of a book whilst still on the facing page.)

The narrative has begun as the words make the subjective realm objective. The implicit is made explicit. Is this fact within fiction? Vice versa? Or fiction within fiction? The diegetic conventions of cinema are immediately dislocated in this play with our attention. Who is the reader or the writer? Even the time frame is uncertain - there is no equilibrium to disrupt. As the book is thrown into the flames, title music begins, resembling a baroque or gothic concerto, but synthesised, and propelled by incongruous disco/rock cadences. The title and credits appear whilst the fire completely engulfs the *mise-en-scène*.

As the music continues apace, the image cuts to a backwards tracking shot, establishing at medium range a refined, middle-aged man riding a bicycle through heavy traffic. The rapid pace of movement, threatening bulk of lorries and motor cars, and the bizarre musical arrangement introduce a brittle, edgy mood, entwined with a filament of comic absurdity that will emerge throughout the narrative. Crossing an iron bridge, the spinning wheels contrast visually with the geometrics of metal girders in a way that recalls Futurist painting - and Argento's previous flamboyant juxtapositions of Art Nouveau curls and Art Deco rectilinear design - visual motifs that embody the clash between sane reason and deranged imagination endemic to his work.

As the music subsides the cyclist's 'destination' is revealed as Kennedy Airport, where, dismounting, he hands his bike to the chauffeur of a Rolls Royce which has apparently

Dislocation and displacement: transsexual Eva Robins/Roberto Coatti as the girl on the beach.

opposite and above:
Maria (Lara Wendel) seeks sanctuary in
the house of a serial killer after being
chased there by a vicious guard dog.

been following behind. Before we even know the character's name and occupation our expectations are confounded, whilst his arrival-as-point-of-departure sets up a pattern of permanent transience. **Tenebrae** vibrates from hereon with a kind of nervy hyperkinesis - even the airport washroom seems 'too much', its tiles luminous with baleful strip-lighting. Emerging from the washroom having changed out of his light-blue tracksuit into a casual blazer and slacks, the man looks relaxed and sophisticated, his neatly groomed slightly greying hair adding to an aura of refinement. A call for 'Peter Neal' is bellowed over the airport intercom (eagle-eyed viewers being perhaps already familiar with the name from the fleetingly glimpsed book cover in the pre-credits sequence); now the smartly dressed man has a name. The double first name has writerly connotations but also suggests possible identity problems. 'Peter' has particular childhood associations (i.e. *Peter Pan, Peter and the Wolf*), and Neal may also be 'kneel' - a motion to subservience. As Neal speaks on the (bright red) telephone at the information desk, he leaves his travelling bag casually several feet away. His call is from a woman, Jane, whom he hangs up on after a short, terse altercation. Unaware that she is in fact calling from a nearby public phone in the airport, he picks up his bag (which may have been moved) and heads for the plane. Their alienation from each other is clearly established. As 'Jane' is given a mysterious all-clear signal by an unspecified female 'friend', she exits the phone cubicle, creating an immediate air of tackily tragic enigma. She has long, dyed-black hair, wears ostentatious dark sunglasses, a fur coat and lots of make-up. Visibly wilting under the weight of her drastic signifiers, 'Jane' looks worried and depressed despite her connotational baggage of strong, mysterious femininity. More conceited than confident, more obsessed than self-possessed, more sick than chic, 'Jane' seems to lack something for which she is trying to compensate. No wonder she seems uneasy! These indexical connotations require familiarity with cinema alone - rendered entirely through cliché and parody, this camp *femme fatale* is recognisable as a construct, and the accompanying pleasure is ironical.

Rome. Is that Peter Neal, looking into a shop window? Impossible! Inside the department store, consumerist affluence is scored to tinny, hysterical muzak and heavy breathing. Another over-made-up woman is observed by the camera, this time stealing a book - 'Tenebrae' by Peter Neal. But, language being phallocentric, she is apprehended by a male - patriarchal power in the shape of The Law. *"Hey, what the fuck...?"* she exclaims, the profanity jarring with her Vogue-model styling. She is able to woo the store detective by offering sexual favours and challenging his masculinity (*"You're not gay, are you?"*). However, a history of compulsive shop-lifting and being repeatedly caught is revealed which marks her as a victim. Walking home, she is chased by an old tramp. The incident begins amusingly but soon turns ugly. After a narrow escape, she is home alone in her breathtakingly stark white showroom of an apartment. Who could live in such a place? Certainly not this woman, who is saved from having to try and relax in this modernistic hellhole by a black-gloved killer who slashes her throat with a straight razor after stuffing her mouth with pages from 'Tenebrae'. A white flash and the hyper-audible whirring of a professional camera indicates that the killer is collecting photographs of his victim. Our

above: Anne (Daria Nicolodi) and Peter Neal (Anthony Franciosa) gaze down into the shadows in a scene from **Tenebrae**.

opposite: Rare pre-release artwork for **Tenebrae**.

below: Convulsions of Terror: Inspector Giermani (Giuliano Gemma) underestimates his quarry.

DARIO ARGENTO

TENEBRAE

A black-gloved nemesis claims his first victim in **Tenebrae**.

awareness of an experience very much other than reality is focused insistently by such devices. As Jacques Lacan suggested, it is the object of perception that acts as a screen, capturing the gaze of the subject. The pleasure of identification with the murderer is admissible during the penetration, though this is then immediately disrupted. With this sudden eruption of violence, the plot begins to emerge, more clearly at first but twisting into stranger and more convoluted forms as further events accumulate.

Unlike the delirious free-wandering of **Suspiria** and **Inferno**, **Tenebrae**'s structure is built on a play between the rigid formal structures of the detective thriller and a variety of weird, jagged displacements. Ambiguous passages that may be dreams, recollections or fevered fantasies are interpolated seemingly at random and without contextual elaboration, whilst the technology of cinematography itself outstrips diegetic events, in a formidable ellipsis that, for instance, has the viewer transfixed for an astonishing, elongated 'moment' by nothing more than the image of slates on a roof, via a louma crane tracking shot. Since the killer has remained unseen and unknown, the camera's escape from the formality of 'point-of-view' lends greater emphasis to the suture through which we may explore the film's symbolic realm and link up the over-determinates. Fragmentation and sliding levels of focus are brought into play as the gaze is methodically guided over the rooftop of a house - perversely thrilling as the objects of identification and desire are removed - whilst one lesbian inhabitant curses and taunts the other over her fling with a man. The pounding music which accompanies the camera on its mad perambulations actually seems to be infuriating the woman on screen. *"Turn it down!"*, she screams distractedly. Upstairs, her lesbian lover lifts the needle from a record with an amplified mechanical click and our perception of the soundtrack is wrenched unexpectedly into the diegetic frame. With dislocation and displacement so highly placed in the film's formal vocabulary, the eerie sunlit beach sequences - dreams, memories or fantasies - become indexical to the actual plot without ever being fully subsumed to it through explanation. (There is a brief thread of connective dialogue, linking the events depicted in the beach sequences to allegations made against Neal, spoken by Inspector Giermani in his *de rigeur* Hitchcockian summary - *"But nothing was ever proven"*.) Here, it seems likely, is *"the fury which tortured him"* rendered visually and without words, the only sounds being the tinkling chimes of a music box warping gradually into spiteful twangs. A woman dressed in a revealing white dress and red heels falls lasciviously to her knees before a group of half-undressed young men in white trousers. Her act of supplication to the surrounding phallus is suddenly rejected violently by one male, who slaps her across the face. The others chase this perpetrator and pin him to the ground. After standing over the prostrate male and spitting on him (seen via a brief identification-with-victim shot), she thrusts the heel of her shoe into his mouth. The scene fades out with woman placed in the position of phallus. Since this symbolic threat displaces patriarchy, it may be assumed that Peter Neal is haunted, like many other men, by the consequences of his inability to conceive of power as a pan-gender phenomenon. If power is exclusively represented as male, under the signification of the phallus, the possibility of female power becomes 'phallicized' by default. The apparent contradiction assumes the form of a neurosis (or psychosis in Peter Neal's case). In **Tenebrae**, the sequence's unconscious repressed signifier becomes a primary source of motivation for Neal.

above and below:
The convulsive beauty of violence:
Jane (Veronica Laria) expires in
an eruption of gore.

Alternatively, this is a male masochistic fantasy in which woman remains the desired object; but if this is so, **Tenebrae** constantly draws attention to this through the stylised, mask-like make-up worn by the women, their estranged acting performances and contradictory emotional responses, and their confusingly similar looks.

Much play is made of the disorientating juxtaposition of contrasts. Even the film's title is an example of this. Meaning 'darkness', it clashes provocatively with what is on the whole a very brightly lit film. The barren, overlit appearance of nature (the beach as surrealist dream), the chic, geometrical interiors with their intense but indirect lighting... even the night scenes are brightly lit, the shiny carapaces of motor vehicles and the sharp lines of designer outfits rendered with crystal precision. Argento has said that the title refers to the darkness of the soul, or the unconscious mind. There are no safe and secure environments; external and internal threats all prevail. Nature becomes a threat as a female character with scant connection to events is corralled into the murderer's lair by the random intervention of a furious dog. It is within spatial construction, within the relationships between things and between people that difference is identified. Peter Neal's motivation is never fully defined. He is said to be insane. The possible reason for this is his being accused of killing a girl during his youth. But the self is always other, constantly engaged in a state of flux or transference. Already the perpetrator (of crimes or otherwise) has shifted (otherness). In Lacan's mirror metaphor it is when the child recognises his reflection in the mirror that the ego develops. But the mirror lies, this sense of the self as a whole is an illusion. This illusion will constantly distort and misguide the subject's identity. Neal's identity crisis seems to be encapsulated in his inability to distinguish between inner and outer reality (boasting of his murder spree to a horrified detective: *"The rest was like writing a book... A BOOK!"*), an entrenched confusion between his Real, Symbolic and Imaginary notions of self. When the cops first intercept Neal in Rome, they let him glimpse a photo of the recently murdered girl. Neal abruptly brushes this aside with a curt *"No!"*. It's possible that at this moment there is a condensation. Peter Neal is jolted into a chain of associated, unconscious signifiers (possibly the childhood memory of the murdered girl).

There is a triadic formula for categorising spatial relation in cinema. 1) Between the people and objects within the frame. 2) Between the camera and the scene within its frame. 3) Between the audience (subject) and the screen (object of the gaze). When Neal's agent Bullmer is murdered, a series of distancing edits disrupt the sense of spatial continuity. Objects and people are seen in close-up, then long-shot; in deep focus, then unclear background. Uncertain of what we are even looking for, our gaze is drawn to a variety of apparently random events taking place in the *piazza* where Bullmer sits. This 'drawing' of the gaze is effected through unconventional means. Instead of demanding

our attention by actively foregrounding intelligible events, the sequence works by drawing out to an unsettling degree an impassive montage of 'casual', unrelated ones. A child plays with a ball, sundry passers-by stroll or cycle through the square, two lovers argue and then split in acrimony (all in virtually inaudible long-shot). A pair of roller-skaters and a pair of joggers add to the sense of chaotic, disassociated movement. Two punks catch Bullmer's eye, as do two men brawling outside a café. This proliferation of pairs stresses the unease of a solitary subject awaiting a rendezvous. There is a sound diegetic explanation for all this artfully sustained elongation of narrative time. We know that Bullmer is waiting to meet someone and events thus far have primed us to be on the look-out for violence at every turn.

The chic geometry, both internal and external, of the psychopath's lair.

The long shots challenge us to foresee how a murder can be committed in broad daylight in such a wide-open public space, and emphasise Bullmer's isolation. Is he safe or vulnerable in his solitary vigil? The modern concrete seat on which he sits resembles a sterile mortuary slab, and makes him look doomed immediately. His physical precariousness is amplified when a child clambers behind him and roots around obscurely beneath the bench. One is reminded of the strategies employed by Michaelangelo Antonioni in his films **Blow Up** and **The Passenger**.

Reality is relative and always other than where it appears. Spatial relations in and outside of the frame are juxtaposed. The viewer might well be alarmed by the changing figures of identification. There is an anxious desire to see what cannot be seen, the space outside of the frame, behind the camera (a desire which is of course present in most of the strategies of the horror cinema). When Bullmer is eventually stabbed with a stiletto blade, a shot at ankle height shows the owner of a pair of red stiletto shoes advance to the crowd of people gathered around the dead man, then veer away again, presumably having recognised him. In this instance the shoes, up till now a harbinger of mysterious trauma, are merely red herrings. A less nerve-wracking, more amusing climax to such spatial tricks follows later. Peter Neal and his young assistant, Gianni, are cruising along in Neal's hired car, talking. When Gianni, who is driving, has a sudden flashback to an earlier scene of violence, the car jolts and a crash is heard. Moments later they are continuing their journey, and a long shot reveals it was the two cars crossing their path that collided.

The graphic violence in **Tenebrae** is pure convulsive beauty, the shock tactic used primarily by the Surrealists to disrupt the subject's complacency. By showing one of the tricks used to create such effects (i.e. Neal's razor which shoots trick blood from the blade) the subject is provoked into thinking about the range of tricks and effects involved in creating the cinematic illusion. There is also another level to such shock effects, indigenous to the splatter movie; the carving up of the body displays the fragmentation of the self, the loss of notions of consistent identity in the world of information overload.

The constant questioning of Neal's responsibility as an artist (from cops, critics, journalists) suggests a transference of identification from the actor to the director. Neal's transient identity shifts between writer/interpreter, detective/psychoanalyst, lover/husband, killer/victim, sane/insane. This endless deconstruction reduces the self to the subject of discourse. Neal's concerned companion, Anne, asks a naïve question - *"How's your head?"* - in the aftermath to Berti's murder. Neal's response is rich and quizzical in the extreme: *"My head? How does my head feel... now that is a very interesting question to contemplate, my head, my head... What head?"*

When Neal kills the critic it is 'for' the Artist. For by what right does the critic judge with authority? The critic is the self-proclaimed interpreter of meaning. Whether he attributes the 'only true' meaning of the work of art to the artist's 'real' intentions or 'discovers' the hidden meaning in the work itself regardless of the artist's proclamations, he claims to be privy to an esoteric code. This involves the critic in a hierarchical system of values (or prejudices) from within which he can confer meaning and aesthetic value. The critic in **Tenebrae** is shown to be intolerant and highly prejudiced. He is a Catholic who believes in abortion, but clearly he feels threatened by difference in sex and sexuality. Women, lesbians, gays are *"human perverts"*. Even when an 'innocent' girl falls victim to his rage, he justifies her 'elimination' to continue his cause. Neal (the artist) is shocked by the critic's code of ethics, defining such differences in more positive terms... until this otherness threatens his own subjectivity. The hardening of Neal's response to the crimes, from appalled curiosity to cold calculation and manipulation, comes after Berti's less-than-subtle threat, which Inspector Giermani helpfully underlines: *"This last note... threatens you personally"*.

opposite top:
Peter Neal (Anthony Franciosa)
finds comfort in chaos in the
closing scenes of **Tenebrae**.

above and opposite bottom:
Inspector Giermani (Giuliano Gemma)
contemplates the killer's latest
gruesome coup de théâtre.

There is the suggestion of an Oedipal power relationship between Peter Neal and the critic Christiano Berti. This mythic/psychoanalytic trope involves the son killing the father in order to inherit (the signification of) the phallus and restore the patriarchal order. But which way does the axe swing in **Tenebrae**? When Neal murders the murderer, one might construe this as the artist's wrenching away of the power of the phallus from the critic. However, a film-maker is unlikely to envisage the relationship between critic and artist in terms so respectful of critical power! (Although the pre-occupation with the relationship is perhaps not surprising when one recalls that Argento - like many French New Wave directors of the late fifties and sixties - began his career as a film critic). Berti's murders are performed as a malignant tribute to Peter Neal, as remarked by the detective, Giermani. Berti's notes informing Neal of the slaughter of each victim are made up of fragments of Neal's own writing (Berti's loyalty to the writer) and one is in Latin (pursuance of his intellectual admiration). He states in one note that the killer will soon be coming after *"the corrupter himself"*. This places the critic in an ambiguous position: idolatrous yet iconoclastic (a typical homosexual position in relation to masculine objects of desire). It is this twisted critical position (admiration soured into hatred) which Neal rejects, definitively, with an axe through his acolyte's head. Neal thus plays the castrating artist/father to Berti's critic/son. He then murders his wife Jane and her lover, the duplicitous agent Bullmer, using Berti's crimes whilst effectively erasing the critic's guilt. As just another loser in the string of victims, Berti is 'absolved' of his responsibility by Neal's actions (and extinguished too as an 'artist of murder'), whilst living on in the palimpsest of Neal's subsequent crimes.

Just as in the palimpsest, where that which has been 'erased' remains as a trace within the superimposed code, Neal then goes on to exhibit traces of Berti's behaviour. Discussing the critic's murder with Inspector Giermani, Neal presents a slick and plausible simulation of innocence, fielding casual but potentially embarrassing questions with ease. *"You didn't get a yellow envelope yet? You will"*, asserts the unsuspecting sleuth, with a bland assumption that the trend is continuing. This confirms to the murderous Neal that he is not under suspicion. Perhaps it also stimulates the arrogance that follows. Giermani flatters Neal by asking sincerely for his help in solving the case; and Neal responds with a speculation which is tantamount to a tempting of fate. *"I just have this hunch that something is missing, a tiny piece of the jigsaw. Somebody who should be dead is alive, or... somebody who should be alive is already dead"*. This breathtaking risk is reminiscent of another taken by the chief protagonist in Edgar Allan Poe's *The Black Cat* who, having successfully evaded suspicion for murder, has his guilt erupt from the unconscious in the form of arrogant bravado: whilst showing police round his home he taps on the wall behind which he has entombed his dead wife, boasting *"These walls are solidly put together!"* Poe's protagonist awakes the eponymous cat, which he'd unintentionally walled up along with the corpse, and its yowls alert the police. Neal is more fortunate, but his words similarly flaunt his involvement as if begging for attention at the possible price of liberty. As such, his remarks feel like echoes of the attention-seeking Christiano Berti, whose megalomaniac urge to boast of his crime to Peter Neal provided the telling detail that ensnared him in the writer's scheme.

The other detail that suggests the trace of Berti 'under erasure' comes with Neal's murder of the 'innocent' Gianni. With the unconscious flirtation of young male jailbait, Gianni shows a sadly misplaced boyish enthusiasm for helping the great writer solve the mysterious crime of Berti's murder. Just as the 'grieving' Berti felt compelled to kill the young, innocent Maria to further his campaign of themed murders, so too does Neal indulge in unprincipled track-covering when he strangles Gianni, after the boy reveals that he's remembered Berti's last words (*"It was me - I killed them all"*). As Gianni ponders the question *"So who killed him?"* he reaches a dangerous springboard - but never makes it to the pool. Neal garrottes him (a method of despatch which has - thanks to William Burroughs - become queasily homo-eroticized).

Argento has always favoured stories which self-consciously foreground the process of deduction and investigation. It is therefore amusing, in a chilly sort of way, to note a sly

top:
Peter Neal's insight into the identity of the
killer marks a turning point in the film's plot.

above:
The "human perverts" of **Tenebrae** mark
themselves down for violent murder.

manipulation of sound technique in this, his most labyrinthine thriller, which perhaps anticipates the way in which critics pour over filmic texts, in order to play the artist's game of hide-and-seek with interpretation just a little further. The key moment of transformation in **Tenebrae** occurs when Peter Neal, Anne and Gianni are ensconced in Neal's hotel room pouring over maps of Rome, scraps of paper and notes from the killer, trying to deduce his identity. Neal re-reads the most recent note - *"I will continue to eliminate the human perverts - soon, now, the corrupter himself"*. With a sudden flash of recognition, Neal recalls that, during their TV interview, Christiano Berti had described the novel, 'Tenebrae', as being *"'About human perversion and its effects on society' - those were his exact words"*. In a flurry of activity, Neal and his cohorts rummage through the papers, consult a telephone directory and locate a map to ascertain where Berti lives (just three blocks away, and very close to where young Maria's body was found). For Neal, the deductive leap is tangibly acute. This is where the plot pivots, with Neal as interpreter of Berti's cryptic statements and notes, achieving symbolic access to the critic's sordid truth. Now he knows both where the critic is 'coming from' and where he lives... Critics examining this sequence for clues to the encrypted structure of **Tenebrae** may feel a shiver of weird, synchronous pleasure as Argento gratuitously adds a doubling echo to the rustling sounds of paper, notes and maps that the trio sift through. It's a dry echo, subtle, without the cavern effect of reverberation... just a creepy doubling of the scrunching of paper. Is this perhaps Argento's gesture of alienated camaraderie, a nod to the restless lovers of the paper-chase? Minds, separated in time, pushing their sensors against either side of the text? Or is it a competitive dry dig of the 'I knew you'd end up here' variety? 'Now wait a minute; this is paranoia', you might think. Perhaps. But isn't it strange that those are Daria Nicolodi's exact words as the echo subsides? At the very least it offers an existential sensation of becoming through the process of puzzle-solving, analogous to the weird moments experienced by Argento protagonists. However, since both critic and artist are struck down by their own insane delusions of grandeur and notions of truth, it is nonetheless left to the reading subject to define meaning.

Of all the oppositions that play across the surfaces of **Tenebrae**, the most compelling may be the antinomical relation between chance and determinism. Thriller writers since Chandler have engaged with this axis of affairs, and it crops up in several notable sequences, such as the way in which a seemingly random chain of events leads inexorably to tragedy: the killer forgets to remove the key from his back door lock; a girl thoughtlessly baits a guard dog which jumps the fence and chases her to the killer's garden; the attack forces her to take refuge in the house using the neglected key to enter; the killer recalls his error whilst on the verge of picking up a new victim and returns home to fetch the key; the girl discovers the killer's secret stash of grisly photos and incriminating paraphernalia; the killer is 'forced' to murder the unfortunate witness. This sequence of events demonstrates the unpredictable action of chance on even the most anally precise of plans, like a virus flooding the pores of a deterministic organism ready to produce chaotic mutation. This process is also the one which governs (if that's the right word) the catastrophic sequence of events at the film's finale.

Anne grows anxious at Inspector Giermani's delay in returning from the house where Peter Neal has killed his wife and faked his own suicide. She doesn't know the cop is dead, felled by Neal's axe. She leaves the safety of the car and runs through pouring rain to the house. Neal stands vigilantly poised with the axe. But as she tries to open the door, it jams on a previously dislodged *objet d'art*. As she pushes harder to dislodge the sculpted cornucopias, Neal impatiently moves behind the door. With a mighty shove, she dislodges the object. It springs suddenly backward, impaling Neal on a formidable steel spike, penetrating his chest and exiting from his back, pinning him to the wall. Blood gushes. On the one hand, this final violence is a prime example of chance mocking the characters: Neal is impaled once again, this time with objective irony; whilst Anne, the pragmatic, affectionate stooge to Neal's covert craziness, becomes a killer. On the other hand, we have the battleground of signification between the sexes. However unconscious her action, it is Anne, the female 'victim', who strikes the final blow. She who thrusts the phallus back against the male, overturning the patriarchal relationship. Neal, symbolically castrated, dying, shocked in disbelief, clutches the spike; desperately attempting to move it. The razor edges slice into his hands, spilling more blood - his final stigmata. She alone, the final survivor, is confronted by his mutilated death-agonies. This final shock is too much, reducing her to a screaming wreck, frenzied beyond the realms of language. Her wailing continues into the end music and credits. Is this the primal scream of her rebirth, beyond the power of patriarchal language? Or is this her final madness beyond the realms of any language, her emptiness, her void, her inability to overcome the despair of anarchy?

The author of the fiction has staged his own death, just like the author within the fiction. The man of action, the artist, the patriarch, the phallus - killed by woman, lack. As with Neal before, we see the trick razor; or so it would seem... Agency has been thoroughly perforated, or - at least - a state of perforation has been acknowledged within the fiction that is Dario Argento. But with Argento as its function, the fiction of the author lives on to revivify alternatives, and potentiate differences, in a myriad of relative meanings.

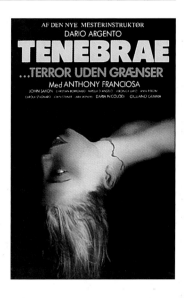

The primal scream: Anne (Daria Nicolodi) sinks into the darkness in **Tenebrae**'s closing image.

Phenomena

Matthew Coniam

ITALY

1985

Wherever the 'Is Dario Argento as good as he used to be?' debate rages, **Phenomena** is one of the films that tends to get caught in the crossfire, with many fans dismissing it as the beginning of the end, others cautiously proclaiming it an under-rated finale to the director's golden period, and Argento himself, contrary bastard that he is, hailing it as his masterpiece. Complicating the issue still further is the fact that the film upon which a large proportion of viewers base their opinions is not **Phenomena** at all, but rather a monstrous abridgement of it called **Creepers**. It was **Creepers** that played in (a few) British cinemas and loiters in the cheap-bins of British video shops.

What constitutes the difference between the two versions has usually been guessed at by the film's detractors. It is often assumed that the film has simply been trimmed for violence and that the remainder of the missing twenty minutes consists of boring, irrelevant talk. Widest of the mark is John McCarty (not an Argentophile) whose *Official Splatter Movie Guide* claims that *"the film has been shorn of some sequences that might have verged on 'kiddie porn'."* In fact, the differences are quite striking, and my review - and especially its conclusion (that the film is undemanding but excellent) - is based on the evidence of the full Italian language version.

Some of the most significant moments lost in the translation include, yes, lots of stagey dialogue, but also an entire scene in which the school doctor subjects Jennifer Connelly's character to a bizarre brain examination (there's a still from this sequence in Maitland McDonagh's *Broken Mirrors, Broken Minds*), a strange bit of narration when she first arrives at the school (much like that which is dubbed over the opening credits of **Suspiria**) and an amazing bit of plot in which Connelly 'sees' that her room-mate has been murdered via psychic empathy with a maggot. Unsurprisingly, virtually every incident of violence has been toned down from the original, which includes more stabbings, a blade shooting from an open mouth, Fiore Argento painfully pulling a pair of scissors out of her hand, more of Daria Nicolodi being attacked by the detective and tons more of her being slashed by the chimp. Taken together, it is quite simply a different movie.

My guess is that Argento saw **Phenomena** as a kind of unofficial 'best of' compilation, a distillation of all his quirks, tricks, obsessions and recurring images; a primer in Argento studies. As with **Trauma**'s anorexia and **The Stendhal Syndrome**'s Stendhal Syndrome, the film equips its young female protagonist with a characteristic that alienates her from society, yet has nothing in particular to do with the plot, in this case the ability to communicate with insects. She is then cast into an intrigue resonant of earlier *gialli*, but in a setting reminiscent of the director's more fantastic works. Supernatural or at least extremely bizarre plot interpolations are manifold, but the resolution is defiantly rationalist.

Critics immune to the film's peculiar charms but familiar with the director's other works tend for this reason to liken the film to a melting pot; an undisciplined stew in which this hitherto most autocratic of auteurs totally abandons the control and balance that so distinguished **Deep Red** or **Suspiria**. Certainly in synopsis the film sounds wild and childish. Is it possible to hack a path through a narrative that includes a deformed, psychotic child, his equally demented killer-mother, a teenage girl given to sleepwalking and the Dolittle Syndrome (who tracks down what she knows to be a vicious killer entirely alone but for the sniffing assistance of a largely animated fly), and a trained chimpanzee who finishes off the villain with a cut-throat razor it finds in a dustbin? Seemingly so arbitrary as well as outré, these aspects of the film confound audiences, and infuriate

opposite top:
The pre-pubescent heroine of **Phenomena** plunges into a pit of decomposing body parts.

opposite bottom:
The rotted, severed head of the first victim is studied for clues to the killer's identity.

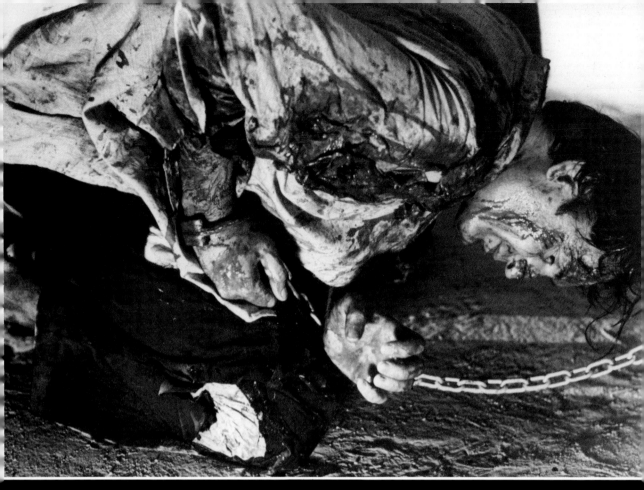

Inspector Geiger (Patrick Bachau) struggles against his chains in the prison-like home of the dysfunctional Bruckner family.

Moments of hideous invention: Jennifer Corvino (Jennifer Connelly) endures the illogical narrative twists of **Phenomena**

Jennifer Corvino (Jennifer Connelly) forms an unlikely alliance with invalid John MacGregor (Donald Pleasance) and his pet chimp.

Insect inside: Jennifer Connelly's telepathic powers manifest themselves.

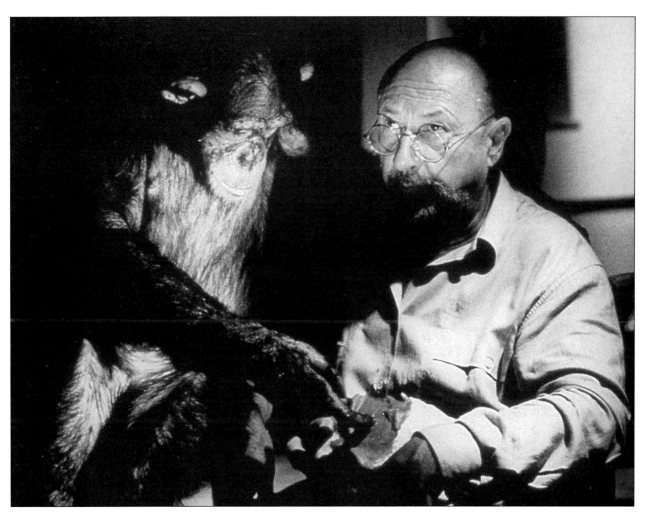

scholars whose defence of the director is precisely that his films can be taken seriously, and analysed with the same degree of sobriety as Hitchcock. Of course, all of Argento's cinema is a whisker short of absurdity - in fact his best films tend to be those which walk the tightrope of realism the most precariously. When the director's concentration and enthusiasm go, in careless works like **Trauma** (and, dare I say it?, **Tenebrae**) the end product tends to fall over that line. But **Phenomena** leaps over it, combining rollercoaster thrills with loud music, gore and that walking symbol of International horror-by-numbers, Donald Pleasence doing a funny voice.

And yet, some of the horror set-pieces are quite simply astounding. The amazing opening sequence (like so much of the film considerably spoiled in the prissy **Creepers** edit) silences any audience with its unfettered wandering camera and catalogue of assaults dealt to Argento's daughter Fiore. (Only at the end, when we see her head plop into a waterfall in long shot does Argento allow the release of sick laughter.) In the similarly *tour-de-force* climax Jennifer Connelly's attempts to escape through the tunnels beneath the floorboards of the killer's house end with her tumbling into a nauseating pit of filth, rotting corpses and squirming maggots. In order to save her, a police detective chained by his wrists to the wall systematically breaks the bones of his own hands. These moments of hideous invention, far from the *"clumsy violence sequences more in the tradition of his crasser countryman Lucio Fulci"* (to quote Kim Newman), strike me as vintage Argento, the neurotically sadistic imagination that conceived the first murder in **Suspiria**, the teeth-smashing of **Deep Red** and the rows of pins in **Opera**, working at full power.

The film continues Argento's preoccupation with visual experimentation. The colour schemes share the insane, baroque richness of **Suspiria**, playing up atmosphere in direct defiance of plausibility and logic. (Note how nocturnal views from windows are not black but lit spectrally blue.) But insane as these images may be, Argento subjects them to their own laws of continuity which are rigidly formalised. In all night-time exterior sequences an ever-present wind blows the trees and whistles on the soundtrack, recalling the howling atmospherics of the Three Mothers films. In contrast, in the daylit exteriors, Argento seems to be playing with a twisted fairy-tale ambience, making mocking use of Hansel and Gretel cottages and romantic lakes. This attention to texture and style gives the film the consistency and shape lacking in its gleefully unhinged plot.

Aside from the dizzying opening camerawork, the most technically provocative aspects of the films are its strictly-speaking irrelevant shots of massing insects. (Argento later revealed that these scenes, at best peripheral to the plot and adding up to little more than a couple of minutes of screentime took four months to shoot.) Though not above all the hoary old tricks, from cartoon animation to pepper on the lens, the shots of the swarming flies attacking the killer mutant, engulfing the front of the school and, from inside, hammering in their thousands against the windows, are splendidly effective, as

DARIO ARGENTO

PHENOMENA

un'esperienza che non potrete mai dimenticare...

Dario Argento

Titanus

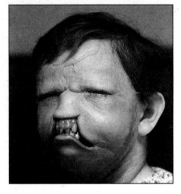

top:
Promotional artwork.

above:
Frau Brückner's mutant child
(Davide Marotta).

right:
Jennifer's scheming peers and emotionally
bankrupt headmistress gain an insight into
her telepathic powers.

superbly realised as the climactic locust-storm in **Exorcist II** and just as unsettling for insectophobes. In fact, Argento has a stylistic field day in this school sequence, additionally rigging up a wind-machine to give Jennifer - placidly intoning *"I love you, I love you all"* to a ring of taunting schoolgirls - the appearance of being simultaneously in a strong breeze and a sealed room. Very odd.

The film's score reveals Argento's shockingly non-discriminating love of 'rock music', festooned as it is with schoolboy stompers from the likes of Motörhead and Iron Maiden, however very little of it actually detracts from the film as is often claimed. Argento always liked to try something new on his soundtracks, from Goblin's rock pieces for **Deep Red** to the unfamiliar instruments and vocal effects of **Suspiria** and the operatic **Inferno**. If anything, the main instrumental portions of the **Phenomena** soundtrack are a decided improvement over the bland synth-score of **Tenebrae**.

In retrospect, the years 1975-76 will be seen as the turning point in Argento's career. The promise of his early *gialli* had reached the perfection of **Deep Red**, and rather than rest on his laurels he attempted something entirely new in **Suspiria**. Both films were triumphant exercises in pure cinema, and rewarded Argento with financial success to match their artistic excellence. Anything that followed would have to be measured against their standard. **Inferno**, though excellent, was basically **Suspiria** part two, while **Tenebrae** tamely rehashed the *giallo* with neither **Deep Red**'s style nor its power. **Phenomena** was at least a brave attempt to try something a little different. To what extent it succeeds is a matter for history and for the individual viewer, but I can't help warming to it.

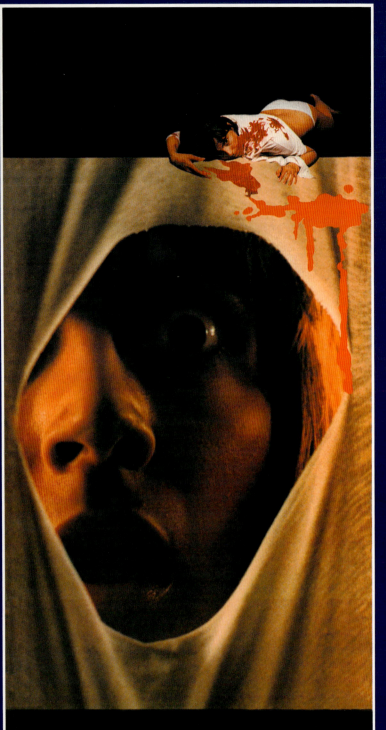

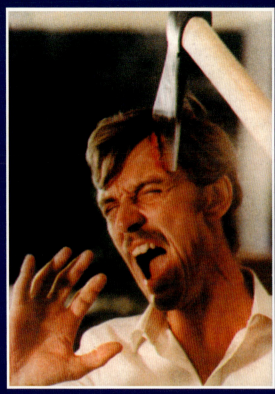

left: Rare promotional artwork for **Tenebrae** under the title 'Shadow'.

above and below: Scenes from **Tenebrae**.

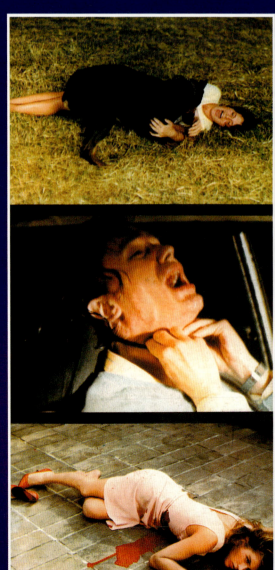

a film by DARIO ARGENTO

SHADOW

starring
ANTHONY FRANCIOSA   DARIA NICOLODI
and with the participation of
GIULIANO GEMMA
directed by
DARIO ARGENTO
Music by
GOBLIN

The red shoes...

above: Jane (Veronica Lavia) receives a gift from a psychopath and...   (below): a young author is subjected to oral rape in **Tenebrae**.

Marion (Mirella Banti) meets **Tenebrae**'s razor-wielding avenger.

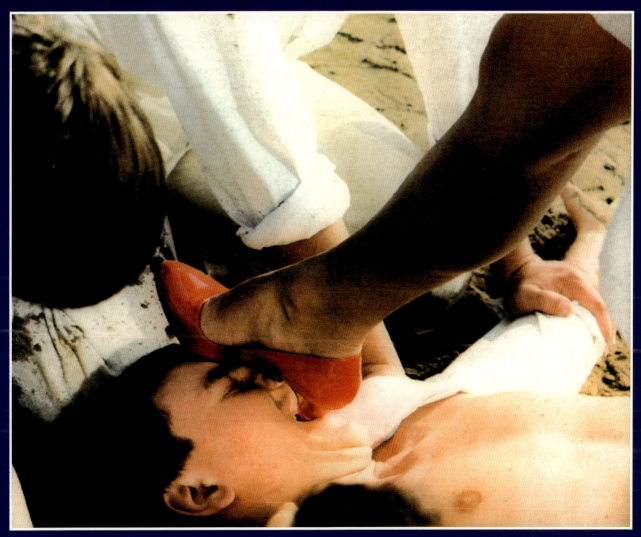

Tenebrae's pivotal flashback sequence.

Italian lobby sheet for **Phenomena**.

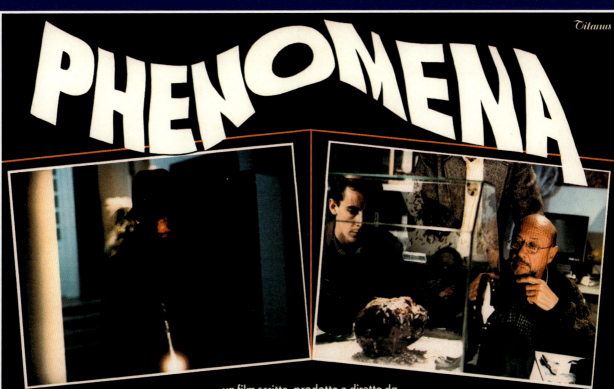

Inspector Geiger watches helplessly as Jennifer is left to wallow in the maggot-infested body parts in **Phenomena**.

An unsuspecting tourist, played by Dario Argento's daughter Fiore, expires amid an impressive display of shattered glass.

Inspector Geiger takes his revenge on the tyrannical Frau Bruckner.

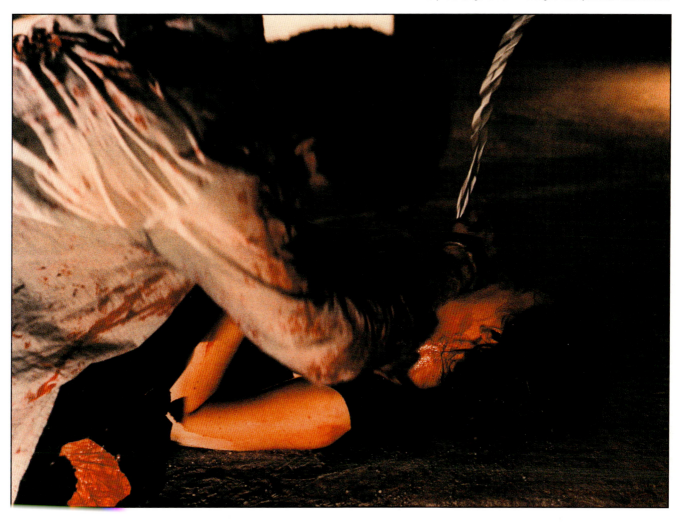

above and opposite: Jennifer Connelly plays Jennifer Corvino in **Phenomena**.

below: Cristina Marsillach in **Opera**.

Inspector Santini makes a desperate attempt to win Betty's affection.

The killer takes aim in a posed publicity shot from **Opera**.

The killer's sexual rival is dispatched in **Opera**.

Mira and Betty prepare to defend themselves against an obsessive opera fan.

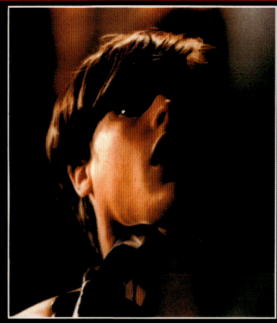

opposite: Look, don't touch: violence, impotence and fetishism come together in an image from **Opera**.

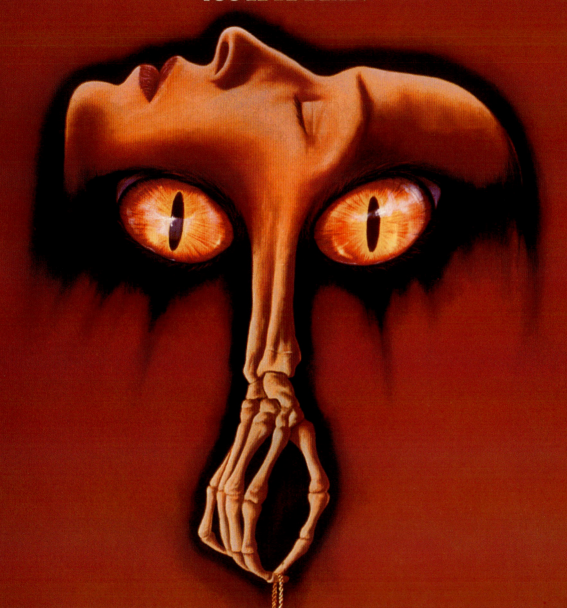

A FILM BY GEORGE ROMERO AND DARIO ARGENTO

"WHEN I WAKE YOU...
YOU'LL BE DEAD."

TWO EVIL EYES

THE CREATORS OF "NIGHT OF THE LIVING DEAD" AND "DAWN OF THE DEAD" GO BEYOND ALL EVIL.

STARRING HARVEY KEITEL · ADRIENNE BARBEAU · RAMY ZADA · SALLY KIRKLAND · MARTIN BALSAM

E.G. MARSHALL · JOHN AMOS · KIM HUNTER · MADELEINE POTTER   MUSIC BY PINO DONAGGIO   SPECIAL MAKE UP EFFECTS BY TOM SAVINI, LTD.

WRITERS GEORGE ROMERO, DARIO ARGENTO AND FRANCO FERRINI   DIRECTORS GEORGE ROMERO AND DARIO ARGENTO

"Still life's my specialty": Rod Usher at work in **The Black Cat**.

Rod's eerie premonition in a dream of pagan ritual.

Opera

Chris Gallant

ITALY

1987

Dario Argento's 1987 masterpiece **Opera** represents his first attempt at adapting Gaston Leroux's classic *The Phantom of the Opera*, the novel which a decade later would provide the basis for a more faithful (albeit considerably less successful) interpretation. While **Phantom** seeks to make unorthodox use of the conventions set through its heritage, **Opera** side-steps all precedents and expectations, effectively disregarding the rule-book altogether. The film stands somewhere between Gothic chiller and Cartesian whodunit, appropriating and negating characteristics of both: it never really provokes fear, the most superficial primary function of the 'terror-Gothic', nor is the identity of its killer sufficiently well concealed to be very difficult to guess, thus paying scant attention to what is traditionally the principal narrative driver of the *giallo*. And yet **Opera** is a singularly compelling film, one which engages at a level that demands rapt attention, inducing in the viewer a compulsion to follow the narrative to the very last frame.

The film begins with the raucous squawking of a truculent raven, one of the many that inhabit the stage of an avant-garde production of Verdi's opera *Macbeth*, due to open imminently at the prestigious Milan Opera House. The temperamental birds are disrupting the rehearsals of the production's equally unprepossessing star, Mara Cecova, who becomes so infuriated that she storms from the building in protest, only to be knocked down by a car. At a moment's notice, young understudy Betty is called upon to take her place on the opening night. In spite of her initial reservations, Betty is a huge hit, shooting to overnight stardom on the first performance. But her new-found fame has brought her an unwelcome admirer, a man who sneaks into the Opera House to ogle her through a pair of opera glasses, before casually impaling an usher who has interrupted his moment of adoration.

Later that night, the hooded psychopath intrudes on Betty's rendezvous with her gentle, sweet-natured lover Stefan. Taking her by surprise, he ties her to a pillar, taping rows of needles beneath her eyes to prevent her from closing them, and then forces her to watch while he butchers Stefan in front of her. But he releases her immediately, and she scurries off to confide in Marco, her director. While Inspector Alan Santini questions Opera House staff the following day, Betty tries to conceal her involvement, disturbed by the similarity between the night's events and the dimly remembered dregs of a recurrent childhood nightmare, which featured the same hooded man. But her tormentor strikes again without delay, binding Betty to a pillar in the costume department of the Opera House and staging another murder before her tortured eyes. That evening, she is forced to fight for her life when she is trapped in her apartment, an ordeal which brings about the death of her maternal agent Mira, who is shot through the eye as she tries to protect her young protégé. Betty escapes, returning to the Opera House, where Marco reveals that he has devised a plan to catch the killer, a plan which will be effected during the next perform-ance. Exhausted, Betty lies napping in her dressing room, when her childhood nightmare returns to haunt her once more. This time she remembers the whole scenario - the hooded killer dispatches a frightened young woman while Betty's mother stands watching, tied to a railing, clearly relishing every moment.

The next performance does indeed bring about the unmasking of the killer - Inspector Santini - but he escapes, badly wounded, and captures Betty once again. Imprisoning her in a storeroom, he reveals that he was once her mother's lover, slaying beautiful young women to appease her cruel sexual predilections, the memory of which has driven him to pursue her daughter in the hope that she too will be willing to play such dangerous

facing page:
Displaced expressions of desire: the
agonized stare of **Opera**'s sadomasochistic
heroine (Cristina Marsillach).

The avant-garde set of **Opera**'s *Macbeth*.

games. The ensuing showdown apparently ends in his death, but this too turns out to be a charade when he later reappears in the Alps, where Betty and Marco have retreated for a holiday. This final confrontation leads to Marco's death before Betty wins an uneasy victory over her maniacal suitor. As the killer is dragged away by the police, she wanders off into the fields, seeking solace in isolation.

At a purely superficial level, what is particularly striking about the iconography of **Opera** is the abundance of S/M imagery. References to sadomasochistic sexuality are frequent - Argento places it centre-stage, rendered in explicit terms for the first time in his career. There is a milieu of sexual abandon, a suggestion that these characters inhabit a social environment where, to put it crudely, anything goes: opera singers are known to be voraciously nymphomaniacal and film directors are widely acknowledged for their depravity. The dynamics of the bondage scenario are introduced gradually over the film's opening third. The first of the killer's memories shows the murder of a young woman in a fairytale-like stone turret, while Betty's mother (at this point unidentified) stands bound somewhere close by. Perhaps she is being forced to watch - it's difficult for us to tell, since she barely reacts to the killing. But the second flashback reveals more. The murder is more explicitly sexualised, the killer drawing back the sheet which covers his sleeping victim, stroking his gloved hand over her naked breast. The complicity of the bound woman is signalled this time - she actually hands him the murder weapon, a distinctive broad-bladed dagger, before allowing him to tie her hands. He strokes her fingers with affection before she strains against the ropes in ecstasy.

By this point in the film, the scenario by which a woman is bound and forced to watch the slaying of another has been described to the extent that we understand it as a sexual game, one in which the bound woman participates gladly, and in which her 'abuser' is a man who loves her. When Betty is forced to witness the murder of Stefan, therefore, the scenario is clearly coded as sadomasochistic bondage fantasy. The apparent difference is Betty's apparent non-cooperation, although the flashbacks have already planted the concept behind the killer's aim in all this - that Betty can be persuaded to collaborate, that perhaps she too might derive a secret pleasure from the S/M scenario, if only she would wake up to the fact. Some of the trappings of S/M culture are already present, Betty's costume for her part as Lady Macbeth comprising an absurd medley of chains, studs, jewels and dark black cloth, the overall visual effect being one which suggests avant-garde dominatrix drag. The stage provides a legitimate reason for having her appear in bizarrely fetishistic costumes. Even off the stage, Betty wears a ring which is shaped like a coiled snake, seen in close-up when she breaks free of the ropes following the murder of Giulia. Maitland McDonagh has suggested that her overnight success is in itself a bad omen, since it implies an unusually strong identification with the role of the manipulative, predatory Lady Macbeth.

The sexual politics of the S/M scenario are themselves a clue. It is often said that in a sadomasochistic 'scene', the masochist exerts the strongest control. It is the masochist who defines limits, places rules on the threshold of pain, judges the boundaries of trust. Suffering, for the masochist, is a well-balanced trade-off between pleasure and punishment, whereby the desire to feel guilty for experiencing pleasure can be indulged.

Ian Charleston as Marco, the opera's sadistic director and soon-to-be ousted contender for Betty's affection.

Pleasure is immediately punished with pain, the urge to feel guilt satisfied. Argento makes it explicitly clear that Betty's co-operation is central to her sexual violation. She must watch. The notion of control, most specifically Betty's control over her predicament, is explored more fully through a shift in roles. The killer is finally humiliated, dragged away in a state of total subjugation, cowering at her feet. His confession in the storeroom reveals his submissive position in the relationship with Betty's mother. While he played the role of the sadist in their sadomasochistic games, he was in a truer sense her slave. The confusion of 'dom'/'sub' roles is identified when he uses his hand to put out a lighted match, confessing *"I'm afraid of suffering"* - in many ways, his suffering at the hands of Betty and her mother seems to be very much part of the fun.

The exchange of roles is not uncharacteristic of S/M fantasy, in which revenge may sometimes play an integral part. The masochist may harbour the fantasy of turning the tables, dishing out punishment and humiliating the oppressor. The 'rape and revenge' film, with plots which revolve around the abuse of an initially defenceless woman who then murders her attackers, allows us to wallow in rape, torture, misogyny and murder guilt-free - the balance will always be restored to a comfortable zero, all guilty parties punished, all heinous crimes avenged. The inherent masochism of identifying with the victim provides us with a legitimate reason for taking gleeful pleasure in the violence she will perpetrate in the narrative's second act. But in many ways, **Opera** denies us that satisfaction. Santini is blinded in one eye by the vengeful ravens, suggesting a promise of greater vengeance to come (previous Argento killers have been decapitated, impaled, sliced up in a satisfying crescendo of violence). For once, Argento disallows the pleasure of payback - Santini is simply carted off by armed police, loaded into a helicopter and whisked away. His humiliation affords no comfort when we discover that he has, in a sense, been victimised all through the narrative, and even far into the past.

The confusion between on- and off-stage fiction becomes a crucial motif. The S/M scenario is, of course, essentially a role-play. Betty is an actress, more than a little accustomed to assuming roles. The events in Betty's private life become steadily more theatrical (her apartment becomes an unfeasible labyrinth in one particular scene, in which both she and the killer appear to become lost), while pointers provided by the production of *Macbeth* seem uncannily accurate. The murders themselves are highly contrived, staged in front of Betty like pieces of hysterical, avant-garde theatre. Role-play and real life become confused. As Santini observes, *"It depends on what you mean by 'reality'."*

The identity of the killer is clear from his first scene. He appears at Betty's dressing room door, gushing complements before assuming his creepy killer whisper (it's a dead give-away - small wonder it was papered over in the English dub). Later he is seen lurking suspiciously outside the dressing room, peering in through the door. The fact that the hooded psychopath turns out to be the handsome Inspector Santini makes him a far more eligible catch than the disfigured phantom of Gaston Leroux's original tale. In fact, he and Betty have been taking part in an oddly misaligned love story from the beginning. Seen in

Pleasure in punishment: Betty (Cristina Marsillach) finds herself caught up in a sadomasochistic scenario, in a scene from **Opera**.

Opening night nerves: Daria Nicolodi as Mira.

above:
Betty (Marsillach) is good - perhaps too good - as the scheming Lady Macbeth.

below:
Alma (Francesca Cassola) and Betty (Cristina Marsillach) share an understanding of the complications of daughterhood.

the context of Santini's S/M fantasy, his stalking of the young star is a heartfelt courting ritual. They are like two lovers who never quite connect. After watching him passionately slicing up her costume in the prop room, we cut to the awkward bedroom scene between Betty and Stefan. Stefan is simply too sweet, too compliant and accommodating. With his boyish, almost adolescent demeanour and his absurd partiality for jasmine tea, he is a dismal substitute for the more complex, passionate, sexually alluring killer. From their earliest scenes, Betty and the nameless psychopath have been identified as two people who are ultimately unfulfilled, the implication being that somehow they should fit together. After all, Betty's frigidity is only dissipated after she has been through the various sadomasochistic rituals with Santini. Only then is she liberated and ready to *"play it sensual"* in *La Traviata*.

Argento has frequently alluded to the film's position against the background of the AIDS crisis, arguing that it occupies a place in a social context in which sexual relations were made problematic. **Opera** is, however, his most heavily sexualised film, decorated with a mass of imagery related to S/M. The emphasis is on frustration - sexual relationships are devoutly desired, such desire manifested in the setting, the iconography and the sexual politics at play between the characters. The role of the sadist in the S/M scenario is often said to be purgative, the principal aim being catharsis. After scrutinising Betty's body through his opera glasses, giving rise to a sadomasochistic memory/fantasy, the killer is driven to blow off steam by impaling one of the ushers on a phallic coat-hook. All of his attacks from then on appear as displaced expressions of desire, attempts to purge and find comfort in catharsis.

The subdued colours, which become central to the visual style, suggest an emotional sterility, although Argento punctuates the surface of his fictive world with wild flashes of bright primaries. Betty is first seen amidst the muted sepia tones of her apartment, although as she settles back to listen to a recording of Verdi's *Macbeth*, the music which will accompany the ensuing drama, the red glow emitted by her hi-fi flickers about her face, its infernal hue anticipating the ordeal to come. The camera roams ceaselessly, at once expressing the film's concern with voyeurism and also drawing attention to the isolation of its characters - we see them, but we also see the space around them, frequently conspicuous in its emptiness. The sense of alienation is crystallised in the scene in which Betty approaches the building which houses her apartment, immediately following the murder of Giulia - movement shifts into slow motion, Betty looks about her in bewilderment, listening to the echoes of a child's crying, and again the scene is painted in dulled down, sterile tones.

But the film's colour-scheme, even if it suggests a superficial monotone, is consistently warm - only in the final scenes (of Betty's betrayal and ultimate victory over Santini) does it touch the aesthetic coldness of **Tenebrae** and **Phenomena**. The depth of human emotion is all there, all the more powerfully expressed in its displacement through colour, *mise-en-scène* and the proliferation of S/M imagery. Ultimately, perhaps this is what makes **Opera** so completely compelling and, for me at least, the most enthralling demonstration of its director's genius, the greatest film of his career. The game of cat and mouse, which the *giallo* traditionally employs as a tactic for generating suspense, here becomes the stuff of weird romance. With **Opera**, Argento delivers an exquisitely crafted masterpiece, a darkly romantic fantasy. It's a slice of sublime, sexualised *grand guignol*, one which makes the cloak-and-dagger antics of Macbeth and his cohorts seem hopelessly tame and anaemic in comparison.

It is worth noting that here the English translation of the film departs from the Italian. The two dubs contain considerable differences, often in dialogue which appears to be pivotal - the oft-quoted line in which Marco refers to his tendency to masturbate before shooting scenes on his horror films is in the English version only, while the line paraphrased above, in which Betty alludes to the sexual degeneracy of filmmakers, is exclusive to the Italian.

Cristina Marsillach in the stunning
Milan opera house.

left:
Dario Argento at work during the making
of **Opera**.

Two Evil Eyes

segment: The Black Cat

Chris Gallant

ITALY

1990

Dario Argento has frequently cited Edgar Allan Poe as one of his principal influences, never more so than through the inevitable hype that attended the production and release of **Two Evil Eyes**, the portmanteau project which houses his film **The Black Cat** (the other 'chapter' is **The Facts in the Case of Mr Valdemar**, directed by George A. Romero). But his attempt to pay off his debt to Poe is not without its complications. **The Black Cat** is an interestingly problematic piece of work. On many levels it fails to deliver, but Argento invests wholeheartedly in the themes which lie at the core of Poe's writing, lending them an inflection which echoes his own highly unique voice.

Rod Usher makes his entrance in a building decorated with the abject remains of dismantled corpses. A naked woman lies bound to a table, sliced in two by a huge pendulum-like blade. Usher is a professional photographer - as he puts it, *"Still life's my speciality"*, a talent which ensures that he is frequently called upon to document the horrors of the baroque crime scenes which are apparently commonplace in Pittsburgh. At home he develops the images born from this latest local atrocity, when his work is interrupted by a black cat, which has apparently been fostered by his lover, Annabel. Their relationship is uncomfortably distant. Annabel is delicate, sensitive, somewhat ethereal, while Rod is a rough, burly, brutish man who seems more at home with the gritty hyper-reality of crime scenes than he is with Annabel's talk of witches and superstition.

Over the coming days a strong antipathy grows between Rod and the cat, a situation worsened by Annabel's excessive protectiveness of her new pet. Driven to distraction by the cat's apparent hatred of him, Rod eventually strangles it, photographing its death throes to provide the front cover of his new book, Metropolitan Horrors, a lurid collection of his most revolting pictures. As Annabel begins to guess the truth, the couple embark on a series of violent arguments, one of which ends with Rod falling into an alcohol-induced slumber and dreaming of a Pagan festival, where he is executed for the murder of the cat. But when Annabel finally spots his book in a shop window, the strangled body of her much-loved pet gracing the cover, she immediately makes arrangements to leave him. Her plans are disrupted, however, when the cat makes a reappearance - an inky feline with identical markings (an obscure white patch on its chest, which seems to reveal the shape of a gallows) has been given to Rod by a woman in a bar. As he sets about putting an end to the animal once and for all, Annabel intervenes and comes to the rescue, causing a confrontation which ends in her death.

Confident that he can escape detection, Rod conceals the body behind a wall in the house and invents a story to explain Annabel's disappearance. But as his neighbours' suspicions are aroused, he becomes trapped by his increasingly elaborate lies. The situation is exacerbated by yet another reappearance by Annabel's cat, although this time Rod succeeds in slicing it with a saw, ensuring that his feline nemesis is finally laid to rest. A visit from the police appears not to phase him in the very least, until an eerie, distorted mewing is heard echoing through one of the walls. As the layer of plaster is hurriedly torn down, Rod's crime is finally revealed. The ever troublesome feline had given birth in Annabel's tomb, and its offspring are now feasting on the remains of their mistress. In the ensuing panic, Rod sets about making his escape from the house by climbing from the window using a rope. His plan fails however, and he slips, the rope tightening around his throat and killing him.

The Black Cat's fascination with the image is signalled from the very beginning. The opening credits are displayed over a shot of a pair of hands, which flick through a collec-

Madeleine Potter, as Annabel,
is directed by Dario Argento.

tion of Usher's photographs. These images become central to the film's iconography, reappearing throughout the narrative. They are stark, dispassionate, monochrome, setting up a contrast with the realm of fantasy and superstition which seems to be Annabel's domain, depicted through Rod's nightmare, which eventually establishes supremacy within the diegetic world. Although Usher at first appears to be no more than a hardened professional, his sensitivity to suffering diminished through experience, he is rapidly revealed as an obsessive, one who not only documents but seeks to engage with the world of 'metropolitan horrors.' In the opening scene he releases the lethal bladed pendulum in order to make his pictures all the more dramatic - even though he seeks to label them *"still life"*, he seems to be trying to take part in the drama of the killing through making the image live. And the cover of his book is a work of horror for which he himself is responsible - the death of the cat. His photography is more than mere social documentary. There is no distance, no objectivity in his attempt to wallow in the physical trappings of death.

Images are ambiguous. Photographs come to be confused with real people (in one scene, Rod fools his neighbours into thinking that Annabel is alive by dressing a dummy with her picture) and Rod's camera becomes an instrument for revealing truth when he is able to use it to 'hear' the secret accusations of Annabel's friends (he watches them mouthing the word "murder" through a telephoto lens). His gruesome documentary photographs seem to serve two primary functions: to provide evidence of past crimes and guilt (Annabel discovers the truth about the death of her cat when she catches sight of the book) and to provide a notion of the horrors to come. The images of death are harbingers of doom, spelling out Rod's ultimate place amongst them from the film's opening shot.

Fate is central to **The Black Cat**'s invocation of Poe. From early on, Rod's Pagan nightmare indicates that he is doomed. Again it is an image, a marking, that spells his fate - the noose which seems to be inscribed in the fur of the cat. *"Your punishment is written here in this white spot,"* Annabel tells him. *"That is your destiny."* The narrative largely depends on Rod's desperate struggle against his destiny for building tension. Following the cat's death, he is dogged by omens which all relate back to his imminent death. Fate, in the films of Argento, is so often suggested through the deployment of doubling in imagery, most famously instituted in the oft-quoted visual 'rhymes' of **Deep Red**. Here, visual echoes of this sort become central, particularly in the recurrence of the image of the noose. Similarly, where Argento ends Rod's nightmare with his being impaled on a phallic pike, he opens the immediately subsequent scene with a crane shot of familiarly pike-like pointed columns in a cemetery. It's not so much a premonition, more of an uneasy reminder, as though what was coded as fantasy in the previous scene has left an ominous remnant in the psychologised landscape of the material world.

Like all Poe protagonists, Rod is haunted, condemned to repeat, never permitted to leave the past behind. The cat refuses to disappear, no matter how many times he kills it, and Annabel's body won't stay hidden within her tomb. To repeat obsessively is to attempt a return to the past, which Freud famously associated with the death drive, the desire to return to inorganic life, in *Beyond the Pleasure Principle*. For Rod, repetition does indeed end in death, and for us the ultimate conclusion that his work, his crimes and his feverish obsessions have all served primarily as rehearsals of his own end.

Although Poe's influence can be detected over the expanse of Argento's career, the attempt to acknowledge this presents limitations. The opening of the film is promising and indeed the first half is impressive overall, but just as it appears to be getting into its stride, it loses its momentum altogether. Although Harvey Keitel's spectacular descent into depravity and inevitable self-destruction is wonderfully true to the character of the archetypal Poe male, many of the ideas suggested by the Poe texts remain only half developed and the references to stories such as *Berenicë* and *The Pit And The Pendulum* primarily present fragmented dead ends.

Although infinitely less elegant than **Opera**, **The Black Cat** nevertheless manages to conjure up an eerie sense of brooding anxiety with its prowling, low-level steadycam photography. Even when not directly assuming the cat's point of view, the camera frequently remains close to the ground, reminding us of the sinister feline's menacing omnipresence.

The Black Cat has its merits, but ultimately its shortcomings lie in the essential flaws of its conception, the constraints of the anthology structure allowing it insufficient space to fulfil its potential, and the story would clearly have worked better as a full-length feature. The result is something of an unfinished portrait, although it stands as a curious, unique and oddly enchanting piece nonetheless.

top:
Annabel and the black cat.

above:
Rod Usher (Harvey Keitel) pursues his
morbid creative instincts in his job as
a crime scene photographer.

Trauma

Adrian Luther-Smith

ITALY/UNITED STATES

1993

"I'm not sure why the critics didn't like this film? ...it really is a traditional Dario Argento movie. Asia plays the role of Aura so well it's frightening. I give this film the highest recommendation". [1]

*"A lot of old crap, for want of a more eloquent phrase, has been written about Dario Argento's **Trauma**, most of it coming from longstanding fans of his work. Much of this nonsense harps on about commercialism, compromise and insists that this is far from the 'classic', earlier films by the stylish Italian director... If this were the first feature by a new director [**Trauma**] would have probably received rave reviews".* [2]

These positive comments from Argento fans are taken from the Internet and indicate that since its almost universally hostile reception in 1993, **Trauma** is slowly building a credible reputation. Initially, the consensus of opinion amongst the director's usually loyal aficionados seemed to be that the film was not only a disappointingly weak entry, it was (worse still) a misguided attempt to appeal to a mainstream horror audience by toning down everything that made an Argento movie so special. Admittedly, it has its faults (which will be considered here in detail), but more than a cursory viewing also reveals certain quirky nuances and a depth of characterisation absent from the director's other work. Besides, it's certainly more stylish than most critics and fans have cared to admit and is undeniably lurid in the best Italian tradition. In the light of the general level of disappointment that has since greeted both **The Stendhal Syndrome** and **Phantom of the Opera** it is time to rehabilitate **Trauma**.

Before considering the film in any depth it is worth noting the background that led up to its production. Understandably frustrated by the poor distribution his films usually received outside his native country, Argento was apparently persuaded by his agent and close associates that making a movie in the U.S. would firmly establish his talent with a wider audience. For despite the critical plaudits and relative financial success achieved by **Deep Red** and **Suspiria**, many Americans had been largely denied the chance to fully appreciate this unique director's work on anything but wretched video releases. **Inferno** had received a scant theatrical release, **Tenebrae** was subjected to scathing cuts and insultingly retitled **Unsane**, whilst **Phenomena** was drastically abridged and crassly renamed **Creepers**. With this back catalogue of cruel disappointments to contend with it is perhaps no wonder that Dario eventually decided that enough was enough.

Not unexpectedly, many of the director's hardcore fans sneered at their Italian idol for 'selling out'. But what they failed to appreciate is that ever since the silent era filmmakers have been tempted by the allure of Tinseltown (or in this case, Minneapolis!). Just a sample of those who have made the transition reads like a roll call of distinction: Michael Curtiz, James Whale, Alfred Hitchcock, Roman Polanski, Paul Verhoeven. Besides, Dario had already acknowledged the power of the U.S. box office by including token American leads in his scenarios for **The Bird With the Crystal Plumage**, **Suspiria**, **Tenebrae** and **Phenomena**. The core scenes of **Inferno** took place in New York, and **Tenebrae** included opening shots in the Big Apple to give the movie transatlantic appeal. But still the obsessives objected; as far as they were concerned **Trauma** was doomed from its inception.

Ironically, the **Trauma** project and his cameo work in John Landis' **Innocent Blood** (1992) proved to be dispiriting experiences for Argento and he remains bitter about

top:
One of the killer's collection of severed heads.

above:
Brad Dourif's head is impaled on a spike at the bottom of a lift shaft, one of the Tom Savini effects deleted from the final cut.

facing page:
Aura (Asia Argento) and David (Christopher Rydell) become entangled in an oedipal romance.

working stateside: *"America can screw itself"*. [3] The highly committed director felt that he had lost control of his own movie during the arduous editing stage, with the producers apparently insisting that blood be kept off screen as far as possible in order to secure an 'R' rating. Such interference is perhaps proof that fans' fears about their idol losing creative control were well founded - and mockingly ironic given that the opening credits announce *'Dario Argento's* **Trauma***'*.

The director's legion of admirers also expressed (understandable) trepidation when faced with the uninspiring title chosen for his latest opus, mainly because it had been used so many times before. **Trauma** was a horror mystery from 1962; a retitle for Maurizio Pradeaux's *giallo* **Passi di danza su una lama di rasoio** (1972); an a.k.a. for James Kenelm Clarke's **Exposé** (1975); the export title for Leon Klimovsky's **Violaçion Fatal** (1977); an a.k.a. for Alberto Negrin's **Enigma rosso** (1978); a cheap slasher by Gianni Martucci (1979); and one of many titles for hospital horror flick **Terminal Choice** (1982).[4] There are certainly others too. **Trauma** also lacks the particular appeal of the director's previous movie monickers (although it's better than the execrable **Two Evil Eyes**). Although a seemingly minor detail, the negative vibe of a well-worn, somewhat clichéd title put many viewers off before they even sat down to watch the movie.

Yet more suspicion arose from the director's decision to cast Asia, his own daughter, in a lead role. This choice appeared odd, especially as the character of Aura is such an overtly sexual one, riddled with Freudian fixations. More disconcertingly, it seemed like a bad case of nepotism. Initially, Asia's performance does indeed come across as somewhat awkward. Her strong Italian accent can also serve to distance the viewer. However, Aura's European intonation is important when one considers that her family are 'outsiders' living in a society that demands homogeny. Indeed, Asia is matchless in a role that reveals many of her father's own neuroses. *"While I was writing the plot and the characters were coming alive I realised that the part of Aura would be perfect for Asia to play. Meanwhile as I wrote the story, Asia understood my choice. She was noticing that I studied her, spying on her. So when I told her she would be the protagonist of my film she already knew. However she has been really good. She really showed a side of her personality and character that even I wasn't aware of"*.[5] It is to Asia's credit that although her suicidal character comes across as understandably vulnerable, she is also seen to be provocative and at times assertive. The remainder of the cast handle their roles well; especially Christopher Rydell who expresses the level of determination demanded by male protagonist roles but also draws upon self-doubt, dependence and ultimately despair. Only Piper Laurie's over-wrought repeat of her dominant, deranged mother figure from **Carrie** seems incongruous.

The film's central mystery, namely what did a sixteen year-old runaway really witness on the stormy night her parents were apparently slaughtered, is the kind of sublime scenario the director had previously worked to masterly effect in **The Bird With the Crystal Plumage** and **Deep Red**. However, unlike these relatively cool, calculated examples of the *giallo* mystery, **Trauma** takes a different, almost hysterical approach to its conundrum and weaves in a romantic element that has also put off many die-hard Argentophiles. In fact, this is one of the most abnormal love stories ever committed to celluloid.

An example of Raffaele Mertes's beautifully textured lighting from the closing scenes of **Trauma**.

The opening murder scene, in which a chiropractor is beheaded by a black-gloved figure (later dubbed 'The Headhunter' by the media) using a specially built electronic guillotine, is shot with the director's customary taste for grisly detail. A rainstorm rages outside the chiropractor's office, increasing the tension within (and providing the first clue to the killer's modus operandi). In the *giallo* tradition, the killer's identity is kept from the audience, although the victim seems sure that she recognises her assailant. *"I never forget a face"*, she asserts, just before her unusual demise. At this point, the exact nature of the murder weapon is kept tantalisingly unclear. It's obvious that the victim is beheaded but the director wisely chooses to show several close-ups of the killer's device rather than allowing the audience a clear gaze at this efficient murder tool. And in a visual reference to his earlier so-called 'animal' trilogy and the finale of **Opera**, Argento shows two lizards being freed by the murderer.

The film's focus then shifts firmly to Aura, an anorexic and volatile sixteen-year-old. Having been saved from suicide by David, a young man, she becomes the pivotal character around whom all the others, including even the killer, must circle. Like many male protagonists in *gialli*, David is impotently caught up in murderous events beyond his own control. Indeed, one of the film's working titles was *Aura's Enigma* (which I person-ally prefer). Despite the fact that she is revealed to be a former drug abuser - and emotion-ally disturbed - it is Aura who takes the lead, with David falling increasingly under her spell. David's growing inability to focus on anything but Aura leads to the break up of his relationship with his pushy newscaster girlfriend Grace (played by Laura Johnson), his absence from work, a renewed drug dependence and his eventual imprisonment by The Headhunter - revealed to be Aura's deeply traumatised mother, Adriana. Only the intervention of an inquisitive young boy saves David from being Adriana's next victim. Significantly, the male 'hero' has placed himself in jeopardy by his fascination with an attractive, albeit youthful woman. A further indication of David's passive role in the proceedings is his inability to detect clues to the killer's identity. It is David's television station colleague Arnie (Ira Belgrade) who realises that The Headhunter only carries out murders during rainstorms. Interestingly, this is the same guy who advises our erstwhile 'hero' about the emotional vulnerability of anorexics, a key theme within the film (and a reflection of Argento's admitted revulsion towards food). Indeed, the director revealed *"...I was anorexic when I was young so I know what it's all about. I had problems with my mother and, until I lived alone, I always had an eating disorder."* [6]

Taking the anorexia theme a stage further, this is a film filled with characters that don't fit into what most people consider 'normal' society. Indeed, Americans might refer to them as weirdos. After all, the 'heroine' is a skinny, suicidal drug addict with a pronounced non-American accent. The 'hero' is an ex-junkie who, rather unbelievably, makes a living drawing sketches for a local TV station (how many sketches might they need every week?). At one point David casually remarks that he has to pretend to be *"a regular person"*. It is no surprise that David automatically makes a mental - and later physical - connection with Aura, especially when he notices tell-tale needle marks on her arms. Even before it is revealed that she is the killer, Aura's mother is also marked out as a 'weirdo', thanks to her paranormal activities as a medium, her pronounced Romanian accent and her decidedly haughty demeanour. Aura's physician, Doctor Judd (Frederic Forrest) acts suspiciously from the moment he appears - not surprisingly, since a typically Freudian revelation later reveals that Aura accidentally witnessed her mother and Judd making love.

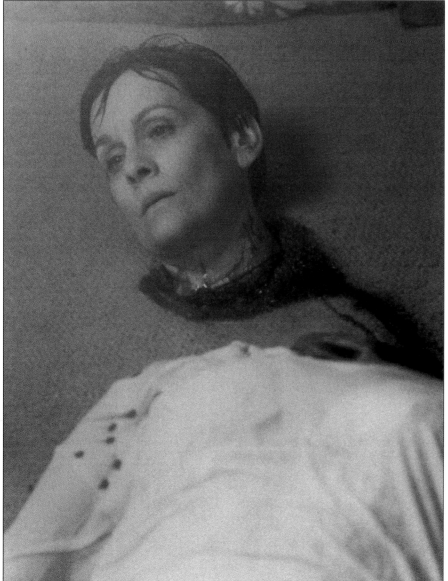

Heads you lose...
top: Maternal monster Adriana Petrescu meets a gruesome end.
left: The not-quite-dead head of one of **Trauma**'s beleagured nurses whispers one last clue.
above: Sinister Dr Judd dons a neck brace in subconscious acknowledgement of the danger posed by the prolific 'Headhunter'.
below: Judd dies to protect the killer's secret.

He wears a neck brace, which is nothing strange in itself, but in a movie where many characters lose their heads, it seems pregnant with meaning. Moreover, Judd has a noticeable speech impediment (making it more difficult for him to communicate 'normally'). Even more curiously, the unorthodox doc uses psychotropic berries to place Aura in a trance like state, from wherein she can recall her traumatic experiences. Hardly standard medical practice, yet necessary if he is to protect his lover Adriana from being revealed as the killer. As in **The Bird With the Crystal Plumage**, Argento suggests that some partners will go to extraordinary lengths to protect their lovers, even when they are aware that they are homicidal. Towards the film's conclusion, David tracks down former Doctor Lloyd (perennial screen loony Brad Dourif), now a junkie who hangs around in the seedy side of town. It turns out that Lloyd was responsible for the accidental beheading of Adriana's new-born infant - during a thunderstorm - and party to the electro-convulsive therapy treatment his medical team used to try to permanently erase the events from the distraught mother's mind.

The guilt associated with this incident leads directly to Lloyd's fall from grace, his drug habit and ultimately his murder at the gloved hands of the vengeful mother. His demise, via a lift shaft, recalls the climax of **Deep Red**. Intriguingly, Lloyd's dope supplier is revealed to be David's ex-girlfriend, Grace. A career woman without a conscience, Grace describes herself as *"a normal responsible person"*, and has no qualms about revealing the whereabouts of runaway Aura to the authorities, labelling her young rival as *"a manipulative little psycho"*. This acts to dissolve the line between **Trauma**'s more obviously disturbed, socially maladjusted characters and the apparently 'respectable' world of career professionals.

The inter-racial lesbian couple (one is Oriental, the other is white) who join the killer's list of victims are also worth noting. Compare this conservatively dressed pair with the overtly sexualized half-naked twosome from **Tenebrae**. The latter duo seem to pander to the heterosexual male fantasy of the sapphic slut (and surely Argento was aware of this?). However, times had changed and so had Dario's approach. The director's fans (mainly male and teenage) had another reason to look back to their idol's glory days, when the screen offered up provocative, scantily clad female victims as slaughter fodder.

As is the case in most *gialli*, the plot mechanics of **Trauma** do not hold up to close scrutiny. After all, in this smokescreen scenario two people who appear to die are later revealed to be alive (though far from well). This approach is perfectly acceptable, indeed, typically Italian, and one of the undoubted attractions of this lurid mystery genre. It is easy to see why such 'trickery' might alienate those viewers who expect more rational plotting and down to earth character motivation. Nevertheless, certain elements of the storyline seem contrived, particularly in the film's later stages. The screenplay was subject to major rewrites by American author T.E.D. Klein, having mutated considerably from the original story conceived by Argento, Franco Ferrini and Gianni Romoli, which perhaps explains the creaky exposition. Whether such tinkering was necessary for reasons of plot coherence or simply the result of interference from the producers is unclear but the end result is definitely no less illogical than most other Italian genre movies.

The film's detractors have also cited the deliberately humorous sections featuring an inquisitive young boy named Gabriel (played by Cory Garven) as evidence that the director was attempting to make the kind of crowd-pleasing film to which his talents were

above:
Artwork from the Japanese novelisation of
Trauma.

right:
Locked in her bedroom, Aura (Asia Argento)
watches as her mother disappears into the
storm.

David (Christopher Rydell) and Aura (Asia Argento) find themselves at the mercy of the Headhunter.

unsuited. This blinkered view conveniently ignores the fact that Argento has always attempted some humour to counterpoint the terror in his movies. For example, in **Four Flies on Grey Velvet** there is a self-deprecating, camp private eye who has never solved a case, and in **Deep Red**, there is much supposedly amusing banter between the two leads, Marc and Gianna. Granted, these comic interludes are not always successfully integrated into the proceedings but they clearly show that such accusations are mistaken. Eventually, Gabriel's boyish interloping proves to be more than a mere comical aside. In fact, the kid's eventual confrontation with the killer provides the film with a typically Italian brutal ending and the scenes of him being menaced by a matriarchal figure have the potential genuinely to offend moral majority types. These scenes are certainly not your average American cinematic fare, and the director had to fight the producers to leave them in the movie. And just as Asia's brief shower scene cannot fail to create a Hitchcockian smile, Gabriel and his binoculars are undoubtedly a peek across to **Rear Window**.

Regrettably, the film's score, by frequent Brian De Palma collaborator Pino Donaggio, is often unsubtle and intrusive. Although his impressive track record, which includes **The Sect** and **Two Evil Eyes**, shows that he has a distinct talent for scoring thrillers, here the horror motifs are somewhat inappropriate, whilst his attempts to introduce 'light' playful portions (such as a piece entitled *Butterflies*) are painfully unsuitable. Certain sections of the score seem to be out of syncopation with the events that unfold on screen. Thankfully, Donaggio's aural accompaniments are not all bad. A Morricone-influenced mix of discordant notes at the point where David is deliriously searching a suburban street for Aura works well, perhaps because of its source inspiration. Aura's theme, a melancholy but haunting melody called *Ruby Rain*, is enriched with an echoing female vocal. This dark folkish piece (for want of a better description) certainly adds depth to the film's emotional charge and helps compensate for some of the composer's more cumbersome contributions. It's especially effective during the moving scene in which David frantically but fruitlessly dives into a moonlit lake in the hope of saving Aura from another suicide bid.

Brad Dourif as Dr Lloyd.

Most intriguingly, as the film ends an unnamed reggae band perform, whilst a skinny young woman dances with them on a suburban veranda. As the skanking beat segues into Aura's theme once more, the camera focuses in on the dancing girl illuminated by bright white light. She shimmers in the incandescent glow, a wind machine causing her hair to take on a life of its own and join the dance. Except for some of the dream sequences in **Phenomena**, this whole scene is quite unlike anything else in the director's canon. Some critics felt this ending was entirely inappropriate.[7] However, I feel that it shows Argento was maturing as a filmmaker and willing to incorporate radically different elements into his work.

It is perhaps ironic, considering the wretchedness of Tom Savini's severed head effects, that the director was persuaded to tone down the amount of viscera shown on screen. Quite why Savini was hired again after his unconvincing work in **Two Evil Eyes** is anyone's guess, particularly when talented Italian technicians such as Gianetto de Rossi could have been brought along for the project. Unfortunately, the supposed Wizard of Gore's strikingly fake creations are a considerable distraction.

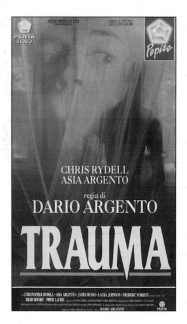

above:
Trauma's Italian video sleeve.

opposite:
Aura's psychotropic fantasy.

The director's disappointed fans have also objected to the rather audacious concept of having a victim's decapitated head whisper a clue to her assailant's identity. Yes, it's plainly unbelievable, but is it any sillier than 90% of what occurs in **Phenomena**? This is fantastical cinema after all. Bizarre images, such as the severed, screaming head of Brad Dourif hurtling down a liftshaft, are typical of the director's *oeuvre*. **Trauma**'s unlikely excesses are surely no more outrageous than the high speed camera Argento used at the conclusion of **Four Flies on Grey Velvet**? Or the ridiculous fountain of blood that sprays from Veronica Lario's obviously fake arm in **Tenebrae**? Or the CGI bullet-through-the-cheeks shot in **The Stendhal Syndrome**?

Although it is clearly very different from the director's previous work, **Trauma** has a particular 'look' all of its own. Raffaele Mertes' cinematography is deliberately softer, accentuating the romantic elements that underly the horrific. The lighting is more subdued, especially for interior shots. Argento illuminated: *"All the interiors represent the human body, the warped psyches of the characters, and are purposely cold, depressing and gloomy"*. The rain-soaked exteriors are lit with incredible precision, revealing just the right amount of visual information whilst concealing dark deeds in torrents of water. Indeed, the film can now be seen to be ahead of its time, anticipating the muted colour schemes and oppressive atmospheres conjured up in Hollywood movies like **Se7en** (1995), **8mm** (1998) and **Stir of Echoes** (1999).

The sheer number of tracking and Steadicam shots in this film is simply breathtaking. The camera seems to glide around buildings and actors with a sense of purpose, confidently moving the narrative forwards. This is a film with lots of movement. We are even forced to frantically follow Aura through a busy restaurant as she rushes to the bathroom to vomit. There are also shots representing a butterfly's point of view conceived using a lightweight micro-Louma crane the director previously employed in an air freshener commercial.

As is the case in all of Argento's films, there are a number of accomplished set pieces, such as the séance scene and subsequent murder of Aura's parents. Every single shot, including some circular pans around the table showing the attendees clutched hands and a glide across the top to focus on Aura's mother, combines to increase the tension. Simple effects, such as a tree lashing against the window and the shadow of torrential rain beating down outside, are well used. The subsequent murder in a cluster of trees is even more effective, particularly when viewed frame by frame via slow motion. As in **Deep Red**, an extremely attentive viewer can spot the murderer on screen but in contrast to that movie, **Trauma** presents this visual information amidst flashes of lightning, claps of thunder and torrential rain. The way these set pieces are presented contrasts with the more calculated, perhaps cruel approach to mayhem the director previously employed (although it could be argued that certain sections of **Phenomena** have the same level of intensity). It is also possible that the use of horror genre trappings (thunder, lightning) served to alienate the director's hardcore audience because they expected a different, perhaps more clinical approach.

Which brings us to the wonderfully grotesque scenes at the Faraday clinic. After classic point-of-view shots of the killer stalking a nurse, we see disturbed patients go into frenzy. David attempts to rescue Aura and is confronted by an elderly female patient forcefully intoning *"You did it. You did it. You did it."* The film's final set piece occurs in the killer's lair. David wanders into a room that has been converted into a sick shrine for Adriana's dead infant Nicholas. Here, Argento creates some of his most exquisite visuals, as our unlikely hero is suddenly propelled into a literal representation of the mind of a grieving but deranged mother. At this point we are shown, as before in **Deep Red**, just how disconcerting a middle-aged female killer can be when compared to the clichéd male psycho.

Unsurprisingly, the combination of oddball characters, a typically barmy plot and over-the-top visuals meant that **Trauma** failed to find its intended mainstream audience. But let's face it, no matter how hard he tried, Dario simply couldn't deliver a crossover movie and that's why his attempt to try something a little radical needs to be given another chance. During the fantasy sequence induced by Judd's psychotropic berries, Aura yanks open a videocassette and drags out the tape within. Those of us who purchased a full screen version of the film on VHS might well want to do the same thing because this is certainly no way to appreciate this lovingly crafted movie.

Thankfully, a letterboxed, stereo version was available for this re-appraisal and it hardly needs stating that seeing the film as it was intended is a revelation. Undoubtedly, a widescreen, Dolby soundtrack release on DVD is inevitable and this shamefully overlooked movie will finally win more of the appreciation it deserves.

Notes

1 - Per Rahlenbeck - Dario Argento - Master of Colors www.argento.vervost.de/argento/review_trauma.html
2 - Rob Dyer - Dario Argento - Master of Colors www.argento.vervost.de/argento/review_trauma.html
3 - Alan Jones - Cinefantastique, Volume 27 Number 8, Illinois, USA, April 1996,
4 - John Stanley's Creature Features Movie Guide Strikes Again - John Stanley, Creatures at Large Press, California, USA, 1994
5 - Argento interviewed by Andrea Giorgi in 1994 www.argento.vervost.de/argento/interview_trauma.html
6 - Mondo Argento - Alan Jones, Midnight Media booklet, Cambridge, England, 1996
7 - Tim Lucas - Video Watchdog No.22, Ohio, USA, March 1994

The Stendhal Syndrome

Robert Daniel

ITALY

1996

"Works of art have power over us. Great works of Art have great power" -
Alfredo, **The Stendhal Syndrome**

"The possibility of Art being deadly really interested me" -
Dario Argento, quoted in *Mondo Argento*

While on the trail of serial rapist and murderer Alfredo Grossi, policewoman Anna Manni succumbs to the Stendhal syndrome, a feverish reaction to the sight of great works of Art, in the Uffizi Gallery. Alfredo recognizes her and, after she experiences a number of art-induced hallucinations, kidnaps and rapes her. Psychologically scarred and spurning her boyfriend Marco, Anna returns to her home town and emotionally barren father. She paints disturbing pictures and recalls a childhood bout of the Stendhal syndrome when visiting the town museum with her deceased mother. Anna is again kidnapped and abused by Alfredo. She manages to defeat him and dumps his body in a river, but is convinced he stalks her still. Upon meeting art student Marie, a boy with whom she falls in love, Anna receives threatening phone calls from Alfredo. When his corpse is discovered and Marie is shot dead in a gallery, Anna's psychiatrist succeeds in piecing the mystery together and calls on her to impart some distressing news. Marco rushes to her apartment to check on her safety, and runs into her nightmare...

Giallo cinema was thirty years old in 1993. Argento's **Trauma** can be seen as a thirtieth birthday present to that sub-genre of thrillers that made his name. **Trauma** is not vintage Argento, however, thirty years of black gloved, leather trenchcoat wearing assassins killing to protect terrible secrets inevitably breeding familiarity with the form. When **The Stendhal Syndrome** was released to almost unanimous scorn, the worst appeared to be confirmed: Argento's aggressive vitality was evident only in retrospectives.

Remarkably, and perversely, **The Stendhal Syndrome** emerges as an Argento triumph. A compellingly bleak deconstruction, and destruction, of stylistic and thematic motifs in his beloved *giallo*, it stands as his densest, most apocalyptic and sexually transgressive film since **Tenebrae**. The premise is pure Argento: protagonists overwhelmed by great works of art plunge into madness. Yet, the syndrome is a genuine malady, deriving its name from the writer Stendhal (real name Marie-Henri Beyle), whose romantic countenance led to his being overwhelmed by beautiful works of art in Florence in 1817, an event he recounted in *Naples and Florence: A Journey from Milan to Reggio Calabria*.

The opening of the film recalls the beginning of **Suspiria**, whilst demonstrating a revision of Argento's visual style. While **Suspiria** intimidated Suzy Banyon with an aggressive colour scheme, this film is visually more subtle, those who label it boring for its lack of saturated colours misunderstanding the director's aims.

When Anna succumbs to the Stendhal syndrome in the Uffizi, the camera behaves in two separate ways. Calmly observing her in wide shot, when it focuses on her or adopts her point of view, the camera becomes erratic and quivering, giddy with movement. The chattering sounds which dominate the soundtrack are located within Anna, unlike some of the wilder aural exhibitions in other Argento films. The colour scheme hardly alters, and this calmer visual sensibility reveals him to be a more sophisticated director than his detractors suggest. Anna's hallucinatory walks into paintings are more controlled than Argento might have once envisioned, even if the first hallucination, in which she kisses a fish, is surreal and deliberately vague.

opposite top:
Anna Manni (Asia Argento) takes a phone call from the beyond the grave in **The Stendhal Syndrome**.

opposite bottom:
Hunter and hunted exchange roles as policewoman Anna Manni (Asia Argento) falls victim to serial rapist Alfredo Grossi (Thomas Kretschmann).

Dario and Asia Argento during the making of **The Stendhal Syndrome**.

Stendhal reacquaints Dario Argento with the possibilities of art on film. During the opening credits, paintings slowly crawl upwards on the right side of the frame. The square images are fitted together in such a way that they resemble a strip of film running through a projector. The relentless scroll of images creates a Stendhal syndrome of its own with this overwhelming barrage of visual information, exascerbated by Ennio Morricone's repetitive and haunting score. This is Argento's most impressive opening since **Opera** and a powerful metaphor for the dangers of art in his work.

Previous Argento killers have been afflicted by madness, which is aggravated by particular works of art. A childish picture of a violent scene in **The Bird With the Crystal Plumage** is a clue to Monica's psychosis, while **Tenebrae**'s first killer takes the book's theme of puritanical punishment as his inspiration. Art, in **The Stendhal Syndrome**, almost becomes a character within the film. Anna's debilitated reaction to the paintings in the Uffizi gallery allows Alfredo to kidnap and terrorize her. Argento's ambivalent attitude toward art is crystallized here: it can blacken the soul. Anna's affliction in the Uffizi obfuscates the investigation, allowing a murderer to kill again.

During the film's opening twenty minutes Anna's amnesia discolours everything with ambiguity. According to the logic of the film, when Alfredo appears reflected in the glass which covers a painting in her bedroom, the temptation is to label his image an hallucination. Argento permits the misconception for a number of seconds, as Alfredo hesitantly hovers behind her. But he grabs her - he *is* in the room - and proceeds to rape her. Once more, art distracts Anna from the danger that lingers two steps behind. Following the rape she begins painting herself. Her retreat into art is an ominous sign: Argento equates murder very closely with art. Murder is cathartic, unleashing repressed demons in the same fashion as the artist does when painting.

The narrational use of paintings here is another departure for the director. Before Alfredo first rapes her, Anna is troubled by a painting in her hotel room, in which the figures appear to chatter. The painting then melts away and she steps through it into a crime scene. Delirious and hallucinatory, this is challenging storytelling. She has stepped into one of her memories, recalling Inspector Manetti's order to travel to Florence and investigate an anonymous tip claiming the killer is there. After twenty minutes of minimal plot exposition, Argento provides the backbone of the story in a daringly surreal fashion. He has been accused of subordinating narrative to *mise-en-scène*, but here he cleverly fuses the two together. Later, in the police headquarters, where the preponderance of paintings makes it more closely resemble an art gallery, Anna steps into another canvas, this one depicting a waterfall. Another bold device, it presupposes the discovery of the killer's lair in a cave by the river and suggests a duality between Anna and Alfredo.

This duality is established further by the sexually violent art which defaces the walls of Alfredo's hideout, closely resembling Anna's disturbingly vaginal paintings. The twinning of victim and victimizer is complete when Anna becomes Alfredo after she kills him, disposing of his body so that she can murder in blissful ignorance. Yet the seeds of her collapse into psychosis have been planted years before. A flashback reveals the infant Anna suffering from the Stendhal syndrome in the town museum. She is doomed from the moment art overwhelms her.

A red herring is fished from the reservoir in **The Stendhal Syndrome**.

Anna (Asia Argento) seeks santuary in the house of her father (John Quentin) but is unable to escape the regime of patriarchal oppression.

The film is fascinating because of the way it deviates from and reconstructs thematic, stylistic and narrational traits that have become Argento trademarks. It can be seen as the first film in which Argento pays full attention to characterisation, characters in his previous films having been subordinate to themes and style. **The Stendhal Syndrome** is a character study, focusing on the degeneration of Anna's personality and sanity. For this reason, Argento's camera rarely leaves her side and most excesses of style can be located with her.

This time, Argento rejects many of the conventions of the *giallo*, most notably the fevered desire to conceal the identity of the killer. The film reveals its murderer at the very beginning, with a neat nod to **Deep Red**: Alfredo, like Marta, is framed amongst works of art, but this killer is not hidden in plain view, he simply stands out in the open. Preconceptions of Argento's work lead the viewer to disbelieve that he is the killer; he is revealed too soon.

The iconography of the *giallo* is largely absent. Neither Alfredo nor Anna don the *de rigueur* leather trenchcoat and black gloves of killers past, and the knife or straight razor is no longer the weapon of choice. The artificiality of this garb would be misplaced here. Alfredo's urbane dress sense, casual trousers and jacket, mark him as being sliced from a different cloth, nonchalantly murdering for pleasure, not killing to conceal past sins.

Rejecting the set-piece nature of previous killings, Argento makes rape and murder small, intimate and ugly. Previous slayings buffered their emotional impact on the viewer with a sheen of fantastic excess. This time, murder disturbs because Argento has stripped away his visual trappings. This is also the first time the director has depicted actual rape, rather than abstracting it as in the infamous bedroom murder in **The Bird With the Crystal Plumage**. Perhaps he felt the subject was too contentious to stylize and opted for a grittier approach. Whatever the reason, the numerous rapes and murders are disturbing, all the more so because of the subdued *mise-en-scène* and the emotional investiture in Anna.

Once the killer is exposed, Argento plays thematic and stylistic games with *giallo* conventions. One initially unusual scene has the killer approach a woman in the street and woo her with a red rose. The scene is shot entirely from his point of view, the victim-to-be talking directly to the camera. With Alfredo revealed as the murderous rapist, having a scene composed of one point of view shot could be mistaken for empty style. However, this sequence follows a scene in which Anna determinedly sprints through a park, as if fleeing from something unsettling and unseen. Although she is not revealed as the second killer until the film's denouement, what is interesting about the POV scene is how she can be suspected of being the face behind the gaze. Suspicions are laid to rest when Alfredo's face is reflected in the bullet which kills his victim, but the film's mirroring of Anna and Alfredo continues.

Asia and Dario Argento in the Uffizi Gallery.

Having revealed the killer early on, the film then kills him surprisingly prematurely. When Anna kills Alfredo, we return to more thematically familiar territory as she continues his work. The *giallo* protagonist is a haunted breed; troubled by a kink in a series of events that skews logic. Here Anna provides that kink by disposing of Alfredo's body so that she can delude herself into believing he is still killing. This guilt transference is common in the *giallo*, as characters blame their unspeakable acts on someone else. Moreover, **The**

Thomas Kretschmann as Alfredo Grossi in **The Stendhal Syndrome**.

Lobby sheets for the Italian release of **The Stendhal Syndrome**.

Anna (Asia Argento) loses herself in confusion and chaos in the closing scenes of **The Stendhal Syndrome**.

Dario Argento and director of photography Giuseppe Rotunno in the Uffizi Gallery.

Stendhal Syndrome reveals what might be about to occur following the climax of other narratives. In **Deep Red** Marc is left staring at his own reflection in a pool of blood and in **Opera** Betty goes decidedly off-kilter in a 'back-to-nature' finale. Anna's tale suggests what happens to these characters after the credits have rolled; none of them are left unscathed by their experiences.

The cinema of Dario Argento depicts a vicious war of the sexes in which gender boundaries blur, characteristics particular to one sex become confused and any victory is always compromised. Murder is eroticized and beyond this an uneasy tension between men and women leads to destruction. In **Four Flies on Grey Velvet** Nina marries Roberto and wants him dead because of his resemblance to her father. This murderous, borderline incestuous impulse stems from Nina's gender confusion, the result of having been raised as a boy by the deranged patriarch.

Sex is infrequent (it's a wonder procreation happens at all) and frigidity is common-place. Both Betty in **Opera** and Aura in **Trauma** are frigid, while Anna's repeated rapes instill in her a loathing of sex. Transsexuality is omnipresent, whether literal as in the uncanny 'dream girl' in the flashbacks of **Tenebrae** (she was played by a transsexual), or in symbolically 'male' acts of murder in which the leather coats and gloves disguise the killer's gender.

The Stendhal Syndrome is fiercely nihilistic with its fatalistic regard for male/female relations. The gun, an even more destructive phallic symbol than the knife, is now the killers' preferred weapon. Alfredo shoots his victims in the face, robbing them of their identity and leaving only their violated sex to recognize them by. Anna stabs Alfredo with rusty bedsprings, before partially blinding him (a symbolic castration), then shoots and bludgeons him to death. Men and women want to destroy each other in this film. When Alfredo rapes Anna, and again when she cuts her hand with broken glass, her blood drips onto a white fabric. This image of virginal deflowerment is demonstrative of the film's concerns: instead of marking Anna's initiation into the world of sex, they open the door to a domain of madness and murder.

Gender roles are frequently blurred. After being raped, Anna desexualizes herself by cutting her hair and, as her brother observes, she now looks like a boy. When Marco, her boyfriend, attempts to court her after months of abstinence, she switches the traditional roles and takes him roughly from behind, dry fucking him until he begs her to stop. For his part, Alfredo adopts feminine characteristics, revealing that it was he who provided Anna with the pivotal tip-off when he later demonstrates a voice disguiser which makes him sound like a woman.

Language is as bitter as any taunt in Argento's previous films. Alfredo beats Anna while demanding that she stays awake, and one of his past victims remarks, *"The sonofabitch was just like my ex-husband."* Language leads to further gender confusion when Anna encounters Marie, a Frenchman with whom she falls in love. Marie (who is an art student, so he's clearly doomed) is amused by Anna's observations that 'Marie' is a girl's name (and other characters make the same mistake), but her affair with him entrenches the male, Alfredo aspect of her personality. When they make love she takes charge, undressing him while he passively complies.

Thomas Kretschmann as serial killer Alfredo Grossi.

After killing Alfredo, she adopts a more feminine persona, donning a blonde wig and white dress in a guise of womanly virtue. Gender responsibility for murder in Argento's films is an infernal Mobius strip. The killers in **The Bird With the Crystal Plumage** and **Four Flies on Grey Velvet** are driven to murder through relationships with men, while the killers in **Tenebrae** and **Opera** kill to take revenge on the women who ridiculed them. **The Stendhal Syndrome** is the first Argento film to feature both male and female killers, crystallizing the dynamics between the sexes in Argento's work. The narrative is permeated by male evil. Anna joined the police force to escape her emotionally sterile, domineering father and Alfredo is the final catalyst for her slide into psychosis.

The Stendhal Syndrome reaffirms Dario Argento's directorial power and proves he remains a formidable genre figure. An underrated film, maligned by those who wanted the fireworks of **Suspiria** or the Cartesian comforts of a more straightforward *giallo*, its positive reappraisal is long overdue. Despite several misfires, Argento has not stood still since **Tenebrae**, and **Stendhal** is a radical testimony to his exciting cinematic growth.

The Nightwatch:
Argento positions the battered corpse of a rape victim, a disturbing memory which emerges from a Rembrandt painting.

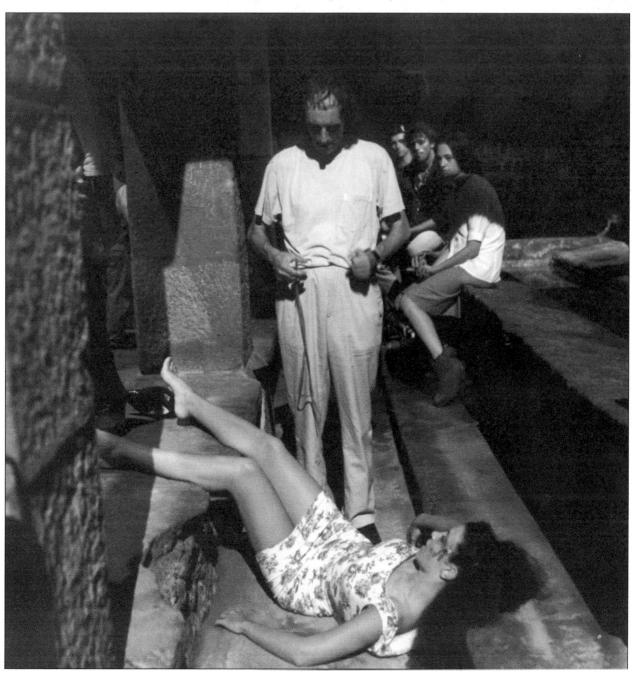

The Phantom of the Opera

Chris Gallant

ITALY/HUNGARY

1998

A number of film theorists have detected a rebirth of the Gothic in *fin de siècle* art, rife with end-of-millennium anxieties and cultural regression, one that closely mimics the emergence of Gothic narratives in the eighteenth century. The truth is, of course, that Gothic never really went away, but as theories on post modernism become steadily de-marginalized, demystified and scripted into popcorn pop culture, in some senses a new Gothic has surfaced, one which is characterised by a double self-awareness, a more intense fascination with its own construction, its own heritage or just, for added accessibility, its own cleverness.

The **I Know What You Did Last Summer** school of 'revisionist' slashers has dressed up its pop-Freudian nightmares in an indelicate slick of irony and post modern posturing, while more recently **The Blair Witch Project** minutely examined the material engineering of modern cinema while squarely positioning the film and filmmakers as recipients of nature's revenge on trespassing culture (how very pre-millennial). In the plethora of tidy, polished, neatly packaged *fin de siècle* Gothic 'revivalists', Argento's adaptation (and remake of remakes) of Gaston Leroux's *The Phantom of the Opera* makes for a rather perplexing, problematic piece of work. Here is a film that chooses to go against the contemporary grain in retelling the original tale in a radically revised form, and yet insisting on dressing it in the period garb of the novel. The trend in period Gothic which emerged in the wake of Coppola's **Dracula** had burnt itself out and **Scream** had by now inaugurated a new Gothic fad which demanded contemporary settings and a cast of hip, streetwise young things to do battle with their very modern monsters.

At a cursory glance it almost appears that Argento has taken an obvious and traditional approach to adapting classic Gothic for the screen. He's adapted it in period and has his version decked out in all the trappings we associate with heritage cinema. Firstly, he couldn't have chosen more reputable and time-honoured source material. He also rekindled his collaboration with Ronnie Taylor (who photographed **Opera** in 1987), a highly respected director of photography with an Academy Award to his name. Julian Sands provides an entirely appropriate lead - in spite of having featured in his fair share of horror flicks (most notably the **Warlock** series), Sands is better known for his work with the likes of Merchant-Ivory and the Taviani brothers. The expectation all this invites is that what Argento is offering is the stuff of high-art, high-culture heritage cinema - James Ivory does classic macabre. What we get, of course, is something altogether different.

Gothic is the literature of revolution, the early Gothic novelists having been prompted partly by the gruesome tales of revolt in France (the Bastille is the Mother of all bad houses). It is fitting, then, that Argento's **The Phantom of the Opera** seems to solicit the association with heritage cinema, only to rebel in characteristically contrary fashion. The first intimation of his revisionist agenda can be seen in the contradictions evident in the film's style. Lavish period décor and elegant gliding camerawork abound, recalling the sensibilities of French art-house, but the inclusion of contemporary experimental techniques is almost jarringly conspicuous. The bleached-out flash-frames of Christine scurrying through subterranean passages are wilfully post-MTV, conspicuously out of keeping with the period tone. One bizarre shot has the camera leap out of the catacombs of the past, breaking through layers of architecture and simultaneously slicing through decades, finally to emerge above ground, outside the Paris Opera House. Again, the effect is one of contemporary, self-conscious slick injected into the ordinarily tradition-obsessed world of classic literary adaptation. Would any other director choose to refer to Bosch with a CGI illusion of pot-

The course of true love ne'er flows easy...
the Phantom in morose mood with his
beloved.

bellied sinners, writhing helplessly in a man-sized rat-trap? The pre-Enlightenment preoccupations of dusty old Feudalistic paintings collide with the hyper-contrived techno-wizardry of the computer generation. Images like this serve to shock us out of the mind-frame of the conventional Gothic of the past and the conventional period cinema of the present, inviting an awareness that while Argento's **Phantom** might frequently draw on the heritage of that mode, this is anything but a conventional interpretation.

From the very first frame, Argento's adaptation signals its disregard for the tradition of Leroux's *Phantom*, its conventions and its most religiously preserved precepts. The opening scene sweeps aside the novel's carefully constructed back-story. The Erik of Gaston Leroux's original tale had a colourful and sinister past, leading back to a vocation as a master executioner in Persia, where he learned the sadistic tricks of his trade. Argento's Phantom (he is never named) is abandoned as a baby, left to float down the river in a basket during a ferocious storm. As he enters the catacombs beneath the Paris Opera House, he is rescued by a family of animatronic rats, who raise him as one of their own.

Years later, the Phantom haunts the corridors and auditorium of the Opera House, skulking in the shadows as young Christine Daée performs alone on the stage, singing to an imaginary audience, long after the crowds have left. Christine is understudy to the untalented and self-obsessed diva Carlotta, the current favourite of the Paris Opera. Enchanted by Christine's voice, the Phantom instigates a series of mishaps, aimed at enabling Christine to usurp the undeserving star. As she falls under his mysterious charm, Christine finds herself torn between the dark, passionate longings which characterise her love for the Phantom and her blossoming affection for long-time admirer Raoul.

The screenplay doesn't entirely restrict itself to the development of this eccentric love story - supporting cast are felled at calculated intervals (although if anything, the murders come across as distractions from the film's core narrative aims), and the authorities inevitably begin to show an interest in the Phantom's grisly carryings-on and set out to hunt him down. At the centre of all this, however, largely tying narrative strands together, is the character of Christine. I have already discussed Christine elsewhere in this volume, although here I shall consider the way in which the Gothic preoccupations which revolve around the heroine extend to other areas of the narrative.

Asia Argento's portrayal of Christine is loaded with all the masochism that is so characteristic of the Gothic heroine. Ann Radcliffe's *The Mysteries of Udolpho* has its female lead, Emily, swoon and weep perpetually, her fragile frame shaken to the core with every twist in arch-villain Montoni's cloak-and-dagger scheme. Similarly, Argento's Christine seems to lapse into unconsciousness at every opportunity, fainting on the stage more than once (*"The emotions must have been too strong for her,"* is the diagnosis of the resident doctor), and collapsing into helpless floods of tears as her boat takes her far away from the doomed Phantom in the final moments of the film. The masochism of the heroine, we gather, is so devoutly to be desired that it almost can't be counted as a handicap at all. In fact, it's a wildly romantic notion - she quite willingly becomes subservient, happily letting go of all inner strength out of her love for her man. Every classic Gothic heroine rides the emotional rollercoaster that is Christine's lot, weeping profusely over the handsome, charming hero-villain (Emily did in *The Mysteries of Udolpho*, driven to tears by Montoni, a cool, seductive bit of nastiness, not untypical of the Gothic mode's highly desirable villains).

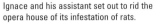

Ignace and his assistant set out to rid the
opera house of its infestation of rats.

Paulette's body is left to fester in the outer reaches of the Phantom's lair.

The heroines of Radcliffe and Leroux are, of course, a far cry from the post-feminist vision of resilient, adolescent femininity on display in contemporary horror cinema. But Christine is still, in a sense, part of a recent progression. She carries a history which exists beyond the boundaries of this particular fiction, since she is necessarily loaded with the connotations of Asia Argento's previous portrayals within her father's *oeuvre*. The casting of recognisable stars in the films of Argento is often pointedly referential, and this collaboration between director and daughter has seen such an unorthodox development that it inevitably collects associations along the way. When Christine stumbles through the underground passageways as she flees from the Phantom's lair, barely able to stay upright and close to lapsing into yet another swoon, one can't help but bring to the experience of watching her an awareness of her past incarnations. The Gothic heroine, as I have discussed, has a long and rich history, but here she inherits a more specific past through the referential significance of Asia. In **Trauma** she was also a victim, a delicate, waif-like anorexic, orphaned and thrust into a nightmarish realm of urban serial murder. One parent is horribly decapitated, the other cruelly imprisons her in the cellar, and her saviour through all this is an unstable man whose love for her compels him to study her like a biological specimen. In **The Stendhal Syndrome** she plays cat and mouse with a ruthless misogynist and finds herself tied to a mattress with wicked-looking wires, where she is beaten, cut and brutally raped. Across the three films in which her father has cast her in a leading role, she has been fetishized, objectified, explored. The Asia Argento who occupies the diegetic worlds of her father's cinema has become a persona which is entirely distinct from that on show in her other films. In **The Phantom of the Opera** she incorporates the history of that persona into her latest embodiment as the masochistic icon of the Argento universe. Needless to say, the superhuman emotional strength which has become a requirement for horror heroines in modern cinema is entirely absent. Christine is what the feisty female leads of the slasher movie aren't allowed to be - she is weak, a state of affairs permissible only because we're engaging with a fictional mode which belongs to the nineteenth century and operates by a different book of rules.

The victims, by and large, are a truly appalling bunch, thoroughly deserving of their fate. One of the most conspicuous flaws in the Argento/Brach adaptation is the way in which it submits to the contemporary horror film's requirement for a spectacular chase, a gory set-piece, something which provides the unambiguous genre brand. A number of characters are injected into the story as dispensable Phantom-fodder, identifiable as soon-to-be-victims from the moment they appear until they meet their inevitable (and inevitably spectacular) deaths. Largely these conventional elements displace Leroux's more chilling inventions (the deadly lasso, the pile of bones in the snow-covered churchyard), changes which have largely to do with Argento's radical rewriting of the Phantom's position as romantic lead. These victims are difficult to mourn. The portly paedophile Opera House Director is a case in point: in one scene he chases after a pre-pubescent dancer, pursuing her as far as the cellars, intent on evil-doing. As his unfortunate quarry hides in the darkness, he stands there, all red-faced, plump and repulsive, whimpering his nasty paedophile overtures, until the Phantom swoops down to murder and partially devour him, dispatching the old man in a cascade of Swiss chocolates, which he had been using as bait, to win the attention of his would-be victim. Alfred and Paulette are punished for

Hidden deep within the catacombs,
The Phantom (Julian Sands) resides
amongst his adoptive family of sewer rats.

their greed, falling foul of the Gothic avenger when they trespass into the catacombs, intent on stealing his hidden treasure. The two Opera House underlings represent a side of humanity of which the Phantom presumably disapproves. Their passion is one which finds its fuel in avarice and the desire for power. It is Alfred who first suggests the raid on the subterranean treasure-trove - Paulette's response is to loosen her clothes and offer repayment in kind, an instance of sex as commerce, which entirely contrasts with the Phantom's mournful longing for Christine. Later, Alfred must affirm his masculine supremacy, revealing the knife which he will carry into the catacombs for protection, ensuring that he will emerge from this adventure the conqueror (Paulette, for her part, will carry the stolen treasure in her knickers). They appear to have been written into the story to represent a variety of facile sexuality against which the Phantom may be compared. Alfred's masculinist posing amounts to little, of course, and when collared by the Phantom, he tries to pass the blame onto *"that whore Paulette"* before he is finally impaled on a phallic stalagmite. All this helps to paint a portrait of the Phantom as a 'good' monster, one who commits these ghastly acts of murder and mutilation only when his victims have pushed their luck so far that they deserve nothing less.

The horrors of the story seem largely to represent a revenge on a society which has become gluttonous and ignorant. The Phantom is a fanatical admirer of beauty, falling in love with Christine for the sound of her voice. But the Opera House itself is an institution corrupted by class snobbery, and opera is a pursuit for the bourgeoisie. The auditorium, stage and backstage are all rife with decadence - blissfully unaware of Christine's talent, staff and stars indulge their bloated egos behind the scenes, while the audiences eat, drink and gossip in the stalls, showing little regard for the activities on the stage. The Phantom is their collective guilty secret, abandoned by parents too impoverished to raise him. He lurks about the Opera House as an ever-present reminder of his exclusion from the world of the privileged and he haunts the inner Mecca of their decadent, self-indulgent realm, surfacing occasionally to punish them for their greed. The Revolution has been and gone, but social evolution has come full circle - the gluttonous rich inhabit the epicentre of art and culture, while the son of paupers is allotted a gloomy existence in the Bastille-like chambers of the caves.

While the Phantom of Gaston Leroux's novel delighted in finding the most eccentric and sadistic means for committing murder, the Argento/Brach screenplay seeks to absolve him as far as possible, something which his position as a romantic lead now demands (in the novel he never got anywhere close to seducing Christine and his love remained unrequited). His lair is bizarrely emblematic of the dichotomy which underscores his character - a lover of beauty, immersed in a world of the grotesque. Deep in the subterranean caverns, his home is adorned with the trappings of art and culture, littered with an eclectic array of ornate props, looted from the sets of the opera. The luxurious trinkets contrast absurdly with the damp, slime-covered walls, an incongruous *mise-en-scène* which appears to both enchant and repulse Christine. Quite how much of the Phantom's murderous activities she is aware of is left unstated, although what seems to disturb her beyond all else is his association with his co-inhabitants, the rats. In one scene she spies on him as he kisses and strokes them, removing his shirt so that the little vermin can scurry around his bare chest. It is no doubt fortunate that she has run away, having seen enough, by the time he unbuckles his belt and starts to loosen his trousers. Whatever happens next is mercifully left out of sight. The scene implies that after making love to Christine, he must enter into some form of sexual union with his adoptive family, marking the impossibility of reconciling his complete rejection of social order with Christine's place within it. In any

left:
Opera house workers Alfred and Paulette
plot the theft of the Phantom's riches.

below:
Asia Argento as Christine and Julian Sands
as The Phantom serve up an overtly
eroticized rendition of the tragic romance at
the centre of Gaston Leroux's original tale.

narrative from the Gothic period proper, this would have signalled the end of their romance, but Argento's interpretation has Christine continue to pine for him, and when she later returns to his world, she appears to accept him back, incestuous rat-sex and all.

The Phantom of the Opera is one of the most memorable of great horror tales. Much like *Frankenstein* or *Dracula*, it has become part of modern folk-mythology. As Argento himself has observed, few people have read the novel in comparison with the vast numbers who are familiar with the story, having heard it second-hand. His radical reinterpretation (it would be truer to say rewriting) thus borders on sacrilege. As such, **The Phantom of the Opera** is a daring and irreverent piece of work, one which is doomed to suffer intense criticism by the very nature of the foundations of its revisionist project. In spite of all its flaws, it is an oddly charming piece. Its contradictions, the pure incongruity of these disparate elements, make an uneasy combination. Argento has knitted together inspiration and influence from across an unusually broad spectrum, the fragments of which can barely be expected to gel. The result is a strange concoction, but one with an appealing quirkiness which is hard to resist.

Sleepless

Chris Gallant

ITALY

2000

To the admirers of Dario Argento, it might come as an unlikely twist that the celebrated master of 'dark dreams' would set out to make a whodunit perfect in its narrative construction, one in which the loose ends, loose structure, proliferation of tangents and narrative digressions familiar from his earlier *gialli* are excised, making way for a more concise, cohesive piece of work. It would perhaps appear to fly in the face of the approach which he has nurtured since the beginning of his career, one which favours the baroque and the dream-like over the narrative solidity of more conventional fare. The appealing quirkiness and lack of rigidity in the telling of the tale is this time replaced with something more tightly constructed. "Finally I am returning to make another *giallo* film," his director's statement begins, "the kind of thriller which is tight [in its construction], mathematical, organised with the precision of a geometric shape."

It wouldn't be difficult to read **Sleepless** as a perfunctory rerun of past successes, stitching the highlights of bygone classics together and honing the result into a more succinct form. The *giallo* is a formula almost entirely founded on the appropriation of familiar ingredients, its iconography, its narrative conventions and characters all pilfered from a whole variety of ancestors. The appeal is in the recipe, its constituent elements having been well worn in earlier traditions. **Sleepless** does, after all, bear an uncanny resemblance to Argento's 1975 film, **Deep Red** - similar story, similar characters, similar locations. Even the music sometimes sounds like a remixed version of the same score. Argento's stories have always borrowed from one another unashamedly, but **Sleepless** treads the line between recycling and reinvention more than most. The product of all this is a delirious work of art, a show of insane bravura the like of which we have not witnessed since **Opera**, made more than a decade before. All creative attention this time is focused on the enigma, the mystery at the core of this particular work. The solving of the enigma, the work of making sense of the puzzle - on all manner of different levels - is what lends the narrative its unity and its driven sense of trajectory.

The film's obsessive concern with the enigmatic is foreshadowed as the opening credits, displayed in white against the black screen, emerge and disappear in time with the rhythm of a Goblin score. NONHOSONNO, the only word to be spelt out in large red letters, appears before us.[1] The first noticeable idiosyncrasy is in the spelling: there are no spaces between the three words 'Non ho sonno'. There's a suggestion of ultra-modernity - to spell without spaces is internet convention, although the pounding rock score is more suggestive of another era, the Seventies perhaps. The joining together of the three words might also serve to lay emphasis on the musical sound they make when they're spoken: *"Non/ho/son/no"*. They're entirely made up of rhyming syllables. Argento has in the past favoured musical-sounding titles for his films: *Pro/fon/do Ro/sso*, *Te/ne/bre*, *Su/spi/ri/a*. Here the rhyme has a childish ring to it: "I can't sleep", an evocative phrase, perhaps suggestive (at a push) of childhood nightmares and infantile anxieties. "And what do children say when they want you to tell them a story?" Argento comments, "I can't sleep…"

The tale begins in Turin, 1983. Inspector Ulisse Moretti enters the home of the Gallo family, who occupy a pokey, working class apartment in a slightly grubby, impersonal building. Thirteen year old Giacomo is still spattered with the blood of his mother, whose mutilated body lies a few feet away, beside her the murder weapon, a musical instrument. The moment of violence has just passed, but the effects, we are left to contemplate, will remain for long into the future. Moretti's promise to the traumatised child says as much:

Death by *cor anglais*: the aftermath of Maria Gallo's murder from the opening scene of **Sleepless**.

"I'll find out who killed your mother, even if it takes the rest of my life."

It is seventeen years later - present day Turin. Angela, a prostitute, is going about her business, striking a deal with a new client over the telephone. Argento's camera moves about her face in extreme close-up, studying her in minute detail - the laughing mouth, the narrowing of the eye, the wry curl of the lips - grotesquely exaggerated, amplified through her thick, mask-like layer of make-up. The fragmentation of Angela's face recalls the famous credits sequence from **Vertigo**, but here the notion of femininity under the scrutiny of the male author evolves in a rather different direction. All is revealed in the following scene. She might have treated the 'deal' with mocking cynicism, but here the tone changes as she sprints across the bedroom, shrieking "No! Not *that!*" in response to her client's instructions. The shadowy figure waves a handful of banknotes at her, instantly securing her co-operation. But as he lies beneath the covers, eerily whispering in his sleep, she makes her escape. In her haste she knocks into a table, scattering its load over the floor, revealing a vicious-looking set of ornate weapons. Gathering her belongings together, she hurries from the apartment.

Already the film has established a train of thought around obscure perspectives. Moretti asks Giacomo to tell him "what you saw" (and the answer is, very little). Angela's eye occupies almost the entire screen while she is talking on the telephone although, frustratingly, we aren't allowed to see her entire face, given only partial, inadequate glimpses of the character we're looking at. She subsequently appears, naked and very much in view in the following scene, but her client seems to exist only as a shadow - there's barely even a suggestion of human form. Even his voice doesn't seem quite real, emerging from the bed as a low grunt. We can, however, see what he sees - a low-level point of view, as he searches for the prostitute in the darkness of the apartment, finally looking out onto the street to see her scurrying away.

And now there's a moment of relief. Angela is on a train, speeding far away from her ogre-like trick, his collection of knives, his dark apartment and his ugly sexual demands. Only now does she realise her mistake - earlier that night, as she hurried to pick up the spilt contents of her bag, she lifted a blue, plastic document wallet from the floor of the apartment. Inside is a collection of photographs, disturbing images of the mutilated bodies of young women, a selection of lurid press clippings and pages of notes, random, garbled scribbles. The moment of recollection when, in a flash, Angela remembers snatching the wallet from the floor, is accompanied by a deafening, thunder-like crash. Understanding comes to us at the same moment - it is too late to replace the pouch of incriminating papers. Angela's fate is sealed.

But there's more. At the back of the pile of loose pages lies a book. The bound volume appears to be a pre-publication manuscript, type-written, bearing the title 'Death Farm' and the author's name, John McKenzie. A flicker of recognition. To Angela, the details she has gleaned from scanning the first few pages of the novel are enough to awaken a dim memory - "the crimes of The Dwarf." The reference is obscure, vaguely comical, disturbing. On the soundtrack, the Goblins strike up a sinister, eerily melodic jingle. The legend of The Dwarf sounds like a fairytale, a notion reinforced when Angela calls Amanda, her trusted confidante, on her mobile phone. The tale of The Dwarf was a local sensation which she remembers from her childhood, a spate of murders in Turin and the arrest of the diminutive suspect. And now, seventeen years later, Angela has stumbled across the identity of the true culprit. Amanda must meet her at the next station, she insists, and together they will deliver the damning cache of evidence to the police.

Moments later, the telephone rings and our worst suspicions are confirmed - Angela's attempt to escape from the clutches of her client has failed. The killer is on her trail, whispering obscene threats. Only now does it occur to us that Argento's account of the evening's events has so far been elliptical. How long did Angela wait on the platform at Turin? How many stations has the train passed since she boarded? Could the killer already be on the train? Angela's compartment is empty and as she steps out into the corridor, the gravity of her predicament becomes clearer. She is the only passenger. The camp hysteria which follows - Angela's flight through the deserted corridor of the train, the short-lived intervention of the ticket inspector, the hyper-contrived lightening bolt which tears through the sky - draws together moments of nervous comedy and nightmarish intensity. Again, perspective is crucial. The killer remains unseen for the majority of the sequence. In breathtaking external shots of the moving train , the figure running in panic, seen through the windows, can be recognised as Angela. Nowhere in the entire train can we even glimpse her pursuer. She is eventually reduced to beating against the windows with bloody fists (having been relieved of one finger) while Amanda waits impatiently at the next platform, and as the train finally pulls into the station, Angela screams her last.

Gloria (Chiara Caselli) takes to the stage with her 'instrument', unwittingly providing the key to a macabre linguistic riddle.

Baffled by the non-appearance of her friend, Amanda boards the train, finds the blue envelope and alights just as it begins to pull away from the platform. Amazingly, she misses all traces of the bloodbath staged only minutes before. There's a suggestion of comedy in the manner in which the packet of evidence becomes pivotal in these opening scenes. It's the ultimate McGuffin (Hitchcock's favourite term for "the thing the spies are looking for", the coveted but otherwise superfluous object which becomes a superficial narrative driver in the chase or hunt). Almost self-consciously, it invites an awareness of its purpose as a crude hook upon which the film's suspense tactics are inelegantly hung. Even its appearance is faintly ridiculous - a shiny, electric blue plastic bag - the killer couldn't have chosen anything more conspicuous in which to hide his guilty secrets. Less loaded with connotations than the cheap, flashy red high-heels in **Tenebrae**, it nevertheless occupies a similar position in the film's aesthetic as an item of absurd, incongruous, camp iconography. Predictably, Amanda drops it as she steps out of the station into the rain-swept car park, tantalising us with the suggestion that further goose-chasing after the lost envelope will ensue. But that would be too easy. Only a few seconds later she goes back to fetch it, but even more bizarrely, her car now appears to be missing. After a heated altercation with a snoozing car park attendant, she finally locates it at the opposite end of the lot and finds shelter from the torrential rain. But within moments, the killer strikes again, putting an end to Amanda's meddling and retrieving the troublesome document wallet.

Not unpredictably, the police are at a loss. The killer appears to have left no clues, no evidence as to his identity. He has even taken the trouble to snip the tips from Amanda's fingers, removing the tell-tale traces of DNA lodged beneath her nails. The only potential clue, we recall, an expensive-looking fountain pen dropped in the parking lot, was quickly appropriated by the indolent car park attendant. Neither can the ticket inspector, recovering from a nasty blow to the head, shed any further light. The only significant detail he recalls is Angela's hysterical allusion to the killer dwarf. The bizarre reference to Turin's celebratedly weird murder case is enough to send Inspector Manni off to visit Ulisse Morretti, now in retirement. But Moretti's memory is failing him and his recollection of the case is incomplete. The infamous dwarf, Vincenzo De Fabritiis, once a writer of *gialli* under the *nom de plume* of John McKenzie, escaped the clutches of the police before he could be arrested. His body was discovered some time later, a bullet buried in his skull. The 'killer dwarf' may have escaped justice, but for Moretti, the case brought fame and promotion.

The police may be floundering, but the elusive maniac is hard at work. Having rescued his cache of murder souvenirs from the clutches of the intervening prostitutes, we watch as he flicks through the pages of 'Death Farm' (so creepy is this character that he even dons black leather gloves in the privacy of his own home, where surely fingerprints are of no consequence). His murderous impulses now freshly reawakened, his eyes fix on a paragraph in the black-bound volume - a line of childish poetry concerning the drowning of a cat. As the tenebrous fingers set about snipping a fragment of paper into a silhouette of the ill-fated feline, the rhythmic thud of a contemporary dance track pre-empts our entry into the multicoloured world of 'Zoo', a Turin discotheque. The camera cuts through the crowd to isolate a young dancer dressed up as a cat, complete with whiskers and pointed ears, hoofing it on the podium. This cat, we can easily conclude, is as good as drowned, and the following sequence sees her hunted down in the now deserted corridors of the club and dispatched in a tank of water.

Moretti's loss of memory is an entirely unexpected revelation. The foundations of the puzzle have been intricately laid, but now the narrative comes to a jarring halt, the trail to the mystery's solution having reached an apparently hopeless dead end. No knew knowledge can be extracted from the killer's most recent activities, all potential clues having been minutely erased, and the one man with in-depth knowledge of his past crimes is lapsing peacefully into dementia, his recollection of the case now reduced to a few paltry crumbs of insight. A new catalyst is called for and the drive towards resolution in this narrative is revived by the re-introduction of Moretti's key witness, Giacomo Gallo, now living in Rome.

Giacomo's return to his home city adds further emphasis to the film's insistent concern with the past, and most specifically with the childhood of its central characters. Giacomo's reluctant return to Turin re-establishes the relationships of his early adolescence. Lorenzo Betti, his childhood companion, has spent a number of years abroad, studying in the States, but little has changed, we gather, over the last seventeen years. Lorenzo's dependence on his wealthy family, which characterised his youth, due principally to continual ill-health, is now mirrored in his adulthood. Still unable to break away from the patterns

Echoing an image from the closing scenes of **Deep Red**, Gabriele Lavia faces his nemesis.

established in his childhood and having failed to attain independence, he is now an employee of his father's law firm. Imprisonment seems to be the key characteristic of this generation - Gloria, a beautiful, talented harpist for whom Giacomo harboured an infatuation years before, is now trapped in an apparently loveless relationship with Fausto, a man many years her senior. He's hopelessly incapable of relating to Gloria or her peers, a fact which becomes painfully obvious when he taunts Giacomo over the legend of the dwarf.

But Gloria's position in this narrative is never anything but secondary. The gendered perspective through which the tale is recounted is perhaps another aspect in which **Sleepless** recalls the *gialli* of the seventies. In more recent years, Argento's central protagonist has almost invariably been female and his films have largely given themselves over to the scrutiny of her sexuality, telling it from her own viewpoint. In particular, **Trauma**, **The Stendhal Syndrome** and **The Phantom of the Opera**, all of which have taken the director's daughter as their focal point, have relegated their male leads to a definite second ranking. Even though Chiara Caselli may be **Sleepless**' billed female star, occupying prime position in its promotional artwork, she doesn't appear until relatively late in the film and even then we see her consigned largely to the background. Giacomo's obsession with Gloria often appears to be an attempt to return to a less traumatic time, a time before his mother's murder - in fact he drops her without a second thought when, later in the film, a turn in events leads him to believe that the killer will never be found.

The subsequent reunion between Giacomo and Moretti draws us into an ever-thickening mesh of twists and counter-twists. The pairing of the young drifter and the elderly sleuth recalls the coupling of father/mentor/son figures in **The Cat O'Nine Tails** and **Tenebrae**, their progress towards the solution of a seemingly insoluble mystery motivated as much by the inherent chemistry of their relationship as it is by the need for closure through the unearthing of truth. The amateur detectives of the traditional *giallo* have often only the most obscure reasons for thrusting themselves into the dangerous hunt for the killer (does it normally fall to a passing witness to solve a crime?), but these two share a common, compelling motive: the murder of Maria Gallo remains unsolved. Neither is convinced of the guilt of Vincenzo De Fabritiis and they remain haunted while the solution continues to evade them. Moretti's obsession with the case is fed by guilt and a sense of having failed. Their relationship is thus one of ambivalence - although Giacomo never explicitly accuses Moretti, he once refers to his investigation as "a hobby".

Through Moretti's inquiries, we discover that the obsessive rituals of the killer's past crimes are being repeated: the placement of paper animal silhouettes beside each of the victims is a continuation of a pattern established in the early eighties. It's all part of a childishly macabre game, each of the victims bearing some resemblance, either physical or through some obscure wordplay, to 'the beasts of the field' which populate a little-known children's nursery rhyme. The rhyme itself, illustrated in a storybook, is found buried within the inevitable 'bad house', a decrepit mansion once occupied by the De Fabritiis family. The building may appear to represent little more than the sad carcass of a former family home, but the characters who once lived there have a disconcerting habit of cropping up like ghosts: Leone, once connected with the De Fabritiis family, now occupies a disused out-building in the grounds, reduced to downing cheap wine and shuffling about his former place of work as a drunken vagrant, and Laura De Fabritiis, devoted mother of the condemned dwarf, returns to the house when the authorities instruct that her son's grave be reopened (he's not there, of course, casting almost impossible doubt on the belief that he ever died). Like Moretti, Laura's inability to bury her past manifests itself in insomnia and she later tells him, "I haven't been able to sleep in seventeen years..."

Also common to the dwarf's original rampage and the bedlam breaking out in modern-day Turin is the killer's mysterious aural signature, which Giacomo recalls through a recurrent flashback to his mother's death. A strange, otherworldly hiss breaks the silence before each of the victims meets their untimely end. It might be no more than an eerie motif of the chaotic Goblin music score but, intriguingly, the characters on the screen seem able to hear it too. But, as Moretti observes, it is the difference between the two murder sprees which deserves the most attention - while the killings of seventeen years ago were centred around a specific geographical area, those of the present are spread across the city. And what, he ponders, could be the significance of the weapon used to kill Maria Gallo, a *Cor Anglais*? Clues come thick and fast, easily identifiable as such, but Argento allows his audience little or no time for deliberation, bolting from one disorienting set piece to the next.

Even more bizarrely, the dwarf himself manages the occasional appearance, in spite of having been dead and buried for almost two decades, emerging from the darkness just before Laura De Fabritiis plunges to her death. Amongst all this, the intervention of what has become a small army of sleuths can't prevent the scheduled slaughter of the remaining farm animals - a bunny-toothed fast food waitress is set upon in the lobby of her apartment block, her face beaten repeatedly against a wall until the offending teeth have been dislodged. And when Gloria dons animal costume for her performance in a local production of Swan Lake, her death seems inevitable. Giacomo hastens to the rescue, apparently arriving at the theatre in the nick of time, but as romance blossoms between our two leads backstage, we discover that the killer's true target, the production's star ballerina, is being garrotted in her dressing room, her head neatly severed in accordance with the requirements of the ghoulish rhyme. The rescue of one of the film's central characters is in itself a variety of subterfuge, for Moretti, who has so far taken the lead in this narrative and seems to carry sole responsibility for solving the puzzle, will that night suffer a fatal heart attack when he comes face to face with the murderous dwarf.

Once again, the narrative seems to have reached a premature state of closure and our

Gloria (Chiara Caselli) and Giacomo
(Stefano Dionisi) seek to enter the killer's
house, under the eerily watchful eyes of
a tattered billboard.

attempt to uncover the answer to the riddle through its characters has been frustrated. The central protagonist is dead, the last of the farm animals has been slaughtered, the killer's predetermined cycle completed and the villain's identity remains a mystery. Resolution seems impossible. And to compound our frustration, the reappearance of the dwarf offers us no greater insight. The premise on which the convoluted enigma has been founded from the very beginning now seems to have been negated. The narrative has defined its own particular brand of logic by invalidating the legend of the dwarf, dismissing it as little more than hysterical folklore. By allowing us to witness his return, the tale seems to have tied itself into an impossible knot. Our own bewilderment is voiced through the character of Giacomo who, having admitted defeat after the death of Moretti, is preparing to leave Turin and return to Rome. But the chain events which will lead to the killer's unmasking is, in a sense perversely, set in motion through coincidence and a chance encounter with Leone brings Giacomo back to the De Fabritiis mansion. There he watches, unseen, as the elderly drunk emerges from beneath the floorboards of his lair, clutching a clockwork toy, a dummy the size of a small man…

The discovery that the dwarf is a crudely constructed mannequin, operated by inserting a lever into its back to prime its clockwork innards, and the (misleading) revelation of Leone's guilt, constitutes a betrayal of the very principles around which the mechanics of this tale have been constructed. The narrative has so far been trading on an illusion of logic and linearity, only to confound us at the very end with a solution founded on sublime absurdity. We could never have guessed the existence of the clockwork dummy, and its introduction in the closing scenes of the film is imbued with a sense of the uncanny. As Freud described in his account of similarly devious manoeuvrings in Hoffmann's The Sandman, the substitution of a lifeless, mechanical object for a living 'character' necessarily generates a powerful sense of unease. One is reminded of Peter Neal's sly reference to Conan Doyle in **Tenebrae**: "When you have eliminated the impossible, whatever remains, however improbable, must be the truth." The 'improbable' in this particular case is a species of narrative cheat ('implausible' would be a more appropriate word), but it remains one aspect in which **Sleepless** is especially adept in its deception, in that it encourages our faith in an artificial construction of 'logic', only to demolish its own precepts at the very end.

Like **Tenebrae**, **Sleepless** repeatedly invokes crime literature, broadly acknowledging its antecedents as it playfully operates outside the rules of classical detective fiction. This time, the literary inspiration behind the violence has passed through more than one pair of hands. Within this fictional world lies another fiction, and within that another: the murders mimic those described by Vincenzo De Fabritiis in his unpublished novel, 'Death Farm', which in turn, with a nod to Agatha Christie, takes its blueprint from the grisly children's rhyme. The supremacy of the author has therefore become lost through the process of retelling. Unlike Peter Neal, this particular killer resists the temptation to write himself into a central role in the drama which erupts between the other characters. Almost in some senses an impostor, he is never as close to the violence or its consequences as Giacomo, Laura De Fabritiis or Moretti, whose lives have all been drastically altered by his actions. One is left to speculate on his inability to relate to humanity from within his own safe, artificial existence, reducing his victims to the level of crude symbolism: pig, cat, swan. Throughout, we gather, he has remained blissfully unaware of the misery he has caused. Equally, one might be tempted to argue that he occupies a position outside of the creative process. He didn't author the mystery himself - he simply cribbed it from a manuscript he once stole from Vincenzo De Fabritiis. But perhaps his true claim to creative input in this saga is his invention of the killer dwarf legend. Ever the petulant infant, he

Moretti contemplates the incongruous
geography of two killing sprees.

Max Von Sydow returns to the horror genre as retired detective Ulisse Moretti, the titular insomniac.

has fulfilled his desire to fabricate his own folklore. He has usurped Vincenzo as the teller of the tale, plagiarising his last, unpublished work and even weaving the unfortunate author into an expanded, more elaborate retelling of his own novel. Vincenzo the dwarf makes the perfect villain in the killer's invented legend. As Laura puts it, he's "a monster twice over: a freak and a murderer." Our discoveries in the killer's workshop in the closing scenes further consolidate his status as 'creator'. It is filled with artificial body parts - prototypes, failures and spare parts of the dummy dwarf. Disembodied hands and heads recall other creators of artificial men, Victor Frankenstein or Geppetto, whilst reminding us of the fantasies of fragmentation associated with schizophrenia, the disunity of identity. Resurrecting the murderous dwarf is the killer's own twist in the 'Death Farm' narrative, and he even goes to the lengths of removing Vincenzo's remains from his tomb. Does he steal the skeleton in order to reinforce belief in the dwarf's guilt? Or is it a form of tribute to the mystery's original author? When the police swarm through the house of horrors at the very end, Vincenzo's dusty remains turn up, carefully tucked away like precious relics.

Of course, not all the elements of this mystery story are within the killer's sphere of control. There are still the clues identified by Moretti, criteria which must be satisfied before a conclusion can be settled upon. Why were the first three murders committed within a single neighbourhood when, seventeen years later, the remaining victims died in places scattered about the city? Why did the murderer remain inactive for almost two decades, between 1983 and 2000? And then there's that ethereal hiss, which might mean something, or nothing at all, but which Giacomo remembers hearing at the scene of his mother's murder. The amiable alcoholic Leone may have been duped into fetching and carrying the midget mannequin, but not all the pieces of the puzzle fall into place until Lorenzo is revealed to be the orchestrator of the dwarf's supposed crimes. Moretti's observations only make sense when we realise that in 1983, the killer was a young boy, unable to travel about as freely as an adult. As Lorenzo himself laughingly points out, there's no evidence that he ever stopped killing after the death of Maria Gallo - he simply moved elsewhere, sent away by his father to continue his education abroad. And the mysterious sound, his signature, can be explained by the hiss of his asthma inhaler. The final clue, written on the hand of the car park attendant, whom he killed in the course of retrieving the missing fountain pen, is an irreverent joke, mockingly pointing to a suspect that his pursuers would never have considered: "I'm a bad little boy."

Just as the various signposts, our obscure clues, fall into place, so other elements on iconographic and symbolic levels begin to add up within the film's internal logic. The invocation of childhood has been central from the beginning. The actual solution to the mystery has been flaunted right from the film's opening scenes. The mischievous, motive-less crimes make a horrible kind of sense when Lorenzo laughingly refers to his rampage as "a game". The revelation that a child was behind the vicious killings of 1983 (another nod to Agatha Christie perhaps, recalling Crooked House) helps to explain why a series of such pointedly pointless murders should have been so meticulously planned.

The theme of childhood is expanded through the insidious distrust of elders, stemming in part from the assumption that the murderer of Maria Gallo must by now be approaching middle age. Not even Moretti is at all times above suspicion. When he turns up promptly at the scene of the nightclub dancer's murder, it can't but occur to us, even if he claims to have heard news of her death on the radio, that his very presence would suggest prior knowledge. Principally however, our distrust is focused on Lorenzo's father and our suspicions rest with him on more than one occasion. He appears to be the owner of the missing fountain pen; he's present in the bar where Lorenzo is poisoned (a subterfuge which Lorenzo planned himself) and he looms threateningly into view when Giacomo investigates the killer's house at the end of the film. His apparent rectitude and his air of sanctimony irresistibly invite speculation as to what disease and corruption might lie beneath the façade of righteousness.

Exactly how much of the truth Signor Betti has uncovered is never made explicit, but there emerges an uneasy complicity between father and son. Betti is a stiflingly protective parent, and not content with controlling his son's adult life, he takes responsibility for his crimes. His final words to Lorenzo, "It wasn't my fault," suggest their exact opposite, hinting at a sense of guilt. It is through his intervention that Lorenzo and Giacomo become separated following the poisoning incident in the bar. Giacomo represents a clear threat because he is of a different class. He's a drifter, most recently a waiter in a Chinese restaurant. Lorenzo, on the other hand, is a member of a more privileged class, for whom murder almost appears to have become a bourgeois blood-sport. But with their wiry frames and their angular features, the two childhood companions even look similar. There's a suggestion of homosexual desire in their camaraderie and Lorenzo almost seems to be inciting Giacomo's participation in Gloria's murder in the final scene. His explanation for luring Giacomo back to Turin, there to relive the horrors of the past, is that it forms a part of his intricate game. The return of Lorenzo's greatest childhood friend and his involvement in his mischief-making is a nostalgic indulgence, reawakening the memories of blissful infancy.

Sleepless' score, in particular, elaborates on this notion of the infantile. An eerie, music box-like jingle becomes the killer's principal theme and the word "monster" echoes on the soundtrack as each of the victims is sought out and hunted down. This killer even speaks in a monster voice, a low, hoarse rasp as he conducts business with the uncooperative prostitute in an early scene. The deep growl which emerges from his bed as she tiptoes out through the front door seems almost too contrived to be 'real' in any diegetic sense and as he skulks in the shadows of the bedroom, he looks like a hunchbacked ogre, completely unidentifiable as the statuesque Lorenzo, as he appears later in the film. In Argento's films there is traditionally almost a detachment of human identity from the symbolic where his murderers are concerned - it is hard to imagine Lorenzo as the shadowy assailant we've been watching. They are like two distinct entities. He has become the monster of his childhood bedtime stories - he is now, in a sense, one of the beasts of the field.

Perhaps related to this is the film's fascination with illusion. There's a suggestion of childish innocence, an infantile belief in magic, in the way in which illusion, both optical and aural, becomes a recurrent theme. There's the high-pitched coughing and choking which accompanies Giacomo's memory of his mother's murder - we assume it comes from her, since our attention is focused on her open mouth, but in fact what we're hearing is the frantic, excited coughing of an asthmatic thirteen year-old. On another level, the sound made by Lorenzo's inhaler becomes so heavily amplified, so stylised on the film's soundtrack, that it becomes virtually unrecognisable (to us anyway) for what it is. The illusion of the mannequin dwarf becomes central to the narrative's resolution, but elsewhere, the motif of optical illusion is repeated in less significant ways. We never discover the source of the strange reflections which look like flames, which distract Giacomo as he enters the killer's kitchen. And one can hardly argue narrative motivation for the bizarre combination of tilting photography and credits which scroll at an identical speed in the closing moments, creating the illusion that the words remain stationary.

The missing fountain pen is put to use, foiling the blackmail schemes of an avaricious car park attendant (Diego Casale).

left:
Pest control: a rabbit-like fast food waitress comes to a particularly messy end against the wall of her apartment block.

below:
The ill-fated bunny rabbit (Barbara Mautino) bares her teeth.

Angela seeks refuge between two carriages
on a deserted late night train.

These things are often conspicuously meaningless - but conspicuous nonetheless. They're strangely inconsequential building blocks in an endlessly deceptive construct.

In addition to the repeated echoes from the childhood of its central 'monster', **Sleepless** continually invokes its own past, its cinematic heritage. Just as the dusty, crumbling De Fabritiis house conjures up a sense of decay, of an era now corrupted by the passing of time, equally it can't help but recall the oddly beautiful ruined villa of **Deep Red**. The references to Argento's 1975 film, to which **Sleepless** is a virtual counterpart (or counterfeit, some of its critics have suggested) are churned out with nostalgia-fuelled abandon. The midget-sized clockwork dummy also made a brief appearance in the earlier film, while Dora's hideous demise pays tribute to that of Glauco Mauri. Giacomo's obscure perspective on his mother's murder provides a neat twist on the horrors which once unfolded before Carlo's eyes one family Christmas, and the film plays mind games with the casting of Gabriele Lavia, placing him in an identical role, but reversing the generation gap to add to the confusion. Looking elsewhere in the Argento filmography, **Sleepless** doffs its cap to **Tenebrae** - a tracking shot which follows a length of carpet to the setting for a spectacular killing recalls the famous Louma crane scene, and the murder of Maria Gallo, with its impotent eye-witness, echoes the gallery sequence from **The Bird With the Crystal Plumage**.

But there's something contrived, wilfully conspicuous about the film's attempt to conjure up a sense of the return of a repressed but unforgotten past. The iconography of 'pastness' is even slightly exaggerated. The stack of paperbacks which Moretti lifts from the De Fabritiis house, for example, all bear gaudy cover designs typical of fifties detective fiction, even though Vincenzo's novels were supposedly written in the early eighties. The majority of the interiors look dated, perhaps by three or four decades, much closer to the Sixties and Seventies than the ultra-modernity of **Tenebrae** or the archaic decor of **Inferno**. The characters and the environment they inhabit seem overwhelmed by the pressure of the past, and their world seems incapable of moving on, as though reflecting their psychology.

Dario Argento's output, over the last ten years or so, has frequently been alluded to as a departure from what was once a less compromising vision. But **Sleepless** delivers on every level on which other recent works have faltered. It's fitting, when one considers the subject matter, that it appeals to our infantile delight in fairytale violence, the spectacular, elaborate puzzles, esoteric symbolism. The director claims that creatively he feels rejuvenated, writing of **Sleepless**, "going back to making a giallo film has given me great pleasure and enthusiasm. I've rediscovered my original vein." Promotional overkill aside, the return of Dario Argento's perpetually confused, quasi-Freudian, infant-oriented monsters exhibits a vibrancy and energy which has been missing for some time. Only time will tell, but this latest success hints at a larger return to form, one that may yet see the long-time artisan of horror stepping in a new direction in the continuing exploration of his unique, extraordinary cinematic vision.

Notes

1.   This review is based on a viewing of the Italian language version of the film, the title of which is **Nonhosonno**.

A Door To Your Nightmares
Dario Argento on TV

Roberto Curti

The young, skinny, dark-haired man with the strange haircut and disquieting eyes, who came out of the darkness, seemed uneasy in front of the camera. His black stare, more often than not, looked away from the viewer, while he almost stumbled on words, clumsily looking for an apt term to describe what he had in mind. Yet his timid, low voice and unhealthy features indelibly stuck in the mind, and you knew that what he was talking about - fear, anguish, anxiety - was suddenly so close to you that you could almost feel it. It was just a matter of minutes.

"You are asking yourselves what 'Door To Darkness' means. Well, it means many things: to open a door that leads to the Unknown, to what we can't understand and therefore frightens us. But to me, this means other things as well. Sometimes it might happen - at least once in a lifetime - that we close a door behind us, and we find ourselves in a dark room, vainly groping for a switch, or trying to open the door again without managing to. And then we have to stay there, alone in the dark, forever. Well, the protagonists of our stories have just closed that door behind their backs."

In 1972, Italian Broadcasting Television (RAI) still retained an almost mythical aura, and allowed its huge audience to know and adore very few idols, since there were only two channels between which to choose for those who preferred spending evenings at home, snoozing on the sofa. Millions of people gathered in front of their TV screens for what was a sort of Pagan rite - prime time. Dario Argento was the new phenomenon of Italian cinema, and his first three films had been box office hits as well as slaps in the face for a somewhat sleepy market largely devoted to ever more baroquely titled spaghetti westerns. He gained the label - both flattering and misleading - of 'The Italian Hitchcock' (by the favourable press, a claim that the vitriol-dipped pens of the more conservative critics had turned into 'Italian would-be Hitchcock'), and his early successes paved the way for a plethora of bizarrely named thrillers. Argento, so apparently naïve and impulsive, almost dominated by the visions and hallucinations that took form in his savage and warped thrillers, was in fact acute and sly enough to jump the gun and conquer the small screen with his own blend of suspense and shock tactics. And it was the right move at the right time, since it allowed him to become an icon, a trademark, a household name - his painfully skinny appearance providing a vivid, startling contrast with Hitch's paunchy silhouette.

The series La porta sul buio consisted of four minifilms, each about an hour long, preceded by an introduction featuring Argento himself, appearing as the host who would take viewers by the hand and lead them through a 'door to darkness', as anticipated by the disquieting image behind the opening credits, and underlined by Giorgio Gaslini's brilliant jazzy score. "These are gialli, but of a new kind. They are different," warned the director, before the first installment, almost as if to prepare the viewers for a challenging experience. Despite his assertions, that was not the truth. At least, not completely. Working for the small screen, Argento had to face several problems: the first, and most relevant, was TV censorship. His films might have drawn crowds thanks to widescreen close-ups of razor wielding maniacs slashing female throats or elaborate slo-mo decapitations, but 'blood' and 'murder' were still words that caused many a thick eyebrow to knit and raise inside the RAI offices. Luigi Cozzi still remembers the long, exhausting meetings and the firm opposition Argento had to face regarding the murder weapon on **Il tram**. Instead of a butcher knife, considered 'too phallic', he eventually had to make do with a hook - which

above:
Promo artwork for the **Giallo** television series, designed by Jacomo.

is just as threatening, but at least doesn't resemble anything sexual... Another difficulty was the one-hour format. Argento had to trim his ideas of every loose end, in the meantime being careful not to go too far with his trademark visual excesses and 'gratuitous' bravura shots. Everything had to be at least digestible for a wider audience that was for the most part different from that of his movies. The results looked very much like the scripts Jimmy Sangster had conceived for Hammer in the early sixties: mechanical, claustrophobic thrillers that revolved around a sole turning point - the twist ending. All things considered, these 'new' *gialli* were not so different from the 'old' ones, if not for the Italian urban setting and some sparse peculiarities that came right from Argento's 'animal' trilogy. That's especially the case with the episodes Argento only supervised. In **La bambola** ("The Doll"), written and directed by Mario Foglietti[1], Mara Venier is menaced by a mysterious stranger (Robert Hoffman) who may or may not be a lunatic escaped from an asylum. Foglietti telegraphs every twist and turn of the plot, turning the movie into a boring affair, enlightened by the presence of a number of reliable familiar faces such as Umberto Raho, Pupo De Luca and Gianfranco D'Angelo (surprisingly, in a serious role, before the plethora of sex-oriented lewd comedies he'd been featured in starting in the mid Seventies). Luigi Cozzi's **Il vicino di casa** ("The Neighbour"), is explicitly Hitchcockian, telling the story of a young couple (Aldo Reggiani and Laura Belli) and their newborn baby, who move into an isolated house by the seaside, only to discover that their upstairs neighbour (Mimmo Palmara) has just disposed of his wife. Cozzi throws in his usual cinephile in-jokes with clips from **Abbott and Costello Meet Frankenstein** as well as his own debut feature **Il tunnel sotto il mondo**, and concentrates on suspense build-ups and jagged editing, making this a sort of dress rehearsal for his following film, **Il ragno** (1975).

Il tram, directed by Argento himself under the pseudonym Sirio Bernadotte, is an expansion of a long sequence originally conceived as part of the script for **The Bird with the Crystal Plumage** [2]. The main theme of the film is, once again, the human eye and its fallibility. A murder takes place inside a street-car: a girl is found dead under a seat after the late night shift. As commissioner Giordani (Enzo Cerusico) soon discovers, nobody noticed anything strange. Increasingly puzzled and upset by what appears to be an impossible murder, Giordani recreates the scene of the crime with the help of the passengers who travelled on the street-car that night and eventually arrests the conductor, who had previously made vain attempts at seducing the girl. But something does not convince him: obsessed by the thought of a vital detail that he might have missed, Giordani starts a personal inquiry with the help of his girlfriend Giulia (Paola Tedesco) [3]. They once again take the late-night street-car, where he finally solves the mystery. Unfortunately the black-gloved murderer is tailing them; he attacks Giordani and knocks him unconscious while Giulia is waiting for him, hidden under a seat, in the depot. The girl is about to fall into the hands of the killer, but is saved at the very last minute.

Alba Parietti in a promotional still for **Giallo**.

Since the very beginning, with the author revealing his fascination for impossible murders, such as those committed in a locked room (a nod to classical mystery writers such as John Dickson Carr, that will later be explicated again in **Tenebrae**), while lead actor Enzo Cerusico appears by his side, both surrounded by darkness, it's obvious that Argento opted for a 'safer' approach. He relies on a popular comedy actor (Cerusico) to build a central protagonist that could retain some of the characteristic traits of Sam Dalmas, Roberto Tobias and Franco Arnò, without becoming unsympathetic for the average viewer. Giordani, in contrast with Argento's heroes in the 'animal' trilogy, is not a completely passive observer, drawn into the mystery by his curiosity or uncertainties. Being a police inspector, investigating is his duty, and that makes him a somewhat 'distant' observer, and thus a feebly motivated hero, who comes to the fore only after the murder has been committed, and cannot therefore be emotionally involved. Argento solves the problem by drawing him as a stubbornly methodical, almost neurotic figure, full of tics and obsessed by the process of repeating, recreating, rethinking the events that lead to the murder almost as if life were a giant film-editing machine. Giordani meticulously gathers all the passengers on the street-car and asks them to repeat every move they made that night, in a vain and patently absurd attempt at reaching the truth. What makes Giordani keep on investigating, even after the apparent culprit has been arrested and put on trial, is not an urge to see justice done, but rather the feeling that 'something' is missing from his all-too-accurate reconstruction - and his insistence on solving the mystery almost costs him and his girlfriend their lives. Once again, the solution is uncovered almost by accident, thanks to an apparently insignificant detail that all of a sudden becomes vital. This duplicity is subtly underlined by the depiction of an anonymous Rome, shot in a semi-documentary style during the first half-hour, which suddenly becomes menacing near the film's ending, when, at night, the street-car strolls along its silent, empty streets. If Argento seems at first concerned with the most stolid and worn-out trappings of the whodunit genre - the 'usual suspects' (the old hag, the elegant gentleman, the slimy employee), police examinations and sparse instances of comic relief (such as the mythomaniac confessing: *"I stabbed her eight times... no, six... maybe five?"* *"Just once"* *"Er... once, sure, but veeery hard!"*) - when the film reaches its climax he finally opens his bag o'tricks. He renders every object insidious and disquieting (for example the streetcar's automatic doors, in a neat image that somehow predates **Suspiria**), introduces the murderer's POV shots (the scene where Giordani is attacked and beaten anticipates a sequence in **Four Flies**) and orchestrates a taut sequence set in the deserted streetcar depot, with Paola Tedesco being menaced by the black-gloved killer. But this time, the motive behind the homicidal hand is not to be found in madness, nor in a chromosome aberration, ultimately depriving the story of its subterranean transgressive potential. The banal truth is a simple crime of passion, which makes the murderer a decidedly forgettable figure, ultimately spared a spectacular, cathartic death and left merely to be arrested.

The last episode, **Testimone oculare** ("Eyewitness"), it is claimed, is based on a true story - another attempt at normalization? - and is introduced by a would-be-funny prologue with Argento himself interviewing a talkative private eye and having to endure the latter's macabre gossip. The film is signed by AD Roberto Pariante but was actually directed by Argento from a script written together with Cozzi. It is stylistically the most intriguing of the series: perhaps by now feeling more at ease with the format, the director allows his camera to go mad and pull out all the stops; not only does he employ his favourite pan and tracking shots, but he goes even further, experimenting with gimmicks like attributing POV shots to inanimate objects, weird camera angles, extreme close-ups *à-la* Sergio Leone, and even a wild psychedelic disco party that looks like a leftover from a warped mondo movie. The final effect is that of saturation, an overdose for the senses which, ultimately, cannot hide the fact that what we are watching is a rudimentary variation on **Diabolique**. Roberta Leoni happens to witness a murder while driving home at night (a girl suddenly falls dead in the middle of the road in front of her car; Roberta discovers that she's been stabbed in the back) but the body goes missing and nobody believes her tale. The story is decidedly routine, as is the persecution she is then subjected to by the murderer, who keeps tormenting her with mysterious phone calls in addition to all the other classic paraphernalia of the lady-in-peril theme. Roberta survives an attempt on her life and eventually barricades herself inside her own house while her husband (Riccardo Salvino) hides outside in the hope of catching the mysterious figure in a black raincoat. However, Roberta soon finds herself besieged by the killer. Here Argento reprises the claustrophobic quality of a central sequence from **The Bird with the Crystal Plumage**, in which Suzy Kendall is menaced inside a grungy building. Argento plays with the evocative power of dark empty rooms, shadows, stairs and doors, and makes the best use of Gaslini's obsessive parade of assorted percussion noises.

Since Roberta is a somewhat unsympathetic character, her tribulations aren't sufficiently interesting, especially given Marilù Tolo's weak performance, while it is worth noting how Argento depicts another decidedly warm figure - that of the commissioner, played by Glauco Onorato, who despite a lack of evidence still believes Tolo's words and finally comes to save her from the none-too-surprising villain: *"Did you really think we*

above:
Alba Parietti, one of the stars of **Giallo**.

policemen were so dim-witted?" Since Argento's police inspectors are usually mere ciphers (with the exception of Morosini in **Bird**, perhaps due less to the film's script than to Enrico Maria Salerno's magnetic personality), this might well be nothing but a sardonic in-joke. Ultimately, **Testimone oculare** is more interesting for the impact it had on the audiences than for its inherent qualities: it certainly was a far cry from the static, opulent Italian TV movies of the time, and its nervous, crafty, energetic approach to 'fear' really did cause a sensation. Argento's claim in introducing the episode: *"I wish you a good night... that is, if you'll manage to sleep"*, was a perfect catch-phrase, and the incredible success of *La porta sul buio* was the final element that made Argento a superstar filmmaker, a figure with the same ardent cult following as that of a rock musician, and eventually a 'mark', a 'product'.

Cut to: Autumn 1987. Argento's latest film, **Opera**, is about to open in theaters, despite a troubled production history and annoying vicissitudes with the board of censors. The director participates in a TV show called *Giallo*, hosted by Enzo Tortora, where Dario reveals his tricks to the public (for example, how to film a fly as he did in **Phenomena**) and supervises a series of svelte mini-whodunits (about twenty minutes each) called *Turno di notte* ("Night Shift") directed by Lamberto Bava and Luigi Cozzi, where viewers are invited to guess the identity of the murderer. Moreover, Argento presents nine short films, *Gli incubi di Dario Argento* ("Dario Argento's nightmares"), about three minutes each. Fifteen years later, many things have changed. Argento is an icon, his name appears above the title on films he only produced (the **Demons** series, for example), assuring big box office results, and his approach towards this new adventure on the small screen is decidedly more iconic.

If *La porta sul buio* followed the route of the *giallo* tradition, the contributions to *Giallo* were more reminiscent of his more recent productions, particularly Lamberto Bava's **Demons**, in courting the Eighties in-your-face approach to horror. Now more aware of his own charismatic presence, Argento plays up to his status of 'Master of Horror' with nonchalant irony. Aided by pale-faced Corallina Cataldi Tassoni [4], he hosts the short films, accompanying them with his unrelenting voice-over, often inter-cutting the action with his ominous features as he straight-facedly exposes the most ridiculous and jaw-dropping twists. His 'Nightmares' are simply grotesque sketches, completely devoid of plot or inner logic, aimed only at showing the audience a number of gloriously excessive gore effects, such as evisceration, eye violation, dismemberment and the like. It's an attitude that mixes an anarchic quest for gratuitous, gruesome details with an exuberant, childish enthusiasm towards the new wave of splatter horror. It's impossible to take seriously stuff like *Addormentarsi* ("Falling asleep"), in which a man is first stabbed in the neck in his bed by someone unseen and then mutates into a giant mouth that eventually devours his pet dog *à la* **Little Shop of Horrors**, to the sound of the Sex Pistols' *'Anarchy In The UK'*, or *Nostalgia Punk*, which ends with a young woman ripping her own belly and exposing her innards in a way that would have made Aristide (**Anthropophagus**) Massaccesi proud. That Argento's tongue is firmly in his cheek is evident also in *Il verme* ("The Worm"), where a pretty girl in bra and panties explores her ample body with a magnifying glass in order to find symptoms of a horrible disease (allowing for abundant close-ups of her buttocks and belly) before eventually gouging out her own infected eye, or *Amare e morire* ("To Love and To Die"), Argento's version of a porn wet dream - girl is raped by masked assailant; girl beds all suspects in order to... erm... collect evidence; girl stabs rapist. Other shorts pay homage to a Ray Bradbury story and (again) to Hitchcock (a two-minute remake of **Rear Window**!). *Riti notturni* ("Nocturnal Rites") is perhaps the most interesting of the lot, mainly because it seemingly draws inspiration from a project Argento was working on at that time, centering on urban voodoo [5], with an ill-fated young couple hiring a Haitian maid who performs strange rites in their flat.

If his goal was to upset the audience, once again he succeeded - lots and lots of angry phone calls from shocked spectators, plenty of media exposure, TV producers asking him to tone down violence. They might have been off-day Argento, but *Gli incubi di Dario Argento* still delivered the goods.

Cut to: The Present.

That was Argento's last foray into the world of the small screen, after a couple of remarkably well-made TV commercials. He has recently appeared as a host, commenting on a number of Alfred Hitchcock classics shown on a pay-TV network [6] - once again his name and Hitch's strictly connected, as if to confirm that old platitude. Looking suavely ethereal while recounting anecdotes on the Master, Argento is now every bit a middle-aged version of the Poe-lookalike we learnt to know so well. His path has taken an entirely different direction to that of his protégés Lamberto Bava and Michele Soavi, now devoted to the cause of TV fiction, and despite rumours of further television projects such as a series of hour-and-a-half movies based on E.A.Poe tales and another dedicated to contemporary urban thrillers, the director has seemingly lost interest in the medium.

Notes

1 - Foglietti co-wrote the basic story for **Four Flies on Grey Velvet** together with Argento and Cozzi.
2 - see Luigi Cozzi, "Dario Argento - il suo cinema i suoi personaggi i suoi miti", Fanucci, Roma, 1991.
3 - Tedesco later starred in Antonio Bido's pastiche of Argentian motifs, **The Cat's Victims** (1977).
4 - An Argento habituée, seen in **Opera** and **Phantom of the Opera**, as well as in Andrea Marfori's trash milestone **Il Bosco 1 / Evil Clutch** (1988).
5 - *"I have a story in mind. Just the basic idea, I'll have to develop it. Anyway, the film will be set in a tropical country, maybe the Caribbeans."* D.A. interviewed by Gianni Vitale, in Sequenze#7, Rosso Italiano 1977/87, Comune di Modena-Uff.cinema, 1988, p30.
*"I didn't do that film because in the meantime there were other movies on the subject, such as **Serpent and the Rainbow, Angel Heart, The Believers**. Voodoo was all the fashion, five films on voodoo in a short time, so I got nervous and eventually dropped the project."* D.A. interviewed by Giorgio Cianfanelli in Dark Star#1, 1989, p7.
6 - Argento had already experienced this role in 1984, when he supervised a cycle of horror movies shown on the Italia1 channel - among them, Romero's **Dawn of the Dead**, of course.

opposite:
Asia Argento as the fragile heroine in **Trauma**.

Nurses conspire to erase Adriana's memory in **Trauma**.

Aura bears witness to an act of revenge in the midst of a rainstorm.

top: Aura's enigma: the icy, austere interior of the killer's house provides the setting for an eerie publicity shot.

left: A voice from the past echoes in the mind of Adriana Petrescu (Piper Laurie).

above: Aura (Asia Argento) embarks on a search for her parents' killer.

below: Dario Argento at work in the two homes of the Petrescu family.

TRAUMA

Dario Argento directs Asia on location.

Anna finds catharsis in art in **The Stendhal Syndrome**.

this page and opposite:
Images from **The Phantom of the Opera**.

un film di **DARIO ARGENTO**

JULIAN SANDS   ASIA ARGENTO

il Fantasma dell'Opera

MEDUSA FILM PRESENTA un film di DARIO ARGENTO • JULIAN SANDS • ASIA ARGENTO "IL FANTASMA DELL'OPERA" • ANDREA DI STEFANO
NADIA RINALDI • CORALINA CATALDI TASSONI • ISTVÁN BUBIK • ZOLTÁN BARABÁS • DIRETTORE DELLA FOTOGRAFIA RONNIE TAYLOR (B.S.C.)
SCENOGRAFIA ANTONELLO GELENG • COSTUMI ÁGNES GYARMATHY • MONTAGGIO ANNA NAPOLI (A.M.C.)
MUSICHE COMPOSTE STRUMENTATE E DIRETTE DA ENNIO MORRICONE • SCENEGGIATURA DI GÉRARD BRACH e DARIO ARGENTO
TRATTO DAL ROMANZO "IL FANTASMA DELL'OPERA" DI GASTON LEROUX
UNA PRODUZIONE MEDUSA FILM REALIZZATA DA GIUSEPPE COLOMBO PER CINE 2000
PRODUTTORE ESECUTIVO CLAUDIO ARGENTO • REGIA DI DARIO ARGENTO
MD153

un film di **DARIO ARGENTO**

JULIAN SANDS   ASIA ARGENTO

il Fantasma dell'Opera

MEDUSA FILM PRESENTA un film di DARIO ARGENTO • JULIAN SANDS • ASIA ARGENTO "IL FANTASMA DELL'OPERA" • ANDREA DI STEFANO
NADIA RINALDI • CORALINA CATALDI TASSONI • ISTVÁN BUBIK • DIRETTORE DELLA FOTOGRAFIA RONNIE TAYLOR (B.S.C.)
SCENOGRAFIA ANTONELLO GELENG • COSTUMI ÁGNES GYARMATHY • MONTAGGIO ANNA NAPOLI (A.M.C.)
MUSICHE COMPOSTE STRUMENTATE E DIRETTE DA ENNIO MORRICONE • SCENEGGIATURA DI GÉRARD BRACH e DARIO ARGENTO
TRATTO DAL ROMANZO "IL FANTASMA DELL'OPERA" DI GASTON LEROUX
UNA PRODUZIONE MEDUSA FILM REALIZZATA DA GIUSEPPE COLOMBO PER CINE 2000
PRODUTTORE ESECUTIVO CLAUDIO ARGENTO • REGIA DI DARIO ARGENTO
MD153

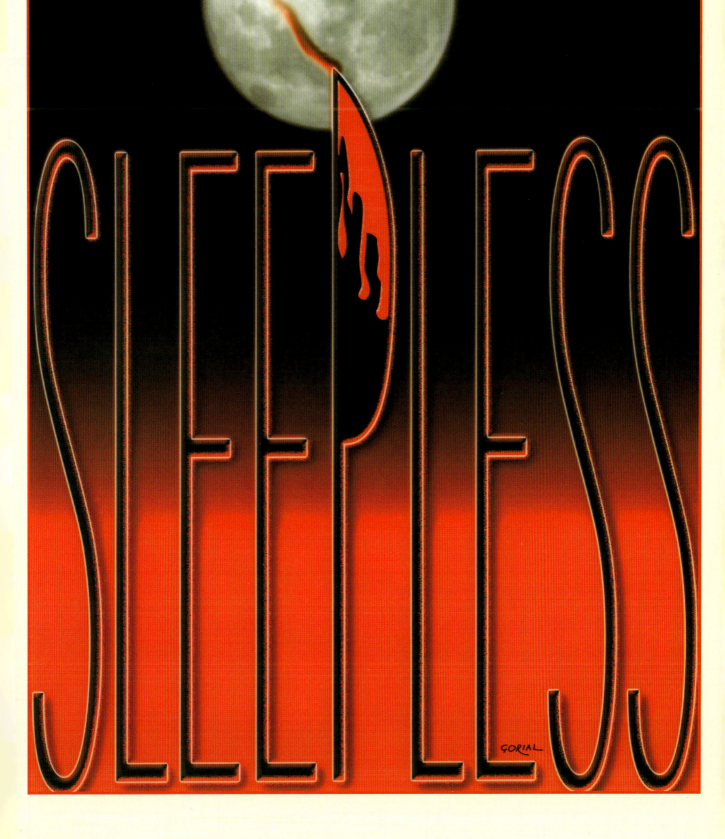

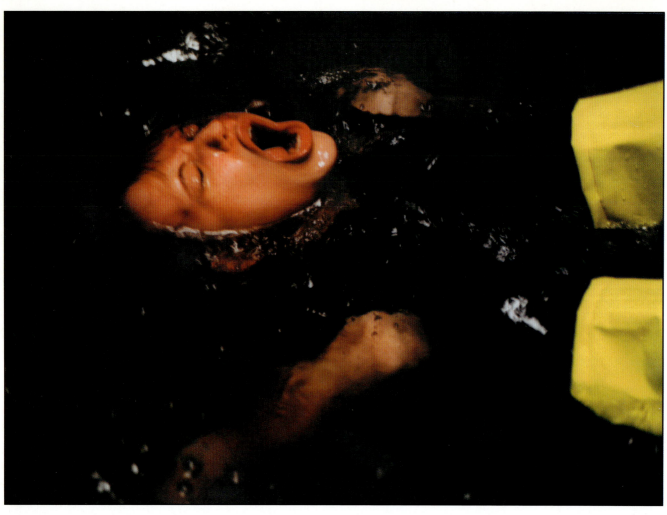

"In the tub for an icy swim and drowning her for just a whim": the grammatically bizarre nursery rhyme claims another victim in **Sleepless**.

An unexpected reunion brings about the death of Laura de Fabritiis (Rossella Falk).

A set of ornate weapons alerts Angela to the intentions of her ogre-like client in **Sleepless**.

Customer satisfaction takes an ugly twist when Angela's new client turns nasty.

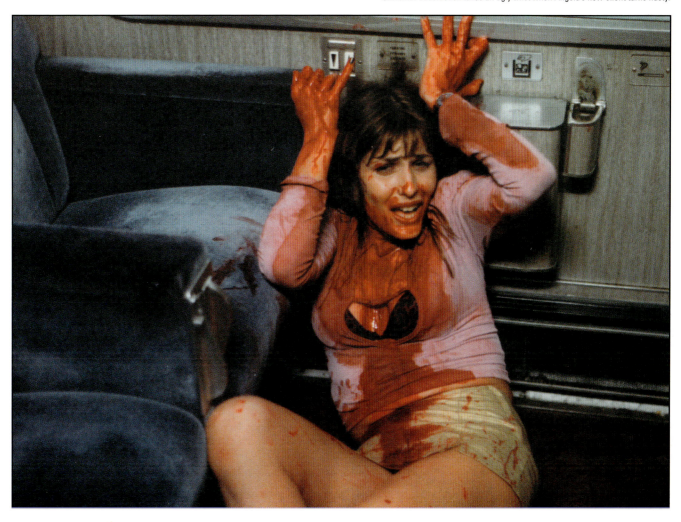

below:
Dario Argento supervises a grisly special effect for **Sleepless**' crucial flashback scene.

below:
Argento directs a scene in the killer's lair.

above: Promotional artwork for George A. Romero's **Dawn of the Dead**.

opposite top: **Sleepless'** bodycount escalates alarmingly as Avv. Betti (Gabriele Lavia) falls in the climactic bloodbath.
opposite middle left: Pass the parcel: the hunt for the elusive blue file draws Amanda (Conchita Puglisi) into the killer's clutches.
opposite middle right: Ulisse Moretti (Max Von Sydow) reinterprets the evidence of one of his former cases.

below: UK theatrical poster for **Demons**.

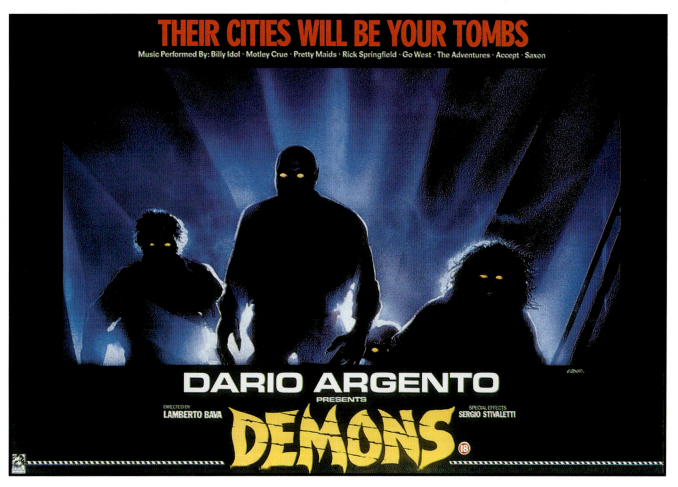

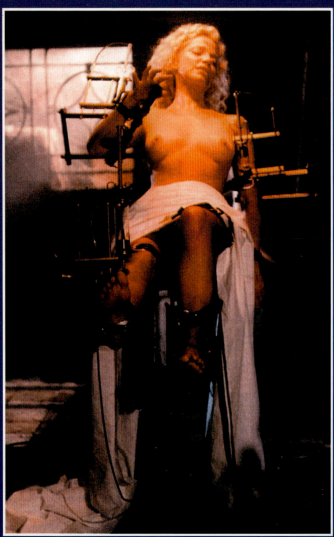

Produced by Dario Argento...

Chris Gallant

Dawn of the Dead (1978)

Since their first uprising in **Night of the Living Dead**, the rebellious walking corpses have grown in number, forming a formidable, seemingly invincible army. Social order has disintegrated amongst the living and many of the by now outnumbered survivors are fleeing from the official communes and rescue centres in search of safer unpopulated areas. Their number includes lovers Fran and Steven, who escape in Steven's helicopter, taking with them two army deserters, Roger and Peter.

The four find their oasis of security in a huge shopping centre, and set about purging their new home of its living dead occupants, sealing it off from the outside world. With whole department stores full of food, clothes and consumer junk at their disposal, they settle down to live out their isolation in luxury. But with the discovery of Fran's pregnancy and Roger's death from an infected zombie bite, their constructed world begins to disintegrate and this temporary security finally collapses when their kingdom comes under attack from a gang of bikers, who break open the doors, exposing their cocooned world to the threat of the outside.

To a large degree, Romero's masterpiece is carried by its wickedly satirical wit, the zomboid shoppers providing endless amusement with their crude mimicking of all-American consumerism. Unable to resist the alluring draw of the deserted mall, they gravitate towards it in their hundreds. Even after death, they never lose their affinity for shopping and simply continue to go through the motions. Innocently they mirror the materialist greed of their living counterparts - even though possessions are now worthless things, Peter and Steven are still willing to risk their lives to protect their shopping mall and its contents from the invading bikers.

The time that has passed since the beginning of the crisis in **Night** is left unspecified, but the living are certainly little better equipped to deal with the confusing upheaval of nature and society. They rapidly become desensitized, however, their survival dependent on attaining a near-impossible detachment from humanity and developing an ability to 'recognize' their undead predators as non-human and unworthy of compassion. There is something powerfully disturbing and utterly transgressive about the scenes of graphic, close-up mutilation. As one character points out, respect for the dead is now a thing of the past and these once-human creatures have become dispensable things to be shot at, disemboweled, beheaded and sliced up for the pure sport or hilarity of it.

The smug machismo of Peter and Roger is their only defense from the horror of their alarming new surroundings, even though it is exactly this macho bravado that proves to be Roger's undoing. Trained survivors, they frequently make the most of their difference from Fran and Steven and, even in death, Steven resents his exclusion from their tough, masculinist world. It is he who leads the zombies to where Fran and Peter have retreated, returning to their secret hideout as though expecting to be welcomed back into the fold of humanity. His last appearance is a poignant one as he shuffles through the door to their hidden apartment, inelegantly twisting his barely operable fingers around his revolver, still trying to be human as identity and consciousness are stripped away.

The pessimism which marked **Night** is less apparent this time. Fran's escape, with Peter and her unborn child, provides a fragile ray of hope. The unavoidable conclusion is

opposite:

left top:
Japanese poster for **The Wax Mask**.

left bottom:
The torturous embalming process used to convert human victims into wax effigies in **The Wax Mask**.

right:
Poster for Michele Soavi's documentary **Dario Argento's World of Horror**.

top:
Cartoon flesh-ripping from **Demons**.

above:
Producer Argento poses for a publicity shot with director George A. Romero, on location for the shooting of influential horror film **Dawn of the Dead**.

that escape is ultimately impossible and there is no such thing as a safe place - humans are just zombies waiting to happen, thus the living carry their inevitable fate with them wherever they run to. It is to their credit that the film's most resilient characters are unwilling to accept the hopelessness of their situation. They cling to the possibility of salvation as they try desperately and unsuccessfully to reach an understanding of their apocalyptic future.

Demons (1985)

"You don't think it's a horror movie, do you? You know, I just hate them," complains Cathy as she accompanies her friend Cheryl to a mystery preview at Berlin's Metropol cinema. Unfortunately for Cathy, it is indeed a horror movie, and as the lights dim, a projector beam cuts across the auditorium, regurgitating an imbecilic stream of Gothic clichés and half-baked horror setpieces in what looks like one of the most unbearable genre films ever made. Its audience is apparently greatly impressed, however, quaking with fear as the 'characters' on the screen fall into the grip of demonic possession and slice each other up with carving knives.

In all the excitement, one member of the audience is herself possessed, sprouting vicious-looking teeth and talons, vomiting bile of various colours and developing some truly horrendous boils, which burst and ooze profusely. Panic-stricken, the terrified patrons make for the nearest exit, only to discover that they have been walled in. As the demonic contagion spreads, Cheryl and her companions find themselves increasingly outnumbered with little chance of escape.

"That's the last complimentary ticket I ever accept," warns one of the dumb teenagers in a moment of sublime understatement. And that about represents the level of intellect we can expect from the characters in **Demons**, prompting one to wonder whether any of them are really worth saving. Personalities fall into two categories, representing what must surely be the ultimate in crude gender stereotyping: the boys tend to stand around being stoic, while the girls run to and fro screaming, waving their hands in the air. Tough, resilient horror heroines may have been the vogue at the time this film went into production, but Cheryl somewhat misses the mark as a feminist icon, spending the majority of the film trailing behind her man, whining *"I can't, I can't!"*, or shrieking *"Do something, George!"* as the demons attack.

Neither does **Demons** score any points for technical genius. Relying entirely on its *coup de théâtre* tactics and Sergio Stivaletti's colourful special effects, much of the film is made considerably worse by its poor photography and sloppy, vulgar lighting. Director Lamberto Bava has fallen a long way since **Macabre**, his brilliant debut, and shows none of the talent for grandiose Gothic horror that was the stock-in-trade of his father. Although a considerable hit in its day, this tragic rehash of **Dawn of the Dead** will surely fade into well-deserved obscurity in the fullness of time.

Demons 2 (1986)

Re-appropriating all the most popular components of the original, the team behind **Demons** sets out to prove that there is enough banal drivel to be milked out of this idea to fill another whole ninety minutes of screen-time. Taking its blueprint from Cronenberg's **Shivers**, **Demons 2** lifts all the gory mayhem from its predecessor and relocates it to a modern apartment block.

Selfish, neurotic good-time girl Sally is having a birthday party in her parents' apartment, but just as the celebrations are getting into full swing, the obnoxious adolescent is possessed by a demon which has crawled out of her television set. Very soon her guests have been reduced to a horde of toothy, slime-covered monsters, and when they finally manage to escape from Sally's locked apartment, they set out to spread their plague through the rest of the building.

The film's principal *raison d'être* is Sergio Stivaletti's messy special effects. In fact this outing is even more heavily laden with blood, goo and tearing flesh than the original, all held together with the laboured predictability of the creakiest script that Argento has ever put his name to. This time the narrative is entirely shapeless, never really getting past plot point one, and its writers have inadvisedly tried to inject a token strand of character through the inclusion of a few scattered 'human interest' subplots, mostly involving families, pregnant wives and doting husbands (*beyond* boring).

Having said that, the film does serve up the occasional pleasant surprise. The scene in which Sally blows out her birthday cake candles while her friends repeatedly chant *"Happy Birthday"*, blissfully unaware of the pandemonium which is about to break out, is wonderfully ominous, while the scene where the soon-to-be-possessed puppy watches corrosive, toxic demon-blood dripping from the ceiling provides at least a flicker of mood and suspense. At least in these scenes Lamberto Bava manages to prove that he isn't entirely devoid of talent and indeed the whole film is, technically and stylistically, markedly superior to the original.

It's difficult to imagine how ninety minutes of pure, uninhibited hysteria can be so utterly tedious, but **Demons 2** seems to fail on virtually every level. Plans for an official third installment fizzled out when 'Cathedral of Demons' metamorphosed into Michele Soavi's **The Church**. We can all breathe a sigh of relief, therefore, as Bava's crazed, hysterical but chronically boring monsters seem finally to have been laid to rest. Let's hope they stay put this time.

Above, below and opposite top: Gory japes from **Demons**, directed by Lamberto Bava.

below: A scene from Michele Soavi's **The Church**, one of the more interesting of Argento's production ventures.

A vision of demonic copulation from
Michele Soavi's **The Church**.

The Church (1989)

Soavi's second feature after **Stagefright**, his conventional but stylish entry in the slasher genre, **The Church** comes across as a rather over-ambitious piece of work. Considerably overplotted, its narrative convolutions have a tendency to lose themselves amongst its bizarre but somewhat clichéd religious imagery.

The film opens with the slaughter of a mediaeval village of witches, whose bodies are piled up in a huge pit and then kept in place by a great Gothic cathedral, which is erected over the mass grave. Leaping forward into the twentieth century, we observe the flurry of activity which now centres around the holy monument: restoration work is taking place, a fashion shoot is being conducted in the aisle and a pack of school children is being given a history lesson beneath its sacred arches.

But the new librarian, greedy for divine knowledge, starts nosing around in the cellar, accidentally releasing a horde of demons. Centuries-old devices grind into motion and the only entrance is mechanically sealed. One by one the cathedral's occupants are possessed and very quickly the entire building is overtaken by the forces of evil.

The expression 'narrative economy' is presumably unknown to the writers of **The Church**. The storyline meanders aimlessly and endlessly: plot points and revelations emerge to wow the participants, only to be forgotten minutes later, and characters seem to drift in and out, none of them ever becoming established as central.

But there are, of course, the setpieces: a young woman is spectacularly nailed to the door with a section of iron fencing, an elderly tourist pulls her husband's head off and uses it to beat against the bells, and a biker escapes from the cathedral through a gap in the floor only to come face to face with an oncoming underground train. All of this is served up with considerable panache, the most impressive scene of all saved for the finale with the destruction of the church.

Although somewhat crippled by its decidedly ropy script, Soavi's film derives some appeal from the inventiveness of its imagery and the quirkiness of some of its gruesome murder tableaux. Although perhaps slightly overstretching himself on this occasion, the director shows considerable flair for the Gothic mode, a talent which was to reemerge, honed and refined, in his later **Dellamorte Dellamore**.

Demonic ecstasies in **The Church**.

The Facts in the Case of Mr Valdemar
from: **Two Evil Eyes** (1989)

"They're coming to get you, Jessica!" whines the decrepit Valdemar as he shuffles around the Dynastyesque sets of **Two Evil Eyes'** first chapter. Romero's camp recycling of **Night of the Living Dead'**s most famous line is an indication of just how badly Valdemar needs a burst of the stylistic mastery on show in his earlier works. Instead the director serves up an uninspired medley of US TV aesthetics, a story which plods at about the same pace as its undead protagonist and a lacklustre collection of characterizations worthy of the most indifferent of daytime soaps.

Scheming Jessica Valdemar is busy preparing for her imminent widowhood, ensuring that her dying husband's fortune is signed over to her before he finally succumbs to his incurable illness. Jessica's partner in crime is her lover, doctor to the immobilized Valdemar, who is able to take control of his cantankerous patient through hypnosis. Their plans go awry however when the old man dies ahead of schedule and, terrified that they might miss their chance to inherit his millions, they decide to preserve the corpse until a more convenient date is reached for his official passing.

above:
The Facts in the Case of Mr Valdemar,
George A. Romero's segment of
Two Evil Eyes.

below and opposite:
Scenes from Michele Soavi's **The Sect**.

Tucked away amongst bags of frozen vegetables, Valdemar is left to rest in peace in the freezer in Jessica's cellar. But the afterlife's a bitch, he discovers, and before long the troublesome geriatric has returned to the land of the living in search of bloodthirsty revenge.

Romero was a bizarre choice of director for an adaptation of Poe, and Valdemar confirms that on this project he's entirely at odds with his subject matter. The trite narrative pays lip-service to the original short story, but little else. Neither is the film invested with any of the director's own trademarks: his striking use of space and editing, the moments of bleak surrealism and dark irony. In fact very little thought seems to have gone into either scripting or technique. Certain sequences try to adopt Hitchcockian suspense tactics, but never does Romero succeed in lifting the level of tension above zero.

Tom Savini's makeup effects are full of his characteristically macabre flair, but all the rotting corpses in the world couldn't accelerate the pace of this leaden pot-boiler. Ultimately, the twin halves of **Two Evil Eyes** make utterly inappropriate bedfellows, coming from two directors whose styles, even at their best, would make an incongruous combination. Romero is sharing screen-time with a filmmaker who is most often accused of putting aesthetics before characterization - the tragedy of Valdemar, however, is that it offers us neither.

The Sect (1991)

A gang of Satan-worshipping bikers invades a hippy commune in the Californian desert to slaughter all its peace-loving, marijuana-zonked inhabitants. Apparently a new age is approaching and the Devil's disciples are just warming up for the birth of the Anti-Christ.

Key to the Satanists' plot is Miriam, a young schoolteacher living in Germany, who crosses the path of an elderly sectarian, knocking him over in her car. She invites him home to recover, but when he dies in her cellar, she finds herself sinking into a confusing and illusory world of sinister omens and mysterious deaths. Little by little the sect's grip on her tightens, until her part in their demonic scheme is finally revealed.

Although perhaps too close to **Rosemary's Baby** to be credited with any great degree of originality, **The Sect** is at least infinitely more tightly plotted and coherent than **The Church**. Nevertheless, there is still some room for a greater degree of narrative unity, and the film would have benefited from being excised of some of its more irrelevant tangents and digressions.

The sets and the art direction are spectacular and the photography is consistently beautiful, if at times a little too slick - eye-catching steadycam fluidity seems to be called upon here especially when there is a paucity of on-screen activity. Soavi this time exhibits a considerable talent for building atmosphere and many scenes are invested with an insidiously eerie sense of nightmarish surrealism. Although clearly in need of a screen-play with more substance and less waffle, the director shows himself to be a truly gifted visual stylist with a genuine affinity for the dream-like and bizarre.

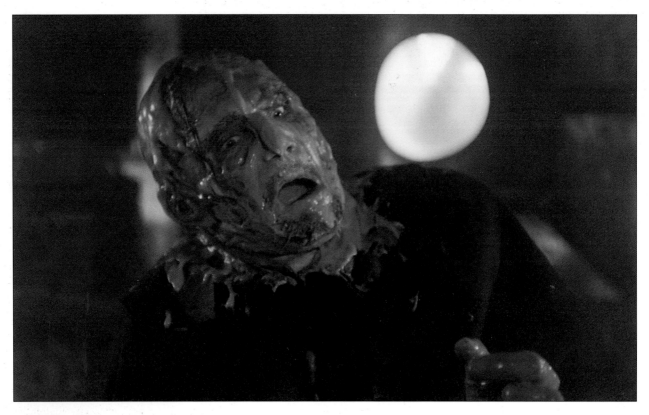

The Wax Mask (1997)

this page and opposite:
Scenes from Sergio Stivaletti's
The Wax Mask, and immediately above,
Dario Argento during filming.

An impressive opening sequence, in which the camera draws back from a view of fireworks over Paris to survey the debris of a particularly messy double murder, gives way to a turgid mass of generic clichés, flat characterizations and show-stopping dialogue howlers.

Years after her parents are viciously butchered, Sonia takes a job as a costume-maker in the macabre Wax Museum. Her employer, Boris, is driven by an all-consuming desire to be recognized as a great artist - and indeed his wax figures do possess a certain lifelikeness. On the eve of her first day's employment, Sonia encounters Andrea, a reporter who is investigating a recent death which occured in the museum. Together they set about unraveling the mystery, gradually making an obscure connection with Sonia's traumatic memory of her parents' deaths.

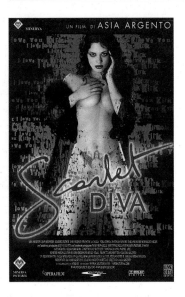

Meanwhile the city is being terrorized by a sinister cloaked assailant, who is responsible for a series of increasingly dastardly and ingenious misdemeanors. All of this leads back to the museum and a shocking revelation: Boris has been cheating by covering corpses with molten wax and passing them off as art. By the time Andrea arrives at the museum, Sonia has already been spirited away to the underground laboratory where the gruesome waxworks are created. Now he must confront the devious Boris and his evil sidekick if he is to save Sonia from becoming another of the museum's ghoulish exhibits.

The roaming steadycam photography and elegant sets with their eerie wax occupants manage to inject the odd moment of suspense or the occasional hint of atmosphere, but for the most part this camp rehash of nineteen-fifties Gothic horror flicks fails to make any great impression. Stivaletti's severed body parts are grotesquely effective but his direction is somewhat less accomplished. Only a few sequences stand out from the surrounding dross, most memorable of which is the sfx bloodbath in which Sonia's father is eviscerated by the metal-handed psychopath, a highlight which is spoiled through being endlessly repeated in flashbacks.

One scene foolishly uses a film poster, 'Man With The Face Of Wax', to allude to bygone horror films and more fondly remembered versions of the same story. Argento, Fulci and Stivaletti have clearly done their best to follow in the footsteps of the grisly, gaudy Vincent Price vehicles of the fifties and sixties and the celebrated chillers of Mario Bava and Riccardo Freda. Sadly, **The Wax Mask** is anything but the Gothic masterpiece its creators set out to produce. Like Boris' creepy statues, it's just a tawdry imitation.

Scarlet Diva (2000)

Nobody could ever accuse Asia Argento of playing it safe. Her first feature as a writer-director is a brash, kitsch, irreverent exercise in self-scrutiny, taking her own experiences as a rising star as its subject matter.

Actress Anna Battista is living in a state of ennui. She's bored with being worshipped, bored with international stardom, bored of being mobbed by armies of rabid fans. Even an award for Best Actress of the Year seems to leave her slightly cold. Her life off-camera consists of drifting around the globe from one major city to the next, deriving cheap thrills from casual sex and drug binges. Having grown tired of the licentious demands of the public and media, with their incessant hunger for nudity and sex, she harbours an ambition to direct her own film and step out of the acting arena.

One night at a rock concert, she falls madly in love with weedy, waif-like singer Kirk and later becomes pregnant with his child. Meanwhile, the promise of a starring role in a new historical epic by Gus Van Sant lures the starlet to Hollywood. The production is a sham, she discovers, a low-budget pot-boiler with a no-name director, and she returns home, more frustrated than before. One evening she comes close to being reunited with the father of her unborn child, when she sees Kirk performing at another concert. This too is revealed to be a delusion, however, when she discovers that he already has a wife and child. She runs out into the street, falling to the ground in tears. She looks up and has a vision, in which she sees Kirk standing above her, surrounded by white light.

Self-criticism is rarely easy. Imagine how **In Bed With Madonna** would have looked, had Madonna written and directed it all herself. Asia Argento's self-portrait is even more self-conscious, and it should come as no great surprise that being a semi-fictionalised videodiary, **Scarlet Diva** emerges as something of a structural disaster. Essentially, it's a non-narrative film, weaving together a series of experiences, thoughts and anecdotes in a single, structureless flow. It has neither a beginning nor a real resolution. In the absence of a narrative proper, the whole rambling affair revolves entirely around Asia herself. She is writer, director, star and subject matter. Presumably the product of all this means more to her than anybody. It can only ever mean less to us.

What Argento does possess is a talent for sharp self-parody. Her deconstruction of stardom through alter-ego Anna is served up with a heavy dose of falling to the ground in tears. It's a thoroughly ambiguous self-portrait. Beneath the celebrity façade, Argento suggests, lies the rebellious, anarchic Anna, the Anna who has sex with strangers in her trailer, who snorts K during photoshoots, the Anna who is never to be seen without a fag hanging out of her mouth. But even that, we can conclude, is just more narcissistic posturing, as much a construction as the surface of glamour which purports to belie it. Argento seems to acknowledge as much through her invocation of grotesque comedy, leading one to speculate that the authentic Anna is the unseen one, the private Anna who rarely reveals herself to the media and is unlikely to emerge for real in self-conscious quasi-autobiographical films like this.

For all these reasons, **Scarlet Diva** is largely too difficult for us to relate to, too remote to maintain our interest. Certain scenes display the director's flair for dark surrealism and her aptitude for black comedy. In a moment of heavy irony, she tells us, "In Italy actresses are like whores. Enough of these shit erotic films. I want to be an artist." As ambitious as **Scarlet Diva** is, one can't help wishing that Asia Argento had chosen to make something that wasn't so completely self-obsessed. Moments of inspiration suggest an emerging talent capable of turning out a darkly engaging film. Maybe next time.

Dario Argento complete filmography

compiled by Julian Grainger

Flug Flight aus Richtung from

BE	486	LONDON
AZ	435	ROM
LH	507	RIO
PA	237	NEW YORK

Dario Argento directs **Suspiria**'s opening scene.

Dario Argento complete filmography (part 1)

APPENDIX

1

films as director

L'uccello dalle piume di cristallo [Italian theatrical/video title]
Das Geheimnis der schwarzen Handschuhe [German theatrical title]
The Bird with the Crystal Plumage [US theatrical & US/UK video title]
The Gallery Murders [UK theatrical title]
L'Oiseau au plumage de cristal [French theatrical title]
Phantom of Terror [alternative US theatrical title]

1970 // Italy & West Germany

Directed by Dario Argento

Cast: Tony Musante (Sam Dalmas, a writer). Suzy Kendall (Giulia/Julia). Enrico Maria Salerno (Inspector Morosini) with Eva Renzi (Monica Ranieri). Umberto Rahi (Alberto Ranieri, gallery owner). Raf Valenti [aka Renato Romano] (Professor Carlo Dover, an ornithologist). Giuseppe Castellano (Monti, Morosini's chief investigator) and with Mario Adorf (Berto Consalvi, an artist) also starring Pino Patti (Faiena, the informer). Gildo Di Marco (Garullo, the pimp). Rosa Toros [Rosita Torosh] (4th victim, 1st photographed at races). Omar Bonaro (one of Morosini's investigators). Fulvio Mingozzi (one of Morosini's investigators). Werner Peters (gay antiques dealer). Karen Valenti (Tina, 5th victim). Carla Mancini. Bruno Erba (one of Morosini's investigators).
[uncredited] Gianni Di Benedetto (Professor Rinoldi, psychiatrist). Reggie Nalder (Needles, an assassin). Liana Del Balzo (old lady in fog). Annamaria Spogli.

Seda Spettacoli (Rome)/CCC Filmkunst (Berlin)
©1970. U - M Film Distributors, Inc. [English language version]

executive producer [for Titanus Distribuzione, uncredited]: Goffredo Lombardo. produced by Salvatore Argento. German co-producer: Arthur Brauner. production manager: Camillo Teti. written by Dario Argento. director of photography: Vittorio Storaro [Eastmancolor - Cromoscope/Technicope]. music by Ennio Morricone. music conducted by Bruno Nicolai. music editor [publisher]: Bixio - Sam (Milan). editor: Franco Fraticell. set dressing & costumes by Dario Micheli. co-costumes [German version]: Anita Schwanst. dialogue director: Robert Rietty. assistant director: Roberto Pariante. script girl [continuity]: Lida Chitarrini. [unit] production manager: Umberto Sambuco. unit managers [German version]: Rudolph Hertzog Jr & Ugo Valenti. administrator: Angelo Tavazza. camera operators: Enrico Umetelli & Arturo Zavattini. make-up man: Pino Ferrante. hairdresser: Lidia Puglia. stills cameraman: Nuova Dial. 1st assistant editor: Cesarina Casini. 2nd assistant editor: Sergio Fraticelli. sound editor: Ken Rolls. sound technician: Carlo Diotallevi. boom man: Eugenio Fiore.

German prints credit the story to Bryan Edgar Wallace however Argento has stated his debt to Fredric Brown's story "The Sreaming Mimi".

Italian visa number: 55555 [16/02/70]. Registro cinematografico: 4.612. Italian takings: L1.650.000.000
Filmed from 25 August 1969 to mid-October 1969 for 7 weeks on location in Rome (Italy) with interiors filmed at Incir - De Paolis Studios (Rome, Italy). Budget: $500,000

Italian theatrical distributor: Titanus Distribuzione (released on 19 February 1970/re-released in 1981). rated: 14. running time: 96 minutes
West German theatrical distributor: Constantin-Film (released on 24 June 1970). rated: 16. running time: 94 minutes
US theatrical distributor: UMC Pictures - a division of Universal Marion Corporation; presented by Sidney Glazier (released in June 1970). rated: GP. running time: 98 minutes
UK theatrical distributor: Eagle Films Ltd. (released in March 1971). rated: X. running time: 94 minutes 22 seconds/8,493 feet
[this was re-submitted to the BBFC by Ango American Film Corp. Ltd. and was passed on 7 March 1983 at 95 minutes 30 seconds having suffered cuts totalling 18 seconds to achieve an '18' rating - presumably it was intended that this would complement the release of "Tenebre"]
French theatrical distributor: Artistes Associés (released on 30 June 1971). rating: none. running time: 102 minutes

Il gatto a nove code [Italian theatrical/video title]
Die neunschwänzige Katze [German theatrical title]
Le Chat à neuf queues [French theatrical title]
The Cat O'Nine Tails [US/UK theatrical & UK video title]

1971 // Italy, West Germany & France

Directed by Dario Argento

Cast: James Franciscus (Carlo Giordani, reporter). Karl Malden (Franco Arnò, "Cookie") and Catherine Spaak (Anna Terzi [Anna Marini]) with Pier Paolo Capponi (Police Superintendent Spimi). Horst Frank (Doctor Braun). Rada Rassimov (Bianca Merusi). Aldo Reggiani (Doctor Casoni) and with Carlo Alighiero (Doctor Calabresi, research analyst). Vittorio Congia (Righetto, newspaper photographer). Ugo Fangareggi (Gigi the loser). Tom [Tommaso] Felleghy (Doctor Esson). Emilio Marchesini (Doctor Mombelli). Fulvio Mingozzi (one of Spimi's men). Corrado Olmi (Brigadier Morsella, one of Spimi's men). Pino Patti (the barber). Umberto Raho (Manuel's ex-lover). Jacques Stany [Stanislav] (Professor Manera) and Stefano Oppedisano (taxi driver). Ada Pometti (a telephonist). Walter Pinelli. Sascha Helwin. Marie Luise Zetha (the starlet photographed at station). Martial Boschero and with Cinzia De Carolis (Lori, Franco's niece). Werner Pochat [Pochath] (Manuel) and also starring Tino Carraro (Professor Fulvio Terzi).
[uncredited] Gianni Di Benedetto (Chief of Police Salmi). Margherita Horowitz (Lori's babysitter).

National General Pictures presents... an Italian/German/French co-production: Seda Spettacoli/Mondial Te. Fi. (Rome)/Terra Filmkunst (Berlin)/Labrador Film (Paris)

screenplay: Dario Argento; based on a story by Dario Argento, Luigi Collo & Dardano Sacchetti; [German version adds] Michael Haller; based on a story by Bryan Edgar Wallace. director of photography: Erico Menczer

This filmography for Dario Argento is arranged by activity and then by date of first public showing in the country of origin. Note that different prints for the same title often provide additional – and sometimes conflicting – information. English language print credits have been used (where available) and if necessary these have been supplemented with data from Italian and other prints.

[Technicolor/Techniscope]. music by Ennio Morricone, conducted by Bruno Nicolai, music publisher: General Music. editor: Franco Fraticelli. art director & wardrobe designer: Carlo Leva. assistant director: Roberto Pariante. production manager: Angelo Iacono [aka Jacono]. Catherine Spaak's dresses are by Luca Sabatelli. production assistants [unit managers]: Carlo De Marchis & Giuseppe Mangogna. camera operator: Roberto Brega. assistant camera operators: Renato Mascagni & Antonio De Castel Terlago. 2nd assistant operator: Maurizio La Monica. script girl [continuity]: Renata Franceschi. [sound] mixer: Mario Ronchetti. boom operator: Eugenio Fiore. chief make-up artists: Giuseppe Ferranti & Piero Mecacci. chief hairdresser: Maura Turchi. assistant make-up: Vincenzo Marchetti. assistant art director: Franco Pedacchia. assistant set dresser: Romeo Costantini. assistant editor: Cesarina Casini. 2nd assistant editor: Sergio Fraticelli. production accountant: Carlo Du Bois. secretary: Roberta Leoni. still cameraman: Firmino Palmieri. gaffer: Rodolfo Flibotto. key grip: Maurizio Micalizzi. sound effects: Luciano Anzellotti. arms adviser: Bruno Ukmar. titles & optical effects: Luciano Vittori. sound: Bernardino Fronzetti. genny operator. Alberto Loreti. synchronization: C.D.S.. dubbing: C.D..

Italian visa number: 57565 [19/1/71]. Registro cinematografico: 4.862. Italian takings L1.141.000.000 (ninth most successful film at the Italian box-office, 1970/71 season)

Filmed in September & October 1970 for eight/nine weeks on location in Berlin (West Germany), Turin & Rome (Italy) with interiors at Cinecittà Studios (Rome, Italy). Budget circa $1 million.

Italian theatrical distributor: Titanus Distribuzione (released on 11 February 1971). rated: 14. running time: 112 minutes
West German theatrical distributor: Constantin-Film (released on 15 July 1971). rated: 18. running time: 91 minutes
French theatrical distributor: Warner Bros. (released in Paris on 11 August 1971). rating: none. running time: 112 minutes
US theatrical distributor: National General Pictures (released in May 1971). rated: GP. running time: 112 minutes
UK theatrical distributor: NGC Distributors Ltd. (released circa May/June 1971). rated: AA. running time: 104 minutes 24 seconds/9,396 feet [submitted @ 112 minutes 41 seconds/10,051 feet]

4 mosche di velluto grigio [Italian theatrical title]

Quatre mouches de velours gris [French theatrical title]
Four Flies on Grey Velvet [US theatrical/video title]
Vier Fliegen auf grauem Samt [German theatrical title]

1971 // Italy & France

Directed by Dario Argento

Cast: Michael Brandon (Roberto Tobias). Mimsy Farmer (Nina Tobias). Jean-Pierre Marielle (Gianni Arrosio, private investigator). Aldo Bufi Landi (coroner). Calisto Calisti (Carlo Marosi). Marisa Fabbri (Amelia). Oreste Lionello (the professor). Fabrizio Moroni (Mirko). Corrado Olmi (gay porter). Stefano Satta Flores (Andrea, raconteur). Costanza Spada [aka Laura Troschel] (Maria Pia, the Tobias' maid) with Francine Racette (Dalia, the Tobias' houseguest) and Bud Spencer [Carlo Pedersoli] (Diomede, English version: Godfrey) supporting cast Dante Cleri (double coffin salesman). Guerrino Crivello (Rambaldi, the neighbour who likes pornography). Gildo Di Marco (the postman). Tom [Tommaso] Felleghy (Commissioner Pini). Leopoldo Migliori. Fulvio Mingozzi (music studio manager). Stefano Oppedisano. Pino Patti (2nd funeral exhibition attendant). Ada Pometti (Amelia). Jacques Stany [Stanislav] (psychiatrist at Villa Rapidi clinic).
[uncredited] Sandro Dori (1st funeral exhibition attendant). Renzo Marignano (2nd funeral exhibition attendant). Gianni Di Benedetto (funeral exhibition visitor). Luigi Cozzi (subway passenger/passerby in front of Roberto's house/masked killer photographing Roberto in theatre).

a film by Dario Argento // produced by Salvatore Argento for SEDA Spettacoli (Rome)/Universal Production France (Paris).
©1972. Seda Spettacoli S.p.A.. [English language version]

produced by Salvatore Argento for SEDA Spettacoli (Rome)/Universal Production France (Paris). production manager: Angelo Jacono. written by Dario Argento. original story: Dario Argento, Luigi Cozzi & Mario Foglietti. lighting cameraman: Franco Di Giacomo. music composed by Ennio Morricone; music conducted by Bruno Nicolai; published by Bixio - Sam. film editor: Françoise Bonnot. production designer: Enrico Sabbatini. assistant director: Roberto Pariante. assistant to the director: Luigi Cozzi. script girl [continuity]: Patrizia Zulini. unit manager: Giuseppe Mangogna. production co-ordinator: Carlo Cucchi. production administration: Carlo Dubois. camera operator: Giuseppe Lanci. special effects: Cataldo Galiano. make-up: Giuliano Laurenti. assistant make-up: Giovanni Morosi. hairstylist: Paolo Borselli. wardrobe: Mina [Giacoma] Manes. assistant operators: Gianfranco Transunto & Mauro Marcheti. assistant art director: Giovanni Viti. assistant costumes: Massimo Lentini. assistant set dresser: Franco Pedacchia. sound engineer: Mario Ronchetti. boom operator: Eugenio Fiore. 1st assistant editors: Alessandro Gabriele, Pietro Bozzo & Catherine Bernard. 2nd assistant editors: Sergio Fraticelli & Bruno Bianchini. sound effects: Luciano Anzellotti. dubbing director [Italian version]: Alberto Piferi. [English language version] recorded by Cinitalia at Fono Roma under the supervision of Nick Alexander.

Italian visa number: 59423 [11/12/71]. Registro cinematografico: 5.048. Italian takings L1.231.000.000

Filmed from 12 July 1971 for nine weeks on location in Turin, Milan and Rome (Italy) with interiors filmed at Incir - De Paolis Studios (Rome, Italy)

Italian theatrical distributor: C.I.C. - Cinema International Corporation (released on 17 December 1971). rated: 14. running time: 105 minutes
French theatrical distributor: C.I.C. - Cinema International Corporation (released in Paris on 21 June 1973). rating: none. running time: 100 minutes
US theatrical distributor: Paramount Pictures (released in August 1972). rated: PG. running time: 101 minutes
UK theatrical distributor: C.I.C. - Cinema International Corporation (released on 11 February 1973). rated: X. running time: 95 minutes 44 seconds/8,526 feet
West German theatrical distributor: C.I.C. - Cinema International Corporation (released on 19 May 1972). rated: 18. running time: 103 minutes

Le cinque giornate [Italian theatrical/video title]

The Five Days of Milan [English-language title] - see footnote, page 112
Five Days in Milan [shooting title]

1973 // Italy

Directed by Dario Argento

Cast: Adriano Celentano (Cainazzo). Enzo Cerusico (Romolo Marcelli, a baker). Marilù Tolo (the countess). Luisa De Santis (the pregnant woman). Glauco Onorato (Zampino). Carla Tatò (the widow) and with Sergio Graziani (Baron Tranzunto) also appearing Germano Altomanni. Salvatore Baccaro (Garafino, a looter). Guglielmo Bardelli. Rolanda Benac. Danny B. Besquet. Ugo Bologna (official at victory celebration). Luca Bonicalzi. Luigi Castejon. Alfredo Ciarpelloni. Lino Cipriani. Angelo Cova. Guerrino Crivello (man with big ears). Agostino Di Berti. Tom [Tommaso] Felleghy (Mariano, contessa's manservant). Vanni Gamerro. Ennio Groggia. Luigi Antonio Guerra. Lorenzo Logli. Manuel Manfredi. Emilio Marchesini (a prisoner). Dante Martini. Loredana Martinez. Fulvio Mingozzi (man at furious debate). Cristina Moranzoni. Ivana Monti (traitor Tranzunto rapes). Stefano Oppedisano (man at debate). Daniele Pagani. Renato Paracchi. Ermanno Pasquini. Claudio Pellegrini. Raffaele Pezzoli. Giorgio Saggioro. Mario Saviane. Claudio Sforzini. Gaetano Scala. Guido Spadea. Damiano Summo. Umberto Tabarelli. Sergio Tardioli. Enzo Ventura.
[uncredited] Dario Argento (bandaged man with Baron Tranzunto). Dante Maggio (old man in jail).

Salvatore Argento presents a film by Dario Argento // a Seda Spettacoli S.p.A. production.
executive producer: Claudio Argento. production supervisor: Angelo Jacono. story: Vincenzo Ungari, Dario Argento & Luigi Cozzi. screenplay: Dario Argento & Nanni Balestrini. director of photography: Luigi Kuveiller [Technicolor]. original music by Giorgio Gaslini. film editor: Franco Fraticelli. art director: Giuseppe Bassan. costumes: Elena Mannini. production manager: Giuseppe Mangogna. 1st assistant director: Sofia Scandurra. 2nd assistant director: Franco Conti. unit managers: Alessandro Calosci & Carlo Cucchi. production secretary: Annamaria Galvinelli. continuity: Nellita Zampieri. cameraman: Ubaldo Terzano & Nino Annunziata. direct sound recording: Amedeo Casati. studio sound recording: Franco Bassi & Danilo Moroni. key make-up: Giuliano Laurenti. key hair stylist: Elda Magnanti. production accountants: Ferdinando Caputo & Carlo Du Bois. stunt co-ordinator: Bruno Ukmar. special effects: Aldo Gasparri. assistant art director: Franco Gambarana. assistant costumes: Maurizio Millenotti. assistant set furnishings: Maurizio Garrone. assistant editors: Pietro Bozza & Sergio Fraticelli. gaffer: Sergio Coletta. key grip: Sergio Emidi. construction manager: Giuseppe Gabrielli. still photography: Vincenzino; Giornalfoto. set dressing & furniture: Rancati (Rome/Milan); Mangiarotti e Spallarossa (Pavia), Preti (Milan); Grilli (Pavia). costume house: G.P. 11 - Tirelli (Rome). wardrobe: Fiorentina (Florence). wigs: Rocchetti. footwear: Arditi. jewelry: Lembo. technical equipment: E.C.E. e Assotecnica. sound effects: Luciano Anzellotti. sound effects editor: Massimo Anzellotti. synchronization by C.D.S. with the collaboration of Cooperativa Doppiatori, directed by Sergio Graziani. historical adviser: Professor Franco Catalano [lecturer in contemporary history at the State University of Milan].
music extracts "La Garza Ladra" by Giacomo Rossini (versione Synthesizer); "ARP Ave Maria" by Johann Sebastian Bach & Charles Gounod - both performed by the orchestra of La Scala di Milano, conducted Giorgio Gaslini; music publishers: Bixio - Sam (Milan).

director originally to have been Nanni Loy. Celentano replaced Ugo Tognazzi in the leading role.

Italian visa number: 63685 [17/12/73]. Registro cinematografico: 5.497.

Filmed from 18 June through August 1973 for 10 weeks on location in Milan and Rome (Italy) with interiors filmed at ICET - De Paolis Studios (Milan, Italy)

Italian theatrical distributor: Euro International Films (released in Rome & Milan on 20 December 1973). rated: 14. running time: 122 minutes

Profondo rosso [Italian theatrical/video title]

Deep Red [UK/US theatrical & UK video title]
The Hatchet Murders [US theatrical re-release title]
Les Frissons de l'angoïsse [French theatrical title]
Sabre Tooth Tiger/Chipsyomega [shooting titles]
Dripping Deep Red [US publicity title]
Suspiria Part 2 [Japanese English language title]

1975 // Italy

Directed by Dario Argento

Cast: David Hemmings (Marc Daly, a music teacher). Daria Nicolodi (Gianna Brezzi, a journalist). Gabriele Lavia (Carlo, jazz pianist). Macha Meril (Helga Ulmann). Eros Pagni (Superintendent Calcabrini). Giuliana Calandra (Amanda Righetti) and with Glauco Mauri (Professor Giordani) and with the participation of Clara Calamai (Marta, Carlo's mother). Piero Mazzinghi (Mario Bardi) and with Aldo Bonamano (Carlo's father). Liana Del Balzo (Elvira, Amanda's housekeeper). Vittorio Fanfoni (cop taking notes). Dante Fioretti (police photographer). Geraldine Hooper (Massimo Ricci). Iacopo Mariani (young Carlo). Furio Meniconi (Rodi, villa caretaker). Fulvio Mingozzi (Agent Mingozzi). Lorenzo Piani (fingerprint cop). Salvatore Puntillo (Fabbroni, a cop). Piero Vida (hungry cop) and the little Nicoletta Elmi (Olga Rodi).
[uncredited] Tommaso Felleghy (surgeon). Salvatore Baccaro (angry man at market). Attilio Dottesio (4th tree specialist). Bruno Di Luia (concerned man in rest room). Mario Scaccia (man being whispered to at psychiatrists' conference).

Glauco Onorato is not in this film.

Rizzoli Film & Salvatore Argento present a film by Dario Argento // a Seda Spettacoli spa (Rome) production [US poster adds] a Lea J. Marks/Radcliffe Associates Ltd. feature film

executive producer: Claudio Argento. production supervisor: Angelo Jacono. story & screenplay: Dario Argento & Bernardino Zapponi. director of photography: Luigi Kuveiller [colour by LV - Luciano Vittori (Rome)]. music by Giorgio Gaslini, recorded by The Goblin; published by Cinevox Record. editor: Franco Fraticelli. art director: Giuseppe Bassan. costume designer: Elena Mannini. production

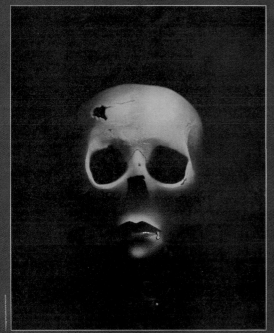

un film di
DARIO ARGENTO

Inferno

SALVATORE ARGENTO
presenta un film scritto e diretto da
DARIO ARGENTO
INFERNO
con la partecipazione di ELEONORA GIORGI – GABRIELE LAVIA – VERONICA LAZAR
LEOPOLDO MASTELLONI – IRENE MIRACLE – DARIA NICOLODI
SACHA PITOEFF con ALIDA VALLI e con LEIGH McCLOSKEY
musiche originali composte e dirette da KEITH EMERSON con la collaborazione di GODFREY SALMON
direttore della fotografia ROMANO ALBANI – scenografia GIUSEPPE BASSAN – montaggio FRANCO FRATICELLI
CLAUDIO ARGENTO con il contributo di RENZO ROSSELLINI
regia di DARIO ARGENTO
TECHNICOLOR – TECHNOVISION
DISTRIBUZIONE PAC PER L'ITALIA CEIAD

Titanus
SALVATORE ARGENTO presenta
un film di
DARIO ARGENTO
TENEBRE

con ANTHONY FRANCIOSA
e con (in ordine alfabetico)
CHRISTIAN BORROMEO – MIRELLA D'ANGELO – VERONICA LARIO – ANIA PIERONI – CAROLA STAGNARO
JOHN STEINER – LARA WENDEL / con / JOHN SAXON / e con / DARIA NICOLODI / e la partecipazione di / GIULIANO GEMMA
direttore della fotografia LUCIANO TOVOLI   musica di SIMONETTI – PIGNATELLI – MORANTE
Edizioni musicali BIXIO C.E.M.S.A. S.p.A. – MILANO   Prodotto da CLAUDIO ARGENTO
TECHNICOLOR – TECHNOVISION   Regia di DARIO ARGENTO   Un film SIGMA Cinematografica – ROMA

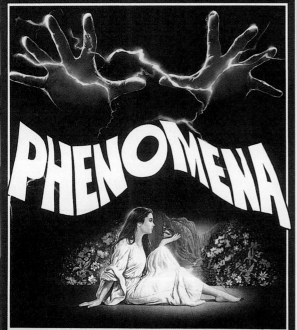

Titanus
un film scritto, prodotto e diretto da
DARIO ARGENTO

PHENOMENA

con JENNIFER CONNELLY
DARIA NICOLODI   con **DALILA DI LAZZARO**   con **PATRICK BAUCHAU**
con **DONALD PLEASENCE** nel ruolo di "John McGregor"
Panavision – Colore Technicolor

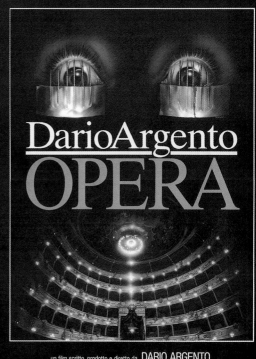

DarioArgento
OPERA

un film scritto, prodotto e diretto da DARIO ARGENTO
"OPERA"
con CRISTINA MARSILLACH – JOHN CHARLESON
URBANO BARBERINI – WILLIAM McNAMARA
ANTONELLA VITALE – BARBARA CUPISTI – CORALINA CATALDI TASSONI
e con DARIA NICOLODI   direttore della fotografia RONNIE TAYLOR (B.S.C.)
sceneggiatura di DARIO ARGENTO e FRANCO FERRINI
una produzione CECCHI GORI GROUP TIGER CINEMATOGRAFICA – A.D.C. in collaborazione con la RAI
regia di DARIO ARGENTO   CDi

manager: Carlo Cucchi. production secretary: Cesare Jacolucci. assistant director: Stefano Rolla. continuity: Vivalda Vigorelli. cameraman: Ubaldo Terzano. assistant cameramen: Antonio Annunziata & Antonio Tonti. 1st assistant editor: Pietro Bozza. 2nd assistant editor: Ernesto Triunveri. sound: Mario Faraoni. boom operator: Eugenio Fiore. key make-up artist: Giuliano Laurenti. make-up artist: Gianni Morosi. hairstylist: Nicla Palombi. administration: Carlo Du Bois. special effects: Germano Natali & Carlo Rambaldi. assistant art director: Maurizio Garrone. set dresser: Armando Mannini. wardrobe: Angela Viglino. gaffer: Sergio Coletta. key grip: Sergio Emidi. construction manager: Aldo Taloni. still photography: Franco Bellomo. set furnishing: G.R.P.; Rancati; Cimino; D'Angelo. costume house: Sartoria Russo. wigs: Rocchetti. shoes: Arditi. jewelery: Lembo. technical equipment: E.C.E. (Rome). transport: Romana Trasporti Cinematografici. stunt team: Giorgio Ricci. special shooting: Guicar (Milan). sound effects: Luciano Anzellotti. sound studio: Palatino (Rome) with the collaboration of C.V.D.. music publishers: Bixio C.E.M.S.A. s.p.a.; Rizzoli Film s.p.a.. negatives: Eastmancolor 5247.

Filmed from 9 September 1974 for 16 weeks on location in Turin & Rome (Italy) with interiors filmed at De Paolis Incir Studios (Rome, Italy)

Italian visa number: 66157 [06/03/75]. Registro cinematografico: 5.828. Italian takings L1.300.000.000

Italian theatrical distributor: Cineriz (released in Rome & Milan on 7 March 1975). rated: 14. running time: 130 minutes
US theatrical distributor [as "Deep Red"]: Directors-Mahler Films (released in June 1976). rated: R. running time: 98 minutes
US theatrical distributor [as "The Hatchet Murders"]: Directors-Mahler Films (released in January 1980). rated: R. running time: 100 minutes
French theatrical distributor: Audi Films/Eurogroup (released in Paris on 17 August 1977). rated: 18. running time: 95 minutes

Suspiria [Italian/German/French/UK theatrical/video title]

1977 // Italy

Directed by Dario Argento

Cast: Jessica Harper (Suzy Bannion). Stefania Casini (Sara) with Flavio Bucci (Daniel, blind pianist). Miguel Bosè (Mark). Barbara Magnolfi (Olga, student who lives in town). Susanna Javicoli (Sonia, Pat's friend). Eva Axen (Pat Hingle, 1st victim). Rudolf Schündler (Professor Milius, author). Udo Kier (Doctor Frank Mandel, psychiatrist) with Alida Valli (Miss Tanner, an instructor) and with Joan Bennett (Madame Blanc, vice-directress of Tam Academy) supporting cast Margherita Horowitz (a teacher). Jacopo Mariani (Albert, Miss Tanner's nephew). Fulvio Mingozzi (airport taxi driver). Franca Scagnetti (Albert's governess [1st servant]). Renato Scarpa (Professor Verdegast). Serafina Scorcelletti (2nd servant). Giuseppe Transocchi (Pavlo, Roumanian handyman). Renata Zamengo (Caroline). Alessandra Capozzi, Salvatore Capozzi, Diana Ferrara, Cristina Latini, Alfredo Rainò & Claudia Zaccari (student dancers).
According to a contemporary report in 'Variety', Daria Nicolodi was replaced by Stefania Cassini when she broke her ankle during shooting.

Salvatore Argento presents a film by Dario Argento - a Seda Spettacoli S.p.A. Rome production

produced by Claudio Argento. production manager: Lucio Trentini. written by Dario Argento & Daria Nicolodi. director of photography: Luciano Tovoli a.i.c. [Eastmancolor/Technicolor/Technovision]. music by the "Goblins" with the collaboration of Dario Argento. film editor: Franco Fraticelli. production designer: Giuseppe Bassan. costumes by Pierangelo Cicoletti. unit manager: Federico Tocci. production co-ordinators: Federico Starace & Massimo Brandimarte. assistant director: Antonio Gabrielli. script continuity: Francesca Roberti. camera operator: Idelmo Simonelli a.i.c.. assistant cameramen: Giuseppe Tinelli a.i.c., Enrico Fontana a.i.c. & Riccardo Dolci. action stills: Francesco Bellomo. 1st assistant editor: Piero Bozza. 2nd assistant editor: Roberto Olivieri. sound recordist: Mario Dallimonti. boom operator: Corrado Volpicelli. re-recording engineer: Federico Savina. make-up supervisor: Pierantonio Mecacci. make-up assistant: Pierino Mecacci. hairstylist: Maria Teresa Corridoni. assistant hairstylist: Aldo Signoretti. assistant art directors: Maurizio Garrone & Davide Bassan. set dresser: Enrico Fiorentini. assistant set dresser: Massimo Garrone. wardrobe mistress: Tiziana Mancini. seamstress: Bertilla Silvestrin. special effects: Germano Natali. production accountants: Ferdinando Caputo & Carlo Du Bois. gaffer: Alberto Altibrandi. key grip: Mario Moreschini. set construction: Aldo Taloni. titles: Studio Mafera. set furnishings: G.R.P.; Rancati; Cimino, D'Angelo; F.R.A. Spa. costume house: Sartoria Anna Mode. wigs by Rocchetti. footwear: Raphael Salato. accessories: Lembo Caracciolo. leather goods: Fendi. camera & lighting equipment: E.C.E. (Rome). international transportation: U.T.I. (Rome). transportation: Romana Trasporti Cinematografici. sound effects: Luciano Anzellotti. unit publicist: Nino Vendetti. recorded in English at International Recording (Rome). dubbing editor: Nick Alexander.
[uncredited] additional music from "Music in Similar Motion" by Philip Glass.

Italian visa number: 69766 [26/01/77]. Registro cinematografico: 6.227. Italian takings L1.430.000.000 (seventh most successful film at the Italian box-office, 1976/77 season)

Filmed from 26 July 1976 for 16 weeks on location in Munich & Bavaria (West Germany) with interiors filmed at De Paolis Incir Studios (Rome, Italy)

Italian theatrical distributor: P.A.C. (released on 1 February 1977, in Rome on 4 February 1977, in Milan on 10 February 1977). rated: 14. running time: 100 minutes
US theatrical distributor: International Classics [20th Century Fox Film Corporation] (released in August 1977). rated: R. running time: 98 minutes
US theatrical distributor (re-release): Joseph Brenner Associates, Inc. (released in 1979). rated: R. running time: 98 m
UK theatrical distributor: EMI Film Distributors Ltd. (released on 28 December 1977). rated: X. running time: 97 minutes 1 second/8,732 feet [BBFC cuts]
West German theatrical distributor: Gloria (released on 5 May 1977). running time: 92 minutes
French theatrical distributor: Les Films Jacques Leitienne (released in Paris on 18 May 1977). rated: 18. running time: 95 minutes

Inferno [Italian/French theatrical & Italian/UK video title]

Horror Infernal [German theatrical title]

1980 // Italy

Directed by Dario Argento

Cast: Leigh McCloskey (Mark Elliot, musicology student). Irene Miracle (Rose Elliot, Mark's sister). Eleonora Giorgi (Sara, a music student). Daria Nicolodi (Countess Elise Delon Van Adler). Sacha Pitoeff (Mr Kazanian, an antiques dealer). Alida Valli (Carol, caretaker). Veronica Lazar (Varelli's nurse). Gabriele Lavia (Carlo, a tv sports writer). Feodor Chaliapin (Doctor E. Varelli, 'Professor Arnold'). Leopoldo Mastelloni (John, Elise's butler). Ania Pieroni (music student with cat). James Fleetwood (cook). Rosario Rigutini (man). Ryan Hilliard (Shadow). Paolo Paoloni (music teacher). Fulvio Mingozzi (1st cab driver). Luigi Lodoli (bookbinder). Rodolfo Lodi (old man in library).

Salvatore Argento presents a film by Dario Argento - produced by Claudio Argento for Produzioni Intersound (Rome) // released by Twentieth Century-Fox Film Corporation
©1980. Twentieth Century-Fox Film Corporation [English language version]

produced by Claudio Argento for Produzioni Intersound (Rome). production administrator: Solly V. Bianco. production manager: Angelo Jacono. story & screenplay: Dario Argento. director of photography: Romano Albani [colour by Technicolor/Technovision - prints by DeLuxe]. music by Keith Emerson; music arranged by [Keith] Emerson and [Godfrey] Salmon; orchestrated & conducted by Godfrey Salmon; published by Bixio C.E.M.S.A. - L.B.G. Artist. film editor: Franco Fraticelli. art director: Giuseppe Bassan. costumes: Massimo Lentini. [1st] assistant director: Lamberto Bava. unit manager: Cesare Jacolucci. production assistants: Anna Maria Galvinelli, Michela Prodan & Saverio Mangogna. 2nd assistant director: Andrea Piazzesi. script supervisor: Maria Serena Canevari. cameraman: Idelmo Simonelli. still photographer: Francesco Bellomo. soundman: Francesco Groppioni. boom man: Giancarlo Laurenzi. make-up: Pierantonio Mecacci. hair stylists: Luciana Maria Costanzi & Giancarlo De Leonardis. set decorators: Francesco Cuppini & Maurizio Garrone. gaffer: Alberto Altibrandi. key grip: Agostino Pascarella. special effects: Germano Natali. underwater sequence: Lorenzo Battaglia. footwear: RS - Raphael Salato. jewelry: "Bulgari". technical equipment: E.C.E. (Rome). US production service: Cinerex Assoc. N.Y.. executive producer: William Garroni. production manager: Andrew W. Garroni. sound effects: Luciano Anzellotti & Massimo Anzellotti. sound effects editor: Attilio Gizzi. sound recording studios: International Recording (Rome). sound mixer: Romano Pampaloni A.T.I.C.. unit publicist: Enrico Lucherini & Ghergo. music publisher: Bixio C.E.M.S.A. (Milan); L.B.G. Artists. music recorded at Trafalgar Recording Studios (Rome). orchestra: Unione Musicisti di Roma. head titles: Studio Verzini.
music extracts "Va pensiero..." from Giuseppe Verdi's "Nabucco" Symphonic Orchestra and Chorus of Rome, Radio Televisione Italiana. chorus conducted by Gaetano Riccitelli, director: Fernando Previtali, courtesy of Fonit Cetra.
[uncredited] assistant cameramen: Michele Picciaredda & Stefano Ricciotti. sound engineer: Mario Dallimonti. special effects: Mario Bava & Pino Leoni. dialogue director [coach]: Neil Robinson. production accountants: Carlo Du Bois, Ferdinando Caputo, Carla Menicocci & Egle Friggeri. wardrobe mistress: Berta Berti. assistant art director: Davide Bassan. assistant set decorator: Massimo Garrone. set painters: Giorgio Palomba & Mauro Tiberi. assistant editor: Piero Bozza. unit publicist: Walter Alford. publicist (Italy): Enrico Lucherini. New York production services: William Lustig.
recorded in Dolby stereo.
music recorded at Trafalgar Recording Studios (Rome) & Compass Point Studios (Nassau, Bahamas). music engineer: Giorgio Agazzi. additional performer on "Mater Tenebrarum" Linda Lee (vocals); on "Taxi ride" and "Cigarette, ices etc." Frank Scully (drums) & Kendal Stubbs (bass). soundtrack available on Cinevox Record (MDF 33/138), distributed by Dischi Ricordi S.p.A..

Italian visa number: 74729 [06/02/80]. Registro cinematografico: 6.642. MPAA #25916.

Filmed from 21 May 1979 for 14 weeks on location in Rome (Italy) with interiors filmed at De Paolis Incir (Rome) & at Elios Studios (Rome); preceded by one week's filming in April 1979 in Manhattan & Central Park (New York, USA). Budget $3 million.

Italian theatrical distributor: Twentieth Century-Fox Italy (released in Rome on 7 February 1980). rated: 14. running time: 107 minutes
US theatrical distribution: 20th Century-Fox Film Corporation (released in August 1986). rated: R. running time: 83 minutes
UK theatrical distributor: Cinecenta (released in September 1980). rated: X. running time: 106 minutes 16 seconds/9,564 feet [BBFC cuts]
French theatrical distributor: 20th Century-Fox (released in Paris on 16 April 1980). rated: 18. running time: 110 mins
West German theatrical distributor: 20th Century-Fox (released on 12 September 1980). running time: 102 minutes

Tenebre [Italian theatrical/video title]

Tenebrae [UK theatrical/video title]
Unsane [US theatrical/video title]
Shadow [Japanese laserdisc title]
Ténèbres [French theatrical title]
Tinieblas [Spanish theatrical title]
Tenebre Der kalte Hauch des Todes [West German theatrical title]

1982 // Italy

Directed by Dario Argento

Cast: Anthony Franciosa (Peter Neal) and with - in alphabetical order Christian Borromeo (Gianni, junior agent). Mirella D'Angelo (Tilde, a journalist). Veronica Lario [aka Myriam Bartolini] (Jane Miccaro, Peter's wife). Ania Pieroni (Elsa Manni, a shoplifter). Eva Robins [Roberto Coatti] (woman on beach). Carola Stagnaro (Inspector Altieri). John Steiner (Cristiano Berti). Lara Wendel (Maria Alboretto, the porter's daughter) with John Saxon (Bulmer, Neal's agent) and with Daria Nicolodi (Anne, Neal's assistant) with the participation of Giuliano Gemma (Captain Giermani) with Isabella Amadeo. Mirella Banti (Marion, Tilde's girlfriend). Enio Girolami (department store detective). Monica Maisani. Marino Masè (John, Peter's chauffeur). Fulvio Mingozzi (Alboretto, the porter). Gianpaolo Saccarola (autopsy doctor). Ippolita Santarelli (a prostitute). Francesca Viscardi.

[uncredited] Michele Soavi (man by swimming pool with fantasy woman). Theresa Russell (voice of Anna [English language version]).

Salvatore Argento presents a film by Dario Argento - a ∑Sigma Cinematografica (Rome) production

produced by Claudio Argento. story: Dario Argento. screenplay: Dario Argento & George Kemp. director of photography: Luciano Tovoli [colour by Technicolor/Technovision]. music by [Claudio] Simonetti, [Fabio] Pignatelli, [Elsa] Morante. film editor: Franco Fraticelli. general production manager: Angelo Iacono [aka Jacono]. art director: Giuseppe Bassan. costume designer: Pierangelo Cicoletti. 1st assistant director: Lamberto Bava. 2nd assistant director: Michele Soavi. continuity: Francesca Roberti. 1st assistant film editor: Pietro Bozza. assistant film editor: Roberto Priori. production manager: Giuseppe Mangogna. production supervisor: Cesare Jacolucci. production secretary: Saverio Mangogna. camera operator: Giuseppe Tinelli. assistant camera operators: Maurizio Piano & Roberto Marsigli. still photographer: Francesco Bellomo. assistant costume designer: Barbara Canevari. sound technician: Mario Dallimonti. boom man: Giancarlo Laurenzi. make-up artist: Pierantonio Mecacci. make-up: Pierino Mecacci. hair stylist: Patrizia Corridoni. set decorator: Maurizio Garrone. assistant set decorator: Massimo Garrone. 1st assistant art director: Davide Bassan. assistant art director: Antonella Caputo. wardrobe mistress: Vanda Caprioli. production accountants: Carlo Du Bois & Ferdinando Caputo. construction coordinator: Aldo Taloni. key grip: Mario Moreschini. gaffer: Francesco Giulivi. electrician: Remo Cartocci. special effects: Giovanni Corridori. props: Giuseppe Pagnotta & Osvaldo Monaco. furnishings: Saporiti-Tommaso Barbi. costumes: Annamode 68. Mr. Anthony Franciosa's clothes are by Carlo Palazzi. John Saxon's clothes are by Franco Tomei. furs & outfits: Fendi-Cesare Piccini. wigs: Rocchetti-Carboni. shoes: Diego Della Valle. craft service: E.C.E. (Rome). transportations: Romana Trasporti Cinematografica. recorded at International Recording (Rome). sound effects: Luciano Anzellotti & Massimo Anzellotti. sound mixer: Romano Pampaloni. unit publicist: Enrico Lucherini & Ghergo. music publisher: Bixio C.E.M.S.A., Milan. negatives: Eastmancolor 5247-5293. titles: Studio Mafera.
our thanks to Sandro Petti for the use of his house.
[uncredited] US production services: William Lustig.

Italian visa number: 78278 [27/10/82]. Registro cinematografico: 7.117.

Filmed from 3 May 1982 on location in/around Rome (Italy) and at Kennedy Airport (USA) with interiors filmed at Elios Studios (Rome, Italy)

Italian theatrical distributor: Titanus Distribuzione (released on 28 October 1982). rated: 18. running time: 101 minutes
UK theatrical distributor: Anglo American Film Distributors Limited (released on 19 May 1983). rated 18 (X). running time: 101 minutes 51 seconds/9.076 feet [BBFC cuts of 4 seconds]
US theatrical distributor: Bedford Entertainment/Film Gallery (released in February 1987). rated R. running time: 100 minutes
French theatrical distributor: Ginis Film/PM Productions (released in Paris on 27 April 1983). rated: 18. running time: 110 minutes
West German theatrical distributor: Atlas (released on 12 October 1984). running time: 96 minutes

Phenomena [Italian/French theatrical & Italian/German video title]
Creepers [US/UK theatrical/video title]

1985 // Italy

Directed by Dario Argento

Cast: Jennifer Connelly (Jennifer Corvino). Daria Nicolodi (Frau Brückner). Dalila Di Lazzaro (head mistress) with Patrick Bauchau (Inspector Rudolf Geiger) and with Donald Pleasence (Professor John McGregor, entomologist) supporting cast Fiore Argento (Vera Brandt, Danish tourist). Federica Mastroianni (Sophie, Jennifer's roommate). Fiorenza Tessari (Gisela Sulzer, girl killed at the school). Mario Donatone (Morris Shapiro, attorney). Francesca Ottaviani (Grubach's nurse). Michele Soavi (Kurt, Geiger's assistant). Franco Trevisi (real estate agent). Fausta Avelli, Marta Biuso, Sophie Bourchier, Paola Gropper, Ninke Hielkema, Mitzy Orsini & Geraldine Thomas (the schoolgirls)
[uncredited] Marisa Simonetti (a schoolgirl). Alberto Cracco (UBS bank teller). Gaspare Capparoni [aka Kaspar Capparoni] (Karl, Sophie's boyfriend). Antonio Maimone (Grubach, EEG doctor). Davide Marotta (Patau, Brückner's son). Fulvio Mingozzi (Mr Sulzer, Gisela's father). Tanga the Chimpanzee (Inge, the chimp).

a Dario Argento Film - a Dacfilm (Rome) production // a Titanus Distribuzione exclusivity
©1984. Dacfilm [English language version]

produced by Dario Argento. written by Dario Argento & Franco Ferrini. director of photography: Romano Albani a.i.c. [Technicolor/filmed in Panavision]. music by special guests Bill Wyman, Iron Maiden, Motorhead, Simon Boswell, Andy Sex Gang, The Goblin, Claudio Simonetti & Fabio Pignatelli. film editor: Franco Fraticelli a.m.c.. production design: Maurizio Garrone, Nello Giorgetti, Luciano Spadoni & Umberto Turco. costumes designed by Giorgio Armani. production executive: Angelo Jacono. 1st assistant director: Michele Soavi. 2nd assistant director: Bettina Graebe. supervising sound editor: Franco Fraticelli. music editor: Piero Bozza. sound editor: Nick Alexander. dialogue coach: Sheila Goldberg. script continuity: Vivalda Vigorelli. production manager: Cesare Iacolucci. production secretaries: Serenella Severini & Fabrizio Diaz. camera operator: Stefano Ricciotti. assistant cameraman: Aldo Bergamini. steadicam supplied & operated by Nicola Pecorini and Co.. action stills: Franco Bellomo. underwater photography: Gianlorenzo Battaglia. 1st assistant editor: Piero Bozza. 2nd assistant editor: Roberto Priori. wardrobe assistants: Marina Malavasi & Patrizia Massaia. set dressers: Rina Villani & Renato Lori. chief production accountant: Ferdinando Caputo. production accountants: Giulio Cestari & Renato Rinaldo. make-up artist: Pierantonio Mecacci. make-up special effects: Sergio Stivaletti. hair stylist: Patrizia Corridori. sound mixer: Giancarlo Laurenzi. gaffer: Alberto Altibrandi. key grip: Agostino Pascarella. chief set builder: Aldo Taloni. set painter: Mario Grilli. construction grip: Giuseppe Pagnotta. stunt co-ordinator: Giorgio Ricci. special stage effects: Tonino Corridori. entomology consultant: Enrico Stella. assistant entomologist: Fabio Dell'Uomo. animals & insects supplied by Maurizio Garrone. special entomological photography: Ferdinando Armati. special optical effects: Luigi Cozzi. stereo sound effects: Studio Anzellotti. the chimpanzee 'Tanga' is owned & trained by Daniel Berquiny. transportation: Romana Trasporti & Cartocci Bros.. cameras & lenses: Panaflex Panavision supplied by A.R.C.O. 2 srl. re-recording: International Recording. re-recording engineer: Danilo Sterbini. wigs supplied by Rocchetti and Carboni. insurance agent: Cinesicurtà. unit publicist: Enrico Lucherini. titles: Moviecam 2000. Dolby sound consultant: Federico Savina. music soundtrack"Phenomena" by Claudio Simonetti; "Flash of the Blade" by Iron Maiden, by kind permission of E.M.I. Records; "Locomotive" by Motorhead, by kind permission of Bronze Records; "The Naked and the Dead" & "You Don't Know Me" by Andy Sex Gang; "The Maggots" by Simon Boswell; "The Insects" by Fabio Pignatelli; "Valley" & "Valley Bolero" by Bill Wyman & Terry Taylor, by kind permission of Ripple Records. record copyright: Cinevox. music soundtrack produced by Vincent Messina for Bixio C.E.M.S.A..
filmed & printed in Eastmancolor Kodak. Dolby Stereo in selected theatres.

Italian visa number: 80393 [25/01/85]. Registro cinematografico: 7.373.

Filmed from August to October 1984 on location in/around Zurich (Switzerland) with interiors filmed at De Paolis IN.CI.R. Studios (Rome, Italy). 2nd unit commenced filming 18 June 1984. Budget $3.8 million.

Italian theatrical distributor: Titanus Distribuzione (released on 31 January 1985). rating: 14. running time: 110 minutes
UK theatrical distributor: Palace Pictures (released on 18 April 1986). rated: 18. running time: 83 minutes [BBFC cuts of 17 seconds].
US theatrical distributor: New Line Cinema (released on 30 August 1985). rated: R. running time: 83 minutes
French theatrical distributor: AM Films (released in Paris on 12 June 1985). rated: 13. running time: 103 minutes
world sales: Intra Films

Opera [Italian theatrical/video title]
Terror at the Opera [US/UK theatrical/video title]
Terror in der Oper [West German video title]

1987 // Italy

Directed by Dario Argento

Cast: Cristina Marsillach (Betty, an understudy). Ian Charleson (Mark, the director). Urbano Barberini (Inspector Alan Santini). Daria Nicolodi (Myra, Betty's agent). Coralina Cataldi Tassoni (Giulia/Julia, wardrobe mistress). Antonella Vitale (Marion, Mark's lover). William McNamara (Stefan Obrini, stage manager). Barbara Cupisti (Signora Albertini). Antonio Juorio (Baddini, theatre manager). Carola Stagnaro (Alma's mother) and with Francesca Cassola (Alma, the little girl) supporting cast Maurizio Garrone (Maurizio, raven trainer). Cristina Giachino (Maria, Marco's assistant director). Gyorivany Gyorgy (Miro). Bjorn Hammer (first cop). Peter Pitsch (the Diva's assistant). Sebastiano Somma (second cop).
[uncredited] Michele Soavi (Daniele Soavi, Santini's assistant).

Vanessa Redgrave was to have played diva Mara Czekova but left the production before any of her scenes were filmed.

produced by ADC Srl/Cecchi Gori Group/Tiger Cinematografica Srl in collaboration with RAI Radio Televisione Italiana

executive producer: Ferdinando Caputo. produced by Dario Argento. production supervisors: Alessandro Calosci & Verena Baldeo. written by Dario Argento. screenplay: Dario Argento & Franco Verrini; based on an original idea by Dario Argento. director of photography: Ronnie Taylor b.s.c. [prints by Technicolor SpA.]. soundtrack [see below]. editor: Franco Fraticelli a.m.c.. production designer: Davide Bassan. art director (Regio Theatre, Parma): Gianmaurizio Fercioni. costume designer: Francesca Lia Morandini. 1st assistant directors: Paolo Zenatello & Antonio Gabrielli. 2nd assistant director: Alessandro Ingargiola. script supervisor: Cinzia Malatesta. unit managers: Olivier Gerard & Fabrizio Diaz. production secretaries: Francesco Marras, Paola Rossi, Angelo Cavallo & Egle Friggeri. camera operator: Antonio Scaramuzza. steadicam operator: Nicola Pecorini. camera assistants: Massimo Intoppa, Ugo Menegatti & Maurizio Lucchini. clapper loader: Roberto De Franceschi. still photographers: Franco Vitale, Roberto Nicosia Vinci & Gianfranco Massa. assistant film editors: Pietro Bozza & Alessandro Gabriele a.a.m.c.. 2nd assistant film editor: Roberto Priori a.a.m.c.. production sound mixer: Giancarlo Laurenzi. boom operator: Stefano Rossi. chief accountant: Renato Rinaldo. accountants: Carlo Du Bois & Federica Zappalà. assistant art director: Antonio Tarolla. set dresser: Valeria Paoloni. property man: Osvaldo Monaco & Maurizio Iacopelli. wardrobe assistant: Enrica Barbano. seamstress: Francesca Grandi. chief make-up artist: Rosario Prestopino. make-up artist: Franco Casagni. hairdresser: Ferdinando Merolla. gaffer: Fernando Massaccesi. chief grip: Ennio Picconi. 2nd unit director: Michele Soavi. 2nd unit directors of photography: Renato Tafuri & Luca Robecchi. 2nd unit camera operator: Enrico Maggi. special effects: Renato Agostini. animatronics: Sergio Stivaletti. assistant: Barbara Morosetti. special effects supplied by Messrs. Antonio & Giovanni Corridori & Germano Natali. Parma Theatre Chorus directed by M. Giovanni Veneri. lyrical music consultants: M. Francesco Miracle & M. Gianfranco Plenizio. Macbeth arias sung by Elisabetta Norberg Schulz (soprano), Paola Leolini (soprano), Andrea Piccini (baritone) & Michele Pertusi (tenor). music performed by the Arturo Toscanini Symphonic Orchestra of Emilia and Romagna & recorded ast the Elite Studio of Seramide (Mn). dubbing mixer: Romano Pampaloni a.t.i.c.. Dolby sound consultant: Federico Savina. sound effects: L.M. Anzellotti. recorded by International Recording Srl (Rome) and Gambit International (London). ADR director: Robert Rietty. publicity: Enrico Luccherini & Gianluca Pignatelli. camera equipment: ECE srl. lighting: ARCO 2. transport: Romana Trasporti Cinematografici. properties supplied by E. Rancati; G.R.P. Postiglione; Dedali Srl (Rome). furnishings: Artigiana Arredatori & E. Tappezzieri. costumes: Costumi D'Arte & Sartoria Ferroni. jewelry: Nino Lembo. wigs: Rocchetti & Carboni. shoes: LCP. birds & animals supplied by Luigi Paro (Milan). animal consultant: Maurizio Garrone. insurance: Cinesicurtà. titles & opticals: Studio A.M. Srl. graphics: Modgraphic Srl di Angelo Modica.
music "White Darkness", "Balance" & "From the Beginning" by Brian Eno & Roger Eno by arrangement with Opal Ltd. (London); "Opera", "Craws" & "Confusion" by Claudio Simonetti by arrangement with BMG Ariola-Walkman srl.; "Opera Theme" &" Black Notes" by Bill Wyman & Terry Taylor by arrangement with Ripple Music Ltd.; "Knights of the Night" & "Steel Grave" are by the group Steel Grave by arrangement with Franton Music/Walkman srl; "No Escape" by the

group Norden Light by arrangement with Sonet; "Lady Macbeth" by Giuseppe Verdi, "Casta diva" from Vincenzo Bellini's "Norma", "Amami Alfredo" &" Sempre libera" from Giuseppe Verdi's "La traviata" sung by Maria Callas by arrangement with Fonit Cetra; "Un bel dì vedremo" from Giacomo Puccini's "Madame Butterfly" sung by Mirella Freni by arrangement with Polygram. music soundtrack records distributed by Cinevox Records.
negative by Eastmancolor Kodak. Dolby stereo in selected theatres.

Italian visa number: 83198 [18/12/87]. Registro cinematografico: 7.728.

Filmed from 25th May 1986 for 15 weeks on location at the Regio Theatre (Parma, Italy), in Rome (Italy), various Rome locations (including at Via Monserrato) (Italy) and in Lugano (Switzerland) with interiors filmed at De Paolis IN.CI.R Studios (Rome, Italy). Budget: $8 million

Italian theatrical distributor: CDi (released on 19 December 1987). rated: 18. running time: 107 minutes [subsequently recut for a '14' rating, running time: 105 minutes]
US theatrical distributor: South Gate Entertainment (released in 1991). rated: R. running time: 90 minutes
UK theatrical distribution: none - although played in February 1990 at the Scala Cinema (London) before its video release

Submitted to the BBFC by Rank Film Distributors Ltd. and passed on 05/01/1990 at 95 minutes 18 seconds with cuts totalling 35 seconds

Due occhi diabolici [Italian theatrical title]

Two Evil Eyes [US theatrical title & UK video title]
Deux yeux maléfiques [French theatrical title]
Los ojos del diablo [Spanish theatrical title]
Due occhi malocchio/Metropolitan Horrors/Poe/Edgar Allan Poe [pre-production titles]

1990 // Italy

Directed by George Romero & Dario Argento

Cast: La verità sul casi di mister Valdemar/The Facts in the Case of Mr. Valdemar Adrienne Barbeau (Jessica Valdemar). Ramy Zada (Doctor Robert 'Bob' Hoffman) with Bingo O'Malley (Ernest 'Ernie' Valdemar). Jeff Howell (policeman) and E.G. Marshall (Steven Pike, Mr Valdemar's attorney). Tom Atkins (Grogan). Christine Forrest (nurse). Chuck Aber (Mr Pratt, the bank manager). Barbara Bryne (Martha). Anthony DiLeo Jr. (taxi driver). Mitchell Baseman (boy at zoo). Larry John Meyers (old man).
Cast: Il gatto nero/The Black Cat Harvey Keitel (Roderick Usher) with Madeleine Potter (Annabel). John Amos (Detective Inspector LeGrand). Sally Kirkland (Eleonora, South of Heaven bartender). Kim Hunter (Gloria Pym). Holter Ford Graham (Christian) and Martin Balsam (Mr. Pym). Julie Benz (Betty). Lou Valenzi (editor). Peggy Sanders (young policewoman @ crime scene). J.R. Hall (2nd policeman). Scott House (3rd policeman). Jeffrey Wild (delivery man). Lanene Charters (Bonnie). Ted Worsley (desk editor). James G. MacDonald (Luke). Jonathan Adams (Hammer). [uncredited] Tom Savini (the monomaniac).

[also featuring] Mario Caputo. Bill Dalzell III. Charles McPherson. Jeff Monahan. Fred Moore. Christina Romero. Ben Tatar.
Norman Douglass, Andy Duppin, David Lomax, Phil Neilson, Mike O'Rourke, Mike Russo & Tom Savini (stuntmen).

Achille Manzotti presents a film by Dario Argento and George Romero - an ADC/Gruppo Bema production

La verità sul casi di mister Valdemar/The Facts in the Case of Mr. Valdemar
directed by George Romero. screenplay: George Romero. director of photography: Peter Reniers [colour by Cinecittà/filmed in Kodak Eastmancolor].
Il gatto nero/The Black Cat
directed by Dario Argento. screenplay: Dario Argento & Franco Ferrini. director of photography: Beppe Maccari [colour by Cinecittà/filmed in Kodak Eastmancolor].
Combined crew: executive producers: Claudio Argento & Dario Argento. music by Pino Donaggio, conducted by Natale Massara. film editor: Pasquale Buba.production designer: Cletus Anderson. costume designer: Barbara Anderson. casting: Elissa Myers, c.s.a. & Paul Fonquet. production supervisor: Andrea Tinnirello. production manager: Fernando Franchi. unit publicist in Italy: Enrico Lucherini & Fantoli. international public relations: Greg Day, Zakiya & Associates. production manager: Carol Cuddy. 1st assistant director: Nick Mastandrea. 2nd assistant director: Maria Melograne & Fred Donatelli. assistants to Dario Argento [uncredited]: Luigi Cozzi & Michele Soavi. director, EPK [uncredited]: Luigi Cozzi. production office co-ordinator: Lisa Bradley. production assistant: Andrew Sands. production accountant: Luciano Tartaglia. interpreter: Bert Bell. production secretary: Allegria Elson. script supervisor: J.S. Shoe. dialogue coaches: Kenneth Gargaro & Burton White. camera operator: Frank Perl. 1st assistant cameramen: Michael Latino & Erik Brown. 2nd assistant cameraman: John Moyer. still photographer: Beth Kukucka. 2nd unit director & steadicam operator [The Black Cat]: Nicola Pecorini. gaffers: Ed Letteri & Fernando Massaccesi. best boy: Frank McGough. electricians: Joe Abelin, Barry Kessler, Brian Haughin & Ted Wiegand. key grip: John Janusek. grips: Nick 'Bomba' Tallo, Rich Sieg, Bart Flaherty & Joseph 'Bruno' Pelle. assistant set designer: Lawrence Bailer. assistant to the production: Mark Worthington. set decorator: Diana L. Stoughton. leadman: Jim Schneider. art department co-ordinator: Gary Kosko. set dressers: Eloise Albrecht & Francine Byrne. prop master: Martin Garrigan. prop department: Thomas Garrigan. props: Norman Beck. set painter: Eileen Garrigan. 1st scenic: Frederika Gray. scenics: Charles Ballew, Nora Cline & Paula Payne. construction co-ordinator: Lou Taylor. chief carpenter: Howard Jones. wardrobe supervisors: Kathy Borland & Nancy Palmetier. wardrobe assistant: Mindy Eshelman. seamstresses: Diane Collins & Debra Marks. make-up artist & hair stylist: Jeannee Josefczyk. make-up assistant: Terrie Godfrey. location manager: Judy Matthews. production sound mixer: Felipe Borrero. boom operator: Tommy Louie. cat wrangler: Chris Peworchik Call. rain effects: J.C. Brotherhood. special make-up effects supervisor: Tom Savini Ltd.. special make-up assistants: Everett Burrel, John Vulich & Will Huff. local casting: Donna Belajac & Christina Romero. extras casting: Staci Blagovich. choreography: Kathy Carthers-Wayne. transportation co-ordinator: John Bergholz. generator man: Fred Pope. transportation captain: Anthony J. Yannone. driver: Edward J. France. assistant editor: Ray Boniker. 2nd assistant editor: John S. Bick. optical effects: Perpetual Motion Pictures. craft services: Grant Rhinehart. production staff in Rome unit manager & post-production co-ordinator: Fabrizio Cico Diaz. production accountant: Carlo Du Bois. 1st assistant editor & music editor: Lorenza Franco. dialogue editor: Cesare D'Amico. ADR editor: Nick Alexander. re-recording mixer: Romano Checcacci. titles & opticals: Studio A.M. - Aldo Mafera. post-production facility: Fono Roma. additional sound effects & foley artists: Luciano Anzellotti & Massimo Anzellotti. insurance brokers: Cine Sicurtà srl. music producers: Faso Edizioni Musicali s.a.s.. [music] performance: Paolo Stefan. music recording: Forum (Rome). music mixer: Sergio Marcotulli. Dolby stereo consultant: Federico Savina. The production thanks Aquarius Transfermation Ltd. (New York).
processing laboratory: Technicolor (Rome & New York). Dolby stereo in selected theatres.

Italian visa number: 85361 [22/01/90]. Registro cinematografico: 8.106.

Filmed from 10 July 1989 to 12 September 1989 [22 days on The Facts in the Case of Mr. Valdemar and 32 days on The Black Cat] on location in/around Pittsburgh (PA, USA). Locations include a Victorian house in Allegheny, Fox Chapel and the Westin William Penn Hotel (Pittsburgh, PA, USA) and the Edgar Allan Poe House in Baltimore (MA, USA). Budget: $9 million.

Italian theatrical distributor: Artisti Associati (released on 25 January 1990). running time: 115 minutes
US theatrical distributor: Taurus Entertainment (released on 25 October 1990). rated: R. running time: 115 minutes
French theatrical distributor: Unirecord (released in Paris on 8 July 1992). running time: 105 minutes

Trauma [Italian/US theatrical & video title]

L'enigma di Aura/Aura's Enigma [shooting titles]
Moving Guillotine [pre-shooting title]
Aura [German video title]

1993 // Italy & the United States

Directed by Dario Argento

Cast: Christopher Rydell (David Parsons). Asia Argento (Aura Petrescu). James Russo (Captain Travis). Laura Johnson (Grace Harrington, newsreader). Hope Alexander-Willis (Linda Quirk). Sharon Barr (Hilda Volkmann, Aura's nurse). Frederic Forrest as (Doctor Leopold Judd) and Piper Laurie (Adriana Petrescu, a medium) special appearance by Brad Dourif (Doctor Lloyd). Dominique Serrano (Stefan Petrescu, Aura's father). Ira Belgrade (Arnie or Artie). Isabell Monk (Georgia Jackson, chiropractor). Cory Garvin (Gabriel Pickering). Terry Perkins (Mrs Pickering, Gabriel's mother). Tony Saffold (Ben Aldrich, tv news reporter). Peter Moore (Mark Leneer). Lester Purry (Sergeant Carver). David Chase (Sid Marigold). Jacqui Kim (Alice). Rita Vassallo (Rita, mannish woman). Stephen D'Ambrose (pale man). Bonita Parsons (prime woman). Gregory Beech (deaf man). Kevin Dutcher (John Miller, timid man). Kathy Quirk (Gare Grayson, redhead). E.A. Violet Boor (Mrs Potter).
Les Exodus, Onesmo Kibira, Innocent Mfalingundi, Charles Petrus & Lance Pollonais (reggae band).
Ky Michaelson & Donna Quinn (stunts).
[uncredited] Fiore Argento (Farraday Clinic receptionist).

Mario & Vittorio Cecchi Gori/Silvio Berlusconi Communications/Overseas Filmgroup present an A.D.C. Produzioni Cinematografiche e Televisive/Overseas Filmgroup (Los Angeles) production
[uncredited] B.N.L. - Sezione Credito Cinematografico e Teatrale
executive producers: T. David Rash & Andrea Tinnirello. produced by Dario Argento. line producer: Chris Beckman. written by Dario Argento & T.E.D. Kline; based on an original story by Franco Ferrini, Gianni Romoli & Dario Argento. director of photography: Raffaele Mertes [colour by Technicolor]. music by Pino Donaggio. editor: Bennett Goldberg. production designer: Billy Jett. costume designer: Leesa Evans. special make-up effects: Tom Savini. casting: Louis Di Giaimo & Ira Belgrade. production manager: Andrew Sands. 1st assistant director: Rod Smith. 2nd assistant director: Phil Elins. 2nd 2nd assistant director: Daniel Carrey. dialogue coach: Paul Draper. assistant designer: Ruth Jessup. additional dialogue: Kirk Gardner. 1st assistant camera: Richard Cantu. 2nd assistant camera: D.J. Harder. additional 2nd assistant camera: Dennis Lynch. still photographer: Carlo Ontal. script supervisor: Dea Hickox. production accountant: Luciano Taraglia. production co-ordinator: Abigail Sheiner. assistant production co-ordinators: Holly Edwards & David Ray Martin. make-up & hair stylist: Desne Holland. make-up & hair: Tracey Roden. assistant make-up & hair: Cheryl Nick. hair stylist for Piper Laurie: Lori Guidroz. wardrobe supervisor: Allyson Brown. wardrobe assistant: Susan Strubel. location manager: Jon Bergholz. assistant location manager: Beth Lundin. art director: Nancy Derby. set decorator: Jaqueline Jacobson. property master: Joel Benton. on-set dresser: Cory Schubert. assistant art director: Michael Morgenthal. gaffer: Michael Marzovilla. best boy electric: Nick Kupkovic. electrics: Michael Flash McDonald & Chris Van Zant. generator operator: Scott Fischel. key grip & dolly girp: Christopher Skutch. best boy grip: Edgar Martin. grips: Neil Williams & Chris Barry. Luma crane operator: Victor Korte. construction co-ordinator: Bob Hedstrom. sound recordist: Paul Coogan. boom operator: Jack Bornoff. stunt co-ordinator: Ky Michaelson. stunt co-ordination (car crash): Jack Gill. Romanian language coach: Michael Lupu. local casting: Barbara Shelton. extra casting: Andrea Wulff. physical effects supervisor: Paul Murphy. physical effects assistant: Jessica Moliter. transportation co-ordinator: Paul Giorgi. transportation captain: Mike Kennedy. assistant editor: Jim Schimmerhorn. special make-up effects: Greg Funk, Will Huff, Christopher Martin & Tom Savini. unit publicists: Nikki Parker & Cid Swank [Denmead Marketing]. set production assistants: David Diamond & Martin Kloner. insurance USA: Cohen Near North Insurance. legal services: Mitchell Silverberg & Knupp. completion bond: Film Finances Italia srl. camera provided by Technovision srl. editing system: Editdroid. film to video transfer: Encore Video. video to laserdisc transfer: Lucas Arts Entertainment Company. 24 FPS video playback: Intervideo, Steve Austin. video assistant support services: Judah Hanna. grip electric equipment: Leggs, Inc.. Pee Wee dolly equipment: Lighthouse, Inc.. videographers: Mike Rivard & Jerome Thelia. sound effects: Interlock. payroll service: Producers' & Artists' Services. travel provided by Northern Lights Travel. post production supervisor: Steve Barnett. music performed by Bulgarian Symphony Orchestra, directed by Victor Ciuckovl.
The Producers wish to thank the Minnesota Film Board and the Minneapolis Film Office.

negative: Eastmancolor Kodak. Dolby Stereo in selected theatres.

Italian visa number: 88494 [10/03/93]. Registro cinematografico: 8.664.

Filmed from 3 August 1992 to 26 September 1992 for eight weeks on location in Minneapolis & St Paul (Minnesota, USA). Budget: $7 million

Italian theatrical distributor: Penta Film (released on 12 March 1993). rated: none. running time: 110 minutes
US theatrical distribution: none. world sales: Overseas Filmgroup

La sindrome di Stendhal [Italian theatrical title]

The Stendhal Syndrome [UK video title]

1996 // Italy

Directed by Dario Argento

Cast: Asia Argento (Assistant Inspector Anna Manni). Thomas Kretschmann (Alfredo Grossi) and with Marco Leonardi (Marco Longhi). Luigi Diberti (Chief Inspector Manetti). Julien Lambroschini (Marie Bale, French research assistant). John Quentin (Mr Manni, Anna's father). Franco Diogene (victim's husband). Sonia Topazio (victim in Florence). Antonio Marziantonio (musuem watchman). Lucia Stara (Viterbo shop assistant) and guest star Paolo Bonacelli (Doctor Cavanna). Lorenzo Crespi (Giulio). Vera Gamma (policewoman). John Pedeferri (hydraulic engineer). Veronica Lazar (Marie's mother). Diano Mario (coroner). Eleonora Vizzini (Anna, as a child). Maximilian Nisi (Luigi). Leonardo Ferrantini (Alessandro Manni, Anna's brother). Sandro Giordano (Fausto). Cinzia Monreale (Mrs Grossi, Alfredo's wife). Michele Kaplan (the Grossi's son). Laura Piattella (40 year old woman). Vincenzo Uccellini (40 year old woman's son). Elena Bermani (30 year old woman). Luca Camilletti (Albergo Porta Rossa porter). Graziano Giusti (2nd coroner). Monica Fiorentini (female doctor in Florence). Giancarlo Teodori (male doctor in Florence). Antonello Murru (1st police officer). Marna Del Monaco (dining car stewardess). Maria Grazia Nazzari (night watch victim). Alexys Schwartz (child's voice)

Scenes featuring Veronica Lazar, Franco Diogene and Michele Kaplan were deleted from the film just prior to its Italian release, apparently to "increase pacing". Their credit remains on all prints.

a Medusa Film production produced by Cine 2000.

produced by Dario Argento & Giuseppe Colombo. line producer: Walter Massi. screenplay: Dario Argento. story: Dario Argento & Franco Ferrini; based on the novel "The Stendhal Syndrome" by Graziella Magherini. director of photography: Giuseppe Rotunno a.i.c. - a.s.c. [colour by Technicolor S.p.A./filmed in Technovision]. music composed, orchestrated & conducted by Ennio Morricone. film editor: Angelo Nicolini. production designer: [Massimo] Antonello Geleng. costumes by Lia Morandini. special visual & digital effects: Sergio Stivaletti. special make-up effects: Franco Casagni. assistant editor: Carla Funari. 2nd unit director: Luigi Cozzi. 2nd unit director of photography: Roberto Girometti. 2nd unit cameraman: Lucio Granelli. 2nd unit grip: Fabio Carussi. assistant directors: Nicolò Bongiorno, Fabrizio Campanella, Filippo Macelloni & Daniele Persica. unit managers: Fiore Argento, Renata Paccariè, Maurizio Pigna & Ruggero Salvadori. production secretaries: Laura Campanelli & Barbara Spoletini. assistant production secretaries: Riccardo Folgore & Tommaso Pantano. production assistant: Riccardo Carinci. dialogue coach: Dianne Jones. camera operator: Gianni Fiore Coltellacci. 1st assistant camera: Lorenzo Tovoli. 2nd assistant camera: Armando Barbieri. assistant operator: Roberto De Angelis. stills photographer: Franco Vitale. script supervisor: Maria Anita Borgiotti. assistant script supervisor: Melissa Strizzi. consulting accountant: Andrea Tinnirello. production accountant: Benito Mancini. make-up: Gloria Pescatore. hair stylist: Ferdinando Merolla. wardrobe assistant: Stefania Svizzeretto. seamstress: Bertilla Silvestrin. set dresser: Giovanni Natalucci. assistant set dresser: Michela Gisotti. props: Giuseppe Pagnotta & Danilo Pagnotta. painter: Claudio Tedesco. carpenters: Dante Precetti & Claudio Quaglietti. gaffers: Renato Sardini & Rodolfo Bramucci. electricians: Giuseppe Bertucci, Alfredo Bramucci, Stefano D'Offizi & Massimiliano Sardini. generator man: Maurizio Cartocci. key grip: Roberto Diamanti. grips: Dario Badia, Claudio Del Gobbo, Mauro Diamanti, Roberto Pecci & Massimo Sergianni. production sound mixer: Carlo Palmieri & Riccardo Palmieri. boom operator: Piero Fondi. crowd marshalls [Florence]: Renzo Cantini, [Viterbo]: Sabine Lucarelli, [Rome]: Alfredo Ruffini. unit publicist [Italy]: Paola Paggetta [abroad]: Corbett & Keene Ltd.. insurance brokers: Studio M for Cinesicurtà S.R.L.. post-production consultant: Lillo Capoano. additional sound effects: Soundtracks S.N.C.. ADR editor: Nick Alexander. music co-ordinator: Claudio Messina (RTI Music). music producer: RTI Music. orchestra: A.M.I.T. - Accademia Musicale Italiana. recorded at Forum Studio (Rome). music mixer: Franco Patrignani. music assistant: Andrea Morricone. special effects: Giovanni Corridori & Co.. assistants to Sergio Stivaletti: Mischa Koopman, Daniele Auber, Dario Rega & Francesca R. Di Nunzio. digital scanning & recording: Cinesite (Europe) Ltd.. post production facility: International Recording. titles & opticals: Penta Studio. sculpture: Cinears S.R.L.; Cemar S.R.L.. costume house: Sorelle Ferroni (Rome). set furnishings: G.R.P.; Arredamenti Cineteatrali. wigs: MAG.GI Palombi Wigs. underwater photography: Marco Manferdini's Video Film [sic]. edited on Lightworks. raw stock: Kodak S.p.A.. camera equipment supplied by Arco Due S.R.L.. lighting equipment: Petracca & Co.. transportation: Fratelli Cartocci; Consorzio Trasporti Cin.. production equipment: Cineservice S.R.L.. telecinema: Augustus Color.
The production thanks Casa Editrice Ponte Alle Grazie; 1st. Liceo Artistico (Rome); The Villa Giulia Etruscan Museum; The Italian National Art Gallery; The Mayor and Municipal Authorities of Florence; The Uffizi Gallery (Florence); The Mayor and Municipal Authorities of Viterbo; Pianeta Benessere, Grand Hotel Salus e Delle Terme (Viterbo); The Mayor and Municipal Authorities of Terni; The Tourist Office (Terni); Enel S.p.A. (Terni); Nucleo Idro Elettrico; Props Management Sabina Palmero; For Intesa & Intesa; Telecom Italia S.p.A.; The Italian State Railways; Nokia Italia S.p.A.; Sidauto S.p.A..
Dolby Digital Stereo SR [Spectral Recording].

Filmed from 17 July 1995 to 15 September 1995 for nine weeks in Florence [including the Uffizi Gallery], Viterbo, Terni & Rome (Italy) with interiors at Cinecittà [Studios] (Rome, Italy). Budget: $3.8 million.

Italian theatrical distributor: Medusa Distribuzione (released in Rome & Milan on 26 January 1996). rated: 14. running time: 119 minutes

Il fantasma dell'opera [Italian theatrical title]

The Phantom of the Opera [export title]
Le Fantôme dell'opera [French theatrical title]

1998 // Italy & Hungary

Directed by Dario Argento

Cast: Julian Sands (The Phantom). Asia Argento (Christine Daaé). Andrea Di Stefano (Baron Raoul De Chagny). Nadia Rinaldi (Carlotta Altieri, the diva). Coralina Cataldi-Tassoni (Honorine, Christine's maid). István Bubik (Ignace, the ratcatcher). Lucia Guzzardi (Madame Gíry). Aldo Massasso (M. Pourdieu, the Paris Opera House's new manager). Zoltán Barabás (Poligny). Gianni Franco (Montluc, journalist with the Gazette Républican). David D'Ingeo (Alfred). Kitty Kéri (Paulette, Alfred's lover). John Pedeferri (Doctor Princard). Leonardo Treviglio (Jérôme De Chagny, Raoul's brother). Massimo Sarchielli (M. Buquet, the girls' teacher). Luis Molteni (Nicolaud, the ex-manager). Enzo Cardogna (Marcel). Antonio Pupillo (Gustave). Domenica Coppolino (Carlotta's mother).
English language version adds: Itala Békés (Carlotta's mother). Claudia Kemenes (Hermine). Csilla Wend (Liza). Réka Pozsgay (Marthe, the little girl). Ferenc Deák B. (Edgar Degas, the artist). Rezsò Ludvigh (Maestro Gounod). David Drucker (Kiki). Gábor Harsay (Marc, Carlotta's manservant). Balázs Tardy (Longuet). Dénes Újlaky (Papin). Sándor Bese (dwarf, Ignace's assistant). Iván Dengyel (Martin). György Szakály (ballet master). Ferenc Rátkai (Pollidori). Podporina Ilona (Rose 'Velvet Lips', a prostitute). Frigyes Hollósi (friend). István Szöczey (Faust). Szabó Benke Róbert (poet #1). Zoltán Rajkai (poet #2). Tania Nagel (mother). Crespo Rodrigo (father). Zsolt Anger (waiter). Zsolt Derecskei (Romeo). Tibor Nemes (Mephisto). Gabor Piroch (Phantom's stunts). Lászlo Petò, Dániel Zdroba & Béla Nemeth (pianists).
Asia Argento's arias were sung by Raffaella Milanesi. Giovanni Cianfriglia, Domenico Cianfriglia, Alessandro Novelli, Mario Novelli, Rocco Russo, Massimo Vanni & Omero Capanna (stunts). György Kivé (Hungarian crew double).

Italian & English language prints differ as to the the actress they credit as playing Carlotta's mother.

a film by Dario Argento // a Medusa Film - Reteitalia production for Cine 2000 [in association with] Focus Film, Budapest [and] Tele + // this film was produced with support from the Presidenza del Consiglio dei Ministri ©1998. Medusa.
executive producer: Claudio Argento. produced by Giuseppe Colombo. Hungarian producer: Áron Sipos. screenplay: Gérard Brach & Dario Argento; based on the novel "Le Fantôme dell'opera" by Gaston Leroux. director of photography: Ronnie Taylor b.s.c. [prints & processing: Cinecittà]. music composed, orchestrated & conducted by Ennio Morricone. editor: Anna [Rosa] Napoli a.m.c.. production designer: [Massimo] Antonello Geleng. costume designer: Ágnes Gyarmathy. special visual effects: Sergio Stivaletti. production supervisor: Tommaso Calevi. 1st assistant director: Alessandro Ingargiola. 2nd assistant director: Enrico Tubertini. production manager: Verena Maria Baldeo. unit manager: Riccardo Folgore. production secretaries: Carla Alonzo & Michela De Porzi. dialogue coach: John Fonseca. casting: Mirta Guarnaschelli u.i.c. & Emma Style. M.D.P. camera operator & steadicam: Marco Pieroni. 2nd camera operator: Giuseppe Tinelli. 1st assistant camera operator: Claudio Zamarion. assistant camera operators: Roberto Gentili, Sacha Ippoliti & Daniele Armeni. video assistant: Monica Bonomi. still photographer: Franco Vitale. script supervisor: Paola Mengoni. production accountant: Marcello Lanza. assistant production accountant & paymaster: Carla Menicocci. key make-up artist: Alessandro Bertolazzi. make-up artist: Paola Gattabrusi. key hair stylist: Massimo Gattabrusi. seamstress: Bertilla Silvestrin. set dresser: Paola Riviello. construction co-ordinator: Giuseppe Cancellara. props: Salvatore Manca. set painter: Santo Spalla. carpenter: Fabrizio Carletti. gaffer: Stefano Marino. electricians: Fabrizio Amendola, Daniele Cafolla, Alberto Rogante, Salvatore Ruberto & Antonio D'Arienzo. key grip: Claudio Diamanti. grips: Luigi Orso, Maurizio Salvatori, Gianluca Ventiru, Vincenzo Mancini & Giuliano Paravano. generator operator: Benvenuto Pedron. production sound mixers: Roberto Alberghini, Umberto Montesanti & Gilberto Martinelli. boom operators: Alfredo Petti & Marco Lazzaro. production drivers: Marcello Colaciello, Domenico Di Pietro, Luciano Scrocca, Luigi D'Ettorre, Paolo Racalbuto & Andrea Regoli. stunt co-ordinator: Riccardo Mioni. [live] action special effects: Danilo Bollettini, Gastone Callori, Massimo Cristofanelli & Ercole Quaglietti for Corr. G & A Cinematografica Srl. Laboratorio Stivaletti crew realization supervisor [supervising producer]: Barbara Morosetti. chief sculptor: Francesca Romana Di Nunzio. sculptors: Carlo Diamantini & Carolina Sorrano. mechanism of animated creatures: David Bracci. mechanism of rat-hunting machine: Simon Blades. models: Arianna Pascazi. animated creatures finishing: Enrico Corradino. special plastic materials: Fabrizio Capponi. post-production shots assistants: Gabriele Magri & Vittorio Magri. [financial] administration: Anna Morosetti. digital effects provided by Apocalypse di S. Stivaletti ['Sergio Stivaletti's Apocalypse']. digital compositing operator: Gaetano Polizzi. 3D operators [animators]: Ugo Frigerio & Gabriele Zuppardo. computer optimization: Antonio Rossi. software: Alias/Wavefront; AVID. computer stations: Silicon Graphics. animals supplied by Maurizio Garrone. animal consultant: Zoo Grunwald di Pasquale Martino. publicity: Studio Nobile - Scarafoni. insurance: Cinesicurtà Srl. completion bond: Film Finances Italia SpA. final sound mix: Fausto Ancillai. studio sound mixers: Angelo Raguseo & Danilo Sterbini. production sound editing: Sound On Line Srl. sound effects editors: Tullio Arcangeli; Roberto Sterbini, Paolo Pucci & Saverio Lancia for Space Sound. Italian version sound credits dubbing by CDL Doppiaggio Edizione srl. dubbing director: Rodolfo Bianchi. assistant dubbing: Viviana Barbetta. dubbing recordist: Roberto Cappannelli. English language version sound credits ADR supervisor: Nick Alexander. English adaptation: Georgina Caspari.
music producer: Claudio Messina (RTI Music). music publisher: RTI Music Srl (Milan). assistant to the composer: Andrea Morricone. orchestra: Roma Sinfonietta. choir: Corale e Coro Giovanile (S. Filippo); directed by Fabrizio Barchi. copyist: Donato Salone. music recorded at Forum - Music Village. music recording: Fabio Venturi. assistant sound: Damiano Antinori. music supervisor & co-ordinator: Enrico De Melis. singing teachers (for Asia Argento): Lilian Zafred, (for Nadia Rinaldi): Stefania Magnifico. music consultant: Cinzia Cavalieri.
AVID supplier: Todomodo. 1st assistant editor: Emanuela Di Giunta. 2nd assistant editor: Maria Cristina Marra. camera equipment supplied by Panalight. lighting equipment: Petracca. transport: Cinetecnica Srl. forwarders: Transor International Srl. travel agency: Islet Viaggi e Turismo. stills laboratory: Fast Photo Service. wigs: Rocchetti & Rocchetti. jewelry & accessories: L.A.B.A.. titles & opticals: Penta Studio. colour timer: Pasquale Cuzzupoli. Dolby consultant: Federico Savina.
production services in Budapest (Hungary): Focus Film. production manager: István Juhász. 1st unit manager: Gábor Rajna. 2nd unit manager: Balázs Endrödy. production assistant: Regina Darányi. runners: Imre Csik & Balázs Kovács.

ACHILLE MANZOTTI presenta

UN FILM DI

DARIO ARGENTO | **GEORGE ROMERO**

DUE OCCHI
DIABOLICI

TECHNICOLOR

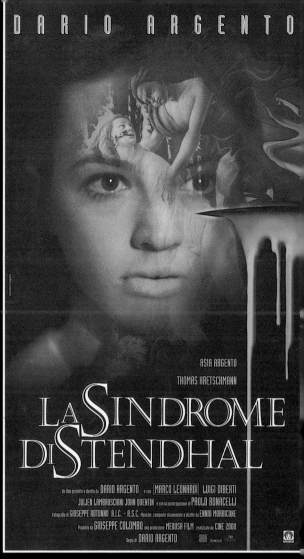

DARIO ARGENTO

ASIA ARGENTO

THOMAS KRETSCHMANN

LA SINDROME
DI STENDHAL

Un film prodotto e diretto da DARIO ARGENTO e con MARCO LEONARDI · LUIGI DIBERTI
JULIEN LAMBROSCHINI JOHN QUENTIN e con la partecipazione di PAOLO BONACELLI
Fotografia di GIUSEPPE ROTUNNO A.I.C. – A.S.C. musiche composte strumentate e dirette da ENNIO MORRICONE
Prodotto da GIUSEPPE COLOMBO una produzione MEDUSA FILM realizzata da CINE 2000

regia di DARIO ARGENTO

PENTA FILM

MARIO & VITTORIO CECCHI GORI presentano

SILVIO BERLUSCONI COMMUNICATIONS

regia di
DARIO ARGENTO

TRAUMA

con CHRISTOPHER RYDELL · ASIA ARGENTO · JAMES RUSSO · LAURA JOHNSON · FREDERIC FORREST

MEDUSA FILM presenta

un film di
DARIO ARGENTO

JULIAN
SANDS

ASIA
ARGENTO

il Fantasma
dell'Opera

MEDUSA FILM presenta un film di DARIO ARGENTO · JULIAN SANDS · ASIA ARGENTO "IL FANTASMA DELL'OPERA" · ANDREA DI STEFANO
NADIA RINALDI · CORALINA CATALDI TASSONI · ISTVAN BUBIK · ZOLTAN BARABAS · DIRETTORE DELLA FOTOGRAFIA RONNIE TAYLOR (B.S.C.)
MUSICHE COMPOSTE STRUMENTATE E DIRETTE DA ENNIO MORRICONE · SCENEGGIATURA DI GÉRARD BRACH e DARIO ARGENTO
TRATTO DAL ROMANZO "IL FANTASMA DELL'OPERA" DI GASTON LEROUX
UNA PRODUZIONE MEDUSA FILM REALIZZATA DA GIUSEPPE COLOMBO PER CINE 2000
PRODUTTORE ESECUTIVO CLAUDIO ARGENTO · REGIA DI DARIO ARGENTO

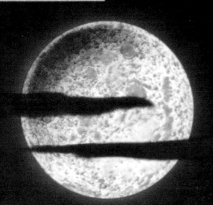

una produzione MEDUSA FILM
realizzata da DARIO ARGENTO e CLAUDIO ARGENTO per la OPERA FILM

il nuovo thriller di
Dario Argento

NONHOSONNO

un film di DARIO ARGENTO "NONHOSONNO" MAX VON SYDOW   STEFANO DIONISI   CHIARA CASELLI   GABRIELE LAVIA
PAOLO MARIA SCALONDRO   ROBERTO ZIBETTI   con la partecipazione di ROSSELLA FALK
direttore della fotografia RONNIE TAYLOR (B.S.C.)   scenografia ANTONELLO GELENG   costumi SUSY MATTOLINI
organizzatore generale TOMMASO CALEVI   montaggio ANNA NAPOLI (A.M.C.)   effetti speciali visivi SERGIO STIVALETTI
musiche dei GOBLIN   edizioni musicali BIXIO C.E.M.S.A. s.r.l.
produttore esecutivo CLAUDIO ARGENTO   soggetto di DARIO ARGENTO   FRANCO FERRINI
sceneggiatura di DARIO ARGENTO   FRANCO FERRINI   con la collaborazione di CARLO LUCARELLI
regia di DARIO ARGENTO

la colonna sonora è incisa su dischi CINEVOX RECORD

SESTITO

www.nonhosonno.it

TELE +   MEDUSA

interpreters: Ildikó Kéri & Réka Belsò. production accountant: Rita Manyai. 1st assistant director: Péter Racz. 2nd assistant director: Rita Nagy. 3rd assistant director: Tamás Mink. art director: Csaba Stork. assistant art directors: János Rauschenberger & Dóra Szentirmai. set construction: István Galambros, Andrea Tóth & Lajos E. Szabo. set dressers: Ferenc Schöffer, Mihály Sütò & Tamás Breier. props: Péter Ujváry, Zoltán Szabo & Zoltán Schöffer. 1st assistant costume designer: Ágnes Endres. 2nd assistant costume designer: Richárd Basa. key seamstress: György Homonnay. seamstresses: Gábor Szabó, Gyula Zambó, Mari Balázs Piri, Dóra Riesz & Andrea Nárai. 1st unit assistant cameraman: Péter Dobrányi. 2nd unit assistant cameramen: Balázs Szinte & Péter Kotschy. production sound mixer: József Kardos. boom operator: Csaba Erös. gaffer: Péter Sidlò. electrician: Sandór (Tücsi) Novak. key grip: Attila Szücs. van driver: Zoltàn Makra. special effects: Péter Szilágyi & Iván Pohárnok. standby special effects: Attila Halász & István Vanek. fight master: Gyula Langer. make-up artist: Ágnes Petrovics. assistant make-up artist: Balázs Novák. hair dresser: István Szücs. cast co-ordinators: Zoltán Baráth & Mari Makó. extras co-ordinator: Sándor Dénes. music consultant: István Mali. consulting speleologist: Péter Adamkó. animal trainer: Péter Huszák. catering: György Herz. production drivers: János Gönczi, Láslo Szamel (Cofi) & Tibor Nyári. minibus driver: Tibor Wallner.
music extracts: "Intermezzo" &" Slow Waltz" from "Sylvia" by Clement Delibes, performed by Slovak Radio Symphony Orchestra, directed by Ondrej Lenard & "Mazurka No 5 in B Flat Major - Op. 7 no 1" from "Vivace" by Frederic Chopin, performed by Sandor Falvay - both (p) & © Nax/EMI Music Publishing Italia Srl.; "Overture - Act I" & "Coro dei folletti"/"The Elves Chorus" - Act V from "Faust" by Charles Gounod, performed by Choeur et Orchestre du Theatre National de l'Opera de Paris, directed by Andre Cfuytens, (p) & © EMI France/EMI Music Italy; "Act I" &" Duet - Act IV" from "Romeo e Giulietta"/"Romeo and Juliet" & "Finale Act II" from "Faust" - all by Charles Gounod and performed by the The Orchestra of the Budapest Opera House, directed by Géza Török; "Bell Song" from "Lakme" by Clement Delibes, performed by The Orchestra of the Budapest Opera House, directed by Géza Török; "Tour Keys" by Maurizio Guarini & Cinzia Cavalieri.
The production thanks: the management and staff of The Budapest Opera House & the management of the Grotte Di Pertosa [Pertosa Caves] in Salerno for their indispensable collaboration.
stock: Eastman. Dolby digital.
Filmed from 19 January 1998 to 17 April 1998 on location at the Budapest Opera House in Budapest (Hungary), in Pertosa (near Salerno, Southern Italy) and in Paris (France) with interiors filmed at the Mafilm facility at Mariassay Studio (Budapest, Hungary) for 10 weeks. Budget: circa $10 million

Italian theatrical distributor: Medusa Distribuzione (released in Rome & Milan on 20 November 1998). rated: 14. running time: 106 minutes

Nonhosonno [Italian theatrical title]
Sleepless [export title]
Insomnia [production title]

Italy // 2000

Medusa Motion Pictures // Medusa Film presents in collaboration with Tele+, a Medusa Film production // produced by Dario Argento & Claudio Argento for Opera Film // a film by Dario Argento

Directed by Dario Argento

Cast: Max von Sydow (Inspector Ulisse Moretti). Stefano Dionisi (Giacomo). Chiara Caselli (Gloria). Gabriele Lavia (Betti, a lawyer). Paolo Maria Scalondro (Inspector Massi). Roberto Zibetti (Lorenzo). Roberto Accornero (Fausto). Barbara Lerici (Angela). Barbara Mautino (Dora). Conchita Puglisi (Amanda). Massimo Sarchielli (Leone, a hobo). Elena Marchesini (Mel). Guido Morbello (the young detective). Aldo Massasso (Cascio, the old detective) <with the participation of> Rossella Falk (Laura de Fabritiis). Diego Casale (Beppe). Alessandra Comerio (Signora Betti). Brian Ayres (magistrate). Daniele Angius (Giacomo, aged 13). Robert Camero (Marco). Luca Fagioli (Vincenzo de Fabritiis). Daniela Fazzolari (Maria Luisa). Aldo Delaude (train guard). John Pedeferri (investigator). Francesco Benedetto (Perlabagagli). Renato Liprando (station master). Elisabetta Rocchetti (fast food girl). Rosella Lucà (Mara).
[uncredited] Antonio Rec (man in discotheque). scenes apparently deleted: Francesca Bettori (Giacomo's mother).

executive producer: Claudio Argento. produced by Dario Argento & Claudio Argento. story by Dario Argento, Franco Ferrini. screenplay by Dario Argento, Franco Ferrini, with the collaboration of Carlo Lucarelli. director of photography: Ronnie Taylor, b.s.c. (colour by Technicolor / prints & processing: Cinnecittà). music by Golbin. editor: Anna Napoli, a.m.c.. art director: Antonello Geleng. costumes: Susy Mattolini. production supervisor: Tommaso Calevi. special visual effects: Sergio Stivaletti. 2nd unit director: Marzio Casa. assistant director (pre-production): Riccardo Cannone. 1st assistant director: Giulietta Revel. 2nd assistant directors: Luca Crivet Brancot, John Anderson Fonseca. casting: Chiara Moretti, Lorella Chiapatti. key grip: Sara Busto. production manager: Gianluca Passone. production manager (Turin): Ladislao Zanin. unit managers: Gianluca Borelli Stracca, Riccardo Folgore. production secretary: Carla Alonzo. assistant production secretaries: Giorgia Pellegrini, Giorgi Turletti, Francesco Beltramme. M.D.P. operator: Roberto Brega. steadicam operator: Giovanni Gebbia. assistant operators: Alessandro Gentili, Ezio Gamba. 2nd assistant operators: Emanuele Leurini, Gianluca Faya, Gina Cuzy. director, making of: Catherine Brelet. assistant director, making of: Cedric Brelet. video operator: Francesco Perri. script supervisor: Fernanda Selvaggi. sound: Tullio Morganti. boom operator: Alessandro Pambianco. music consultant: Cinzia Cavalieri. production administrator: Marcello Lamza. administrator/cashier: Erika Taloni. cashier: Maria Rita Gagliano. key make-up: Alfredo Marazzi. make-up: Graziella Tosti. key hair stylist: Massimo Cattabrusi. hair stylist: Samantha Mura. assistant costumes: Patrizia Bernardini. 2nd assistant costumes: Paola Ronco. seamstress: Francesca Campanella. assistant art directors: Sabrina Dassani, Chiara Alessio. 2nd assistant art director: Gloria Saya. set dresser: Francesca Bocca. assistant set dresser: Maria Castravilli. gaffer: Stefano Marino. electricians: Gianfranco Soro, Fiore Beltrame, Antonio Marchese, Mirco Fincato, Emanuele Miroglio. key grip: Vincenzo Pontil-Scala. grips: Leandro Pagano, Angelo Pace, Antonio Ascione, Enrico Loyato, Andrea Arnaud, Saverio Moggio. generator operators: Marcello Colaciello, Benvenuto Pedron. drivers: Dario Di Gioia, Pietro Rutigliano, Emidio Prioletta, Massimo Giovanetti, Roberto De Persid, Giuseppe Abatangelo, Cristiano Sergioli, Fernando Meluzzi, Riccardo Altobelli, Vincenza Trentanello. properties: Giancarlo Pagani, Salvatore Manca. assistant properties: Enrico Mandirola, Flavio De Simone, Pasquale Scognamiglio, Mauro Franco, Amaranta Flagelli. construction managers: Franco Ragusa, Massimo Cristofanelli, Gastone Callori. stunt co-ordinator: Riccardo Mioni. stuntman: Alessandro Novelli. live action special effects: Corr. G. & A. Cinematografica. still photography: Fast Photo Service; taken

by Franco Vitale. publicity: Francesca De Michele. assistant to Max von Sydow: Catherine Brelet. insurance: Cinesicurtà. dubbing by CDL. dubbing director: Rodolfo Bianchi. assistant dubbing: Liselotte Parisi. dubbing recordists: Alessandro Mastroianni, Marco Di Vittorio. synchronization: Fono Roma. (direct) sound editing: Sound on line s.r.l., Lilio Rosato. sound mixer: Claudio Chiossi. sound effects: Dream Sound di Tullio Arcangeli. assistant effects: Piergiorgio De Luca. sound effects: Alvaro Gramigna. harpists: Sara Terzano, Marina Curasì. music composed & produced by Goblin - Claudio Simonetti & Fabio Pignatelli - Acquario Studio (Rome); DHS Studio (Rome). music recording engineer: Massimo Sinceri. music publisher: Bixio C.E.M.S.A. s.r.l.. soundtrack published by Cinevox Record. stock: Kodak.
AVID furnished by Todomodo di Anna Napoli. assistant editors: Maria Cristina Marra, Alessandro Di Cola. visual effects by Apocalypse by Sergio Stivaletti. Apocalypse staff: supervising director: Barbara Morosetti. sculptor: Francesca Romana Di Nunzio. meccanismi: David Bracci. assistants: Gabriele Magrì, Vittorio Magrì. CG modelling & 3D compositing: Gabriele Zuppardo. paint & compositing: Elena Angeletti. technical equipment: Panalight. lamps & gels: Eurolight '99. transport: Cinetecnica. shipping: Massimo Toreti, International Movie Service. catering: Gastronomia, Marina Assandri (Turin). travel agents: Blue World s.r.l. (Rome), SSilbago Viaggi (Turin). costumes: Annamode 68', Sartoria Cine-Teatrale Norienzo. set construction: Nuova Scenografia Belsole. titles & opticals: Penta Studio. colour timer: Pasquale Cuzzpoli. Dolby consultant: Massimo Puccio. recorded in Dolby Digital.
the production thanks: Regione Piemonte; Patrocinio della Città of Turin; Film Commission (Turin); Fiat Auto S.p.A. (Turin), Ferrovie dello Stato S.p.A.; Grandi Stazioni S.p.A.; Satti S.p.A. Torinese Trasporti Intercomunali; Polizia di Stato - questura di Turin et al. [soundtrack] tbc

"Filastrocca del Fattore" written by Asia Argento.

Filmed from 15 May 2000 for nine weeks on location in Turin (Italy) and at Euphon Studios (Turin, Italy)

Italian theatrical distributor: Medusa Distribuzione (released on 5 January 2001, Rome premiere: 6 January 2001, general release: 12 January 2001). rated: 14. running time: 117 minutes Italian DVD distributor: Medusa (released on 4 July 2001). rated: 14. running time: 113 minutes (R2. languages/subtitles: Italian/English. aspect ratio: 1.77:1. special features: theatrical trailer, 15 minute making-of).

As director for television

Il tram [episode title]
La porta sul buio di Dario Argento [series title]

1973 // Italy

Directed by Sirio Bernadotte [Dario Argento]

Cast: Enzo Cerusico (Commissario Giordani). Paola Tedesco (Giulia) and with Pier Luigi Aprà (the main suspect). Gildo Di Marco. Tom Felleghi (older man). Marcello Fusco. Luciana Lehar. Emilio Marchesini (Marco Roviti). Fulvio Mingozzi (a cop). Corrado Olmi (Morini, a cop). Salvatore Puntillo (moustached man). Maria Tedeschi. Pietro Zardini.

introduced by Dario Argento & Enzo Cerusico

RAI Radiotelevisione Italiana presents a SEDA Spettacoli S.p.A. (Rome) production

[producer: Dario Argento]. story & screenplay: Dario Argento. director of photography: Elio Polacchi [prints & processing: Telecolor (Rome)]. original music by Giorgio Gaslini. editor: Amedeo Giomini. costume designer & art director: Dario Micheli. assistant director: Roberto Pariante. production manager: Giuseppe Mangogna. unit manager: Carlo Cucchi. production secretary: Tomasso Alvieri. cameraman: Nino Annunziata. assistant cameraman: Luigi Conversi. sound: Mario Ronchetti. boom operator: Eugenio Fiore. continuity: M. Grazia Baldanello & Maria Agostini. assistant art director: Maurizio Garrone. assistant editor: Piero Bozza. 2nd assistant editors: Nadia Mazzoni & Tommaso Gramigna. production accountants: Ferdinando Caputo & Carlo Dubois. make-up: Cristina Rocca. hairstylist: Ida Alacino. wardrobe: Marcella Moretti. still photography: Roberto Canevari (Nuova Dial). key grip: Guglielmo Maga. property master: Augusto La Valle. construction manager: Giuseppe Gabrielli. gaffer: Orazio Sinacore. generator operator: Ferdinando Cartocci. sound effects: Anzellotti. titles & opticals: Studio Verzini. synchronization directed by [Domenico] Mimmo Palmara for SINC Cinematografica. mixage: Venanzio Biraschi, recorded by Fono Roma using Western Electric equipment. Italian version: Cinitalia Edizioni. technical equipment: Janiro S.r.l.. costume house: Ferroni. wigs: Rocchetti. furnishings: Cimino Cine Arredamento Rancati. hangings: Alfredo D'Angelo. sound recording: Fono Roma. music publisher: Bixio Sam (Milan).
negatives: Eastmancolor Kodak.

running time: 52 minutes 12 seconds

Testimone oculare [episode title]
La porta sul buio di Dario Argento [series title]

1973 // Italy

Directed by Roberto Pariante [actually Dario Argento]

Cast: Marilù Tolo (Roberta Leoni). Riccardo Salvino (Roberta's husband). Glauco Onorato (police inspector). Altea De Nicola. Luigi Pagnani Fusconi.

introduced by Dario Argento

RAI Radiotelevisione Italiana presents a SEDA Spettacoli S.p.A. (Rome) production

[producer: Dario Argento]. story: Dario Argento. screenplay: Dario Argento & Luigi Cozzi. director of photography: Elio Polacchi [prints & processing: Telecolor (Rome)]. original music by Giorgio Gaslini. editor: Amedeo Giomini. costume designer & art director: Dario Micheli. production manager: Giuseppe Mangogna. unit manager: Carlo Cucchi. production secretary: Tomasso Alvieri. cameraman: Nino Annunziata. assistant cameraman: Luigi Conversi. sound: Mario Ronchetti. boom operator: Eugenio Fiore. continuity: Nellita Zampieri. assistant art director: Maurizio Garrone. assistant editor: Piero Bozza. 2nd assistant editors: Nadia Mazzoni & Tommaso Gramigna. production accountants: Ferdinando Caputo & Carlo Dubois. make-up: Cristina Rocca. hairstylist: Ida Alacino. wardrobe: Marcella Moretti. still photography: Roberto Canevari (Nuova Dial). key grip: Guglielmo Maga. property master: Augusto La Valle. construction manager: Giuseppe Gabrielli. gaffer: Orazio Sinacore. generator operator: Ferdinando Cartocci. sound effects: Anzellotti. titles & opticals: Studio Verzini. synchronization directed by [Domenico] Mimmo Palmara for SINC Cinematografica. mixage: Venanzio Biraschi, recorded by Fono Roma using Western Electric equipment. Italian version: Cinitalia Edizioni. technical equipment: Janiro S.r.l.. costume house: Ferroni. wigs: Rocchetti. furnishings: Cimino Cine Arredamento Rancati. hangings: Alfredo D'Angelo. sound recording: Fono Roma. music publisher: Bixio Sam (Milan).
negatives: Eastmancolor Kodak.

running time: 52 minutes 49 seconds

The Wax Mask

The Sec

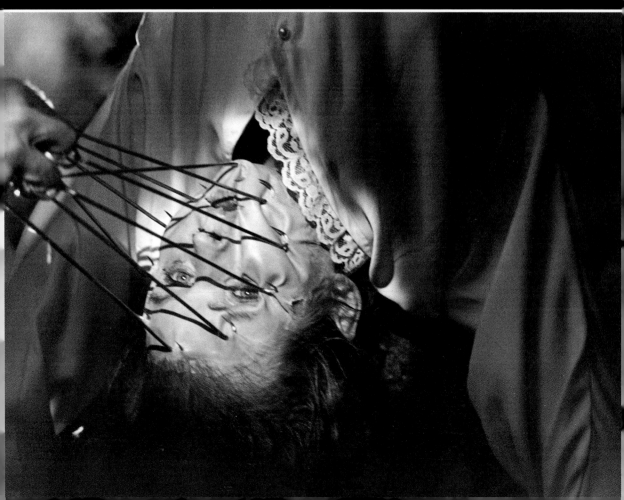

Dario Argento complete filmography (part 2)

Argento as writer or producer

Qualcuno ha tradito [Italian theatrical title]
Requiem pour une canaille [French theatrical title]
Every Man is My Enemy [export title]
Null Uhr sieben kommt John Harris [German theatrical title]

1967 // Italy & France
Directed by Frank Shannon [Francesco Prosperi]

Cast: Robert Webber (Tony Costa). Elsa Martinelli (Laureen) with Jean Servais (Jean, Tony's old friend). Marina Berti (Ann, Jean's wife). Franco Giornelli (Coco Hermann) with Pierre Zimmer (Gabriel Blondel, Tony's old army buddy). Ennio Balbò (the professor). E. Michael Messina [Emilio Messina] (Willy, "the bullseye"). Pierre Marty. [uncredited] Umberto Raho (drug dealer).

a Tiki Film (Rome)/Greenwich Film Productions (Paris) co-production

produced by F. [Francesco] M. Thellung. production manager: Louis [Luigi] Millozza. original story & screenplay: Franco Prosperi & Gianni [Giovanni] Simonelli. screenplay collaborators: Dario Argento & Raimondo De Balzo. director of photography: Sante Achilli [Kodakcolor]. music composed & directed by Piero Morgan [Piero Piccioni]; music published by General Music [Rome]. editor: Ruggero Mastroianni. art director & costumes: Dario Micheli. continuity: Liana Ferri. assistant director: P. [Paul] Nuyttens. cameraman: Ubaldo Terzano. 1st unit manager: Robert Menks. 2nd unit manager: Roberto Cuomo. make-up: Nilo Jacoponi. hair stylist: Amalia Paoletti. assistant costumes: Francesca Romana Cofano. assistant editor: Romana Fortini. sound: Alessandro Sarandrea. sound re-recording: Mario Morigi. dialogue & post-synchronisation [English language version] by Gene Luotto. film processing by Istituto Luce.
theme music for "Laureen" by Armanni & [Stelvio] Cipriani.

Italian visa number: 49422 [28/06/67]. Italian takings L165.000.000

Filmed on location in Marseilles (France) and Miami (USA) with interiors filmed at Cinecittà Studios (Rome, Italy)

Italian theatrical distributor: I.N.C. [Ital-Noleggio Cinematografica] (released on 24 August 1967). rated: 14. running time: 98 minutes
French theatrical distributor: C.F.D.C. (released on 14 August 1968). rated: 18. running time: 89 minutes
West German theatrical distributor: Gloria Filmverleih (released on 29 December 1967). rated: 18. running time: 88 minutes

Oggi a me... domani a te [Italian theatrical/video title]
Today it's Me... Tomorrow You! [UK theatrical/video title]
Today We Kill... Tomorrow We Die! [US theatrical/video title]
Heute ich... morgen du [German theatrical title]
Cinq gachettes d'or [French theatrical title]

1968 // Italy
Directed by Tonino Cervi

Cast: Montgomery Ford [Brett Halsey] (Bill Kiowa) with Bud Spencer [Carlo Pedersoli] (O'Bannion). Wayde Preston (Jeff Milton). Jeff Cameron [Giovanni Scarciofolo] (Moreno). Stanley Gordon (Little Jack). Diana Madigan (Mirana Kiowa). Doro Corrai [Teodoro Corrà] (gunseller). Vic Gazzarra [Victoriano Gazzara] (Bunny Fox). Aldo Marianecci (Peter). Michele Borelli (prison director). Umberto Di Grazia (2nd-in-command). Franco Pechini (sheriff). Nazzareno Natale and with William Berger) (Francis 'Colt' Moran) and with Tetsuo Nakadai (James Elfego). [uncredited] Franco Gulà (old man in saloon). Pietro Torrisi & Riccardo Petrazzi (Elfego henchmen).

P.A.C. [Produzione Atlas Consorziate]/Splendid [Film] (Rome)

director of production: Lucio Trentini. story & screenplay: Dario Argento & Tonino Cervi. director of photography: Sergio D'Offizi [Eastmancolor - color prints by Boschi]. music composed & directed by [Angelo] Francesco Lavagnino; published by C.A.M.. editing: Sergio Montanari. scenes [art director]: Carlo Gervasi. assistant director: Mauro [Maurizio] Sacripante. action [stunt co-ordinator]: Nazzareno Zamperla. cameraman: Giuseppe Gatti. assistant cameramen: Salvatore Caruso & Remo Grisanti. production unit [unit manager]: Franco Cuccu; [continuity]: Giuliano Principato & Federico Starace; [cashier]: Anita Galassini. costumes: Giorgio Desideri. sound: Vittorio De Sisti. boom operator: Salvatore Melaranci. make-up: Rossana Caporricii. assistant editors: Marcello Olasio & Roberto Gianandrea. dubbing: Cinelatina. costumes produced by Giarlo. wigs by Carboni. set decoration: Set Dedalo. weapons: Baciucchi. equipment: Massaccesi.
song: "Che gioia vivere"

Italian visa number: 51163 [26/03/68]. Registro Cinematoghrafico: 4.197. Italian takings L1.019.000.000

Interiors filmed at Elios Studios (Rome).

Italian theatrical distributor: P.A.C. (released on 28 March 1968). rating: none. running time: 93 minutes
West German theatrical distributor: Inter (released on 19 November 1968). rated: 18. running time: 95 minutes
French theatrical distributor: Warner Bros. (released on 11 June 1969). rating: none. running time: 94 minutes
US theatrical distributor: Cinerama [- presented by Herman Cohen] (released in June 1971). rated: GP. running time: 95 minutes
UK theatrical distributor: Miracle Films Ltd (released on 11 May 1969). rated: X. running time: 95 minutes 42 seconds/8,523 feet [BBFC cuts]

Comandamenti per un gangster [Italian theatrical title]
Poslednji obracun [Yugoslavian theatrical title]
L'Enfer avant la mort [French theatrical title]
Hölle vor dem Tod [German theatrical title]
Commandments for a Gangster [translated title]

1968 // Italy & Yugoslavia
Directed by Alfio Caltabiano

Cast: Lee Tadic [Ljuba Tadic] (Northon) and Al Northon [Alfio Caltabiano] ("five cents") <with> Dan May [Dante Maggio] (the old man). Rade Markon [Rade Markovic]. Nick Ballantine. John Janick [Jovan Janicijevic] Sir John. Gene Maras [Giancarlo Marras]. Joe Rast. Arion Lavrick. Ivan Giovanni Scratuglia c.s.c. (2nd man murdered on seafront). Gaetano Gabadi. Licio Carrara with a special appearance by Olivera [Olivera Vukotic].
[uncredited] Dusan Janicijevic. Sergio Mioni.

Salvatore Argento presents a Triumph Film 67 Prodi Cinematografico (Rome)/Avala Film (Belgrade)

produced by Salvatore Argento. production manager: Salvatore Vizzini Bisaccia. story & screenplay: Alfio Caltabiano & Dario Argento. director of photography: Mile Markovic [Milorad Markovic] (Telecolor / Kodakolor). music: Ennio Morricone, orchestrations by Bruno Nicolai, published by C.A.M.. editor: Eugenio Alabiso. art directors: Ivkov [Dragoljub Ivkov] & Luciana Marinucci. costume designer: Luciana Marinucci. cameraman: Emilio Varriano. underwater cameraman: Tomaso Manunza. titles: Libratti.
song Solo nostalgia by Ennio Morricone & Audrey Nohra is sung by Jane Reilly.

Italian visa number: 51254 [04/04/68]. Registro cinematografico: 4.230. Italian takings L80.000.000

Filmed on location in Yugoslavia & Italy

Italian theatrical distributor: D.C.I. (released on 22 May 1968). rated: 18. running time: 96 minutes
Yugoslavian theatrical distribution: 1968
French theatrical distributor: Eclair Journal (released on 7 January 1970). rating: none. running time: 80 minutes
West German theatrical distributor: Inter-Verleih Film-Gesellschaft (released on 20 December 1968). rated: 18. running time: 92 minutes

Commandos [Italian/UK/French theatrical/video title]
Himmelfahrtskommando El Alamein [German theatrical title]
Sullivan's Marauders [US theatrical/video title]
Los chacales del desierto [Spanish theatrical title]
Mit Eichenlaub und Schwertern [German theatrical title]

1968 // Italy & West Germany
Directed by Armando Crispino

Cast: Lee Van Cleef (Sergeant Sullivan). Jack Kelly (Captain Valli) with Giampiero Albertini (Aldo). Marino Masè (Lieutenant Tommasini, captured Italian soldier). Götz George (Oberleutnant Rudy Kasper). Pier Paolo Capponi (Corbi). Ivano Staccioli (Rodolfo). Marilù Tolo (Adriana) and Akim Berg [Joachim Fuchsberger] (Oberleutnant Heitzel Agen, "the professor") other players - in alphabetical order Heinz Reincke (Unteroffizier Hans). Helmut Schmid (wounded German soldier). Otto Stern (Hauptmann Braumann). Pier Luigi Anchisi (Riccio). Gianni Brezza (Marco, captured Italian soldier). Duilio Del Prete (Bruno, captured Italian soldier). Emilio Marchesini (Antonio). Biagio Pelligra (Carmelo). Lorenzo Piani (Bianca, the nervous commando). Giacomo Piperno (Vincenzino). Romano Puppo (Dino, Sullivan's right hand man). Franco Cobianchi (Abu Ali). Mario Ferlazzo (sergeant on watch). Mauro Lumachi. Gianni Pulone c.s.c. (Mario). Ivan Scratuglia c.s.c. (Italian soldier).

an Italo-German co-production: P.E.C. [Produzione Esecutiva Cinematografica] S.p.A. (Rome)/C.C.I. [Compagnia Cinematografica Internazionale] S.p.A. (Rome)/C.C.C. [Filmkunst] (Berlin)
©P.E.C. S.p.A./C.C.I. S.p.A./C.C.C. [English language version]

produced by [Enrico] Chroscicki & [Alfonso] Sansone. production manager: Franco Palaggi. story: Don Martin & Arthur Brauner. screenplay: Lucio Battistrada, Armando Crispino, Stefano Strucchi & Dario Argento; based on a story by Menahem Golan. director of photography: Benito Frattari [colour by Eastmancolor - Cromoscope]. music composed & conducted by Mario Nascimbene; recorded & published by Bixio Sam (Milan). editor: Daniele Alabiso. set designer: Alberto Boccianti.
[uncredited] German co-producer: Arthur Brauner. German production manager: Dr. Götz-Dieter Wulf. costume designer: Enzo Bulgarelli. assistant director: Vito Minore. 2nd assistant director: Eugenio La Penna. cameraman: Silvio Fraschetti. sound: Bruno Moreal & Raul Montesanti. dubbing: C.D.C..

Italian visa number: 52688 [12/11/68]. Registro cinematografico: 4.259. Italian takings L154.000.000

Filmed in July & August 1968 on location in Sardinia (Italy) with interiors filmed at Incir - De Paolis Studios (Rome, Italy)

Italian theatrical distributor: Titanus Distribuzione (released on 19 November 1968). rating: none. running time: 122 minutes
West German theatrical distributor: Columbia (released on 8 August 1969). rated: 18. running time: 88 minutes
French theatrical distributor: C.F.D.C. (released on 2 July 1969). rating: none. running time: 112 minutes
UK theatrical distributor: 20th Century-Fox Film Co. Ltd (released circa February 1972). rated: X. running time: 89 minutes 53 seconds/8,000 feet

La rivoluzione sessuale [Italian theatrical title]
Seid nett aufeinander [German theatrical title]
La Révolution sexuelle [French theatrical title]
The Sexual Revolution [translated title]

1968 // Italy
Directed by Riccardo Ghione

Cast: Marisa Mantovani (Marcella Segre). Ruggero Miti (Giorgio Segre). Riccardo Cucciolla (Emilio Missiroli). Christian Alegny (Cesare). Laura Antonelli (Liliana). Gaspare Zola. Maria Luisa Bavastro (Nanna). Giulio Girola (Dino Segre). André José Cruz (Tony). Lorenza Guerrieri (Rita). Guy Heron (Marco). Maria Rosa Sclauzero. Maria Montero. Rosabianco Scerrino. Leo Gavero.

Italo Zingarelli presents a West Film production

executive producer: Roberto Palaggi. produced by Italo Zingarelli. story: Riccardo Ghione, based on the novel by Wilhelm Reich. screenplay: Dario Argento & Riccardo Ghione. director of photography: Alessandro D'Eva [Eastmancolor]. music by Teo Usuelli. editor: Attilio Vincioni. art director: Giulio Cabras. costumes: Maria Gelmetti. production manager: Sergio Borelli. assistant director: Anna Maria Sbordoni. make-up artist: Franco Schioppa. sound: Mario Morigi.
film processed by S.P.E.S. (manager: E. Catalucci).

Italian visa number: 52242 [29/10/68]. Registro cinematografico: 4.280. Italian takings L290.000.000

Filmed circa May/June 1968 on location in Italy

Italian theatrical distributor: Delta (released on 21 November 1968). rated: 18. running time: 92 minutes
West German theatrical distributor: Düssel (released on 16 January 1970). rated: 18. running time: 92 minutes
French theatrical distributor: Dis./Ass. (released on 24 June 1970). rating: none. running time: 91 minutes

C'era una volta il west [Italian theatrical/video title]
Once upon a Time in the West [US/UK theatrical/video title]
Spiel mir das Lied vom Tod [German theatrical title]
Hasta que llego su hora [Spanish theatrical title]
Il était une fois dans l'Ouest [French theatrical title]
Once upon a Time... in the West [shooting title]

1968 // Italy & the United States
Directed by Sergio Leone

Cast: Claudia Cardinale (Jill McBain). Henry Fonda (Frank). Jason Robards (Cheyenne). Charles Bronson (Harmonica). Gabriele Ferzetti (Mr Morton, railroad businessman). Paolo Stoppa (Sam, Jill's driver) guest stars Woody Strode (Stony, Frank's hired killer #1). Jack Elam (Snakey, Frank's hired killer #2). Keenan Wynn (sheriff of the county). Frank Wolff (Brett McBain). Lionel Stander (tavern proprietor).
[uncredited] Aldo Berti (Frank's man #3 playing poker). Federico Boido (foxy-faced man in tavern). Francisco Braña (Frank's man #2 at auction). Luigi Ciavarro (deputy wearing dark hat escorting Cheyenne after auction). Spartaco Conversi (Frank's grey-bearded gunman on train with Morton). Bruno Corazzari (Cheyenne's man #2). John Frederick (Frank's assassin #2 sent to kill Jill @ ranch). Claudio Mancini (Harmonica's elder brother). Dino Mele (young Harmonica). Antonio Molino Rojo (Frank man @ auction). Al Mulloch (Knuckles, Frank's hired killer #3). Tullio Palmieri (Flagstaff lumber salesman). Renato Pinciroli (1st bidder @ auction). Aldo Sambrell (Frank's man @ station #1). Enzo Santaniello (Timmy McBain). Simonetta Santaniello (Maureen McBain). Ivan G. [Giovanni] Scratuglia. Benito Stefanelli (Frank's key henchman). Luukialvana 'Luana' Kalaeloa Strode (indian woman at station). Fabio Testi (Frank man @ auction). Marco Zuanelli (Wobbles, Frank's contact).
Luigi Magnani. Marilù Carteny. Paolo Figlia. Sandra Salvatori. Dino Zamboni. Livio Andronico. Stefano Imparato. Umberto Morsella. Conrado Sanmartin (official @ Brett McBain's funeral). Claudio Scarchilli. Salvo Basile. Frank Leslie. Enrico Morsella.

the following two actors were listed during production: Robert Hossein. Eduardo De Filippo.
originally cast prior to start of production: Enrico Maria Salerno. Robert Ryan.

Paramount - a Gulf+Western Company // a Sergio Leone film // a Rafran [Cinematografica] - [Finanziaria] San Marco production

©1969. Paramount Pictures Corporation [English language version]

executive producer: Bino Cicogna. produced by Fulvio Morsella. production supervisor: Ugo Tucci. production manager: Claudio Mancini. screenplay: Sergio Donati & Sergio Leone; from a story by Dario Argento, Bernardo Bertolucci & Sergio Leone. [English] dialogue by Mickey Knox. director of photography: Tonino Delli Colli [Techniscope/Technicolor]. music composed & conducted by Ennio Morricone. editor: Nino Baragli. sets & costumes by Carlo Simi. 1st assistant director: Giancarlo Santi. make-up supervisor: Alberto De Rossi. make-up: Giannetto De Rossi. hairdresser: Grazia De Rossi. sound engineers: Claudio Maielli, Elio Pacella & Fausto Ancillai. costumes by Western Costume; Safas; Antonelli, Pompei. special effects: Bacciucchi. sound effects: Luciano Anzilotti, Italo Cameracanna & Roberto Arcangeli. editing, mixing & synchronization by NIS with the participation of C.D.C.. music edited [published] & recorded by R.C.A. S.p.A.. The producers are grateful to the Navajo Tribal Council for their hospitality in their territories in Arizona and Utah.
[uncredited] assistant editors: Andreina Casini. & Carlo Reali. wardrobe: Marilù Carteny. set decorator: Carlo Leva & Raphael Ferri. assistant art director: Enrico Simi. assistant set dresser: Antonio Palombi. 2nd assistant director: Salvo [Salvatore] Basile. unit managers: Camillo Teti & Manolo Amigo. production secretaries: Glauco Teti & Giorgio Risi. continuity: Serena Canevari. cameraman: Franco Di Giacomo. assistant cameraman: Giuseppe Lanci. stunt co-ordinator: Benito Stefanelli. still photography: Angelo Novi. assistant make-up: Feliziano Ciriaci. assistant hairdresser: Antonietta Caputo. co-special effects: Giovanni Corridori. administration: Raffaele Forti. wardrobe: Valeria Sponsali. key grip: Franco Tocci. gaffer: Alberto Ridolfi. wigs: Rocchetti. set furnishings: Cimino.

Italian visa number: 52908 [20/12/68]. Registro cinematografico: 4.207. Italian takings L2.503.669.000 (fifth most successful film at the Italian box-office, 1968/69 season)

Filmed from 8 April 1968 on location in Almería & Guadix (Spain - for two months) & Monument Valley in Utah, Arizona and Mesa Verde in Colorado (USA - for one month) with interiors filmed at Cinecittà Studios (Rome, Italy). Budget: $5,000,000

Italian theatrical distributor: Euro International Film (released on 21 December 1968). rating: none. running time: 165 minutes
US theatrical distributor: Paramount (released in May 1969). rated: M. running time: 165 minutes

West German theatrical distributor: Paramount Pictures (released on 14 August 1969). rated: 16. running time: 164 minutes
UK theatrical distributor: Paramount Film Service Ltd. (released on 31 August 1969). rated: A. running time: 144 minutes/12,960 feet
UK theatrical re-release distributor: Paramount Film Service Ltd. (released in 1982). rated: AA. running time: 167 minutes 6 seconds/15,039 feet
French theatrical distributor: Paramount Pictures (released in 1969). running time: 150 minutes

Une corde, un colt [French theatrical title]
Cimitero senza croci [Italian theatrical/video title]
Cemetery without Crosses [UK video title]
Una cuerda, un colt [Spanish theatrical title]
Friedhof ohne Kreuze [German theatrical/video title]
Cemitério sem cruzes [Brazilian theatrical title]

1969 // France & Italy
a film by Robert Hossein

Cast: Michèle Mercier (Maria Caine). Robert Hossein (Manuel) with Lee Burton [Guido Lollobrigida] (Thomas Caine) and with Daniel Vargas (Pa Rogers). Serge Marquand (Larry Rogers). Pierre Hatet (Franck Rogers). Philippe Baronnet [Frugues] (Bud Rogers). Pierre Collet (the sheriff). Ivano Staccioli (Vallee, a rancher). Béatrice Altariba (saloon woman) with Michel Lemoine (Ely Caine) and Anne-Marie Balin ([French version] Johanna, [English version] Diana - Rogers' daughter).
[uncredited] Benito Stefanelli (Ben Caine, Maria's husband). Cris Huerta (hotel desk clerk). Ángel Álvarez (the bartender). Álvaro de Luna (deputy sent to bring back Maria from the Caine ranch). Charly Bravo [Ramón Carlos Mirón-Bravo] (Sam Vallee). José Canalejas (2nd Vallee man). Lorenzo Robledo (one of Rogers' men).

a film by Robert Hossein // an French-Italo co-production: Loisirs Du Monde S.A. (Paris)/Films Copernic (Paris)/Fono Roma (Rome)

executive producers: Jean-Charles Raffini & Jean-Pierre Labatut. unit manager: Jean Mottet. story & screenplay: Robert Hossein, Claude Desailly & Dario Argento. director of photography: Henri Persin [Eastmancolor by Telecolor]. music by André Hossein; published by "La Compagnie". film editor: Marie-Sophie Dubus. sets by Jean Mandaroux. assistant director: Tony Aboyantz. stunt director: Benito Stefanelli. cameraman: Gilles Bonneau. in charge of production: Robert Porte. assistant cameraman: Jean Castagnier. script girl [continuity]: Hélène Sebillotte. special effects: Rosine Delamare. hairstylist: Jacqueline Juillard. make-up: Maguy Vernadet. administration: Jacqueline Dove. assistant [film editor]: André Davanture. sound: Guy Villette. sound studio: Fono Roma.
theme song: "Rope and the Colt" performed by Scott Walker.

Italian visa number: 53374 [08/03/69]. Italian takings L613.356.000

Filmed from 8 January to 30 March 1968 on location in Almeria (Southern Spain)

French theatrical distributor: Fernand Rivers (released on 25 January 1969). rating: adults. running time: 90 minutes
Italian theatrical distributor: Euro International Film (released on 19 April 1969). rating: none. running time: 90 minutes
West German theatrical distributor: Apollo (released on 27 February 1970). rated: 16. running time: 84 minutes

Metti, una sera a cena [Italian theatrical/video title]
Disons, un soir à dîner [French theatrical title]
The Love Circle [UK theatrical title]
One Night at Dinner [US theatrical title]

1969 // Italy
Directed by Giuseppe Patroni Griffi

Cast: Jean-Louis Trintignant (Michele, the writer). Lino Capolicchio (Ric). Tony Musante (Max, an actor). Florinda Bolkan (Nina, Michele's wife) with the participation of Annie Girardot (Giovanna).
Silvia Monti (actress at press conference). Milly (singer). Adriana Asti (stepdaughter). Titina Maselli (mother). Ferdinando Scarfiotti (son). Claudio Carrozza (baby). Nora Ricci (1st actress). Mariano Rigillo (comedian). Antonio Jaia (1st young actor).

a film produced by Marina Cicogna & Giovanni Bertolucci for [Finanziaria] San Marco/Red Film

produced by Marina Cicogna & Giovanni Bertolucci. screenplay: Dario Argento & Giuseppe Patroni Griffi with the collaboration of Carlo Carunchio; based on the play of the same name by Giuseppe Patroni Griffi. director of photography: Tonino Dello Colli [Technicolor/Technicope]. music by Ennio Morricone; conducted by Bruno Nicolai; published by Bixio Sam (Milan). soundtrack available on Cinevox Record. editor: Franco Arcalli. art director: Giulio Coltellacci. production manager: Aldo U. Passalacqua. assistant director: Carlo Carunchio. continuity: Serena Canevari. cameraman: Franco Di Giacomo. unit manager: Nicola Venditti. production secretaries: Attilio Viti & Alberto Casati. production accountant & paymaster: Pietro Sassaroli. make-up: Franco Corridoni. hair stylist: Rosa Luciani. sound: Giorgio Minoprio. assistant editors: Olga Pedrini & Gabriella Cristiani. assistant cameramen: Giuseppe Lanci & Roberto Forges Davanzati c.s.c.. assistant art director: Claudio Giambanco c.s.c.. assistant set dresser: Gianni Silvestri. assistant costumes: Metka Koschak. costumes supplied by Sartoria Mayer. furs provided by Pendi Alta Moda (Rome). publicity: Enrico Lucherini, Margherita Rossetti & Matteo Spinola. special [sound] effects recorded with 'Organo Thomas'. original soundtrack available on Cinevox Record. sound recording: Westex recording. recorded at the studios of Fono Roma with the participation of C.DC.. dubbing director: Mario Maldesi; mixage: Franco Bassi.
with thanks to Luigi Pirandello for use of "Sei personaggi in cerca d'autore"/"Six Characters in Search of an Author"
songs: "Il tango del magnaccia" by P. Carpi, performed by Milly; "Metti, una sera a cena" (Hurry To Me) by Fishman & Ennio Morricone, performed by Sandpipers.

Italian visa number: 53517 [29/03/69]. Registro cinematografico: 4.392. Italian takings L1.428.237.000

Filmed in autumn 1968 on location in Milan (Italy) with interiors filmed at De Paolis - I.N.C.I.R. Studios (Rome, Italy)

Italian theatrical distributor: Euro International Film (released on 3 April 1969). rated: 18. running time: 125 minutes
French theatrical distributor: Corona (released in 1970). running time: 125 minutes
UK theatrical distributor: Cinecenta (released in July 1970). rated: X. running time: 108 minutes/9,270 feet [BBFC cuts]
US theatrical distributor: International Co-productions (released in November 1971). rated: R. running time: 110 minutes

Probabilità zero [Italian theatrical/video title]
Probability Zero [US/UK theatrical/video title]
Les héros ne meurent jamais [French theatrical title]

1969 // Italy
Directed by Maurizio Lucidi

Cast: Henry Silva (Duke) with Luigi Castellato (Carlo 'Charley' Sardi). Riccardo Salvino (Hans Liedholm). Ezio Sancrotti (Captain Sam Schultz, from Norway) and Franco Giornelli (John MacHarding, a Scottish mountain climber). Vittorio Andrè (Professor Schwartz). Marco Bogliani. Maria Cristina Farnese. Paolo Magalotti (tall, bearded OSS officer). Fulvio Mingozzi (British intelligence officer). Tony Roico with Peter Martell (Pietro Martellanza) (Sam, the Brit) and Katia Christine (Kristy) and with the participation of Renato De Carmine (Major Horst) and Marco Guglielmi (Captain Kreug)
[uncredited] Bill Vanders (OSS officer).

Auriga Film '68

a film produced by Salvatore Argento & Dario Argento. director of production [production supervisor]: Camillo Teti. production manager: Enzo Mazzucchi. story: Dario Argento. screenplay: Dario Argento, Maurizio Lucidi, Giuseppe Mangione & Vittoriano Vighi. director of photography: Aldo Tonti [Eastmancolor]. music composed by Carlo Rustichelli; conducted by Bruno Nicolai. editor: Alberto Gallitti. art director: Alberto Boccianti. assistant director: Aldo Lado. set dressing: Claudio Cinini & Giorgio Bertolini. wardrobe: Luciana Marinucci. special effects: Nicola Balini. production secretary: Sergio Bollino. cameraman: Maurizio Cipriani. assistant cameraman: Gianni Maddaleni. script girl [continuity]: Marisa Casale. assistant editor: Gasparina Maroni. make-up: Eligio Trani. hair dressing: Clementina Battello. sound engineering: Carlo Diotallevi. models: Carlo De Marchis. properties: S.E.T. Rancati. footwear: Pompei. costumes supplied by Casa D'Arte Firenze. weapons: Battistelli. lighting equipment: A.T.C. electronic & radar equipment: Soc. Derica.
[uncredited] 2nd assistant editor: Roberto Gianandrea.

Italian visa number: 53313 [26/02/69]. Registro cinematografico: 4.370. Italian takings L165.800.000

Filmed circa September/October 1968 on location in Dalmazia, Ponza and Palmarola (Italy) with 2nd unit work in Norway. Interiors shot at De Paolis - Incir Studios (Rome, Italy)

Italian theatrical distributor: Euro International Film (released on 7 May 1969). rating: none. running time: 95 minutes
French theatrical distributor: SNA (released in Paris in 1970). running time: 95 minutes

La legione dei dannati [Italian theatrical/video title]
La brigada de los condenados [Spanish theatrical title]
Die zum Teufel gehen [German theatrical title]
Battle of the Commandos [US theatrical/UK video title]
The Legion of the Damned [prospective UK theatrical title]
La Légion des damnés [French theatrical title]
La legión de los condenados [Spanish shooting title]
Die Legion der Verdammten [alternative German title]

1969 // Italy, Spain & West Germany
Directed by Umberto Lenzi

Cast: Jack Palance (Colonel Charlie MacPherson) with Tom Hunter (Captain Burke, the American). Robert Hundar [Claudio Undari] (Raymond Stone, commando). Wolfgang Preiss (Colonel Ackermann). Helmuth [Helmut] Schneider (Sam Schirer, 'the anarchist'). Lee Burton [Guido Lollobrigida] ('Count' Carlisle, commando). Aldo Sambrell (Sergeant Rabindra, MacPherson's second). Diana Lorys (Jeanine, French woman). Franco Fantasia (Marc, Maquis leader). Gerard Herter (Stürmführer Hapke, SS officer). Mirko Ellis (Major Ardler). Bruno Corazzari (Frank Madigan, commando). [Antonio] Molino Rojo (Albert Hank, commando). Lorenzo Robledo (Bernard Knowles, commando) and with Curd Jurgens as guest star (General von Rylov).
[uncredited] John Stacy (the general, MacPherson's commanding officer). Luis Induni (Pierre, Jeanine's lover). Guillermo Méndez (Maquis contact in village).

a Tritone Filmindustria Roma/Eguiluz (Madrid)/Hape Film (Munich) co-production
©1969. Tritone Filmindustria [English language version]

executive producers: Bruno Bolognesi & Ignacio Gutierrez. executive production manager: Adriano Merkel. story: Stefano Rolla & Romano Moschini. screenplay: Dario Argento, Rolf Grieminger & Eduardo M. [María] Brochero. dialogue by Ugo Moretti. director of photography: Alejandro Ulloa [Tecnostampa]. music by Marcello Giombini; published by Nazionalmusic (Milan). editor: Giese Rohm. architect [set designer]: Jaime P. [Perez] Cubero. set designer: Piero Filippone. costumes: Luciano Sagoni. make-up: Raoul Ranieri. assistant director: Wolf Duschl. script supervisor: Fanny Wessling. unit managers: Mario Campolunghi & Ramon Sanz. set secretary: Lamberto Andreani. cameraman: Mario Sbrenna. sound engineer: Leopoldo Rosi. mixing: Bruno Moreal. synchronization (Italian version): N.C.. dubbing: C.DC..
additional post-production [US version]: Paragon Films. producer: Don Hulette. supervisor: Ronald Stein.

Italian visa number: 54301 [08/08/69]. Registro cinematografico: 4.4.76. Italian takings L211.500.000

Filmed from January to March 1969 on location in Madrid and the sierra of Guadarrama (Spain), Rome and the military base at Taranto (Italy) and London (the United Kingdom) with interiors filmed at Studio Dear Film (Rome, Italy)
Italian theatrical distributor: Titanus (released on 12 August 1969). rating: none. running time: 93 minutes
West German theatrical distributor: Alpha (released on 17 April 1970). rating: none. running time: 93 minutes
French theatrical distributor: Marbeuf (released on 17 June 1970). running time: 92 minutes
US theatrical distributor: NTA. rated: PG-13

Un esercito di 5 uomini [Italian theatrical title]
The Five Man Army [US/UK theatrical/video title]
Die Fünf Gefürchteten und ein Hallelujah [German theatrical title]
Cinq hommes armés [French theatrical title]
Carabina 30/30 [shooting title]

1969 // Italy
Directed by Don Taylor [Italian prints] Italo Zingarelli

Cast: Peter Graves (Dutchman). James Daly (Captain Augustus Bennett, dynamite expert). Bud Spencer [Carlo Pedersoli] (Mesito, a glutton). Nino Castelnuovo (Luis Dominguez, acrobat) and Tetsuo Tamba (Samurai, the swordsman) with Claudio Gora (Manuel Esteban). Carlo Alighieri (Captain Gutierrez). Giacomo Rossi Stuart (Mexican officer). Dan Sturkie (carnival barker). José Torres (Mexican spy). Marino Masè (stoker on train). Annabella Andreoli (Perla, Mexican woman) and Daniela Giordano (Maria).
[uncredited] Steffen Zacharias (Augustus' opponent in poker game). Gigi Bonos (the priest). Dante Cleri (puebla mayor). Fortunato Arena (head of Mexican firing squad). Pietro Torrisi (2nd Mexican officer). Osiride Pevarello (bearded singing Mexican).

the film's press kit incorrectly lists Marc Lawrence as the actor playing the carnival barker

Metro Goldwyn Mayer presents an Italo Zingarelli production [for Tiger Film] // a Metro Goldwyn Mayer release
©1969. Metro-Goldwyn-Mayer Inc. MPAA: 22138 [English language version]

produced by Italo Zingarelli. screenplay: Marc Richards & Dario Argento. director of photography: Enzo Barboni [Metrocolor/Technicolor - in Deltavision]. music by Ennio Morricone. editor: Sergio Montanari. art director & costume designer: Enzo Bulgarelli. production manager: Franco Palaggi. assistant director: Stefano Rolla. sound editor: Eraldo Giordani. camera operator: Sergio Bergamini. set decorator: Ennio Michettoni.
[uncredited] executive producer: Roberto Palaggi. music director: Bruno Nicolai; music published by Ariete - West. unit manager: Luciano Pesciaroli. production secretary: Ruggero Capelli. continuity: Maria Luisa Rosen. special effects: Sergio Chisui. dialogue director: Raffaele Mottola. sound assistant: Antonio Bramonti. costume assistant: Luciano Sagoni. make-up: Massimo Giustini. property master: Mario Belocchi. wardrobe: Pasqualino Sindici. hairstylist: Salvatore Cotroneo. make-up assistant: Sergio Petruzzelli. stills photographer: Roberto Biciocchi. unit publicist: Walter Alford. stuntman (Italy): Alessandro Ferrau. assistant editor: Nadia Bonifazi. sound mixer: Gianni D'Amico.
song: "Muerte donde vas?" [Death Where Are You Going?] by Ennio Morricone & Radici.

Italian visa number: 54748 [09/10/69]. Registro cinematografico: 4.468. Italian takings L365.000.000

Filmed from 3 March 1969 for 12 weeks on location in the village of Polopos and other Sierras locations and in Almeria (Spain) and in Fiumicino, in Capranica in the Central Apennines near Viterbo, at the quarry in Grottarossa, on a farm near Lake Bracciano and in Ostia (Italy) with interiors filmed at Incir - De Paolis Studios (Rome, Italy)

Italian theatrical distributor: Delta Film (released on 16 October 1969). rating: none. running time: 105 minutes
US theatrical distributor: Metro-Goldwyn-Mayer, Inc. (released in Feburary 1970). rated: GP. running time: 105 minutes
West German theatrical distributor: MGM (released on 26 March 1970). rated: 16. running time: 105 minutes
French theatrical distributor: MGM (released in Paris in 1970). running time: 105 m.
UK theatrical distributor: MGM Pictures (released on 18 January 1970). rated: A. running time: 105 minutes 57 seconds/9,445 feet [BBFC cuts]

La stagione dei sensi [Italian theatrical title]
The Season of Senses ['Films and Filming' title]

1969 // Italy & West Germany
Directed by Massimo Franciosa

Cast: Udo Kier (Luca). Laura Belli (Monica). Edda Di Benedetto (Claudia). Eva Thulin (Michèle). Suzanne Von Sass (Marina). Gaspare Zola (Peter). Ugo Adinolfi (Marco). Andreina Paul.

Italo Zingarelli presents a co-production: West Film (Rome)/Rapid Film (Munich)/A. & P. Film (Munich)

produced by Italo Zingarelli. story: Amedeo Pagani, Pier Giuseppe Murgia & Barbara Alberti. screenplay: Barbara Alberti, Dario Argento, Franco Ferrari & Peter Kintzel. director of photography: Alessandro D'Eva. music composed & conducted by Ennio Morricone. editor: Sergio Montanari. art director: Franco Bottari.
songs: "Tell Me Tell Me" & "Laila Laila" by Audrey Nohra & Ennio Morricone are sung by Patrick Samson; "Una voce allo specchio" & "Sospendi il tempo" by Ennio Morricone with the voice of Edda Dell'Orso.

Italian visa number: 54799 [11/10/69]. Registro cinematografico: 4.409. Italian takings L130.000.000

Filmed circa September/October 1968

Italian theatrical distributor: Delta Film (released on 22 October 1969). rated: 14. running time: 86 minutes
West German theatrical distribution: none.

Dawn of the Dead [US/UK theatrical/video title]
Zombi [Italian theatrical/video title]
Zombies Dawn of the Dead [UK theatrical title]
Zombie [German theatrical title]
Zombie Le Crépuscule des morts-vivants [French theatrical title]
Zombie Dawn of the Dead [Dutch video title]

1978 // the United States & Italy
Directed by George A. Romero

Cast: David Emge (Stephen). Ken Foree (Peter). Scott H. Reiniger (Roger). Gaylen Ross (Francine). David Crawford (Doctor Foster). David Early (Mr Berman). Richard France (scientist). Howard Smith (TV commentator). Daniel Dietrich (Givens). Fred Baker (commander). Jim Baffico (Wooley). Rod Stouffer (young officer on roof). Jese Del Gre (old priest). Clayton McKinnon & John Rice (officers in project apartment). Ted Bank, Patrick McCloskey, Randy Kovitz & Joe Pilato (officers at police dock). Pasquale Buba, Tom Savini, Tony Buba, Marty Schiff, "Butchie", Joe Shelby, Dave Hawkins, Taso Stavrakos, Tom Kapusta, Nick Tallo, Rudy Ricci & Larry Vaira (motorcycle raiders). Sharon Ceccatti, Pam Chatfield, Bill Christopher, Clayton Hill & Jay Stover (lead zombies). Tom Savini & Taso Stavrakis (stuntmen). Leonard DeStefans, John Konter & Carl Scott (truck stunt drivers).
[uncredited] George A. Romero (TV director). Christine Forrest (TV producer). Tom Savini (Blades). Taso Stavrakos (Sledge). John Amplas (Puerto Rican on rooftop/zombie that gets an arm pulled off/zombie thrown over balcony by Tom Savini). John Harrison (screwdriver zombie). Jeannie Jefferies (blond zombie who attacks Roger in truck). Jim Krut (helicopter zombie). Lenny Lies (machete zombie). Sukey Raphael & Roy Frumkes (other zombies).

[US version] Herbert R. Steinman and Billy Baxter present a Laurel Group production in association with Claudio Argento & Alfredo Cuomo
[Italian version] a film written and directed by George A. Romero // a Laurel Production // a United Film Distribution release
©1978. Dawn Associates

produced by Richard P. Rubinstein. written by George A. Romero. script consultant: Dario Argento. director of photography: Michael Gornick [(US) colour by Technicolor New York (Italy) filmed in Eastmancolor/Technospes]. original music/sound track: The Goblins (in collaboration) with Dario Argento. editor: George A. Romero. lighting: Carl Augenstein. costumes: Josie Caruso. Production Coordinators. make-up & cosmetic special effects: Tom Savini. 1st make-up assistants: Nancy Allen & Jeannie Jefferies. set decoration: Josie Caruso & Barbara Lifsher. wardrobe: Michele Martin. assistant director: Christine Forrest. continuity: John Rice. casting: John Amplas. production manager: Zilla Clinton. assistant producer: Donna Siegal. unit manager: Jay Stover. business manager: Vince Survinski. graphics: Joseph Eberle. explosive effects: Gary Zeller & Don Berry. weapons co-ordinator: Clayton Hill. weapons: The Plastic Factory. assistant cameraman: Tom Dubensky. still photography: Katherine Kolbert. casting assistants: Ellen Hopkins & Michael Lies. assistant editor: Kenneth Davidow. sound: Tony Buba. key grips: Nick Mastandrea & Cliff Forrest. slate: Diane Donati. publicity: Renee Furst. publicity assistant: Francine Davidoff. grips: Dan Bertha, Bradley Drumheller, Lenny Lies, Clayton McKinnon, Ken Nagin & Daniel Silk. boom man: Robert Williams. distribution consultant: Ben Barenholtz. additional soundtrack: Dario Argento. production assistants: Leslie Augenstein, Sharon Ceccatti, Margarida Delgado, Ed Letteri, Dan Lupovitz & Diane Westerman. helicopter services: Royale Helicopter, Inc.. helicopter pilot: Barth Bartholomae. mall liaison: Bill Wagner. mall security: Jim Barger. insurance: Rogal & Company. film shipping: C & L Shipping. production accounting: Charles Forman, Wechler Meyers Wolsh. equipment: F & B Ceco (New York). sound transfers: Aquarius Sound. production services: The Latent Image, Inc., The Ultimate Mirror, Ltd., Laurel Tape & Film, Inc.. hi-fi equipment: The Listening Post, Inc.. fur coats: Lupovitz Furs. home furnishings: Wickes Furniture. costumes: Brooks Van Horn (Maiers, Pittsburgh). re-recording mixer: Richard Dior, Trans/Audio, Inc.. hairstyles: Hairtique. optical effects: Exceptional Opticals. optical consultant: Arthur J. Canestro. titles by Jean Bertl, Karen Levy, Jose V. Gallardo & James Chai. Technicolor advisers: Otto Paoloni & Joey Violante.
Produced with the co-operation of Robert Cox; Marvin Lieber; Miguel Lisenberg; Oxford Development Co.; Pennsylvania National Guard (1st Battalion, 10th Field Artillery); Pittsburgh Housing Authority; Pittsburgh Explorers Club; Resource Investments, Inc.; Alvin Rogal; Frank Rubinstein; Irvin Shapiro; Max Toberoff; Susan Vermazen.
soundtrack available on Varese Sarabande Records [#VC 81106]. novelization by George A. Romero & Susanna Sparrow; published by St. Martin's Press (1978).
Italian version additional credits
dialogue adaptation: Alberto Piferi. assistant editor: Piero Bozza. sound re-recording: Fausto Ancillai. music re-recording: Giorgio Agazzi. titles: Studio Mafera. Italian dubbing by CD (Cooperativa Doppiatori). dubbing director: Sergio Graziani. recording: International Recording. soundtrack recorded at Cinevox Record (Rome). [uncredited] editor & post-production supervisor: Franco Fraticelli.

Filmed from 13 November 1977 through February 1978 for nine and a half weeks on location at Oxford Development's Monroeville near Pittsburgh and an abandoned tenement building in downtown Pittsburgh and at the studios of an independent UHF station in Pittsburgh (Pennsylvania, USA). Budget: $1,500,000

US theatrical distributor: UFDC - United Film Distribution Company (released in April 1979). rating: none. running time: 126 minutes [director's cut] 137 minutes
Italian theatrical distributor: Titanus Distribuzione (released in Milan on 2 September 1978, in Rome on 7 September 1978). rated: 18. running time: 119 minutes
UK theatrical distributor: Target International Films Ltd. (released on 29 June 1980). rated: X. running time: 125 minutes 25 seconds/11,288 feet [BBFC cuts]
West German theatrical distributor: Neue Constantin-Film (released on 2 August 1979). rated: 18. running time: 118 minutes
French theatrical distributor: René Chateau (released in Paris on 18 May 1983). rated: 18. running time: 115 minutes

Demoni [Italian theatrical/video title]
Demons [US theatrical & US/UK video title]
Démons [French theatrical title]
Dämonen 2 [German theatrical title]
Demons 1 [alternative title]

1985 // Italy
Directed by Lamberto Bava

Cast: Urbano Barberini (Giorgio/George, Ken's pal). Natasha Hovey (Sharon/Sharel). Karl Zinny (Ken, George's pal). Fiore Argento (Hannah, Tom's girlfriend). Paola Cozzo (Kate/Kathy). Fabiola Toledo (Carmen, 1st girl with Tony). Nicoletta Elmi (Ingrid, the usherette). Bobby Rhodes (Tony) supporting cast Stelio Candelli (Frank, Ruth's husband). Nicole Tessier (Ruth, Frank's wife). Geretta [Marie] Giancarlo (Rosemarie, 2nd girl with Tony). Guido Baldi (Tommy, Hannah's boyfriend). Bettina Ciampolini. Giuseppe Cruciano (Hot Dog). Sally Day. Eliana Hoppe (woman in tent, horror film). Jasmine Maimone (Nancy, horror film). Marcello Modugno (Bob, horror film). Peter Pitsch (Baby Pig). Pasqualino [Lino] Salemme (Ripper, driver of car). Enrica Maria Scrivano. Alex Serra (Werner, Liz's father). Michele Soavi (man in black distributing tickets/Jerry, horror film). Claudio Spadaro (Liz's lover).
[uncredited] Goffredo Ungaro (Kurt's dad, jeep driver). Giovanni Frezza (Kurt, boy in jeep). Lamberto Bava (large man, 1st to get off subway train). Sami Habib Ahmed (demon emerging from Kathy).

produced by Dario Argento for DACFILM, Rome.
©1985. DACFILM, Rome [English language version]

produced by Dario Argento. original story: Dardano Sacchetti. screenplay: Dario Argento, Lamberto Bava, Dardano Sacchetti & Franco Ferrini. director of photography: Gianlorenzo Battaglia. music by Claudio Simonetti. additional music by Rick Springfield, Motley Crue, Pretty Maids, Go West, The Adventures, Billy Idol, Accept & Saxon. supervising film editor: Franco Fraticelli a.m.c.. film editor: Piero Bozza. production design: Davide Bassan. costumes: Marina Malavasi & Patrizia Massaia. production manager: Eros Lafranconi. assistant director: Michele Soavi. dubbing editor: Nick Alexander. script continuity: Daniela Tonti. unit manager: Guido De Laurentiis. production secretaries: Fabrizio Diaz & Rita Friggeri. special make-up creations: Sergio Stivaletti. special make-up assistants: Barbara Morosetti & Sami Habib Ahmed. make-up artist & special make-up effects: Rosario Prestopino. make-up assistant: Giacinto Bretti. special construction models: Angelo Mattei. special stage effects: Corridori & Co.. assistant cameramen: Enzo Frattari, Claudio Nannuzzi, Daniele Cimini & Federico Martucci. action stills: Franco Bellomo & Gianfranco Caira. production accountant: Ferdinando Caputo. paymaster: Renato Rinaldo. hairstyles: The Sargassis. supervising hairdresser: Teodora Bruno. assistant set dresser: Livia Pascucci. sound mixer: Raffaele De Luca. boom operator: Angelo Amattulli. 1st assistant editor: Roberto Priori. 2nd assistant editors: Sergio Fraticelli & Fabrizio Fraticelli. gaffer: Cristo Verrillo. key grip: Franco Serantoni. prop master: Maurizio Jacopelli. seamstress: Carla Latini. transportation: Romana Trasporti & Co.. lighting camera equipment: Ciack Italia. re-recording: International Recording. re-recording engineer: Romano Pampaloni. Dolby sound consultant: Federico Savina. special sound effects: Studio Anzellotti. wigs: Rocchetti - Carboni. insurance consultants: Cinesicurtà. unit publicist: Enrico Lucherini. music producers: Universo Film. the original soundtrack is recorded on R. C. A. records. titles & opticals: Aldo Mafera.
soundtrack: "Demon" performed by Claudio Simonetti (Universo Film/RCA), "Killing" performed by Claudio Simonetti (Universo Film/RCA), "Out of Time" performed by Claudio Simonetti (Disaster Universo Film/RCA), "Walking on the Edge" performed by Rick Springfield (courtesy of RCA records), "Save Our Souls" performed Motley Crue (courtesy of Elektra Asylum Records by arrangement with Warner Special Products), "Night Danger" performed by Pretty Maids (courtesy of CBS Denmark), "We Close our Eyes" performed by Go West (courtesy of Chrysalis), "Send my Heart" performed by The Adventures (courtesy of Chrysalis), "White Wedding" performed by Billy Idol (courtesy of Chrysalis), "Fast as a Shark" performed by Accept (courtesy of Breeze Music), "Everybody Up" performed by Saxon (courtesy of EMI Records Ltd.).
[US version additional credits] post-production: Lajon Productions, Inc.. US post-production supervisor: Lawrence Applebaum. creative sound design: Burton Lee Harry, Dennis Patterson, Gabrielle Gilbert & Joe Earle.
processing laboratory: Luciano Vittori. film raw stock: Eastmancolor Kodak. Dolby stereo in selected theatres.

Italian visa number: 80955 [04/10/85]. Registro cinematografico: 7.493.
Filmed in June & July 1985 for nine weeks on location in West Berlin (Germany) and at a derelict theatre near De Paolis Studios (Rome) with interiors filmed at IN. C. I. R. De Paolis Studios (Rome, Italy). Budget: $1.8 million
Italian theatrical distributor: Titanus Distribuzione (released on 4 October 1985, released in Rome & Milan on 5 October 1985). rated: 18. running time: 95 minutes
US theatrical distributor: Ascot Entertainment Group (released on 30 May 1986). rating: none. running time: 89 minutes. catalogue number: 9573.
French theatrical distributor: Actrum Films (released in Paris on 1 October 1986). rated: 18. running time: 95 minutes
UK theatrical distribution: none [although submitted to the BBFC by Avatar Communications Ltd. in January 1987 - rated 18 at 86 minutes 16 seconds after cuts totalling 2 minutes 4 seconds - and screened for some sections of the British press, the UK cinema release was apparently cancelled at the last minute]

Demoni 2... L'incubo ritorna [Italian theatrical/video title]
Demons 2 [UK theatrical & US/UK video title]
Daemonen 2 [Dutch video print title]
Dämonen [German theatrical/video title]
Demons 2 The Nightmare Begins/Demons 2 The Nightmare Continues [alternative titles]

1986 // Italy
Directed by Lamberto Bava

Cast: David Knight (George). Nancy Brilli (Hannah, David's wife). Coralina Cataldi Tassoni (Sally). Bobby Rhodes (Hank, gym instructor). Asia Argento (Ingrid Haller). Virginia Bryant (the prostitute). Anita Bartolucci (woman with dog). Antonio Cantafora (Mr Haller, Ingrid's father). Luisa Passega (Helga Haller, Ingrid's mother). Davide Marotta (little boy demon). Marco Vivio (little boy). Michele Mirabella (man wearing glasses). Lorenzo Gioielli. Lino [Pasqualino] Salemme (the security guard). Maria Chiara Sasso (partygoer with camera). Dario Casalini (Teddy).

Andrea Garinei (young partygoer waiting for Jacob). Luca De Nardo. Angela Frondaroli. Caroline Christina Lund. Karen Gennaro. Marina Loi. Silvia Rosa. Monica Umena. Lorenzo Flaherty. Fabio Poggiali (young partygoer). Andrea Spera. Pascal Persiano. Robert Chilcott. Eliana Hoppe (Ulla). Yvonne Fraschetti. Bruno Bilotta (Jacob, the driver). Furio Bilotta (man in back of car). Giovanna Pini (frightened woman in garage). Stefano Molinari (the 1st demon). Pasquale Valente. Kim Rhone. Annalie Harrison.
[uncredited] Lamberto Bava (Sally's father).

produced by D.A.C. Film s.r.l. (Rome)

written by Dario Argento, Lamberto Bava, Franco Ferrini & Dardano Sacchetti. director of photography: Gianlorenzo Battaglia. music by Simon Boswell, The Smiths, The Cult, Art of Noise, Peter Murphy & Dead Can Dance. supervising editor: Franco Fraticelli a.m.c.. film editor: Pietro Bozza. art director: Davide Bassan. costume designer: Nicola Trussardi. mechanical creations & transformations: Sergio Stivaletti. special make-up effects: Rosario Prestopino. production manager: Guido De Laurentiis. executive producer: Ferdinando Caputo. unit publicists: Enrico Lucherini & Gianluca Pignatelli. assistant director: Fabrizio Bava. casting: Roberto Palmerini. script continuity: Francesca Ghiotto. unit managers: Antonio Saragò & Fabrizio Diaz. dialogue editor: Nick Alexander. production secretaries: Paola Rossi, Egle Friggeri & Andrea Caputo. chief make-up artist: Rosario Prestopino. make-up: Giacinto Bretti. special action effects: Corridori & Co. mechanical creation assistant: Barbara Morosetti. camera operator: Guido Tosi. assistant cameramen: Stefano Falivene & Federico Martucci. action stills: Francesco Bellomo. production accountant: Renato Rinaldo. set dresser: Valeria Paoloni. sound mixer: Raffaele De Luca. assistant editors: Alessandro Gabriele & Fabrizio Fraticelli. gaffer: Domenico Caiuli. key grip: Franco Micheli. prop master: Maurizio Iacopelli. transportation: Romana Trasporti. camera & lighting equipment: Ciak Italia. cameras: Technovision E. C. E.. re-recording: International Recording. re-recording engineer: Romano Pampaloni. Dolby sound consultant: Federico Savina. wigs: Rocchetti & Carboni. accessories: Lembo. insurance consultants: Cinesicurtà. titles & opticals: Aldo Mafera.
processing laboratory: L. V. Luciano Vittori. optical film stock: Eastmancolor Kodak. Dolby stereo in selected theatres.

Italian visa number: 81851 [01/10/86]. Registro cinematografico: 7.638.
Filmed from 26 May 1986 on location in Rome (Italy) with interiors filmed at De Paolis - IN.CI.R. Studios (Rome, Italy).

Italian theatrical distributor: Titanus Distribuzione (released on 9 October 1986). rated: 14. running time: 91 minutes
UK theatrical distributor: Avatar Communications Ltd. (released on 18 September 1987). rated: 18. running time: 91 minutes 8 seconds [no BBFC cuts]
West German theatrical distributor: Alemannia/Elysee (released on 9 July 1987). running time: 82 minutes

La chiesa [Italian theatrical/video title]
The Church [US theatrical/video title]
El engendro del diablo [Spanish theatrical title]
Demons 3 Return to the Land of the Demons/Cathedral of Demons/Demon Cathedral [pre-production titles]

1989 // Italy
Directed by Michele Soavi

Cast: Hugh Quarshie (Father Gus). Tomas Arana (Evan, a librarian). Feodor Chaliapin (the bishop). Barbara Cupisti (Lisa, restoration expert). Antonella Vitale ("princess", model bride). Giovanni Lombardo Radice (reverend). Asia Argento (Lotte, Sacristan's daughter). Roberto Caruso (Freddie, Joanna's boyfriend). Roberto Corbiletto (Hermann the Sacristan, Lotte's father). Alina De Simone (Lotte's mother). Olivia Cupisti (Mira, Dark Ages witch). Gianfranco De Grassi (the accuser - dark ages). Claire [R.] Hardwick (Joanna). Lar Jorgensen [Lars Bodin-Jorgensen] (Bruno, groom model). John Karlsen (Heinrich). Katherine Bell Marjorie [Katherine Bell] (Heinrich's wife). Riccardo Minervini (older of schoolboy best friends). Enrico Osterman [Ostermann] (the torturer). Micaela Pignatelli (fashion shoot photographer). Patrizia Punzo (Miss Brückner, school teacher). John Richardson (the architect). Matteo Rocchietta [Matthew Rocchietta Wilson] (younger of schoolboy best friends).
[uncredited] Michele Soavi (1st cop at Lisa's house).
ADC - Cecchi Gori Group - Tiger Cinematografica - Reteitalia [Segrate (MI)]

production executive: Giuseppe Mangogna. story: Dario Argento & Franco Ferrini. screenplay: Dario Argento, Franco Ferrini & Michele Soavi. director of photography: Renato Tafuri [filmed in Eastman Kodak]. original music: Keith Emerson & The Goblins. film editor: Franco Fraticelli. production design: [Massimo] Antonello Geleng. costumes: Maurizio Paiola. assistant director: Filiberto Fiaschi. assistant to the director: Claudio Lattanzi. script continuity: Marisa Calia. stunt co-ordinator: Arnaldo Dell'Aqua. unit manager: Saverio Mangogna. production secretaries: Daniela Rocco & Ezio Maggi. camera operators: Alessandro Carlotto & Enrico Maggi. assistant cameramen: Alfonso Vicari & Maurizio Cremesini. stills photographer: Franco Vitale. 1st assistant editor: Piero Bozzo. 2nd assistant editor: Roberto Priori. production sound mixer: Giulio Viaggiani. boom operator: Claudio Paolucci. production accountant: Carlo Du Bois. bookkeeper: Antonella Villanti. paymaster: Carlo Cestari. set dresser: Caterina Napoleone. assistant set designer: Daniela Giavonnoni. props: Osvaldo Monaco & Fabio Altamura. wardrobe assistant: Claudio Antonucci. dressmaker: Carla Latini. make-up artist: Rosario Prestopino. make-up: Franco Casagni & Laura Borzelli. hair stylists: Piero Cucchi & Assunta Emidi. gaffer: Fernando Massacessi. key grip: Augusto Proietti. set construction chief: Aldo Taloni. special effects: Renato Agostini. special effects creations: Sergio Stivaletti, assisted by Barbara Morosetti. special Stage effects: A & G Corridori. production Equipment: Ciakitalia. camera equipment: Technovision. lighting equipment: Franco Petracca & Co. wigs: Rocchetti & Carboni. costume houses: Sartoria Izzo, Neriteatromoda, GP11. footwear: LCP. set furnishing: E Rancati, GRP, GR Postiglione, Dedalo, Cinears, Immaginotera. carpeting: Artigiana Arredatorie e Tappezzieri. costume Jewellery: Laba. insurance brokers: Cinesicurtà. transportation: Romana Trasporti, Cinematografici. animals supplied by Marco Stefanelli & Grunwald Martino P.. titles & opticals: Studio AM. English dialogue: Nick Alexander. additional sound effects: Sountrack, L & M Anzellotti. soundtrack supervisor: Vincent Messina. music produced by Bixio - CEMSA. unit publicity: Enrico Lucherini & Gianluca Pignatelli.
songs: Philip Glass, Martin Goldray, The Goblins, Zooming on the Zoo, Definitive Gaze, Simon Boswell.

processing lab: Technicolor

originally to have been directed by Lamberto Bava. Early versions of script written by Dardano Sacchetti & Lamberto Bava.

Italian visa number: 84503 [10/03/89]. Registro cinematografico: 7.974.

Filmed from early September to November 1988 on location in Budapest (Hungary) [5 weeks] and Hamburg (Germany) with interiors filmed at De Paolis Studios (Rome, Italy) and R.P.A. Studios (Rome, Italy) for a total of eleven weeks. Budget $3 and a half million

Italian theatrical distributor: Cecchi Gori (released on 10 March 1989). running time: 103 minutes

La setta [Italian theatrical title]

The Sect [UK video title]
The Devil's Daughter [US video/laserdisc title]
La secta [Spanish theatrical title]

1991 // Italy & Germany
Directed by Michele Soavi

Cast: Kelly Curtis (Miriam Kreisl). Herbert Lom (Moebius Kelly). Maria Angela Giordano (Katryn, Elv: Katherine). Michel Adatte (Frank Pernath). Carla Cassola (Doctor Pernath). Angelika Maria Boeck (Mrs Claire Henri). Giovanni Lombardo Radice (Martin Romero). Niels [Nils] Gullov (Mr Henri) with Tomas Arana (Damon) and with Donald O'Brien (Justice Jonathan Ford). Yasmine Ussani (Samantha Heinz, one of Miriam's pupils). Paolo Pranzo (Steven). Richard Sammel (Jack, truck driver). Ralph Bola Mustapha (2nd truck driver). Erica Sinisi (Sara). Dario Casalini (Mark, a hippy). Fabio Saccani (bald pickpocket on tube). Vincenzo Regina (male nurse). Giovanna Rotellini (1st midwife). Chiara Mancori (2nd midwife). Carmela Pilato (woman of the sect).

Dario Argento presents a film by Michele Soavi produced by Mario & Vittorio Cecchi Gori and Dario Argento for Penta Film/ADC Silvio Berlusconi Communications

executive producer: Andrea Tinnirello. produced by Mario Cecchi Gori, Vittorio Cecchi Gori and Dario Argento. production manager: Fernando Franchi. written by Dario Argento, Giovanni Romoli & Michele Soavi. director of photography: Raffaele Mertes [colour: Technicolor spa]. music by Pino Donaggio; recording studios: Bixio C.E.M.S.A.; Chappell Recorder Music. film editor: Franco Fraticelli a.m.c.. production manager: Fernando Franchi. production designer: M. [Massimo] Antonello Geleng. costumes by Vera Cozzolino. assistant director: Marco Guidone. 2nd assistant director: Enrico Grassi. script girl [continuity]: Francesca Roberti. dialogue coach: William Quarshie. stunt coordinator: Arnaldo Dell'Acqua. unit managers: Patrick Carrarin, Fabrizio Cico Diaz & Egle Friggeri. camera operator: Camillo Sabatini. underwater cameraman: Mario Bagnato. steadicam operators: Nicola Pecorini, Giovanni Gebbia & Sebastiano De Pascalis. assistant camera operator: Frabrizio Papale. still photographer: Franco Vitale. 1st assistant film editor: Adriana Benedetti. 2nd assistant film editor: Alessandra Guerra. sound mixer: Giancarlo Laurenzi. boom operator: Claudio Morra. chief account cashier: Archimede Orlando. set dresser: Giacomo Calò Carducci. props: Osvaldo Monaco & Sebastiano De Caro. painter: Giancarlo Sensidoni. wardrobe assistant: Roberta Cucciolla. seamstress: Mirella Pedetti. make-up: Rosario Prestopino. make-up assistant: Laura Borzelli. hairdresser: Iolanda Angelucci. chief gaffer: Giovanni Galasso. chief grip: Roberto Mareschini. special effects: Massimo Cristofanelli. fantasy creatures created & realised by Sergio Stivaletti. fantasy creatures assistance: Barbara Morosetti. on set special effects: Fratelli Corridori.
production equipment: Arco Due srl. lighting equipment: Franco Patracca & C. sas. wigs: Rocchetti e Carboni srl. costume house: Gi.Elle - Gabriella Lo Faro. footwear: Arditi. set furnishings: E. Rancati snc; G.R.P. di G.R. Postiglione, snc; Dedalo srl.; La Teca dell'Immaginario. carpets: Sanchini. flowers & plants: Vivai e Piante V. Rossiello. insurance broker: Cinesicurtà srl. transportation: Fratelli Cartocci. animals on set: Maurizio Garrone. sound effects: Sound Track. titles & optical effects: Studio A.M. srl; Aldo Mafera. post production supervisor: Lillo Capoano. [sound] studios: Fono Roma. soundtrack produced by Gianni Dell'Orso. music producers: Bixio C.E.M.S.A. unit publicists: Enrico Lucherini & Gianluca Pignatelli. The Production wish to thank Frankfurter Filmproduktion for their collaboration in Frankfurt.
songs: "A Horse with No Name" by Dewey Bunnell; published by Warner Bros. Music, courtesy of Warner Bros Music Italy America; "Don't Leave Me Alone" by W.L. Wilson, B.S. Mason & D.R. Pfrimme; published by Chappell Recorded Music/Flipper srl.
negative: Eastmancolor Kodak.

Italian visa number: 86465 [01/03/91]. Registro cinematografico: 8.307.

Filmed from September 1990 to mid-November 1990 on location in Frankfurt (Germany) and in the Marino Hills outside Rome (Italy) with interiors filmed at De Paolis Studios (Rome, Italy). Budget: $2 million

Italian theatrical distributor: Penta Film (released on 1 March 1991). rated: 14. running time: 115 minutes

M.D.C. Maschera di cera [Italian theatrical title]

The Wax Mask [UK video title]
La maschera di cera/Il terrore della maschera di cera/The Terror of the Wax Mask [shooting titles]

1997 // Italy & France
Directed by Sergio Stivaletti

Cast: Robert Hossein (Boris Volkoff, museum curator). Romina Mondello (Sonia Lafont/Marta Volkoff). Riccardo Serventi Longhi (Andrea Conversi, reporter with 'Il Messagero'). Gabriella Giorgelli (Francesca, Sonia's aunt). Umberto Balli (Alex, Volkoff's assistant & designer). Valery Valmond (Georgina, a prostitute). Gianni Franco (Inspector Palazzi). Antonello Murru (museum caretaker). Daniele Auber (Luca). Romano Iannelli (pathologist). Rosa Pianeta (Anna's mother). Sonia Topazio (nurse). Massimo Vanni (Victor, Marta's 2nd husband). Omero Capanna (the monster) and with Aldo Massasso (Inspector Lanvin). Sabrina Pellegrino (Elena/Elaine). Giuseppina Lo Vetro (the madame). Luca Memè (Giovanni). Goffredo Unger [Goffredo Ungaro] (the puppeteer). Stefania Fidotti (Anna, the little girl). Loretta Cester (girl in waiting room). Salvatore Cammuca (gypsy). Maria Asiride, Ginevra Casini, Caterina Cuomo, Angela D'Ambra, Federica Leuter, Antonella Sannite, Elena Marchesina, Michela Paolucci, Elisabetta Rocchetti & Andreina Sirena (madame's girls).
[uncredited] Sergio Stivaletti (brothel client).

Presented by Fulvio Lucisano for I.I.F. Italian International Film // Dario Argento presents a Cine 2000 production in collaboration with Mediaset // a co-production with France Film International // made with the assistance of The Ministers Council - Department of the Arts and with the collaboration of The Banca Nazionale del Lavoro (section for Cinema and Theatre SpA)

produced by Giuseppe Colombo. production manager: Tommaso Calevi. story: Dario Argento, Lucio Fulci & Daniele Stroppa. screenplay: Lucio Fulci & Daniele Stroppa. director of photography: Sergio Salvati a.i.c. [prints & processing: Augustus Color S.A.S.]. music composed by Maurizio Abeni. editor: Paolo Benassi (on Avid). art direction: [Massimo] Antonello Geleng. costumes: Stefania Svizzeretto. special visual & sculptural effects created by Sergio Stivaletti. special make-up effects: Benoit Lestang. dialogue recorded by Gambit International, directed by Robert Rietti. financial consultant: Paolo Di Gravio. assistant director: Michele Salimbeni. 2nd assistant director: Giuseppe Cerabino. unit manager: Cristina Romagnoli. production secretary & post-production supervisor: Riccardo Folgore. assistant production secretary: Stefano Voltaggio. key production assistant: Mauro Nobili. production assistants: Massimiliano Di Giuliani, Cristiano Di Meo, Claudio Ionni, Giuseppe Gambella, Corrado Mantoni & Giancarlo Rebiscini. cameraman: Franco Bruni. 1st assistant camera: Gianfranco Torinti. 2nd assistant camera: Federico Angelucci. steadicam operators: Giovanni Canevari & Pietro Plaia. still photography: Franco Vitale. script supervisor: Maria Rosaria Cilento. production accountant: Benito Mancini. key make-up: Bernadette Grampa. key hairstylist: Bruno Benjamin Ruas. assistant costumes: Luca Grande. wardrobe: Bertilla Silvestrin. assistant art director: Antonella Fulci. set decorator: Giacomo Calò Carducci. assistant set decorator: Francesca Romana Tomassini. props management: Media Show Time, Laura Fiorucci & Tiziana Bonacchi. property masters: Giuseppe Cancellara & Maurizio Iacopelli. assistant props: Paolo Iacopelli, Giuseppe Quinizi & Roberto Petroni. set dressers: Franco De Masi, Barbara Morosetti & Fabio Unger. gaffer: Stefano Marino. electricians: Giovanni Maria Gambella, Gianni Gentili, Giuseppe Meloni, Marco Raimondi, Luigi Pasqualini, Gianluca Terlizi & Severino Tramontani. generator operators: Marco Cartocci, Carlo Lamoratta & Mario Lamoratta. key grips: Roberto Bagalà & Claudio Pezzotti. grips: Massimiliano Anzellotti, Fabio Caramico, Patrizio Emidi, Sergio Gabrielli, Luciano Giuseppone, Waslter Pavia, Sergio Rossi & Ivano Rugieri. sound: Riccardo Palmieri. boom operator: Piero Fondi. crowd scenes: Silvia Spoletini. unit publicist (production): Paolo Paggetta. unit publicist (distribution): Annarosa Morri. insurance: Studio M for Cinesicurtà Srl.. Italian version consultant: Lorenzo Ciccorelli. assistant editors: Flora Elisa Algeri Bricoli & Letizia Caudullo. sound effects: Studio 16. dubbing director: Aldo Massasso. music publisher: EMI Muisc Publishing Italial Srl. orchestra director & orchestrations: Maurizio Abeni. [music] recordist: Marco Streccioni. music production assistant: Roberto Bongiovanni. special effects & computer graphics: Sergio Stivaletti. Studio Stivaletti crew, life casts & special effects make-up: Barbara Morosetti & Benoit Lestang. asistant: Misha Koopman. Italian version recording: International Recording. mixage: Fausto Ancillai. titles & opticals: Penta Studios. artistic supervisor & sculptor: Francesca Di Nunzio.
catering: Ristorante 'Da Gigi' di Luigi Parrillo. construction: In Scena Srl; Ditta Cori Carlitto Amedeo. costume suppliers: Annamode 68; Sartoria Teatrale e Cinematografica Roma; 'Il Costume' (Rome); N.H.S. Srl - Costumi Teatrali Roma; Nori Enzo Sartoria Abbigliamento Forniture Militari; Sorelle Ferroni & C. Srl; Stamigna Bazar SNC; Nicolosi Salvatore. set furnishings: Cine Ottocento Srl; Arredamenti Cineteatrali G.R.P.; Sanchini Srl; E. Rancati Srl; Pagliaro Giancarlo. footwear: Arditi; C.C.T. Srl - Calzature Cineteatrali. jewelry: Gioielli L.A.B.A. Roma.
Paris crew production assistant: Alain Tourriol; cameraman: Jean François Gondre; French unit director: Charles Lahaye; assistant costumes: Françoise Lotiron; generator operator: Abdel Meziane; electrician: Jerome Pezinni; gaffer: Franck Coquet; key grip: Albert Bonomi. mag stock: Sound Service di Frugis Stefania. technical equipment: Arco Due Sr.l.. lights: Ditta Petracca. transport: Fratelli Cartocci; Consorzio Trasporti Cin..
The production thanks: Banca Nazionale del Lavoro Settore 35 Roma Nord.; Banca Nazionale del Lavoro Ag. 22 di Roma; La Sortoria del Terziere Mezule di Narni; L'Accademia di Costume e Moda di Roma; Helen Marlen Srl; Zanaboni S.N.C.; Banci Firenze Srl; Richard Ginori 1735; Nason Moretti Srl.
negatives: Kodak S.p.A.. Dolby in selected theatres.
Dedicated to Lucio Fulci.

Filmed from 9 July to 13 August 1996 on location in Via Cola di Rienzo and other Rome locations (Italy). Special effects filmed at the Stivaletti studios on Via Tor Cervara (outskirts of Rome). Budget $3 million

Italian theatrical distributor: IIF - Italian International Film (released in March 1997). rated: 18. running time: 98 minutes
French theatrical distribution: none

Scarlet Diva

2000 // Italy
Directed by Asia Argento

Gianluca Curti presents a film distributed by Gruppo Minerva International // Minerva Pictures presents a film by Asia Argento // an Opera Film production in collaboration with Cinema Stream

Cast: Asia Argento (Anna Battista). Jean Shepherd (Kirk Vaines). Herbert Fritsch (Aaron Ulrich). Gianluca Arcopinto (Doctor Pascuccia). Joe Coleman (Mr. Paar). Francesca d'Aloja (Margherita). Véra Gemma (Veronica Lanza). Justinian Kfoury (J bird). Daria Nicolodi (Anna's mother). Schoolly D (Hash-man). Selen (Quelou). Alessandro Villari (Hamid) <and with the participation of> Leo Gullotta (Doctor Vessi) <and with> Paolo Bonacelli (Swiss journalist). Vanessa Crane (Luke Ford). David D'Ingeo (Adam). Jeff Alexander (Tyrone). Robert Sommer (acting playing Caesar). Gloria Pirrocco (Anna as a child). Edoardo Servadio (Alioscia as a child).

Deborah Restante (Simona). Massimo De Lorenzo (drunk). Giovanna Papa (fast food woman). Taiyo Yamanouchi (Japanese). Angelica Di Majo (pierced girl). [originally cast] Blixa Bargeld. Sergio Rubini.

presented by Dario Argento & Claudio Argento. executive producer: Claudio Argento. produced with the collaboration of Gianluca Curti, Stefano Curti & Adriana Chiesa Di Palma. production manager: Gianluca Passone. written by Asia Argento. director of photography: Frederic Fasano. original music: John Hughes; published by Strag. editor: Anna Napoli, a.m.c.. art director: Alessandro Rosa. costumes: Susy Mattolini. sound supervisors: Lilio Rosato, Andrea Lancia. visual effects supervisor: Sergio Stivaletti. 1st assistant director: Alessia Cerasaro. 2nd assistant director: Massimo Sagramola. unit manager: Mauro Mobili. production secretaries: Carla Alonzo, Danilo Santori. M.d.P. camera operator: Frederic Fasano. steadicam operators: Marco Pieroni, Giovanni Canevari. assistant operators: Alessandro Metere, Davide Stampa. backstage operator: Jean-Paris. script supervisor: Renata Salvatore. administration: Erika Taloni. cashier: Maria Rita Gagliano. key grip: Luigia Spoletini. make-up: Claudio Noto, Daniela Mattia. hairdresser: Salvino Palmieri. assistant costumes: Lavinia Giordani. assistant art director: Massimiliano Sturiale. property master: Marco Priori. gaffer: Delio Catini. electricians: Stefano Martino, Massimo Modaffari, Luigi Angelini. grips: Tarcisio Diamanti, Gianpaolo Bosi. assistant grip: Roberto Di Odoardo. driver: Emidio Prioletta. sound: Mirko Perri. boom operator: Flavio D'Andrea. construction manager: Claudio Quaglietti. special effects: Corr. G & A Cinematografica s.r.l.. 1st assistant editor: Maria Cristina Marra. 2nd assistant editor: Francesca Genevois. effects created by Apocalypse di Sergio Stivaletti. Apocalypse staff: production supervisor: Barbara Morosetti. sculptor: Francesca Romana Di Nunzio. mechanical: David Bracci. set assistants: Gabriele Magri, Vittorio Magri. 3D modelling & compositing: Gabriele Zuppardo. [digital] paint & compositing: Elena Angeletti. still photography by Fast Photo Service, photographed by Franco Vitale. animal suppliers/consultants: Zoo Grunwald. animal trainer: Pasquale Martino. unit publicist: Francesca De Michele. insurance: Cinesicurtà s.r.l.. integrazioni dialoghi a cura della Mar International. dubbing director: Roberta Paladini. dubbing assistant: Viviana Barbetta. studio recording: Sound Art 23 s.r.l.. dubbing recordist: Valerio Brini. direct sound editors: Lilio Rosato, Marco Giacomelli. mixage: Andrea Lancia. Andrea Malavasi. sound effects: Space Sound On Line s.a.s. by Tullio Arcangeli, Roberto Sterbini, Paolo Pucci, Saverio Lancia. music synchronization & editing: Cinzia Cavalieri. John Hughes' music recorded & mixed at Hefty studio in Chicago by John Hughes. vocals, Rhodes: John Hughes, guitar: Dan Snazelle; percussion: John McEntire; basso: Erick Bocek; vibraphone: Rick Embach; trombone: Phil Ranelin; guitar: Victor Villareal; violoncello: Brandon Vamos; violin: Simin Ganatra; keyboards: Scott Herren; percussion: Dave Pavkovic; vocals: Ruta Hughes. incidental music by Lory D and excerpts by Jean Shepherd were recorded at "No Man's Land" studio in Rome. titles & opticals: Penta Studio. prints & processing [logo] Cinecittà. digital crew: Silvia Cipparoli, Fabrizio Carraro, Stefano Ballirano, Marina Di Patrizi. colour grader: Pasquale Cuzzupoli. Dolby consultant: Federico Savina. Dolby Digital. filming equipment: Sony 12 Bit Digital Betacam (Sony Italia S.p.A.). digital stock: Sony Digital Betacam: C.I.C. Distribuzione s.r.l.. audio equipment hire: Rita Di Tommaso. Avid editing studio: Grande Mela. technical equipment: Panalight s.r.l.. lenses: Cannon Prime Lenses: Trans Audio Video s.r.l. lamps & gels: Ditta Petracca di Alessio Petracca. transport: Cinetecnica s.r.l.. shipping: Cecchetti Speedcoop s.c.a.r.l. catering: Ristorante "Da Gigi" s.r.l.. costume house: Annamode 68 s.r.l.. travel agent: Blue World s.r.l.. vehicles: Coop. Prati.
the producers thank: Il Gruppo Autogrill; Discoteca Alien; T - Bone Station (di Via Flaminia N. 573, Rome); SA.MO.CAR.. Asia Argento thanks: Giovanni Veronesi; Fabio Camilli; Peppe Lanzetta; Dolce e Gabbana; Bryan Enk; Asia Argento Fan Club; Alessio Manna; Beniamino Catena; Ruta Hughes; the great Phil Ranelin - all the musicians for keeping it real in the soundtrack - Lucio Nicolodi.
[soundtrack] "Supernatural" by Lory D, Ruvolo, Curti; "Ghettoreverse", "Granulator K", "Fantasy Drums" by Lory D, Ruvolo; "Illusion", "Passing Through" by Jean Shepherd, Ruvolo, Curti, sung by Jean Shepherd - all published by Strag; "Che bella cosa sei" by Fred Buscaglione, Leo Chiosso, sung by Fred Buscaglione, published by EMI Publishing; "Wild is the Wind" by Dmitri Tiomkin, Ned Washington, Jungmichel, sung by Nina Simone, published by Polygram.

dedicated to Anna

[credited during production] executive producers: Dario Argento & Claudio Argento. director of photography: Beniamino Catena. music: Blixa Bargeld, Lory D & John Hughes III.

Filmed from 27 September 1999 for five weeks on location in New York (USA), London (UK), Paris (France), Amsterdam (Holland) and Rome (Italy).

©2000. Opera Film s.r.l..

Italian theatrical distributor: Minerva Pictures (released in Rome & Milan on 26 May 2000). rated: 14. running time: 90 minutes / 2,417 metres Italian video distributor: Minerva Video. rated: 14. running time: circa 87 minutes. catalogue number: MVB 20025

Other work for television

La bambola [episode title]
La porta sul buio di Dario Argento [series title]

1973 // Italy
Directed by Mario Foglietti

Cast: Robert Hoffmann. Mara Venier. Gianfranco D'Angelo. Erika Blanc. Maria Teresa Albani. Pupo De Luca. Umberto Raho. Luciano Bonanni.

introduced by Dario Argento

RAI Radiotelevisione Italiana presents a SEDA Spettacoli S.p.A. (Rome) production

[produced by Dario Argento]. story & screenplay. Marcella Elsberger & Mario Foglietti. director of photography. Elio Polacchi [prints & processing: Telecolor (Rome)]. original music by Giorgio Gaslini. editor: Amedeo Giomini. costume designer & art director: Dario Micheli. production manager: Giuseppe Mangogna.

unit manager: Carlo Cucchi. production secretary: Tomasso Alvieri. cameraman: Nino Annunziata. assistant cameraman: Luigi Conversi. sound: Mario Ronchetti. boom operator: Eugenio Fiore. continuity: Nellita Zampieri. assistant art director: Maurizio Garrone. assistant editor: Piero Bozza. 2nd assistant editors: Nadia Mazzoni & Tommaso Gramigna. production accountants: Ferdinando Caputo & Carlo Dubois. make-up: Cristina Rocca. hairstylist: Ida Alacino. wardrobe: Marcella Moretti. still photography: Roberto Canevari (Nuova Dial). key grip: Guglielmo Maga. property master: Augusto La Valle. construction manager: Giuseppe Gabrielli. gaffer: Orazio Sinacore. generator operator: Ferdinando Cartocci. sound effects: Anzellotti. titles & opticals: Studio Verzini. synchronization directed by [Domenico] Mimmo Palmara for SINC Cinematografica. mixage: Venanzio Biraschi, recorded by Fono Roma using Western Electric equipment. Italian version: Cinitalia Edizioni. technical equipment: Janiro S.r.l.. costume house: Ferroni. wigs: Rocchetti. furnishings: Cimino Cine Arredamento Rancati. hangings: Alfredo D'Angelo. sound recording: Fono Roma. music publisher: Bixio Sam (Milan).

negatives: Eastmancolor Kodak.

running time: 58 minutes 53 seconds

Il vicino di casa [episode title]
La porta sul buio di Dario Argento [series title]

1973 // Italy
Directed by Luigi Cozzi

Cast: Aldo Reggiani (the man). Laura Belli (the woman). [Domenico] Mimmo Palmara (the neighbour). Alberto Atenari.

introduced by Dario Argento

RAI Radiotelevisione Italiana presents a SEDA Spettacoli S.p.A. (Rome) production

[produced by Dario Argento]. story & screenplay: Luigi Cozzi. director of photography: Elio Polacchi [prints & processing: Telecolor (Rome)]. original music by Giorgio Gaslini. editor: Alberto Moro. costume designer & art director: Dario Micheli. assistant director: Roberto Pariante. production manager: Giuseppe Mangogna. unit manager: Carlo Cucchi. production secretary: Tomasso Alvieri. cameraman: Nino Annunziata. assistant cameraman: Luigi Conversi. sound: Mario Ronchetti. boom operator: Eugenio Fiore. continuity: Nellita Zampieri. assistant art director: Maurizio Garrone. assistant editor: Piero Bozza. 2nd assistant editors: Nadia Mazzoni & Tommaso Gramigna. production accountants: Ferdinando Caputo & Carlo Dubois. make-up: Cristina Rocca. hairstylist: Ida Alacino. wardrobe: Marcella Moretti. still photography: Roberto Canevari (Nuova Dial). key grip: Guglielmo Maga. property master: Augusto La Valle. construction manager: Giuseppe Gabrielli. gaffer: Orazio Sinacore. generator operator: Ferdinando Cartocci. sound effects: Anzellotti. titles & opticals: Studio Verzini. synchronization directed by [Domenico] Mimmo Palmara for SINC Cinematografica. mixage: Venanzio Biraschi, recorded by Fono Roma using Western Electric equipment. Italian version: Cinitalia Edizioni. technical equipment: Janiro S.r.l.. costume house: Ferroni. wigs: Rocchetti. furnishings: Cimino Cine Arredamento Rancati. hangings: Alfredo D'Angelo. sound recording: Fono Roma. music publisher: Bixio Sam (Milan).
negatives: Eastmancolor Kodak.

running time: 55 minutes 57 seconds

Fiat cromo

1986 // Italy
Directed by Dario Argento. director of photography: Ronnie Taylor.
produced by BRW (Milan)
Advertisement for Fiat Auto.

Giallo La tua impronta del venerdì [Italian television series title]

1987/88 // Italy
Directed by Enzo Gatta

created by Enzo Tortora & Anna Tortora. writers: Laura Grimaldi, Marco Tropea & Dardano Sacchetti. photography: Angelo Pacchetti. music by Manuel De Sica; conducted by Enzo Tortora & Dario Argento. art director: Armando Nobili. hosts: Enzo Tortora, Dario Argento & Alba Parietti

This was a magazine format television series in which Argento and his two co-presenters hosted a series of items which ranged from interviewing members of the public to demonstrations in the studio of how some of Argento's landmark on-screen murders were created.
Two elements of the series were pre-filmed:

1) a series of nine three-minute films written and directed by Dario Argento himself:
La finestra sul cortile
Riti notturni
Il verme
Amare e morire
Nostalgia punk
La strega
Addormentarsi
Sammy
L'incubo di chi voleva interpretare l'incubo di Dario Argento

2) **Turno di notte**, a series of fifteen films created and supervised/produced by Dario Argento for A.D.C. s.r.l..
These giallo-style thrillers, each running about 13 minutes, were linked together by four common characters, all employees of the Calypso taxi firm.

Regular cast: Antonella Vitale (Calypso #1). Matteo Gazzolo. Franco Cerri. Lea Martino (the contoller).
Regular production credits: production supervisor: Piero Amati. director of photog-

raphy: Pasquale Rachini (colour by Telecolor). editor: Piero Bozza. art director: Maurizio Garrone. costumes: Marina Pistolesi.

E' di moda la morte (directed by Lamberto Bava)
guest cast: David Brandon. Vanni Corbellini. Matteo gazzolo.
Heavy Metal (directed by Lamberto Bava)
guest cast: Vittoria Zinny. Maurice Poli.
Buona fine e miglior principio (directed by Lamberto Bava)
guest cast: Stefano De Sando (). Maurice Poli (father). Clelia Rondinella (daughter). Victoria Zinni (mother).
Giubetto rosso (directed by Lamberto Bava)
guest cast: [Marie] Gioia Scola. Lino Salemme.
Il bambino rapito (directed by Lamberto Bava)
guest cast: Ippolita Santarelli.
Babbo Natale (directed by Lamberto Bava)
guest cast: Luciano Bartoli. Mauro Bosco. Stefano De Sando. Stefano Sabelli. Maria Chiara Sasso. Sergio Testori.
L'impronta dell'assassino (directed by Luigi Cozzi)
guest cast: Mirella D'Angelo. Sandra Collodel. Anita Bartolucci. Elena Fanucci. Brett Halsey. Stefano De Sando.
Ciak si muore (directed by Luigi Cozzi)
guest cast: Corinne Cléry. Loris Loddi. Pasquale [Pascal] Persiano. Eleonora Pariante. Roberto Cecacci. Stefano De Sando [uncredited] Michele Soavi.
Sposarsi è un po' morire (directed by Luigi Cozzi)
guest cast: Bruno Bilotta. David Dingeo. Claire Hardwick. Carla Turazza.
Delitto in rock (directed by Luigi Cozzi)
guest cast: Gianni Miani. Cinzia Farolfi.
L'evasa (directed by Luigi Cozzi)
guest cast: Micaela Pignatelli.
La casa dello Stradivari (directed by Luigi Cozzi)
guest cast: Jinny Stefan. Jasmine Maimone.
Giallo Natale (directed by Luigi Cozzi)
guest cast: Asia Argento. Daria Nicolodi. Giada Cozzi.
Via delle Streghe (directed by Luigi Cozzi)
guest cast: Elena Pompei. Bruno Corazzari. Susanna Martinkova.
Il taxi fantasma (directed by Luigi Cozzi)
guest cast: Sonia Viviani.

produced by RAI Radiotelevisione Italiana
Italian television distributor: Rai-2, shown on Friday evenings at 20.30 from October 1987 to January 1988

Gled Pyramid

1992 // Italy
Directed by Dario Argento.
Produced by Mercurio Cinematografica for Verba D.D.B. Needham.
Advertisement for Johnson Wax.

Vicolo cieco

1999 // Italy
Directed by Dario Argento.
Produced by RBA Production for Roberto Gorla. creative director: Roberto Gorla.
running time: 30 seconds.
Short film for Aima (Associazione Italiana Malattia di Alzheimer)

Documentaries about Argento

World of Horror Il meglio di Dario Argento [Italian video title]
Dario Argento's World of Horror [US/UK video/US DVD/laserdisc title]

1985 // Italy
Directed by Michele Soavi

executive producers: Dacfilm (Rome).
interviewees: Dario Argento. Luciano Tovoli.

footage of:
Flavio Bucci (on set of "Suspiria" in Munich); Dario Argento & The Goblins (during editing/scoring of "Suspiria"); Tom Savini (on the Pittsburgh set of "Dawn of the Dead"); Dario Argento & crew (on set of "Tenebre"); Dario Argento, Jennifer Connolly, Donald Pleasence, Fiore Argento, Maurizio Garrone, Sergio Stivaletti, Davide Marotta, Patrick Bauchau & Michele Soavi (on set of "Phenomena"); Dario Argento (on set of "Demons").

written by Michele Soavi. directors of photography: Gianlorenzo Battaglia, Stefano Ricciotti & Enrico Cortese. film editor: Piero Bozza. production manager: Fabrizio Diaz. assistant director: Claudio Lattanzi. assistant cameraman: Aldo Bergamini. assistant editor: Roberto Priori. sound editor: Nick Alexander. sound mixer: Giancarlo Laurenzi. make-up: Antonio Altavilla. production accountant: Renato Rinaldo. grips: Augusto Pascarella & Giancarlo Moreschini. electricians: Mario Massacesi & Maurizio Di Stefano. titles & opticals: Aldo Mafera.
The production would like to thank: Claudio and Salvatore Argento; Titanus - U.I.P. - Merope - Intrafilms; Brando Giordani - R.A.I. and Rete Italia; Panavision; Arco 2 Roma; Bixio C.E.M.S.A.; Claudio Simonetti - Giancarlo Meo; Luciano Tovoli; Romano Albani; Sergio Stivaletti; Luciano and Massimo Anzellotti for sound effects; The crews of "Suspiria", "Tenebre" & "Phenomena" And all those who have contributed to the making of this film.
a special thanks to: The Goblins [Sleepwalking], The Goblins [Suspiria], Keith Emerson [Inferno], Keith Emerson [Mater Tenebrarum], Claudio Simonetti, Elsa Morante & Fabio Pignatelli [Tenebre], Simon Boswell [The Maggots], The Goblins [The Wind], Claudio Simonetti [Demons], Claudio Simonetti [Killing], Iron Maiden [Flash of the Blade], The Goblins [Dawn of the Dead], Bill Wyman & Terry Taylor [Valley], The Goblins [Deep Red], Claudio Simonetti [Phenomena], The Goblins [Elena Morcos].
films excerpts: The Bird with the Crystal Plumage © 1971; The Cat O' Nine Tails ©1971; Four Flies on Grey Velvet ©1971; Deep Red - Suspiria 2 ©1975; Suspiria

©1977; Inferno ©1980; Tenebre ©1982; Phenomena - Creepers ©1984; Zombie: Dawn of the Dead ©1979; Demons ©1985.
laboratories: Luciano Vittori, Technicolor & Telecolor

running time: 75 minutes

Protagonisti del cinema italiano Dario Argento [Italian video title]

1989 // Italy
produced by Etabeta (Rome)

series editor: Valerio Caprara. editorial co-ordinator: Mario Canale. editors: Pietro D'Orazio & Marco Trivelli. music: Ennio Morricone, Goblin, Giorgio Gaslini & Claudio Simonetti.

interviewees: Susy Blady, Enrico Magrelli, Stefania Casini

running time: 60 minutes

This was one of a series of eight programmes released under the umbrella title "I grandi registi" [The Great Directors].
The others titles were:
Bernardo Bertolucci
Il fantastico Nuti
Il grande Troisi
L'incontenibile Villaggio
L'incredibile Benigni
L'irrestibile Verdone
Marco Ferreri.

Il mondo di Dario Argento 2 [Italian video title]
Dario Argento Master of Horror [UK video title]

1991 // Italy
Directed by Lewis Coates [Luigi Cozzi]

with Dario Argento

DB Media presents // produced by ADC srl (Rome) for SA.MA Film.
©1991. ADC s.r.l.

executive producer: Lillo Capoano. written by Luigi Cozzi. additional text by Fabio Giovannini. lighting cameraman: Arcangelo Lannutti. film editor: Vittorio Viscardi. visual co-ordinator: Maria Letizia Sercia. RVM: Franco Zeppieri. artistic organization: Cico Diaz. editing, dubbing & synchronization: Cometa s.n.c..
film excerpts: Tenebre (Unseen); Opera (Terror at the Opera); La chiesa (The Church); Due occhi diabolici (Two Evil Eyes); La setta (The Sect).

interviews filmed at Dario Argento's "Museo degli Orrori" at Profondo Rosso (Roma, Italy).
running time: 90 minutes

Il mondo Dario Argento n.3 Il museo degli orrori di Dario Argento [Italian video title]

1997 // Italy
Directed by Luigi Cozzi

Dario Argento with the participation of Asia Argento. Bill Wyman. Lamberto Bava. Riccardo Freda. Antonella Vitale. Vittorio Giacci. Matteo Gazzolo. Jennifer Connelly. Fiore Argento. Tom Savini. Alba Parietti. Enzo Tortora. Daria Nicolodi. Barbara Steele. Elena Pompei & Claudio Simonetti.

Profondo Rosso presents a Profonfo Rosso S.a.s. production
©1997. Profonfo Rosso S.a.s.

original concept, story & credits: Lewis Coates [Luigi Cozzi]. dialogue collaboration: Nicola Lombardi. music: Claudio Simonetti, Bill Wyman, Ennio Morricone & I Goblin. editor: Vittorio Viscardi, Cometa S.n.c.. art director: Davide Bracci. special make-up equipment: Franco Casagni. archive research: Maria Letizia Sercia.
with the participation of the Cittadino dello Spazio, del Mostro della Laguna Nera e del Figlio di King Kong
video excerpts:Phenomena photography: Romano Albani, director: Dario Argento; The Valley director: Michele Soavi; Heavy Metal photography: Pasquale Rachini. screenplay: Dardano Sacchetti. director: Luigi Cozzi.

Filmed on location in Rome (Italy)

running time: 105 minutes 52 seconds

Dario Argento's documentary appearances

1978 **La macchina cinema** (IT) film makers: Silvano Agosti, Marco Bellocchio, Sandro Petraglia & Stefano Bulli. DA was interviewed in this five-part television documentary series. Shown on RAI-2 from 01/11/1978.
1991 **Fear in the Dark** (UK/US) director: Dominic Murphy. DA was interviewed in this television documentary
1993 **This is Horror Special** (US) DA was interviewed in this made-for-video documentary

Dario Argento's feature film appearances

1966 **Scusi, lei è favorevole o contrario?** (Italy) director: Alberto Sordi. DA appears in an uncredited bit role as a young priest
1973 **Le cinque giornate** (Italy) director: Dario Argento. DA makes an uncredited appearance as one of Baron Tranzunto's gang, seen in a brief shot wearing bandages around his head.
1992 **Innocent Blood** (USA) director: John Landis. DA appears as a paramedic
1995 **Il cielo è sempre più blu**/Bits and Pieces (Italy) director: Antonello Grimaldi. DA appears as a man sitting on a park bench confessing to a Franciscan monk

As has been reported elsewhere, DA frequently 'cameos' as the murderous hands of the various killers in his own gialli.

Dario Argento's documentary appearances

1978 **La macchina cinema** (IT) film makers: Silvano Agosti, Marco Bellocchio, Sandro Petraglia & Stefano Bulli. DA was interviewed in this five-part television documentary series. Shown on RAI-2 from 01/11/1978.
1991 **Fear in the Dark** (UK/US) director: Dominic Murphy. DA was interviewed in this television documentary
1993 **This is Horror Special** (US) DA was interviewed in this made-for-video documentary

The productions of Seda Spettacoli (co-owned by Salvatore Argento and Dario Argento)

1970 **L'uccello dalle piume di cristallo** / Das Geheimnis der schwarzen Handschuhe/The Bird with Crystal Plumage (Italy/West Germany) director: Dario Argento. made by Seda Spettacoli/CCC Filmkunst (Berlin)
1971 **Il gatto a nove code** / Die Neunschwänzige Katze/Le Chat à neuf queues/Cat O'Nine Tails (Italy/West Germany/France) director: Dario Argento. made by Seda Spettacoli/Mondial Te.Fi. - Televisione Film/Labrador Films, Paris (France)/Terra Filmkunst, München/Berlin (Germany)
1971 **Er Più Storia d'amore e di coltello** (Italy) director: Sergio Corbucci. made by Seda Spettacoli/Mondial Te.Fi. - Televisione Film/Clan Celentano Films
1971 **4 mosche di velluto grigio** / Quatre mouches de velours gris/Four Flies on Grey Velvet (Italy/France) director: Dario Argento. made by Seda Spettacoli/Universal Productions France, Paris (France)
1973 **Le cinque giornate** (Italy) director: Dario Argento. made by Seda Spettacoli
1973 **La porta sul buio di Dario Argento** [four-episode television series]
        Testimone occulare (Italy) director: Roberto Pariante [actually Dario Argento]
        Il tram (Italy) director: Sirio Bernadotte [Dario Argento]
        Il vicino di casa (Italy) director: Luigi Cozzi
        La bambola (Italy) director: Mario Foglietti
1974 **Antoine et Sébastien** (France/Italy) director: Jean-Marie Périer. made by Fildebroc (Paris)/Seda Spettacoli
1974 **L'albero dalle foglie rosa** (Italy) director: Armando Nannuzzi. made by Seda Spettacoli
1975 **Profondo rosso**/Deep Red (Italy) director: Dario Argento. made by Seda Spettacoli
1976 **Carioca Tigre** (Italy/Brasil) director: Giuliano Carnimeo. made by Centro Produzioni Cinematografiche Città di Milano/Seda Spettacoli/Cinematica Prod. Cinematográficas (Rio de Janeiro)
1977 **Suspiria** (Italy) director: Dario Argento. made by Seda Spettacoli

The Productions of Dacfilm (Rome) (owned by Dario Argento)

Dacfilm was the sole producer of the following films:
1984 **Phenomena**/Creepers (Italy) director: Dario Argento
1985 **Demoni**/Demons (Italy) director: Lamberto Bava
1985 **Dario Argento's World of Horror** (Italy) director: Michele Soavi
1987/1988 **Giallo La tua impronta del venerdì** (Italy) director: Enzo Gatta (for television)

Live work

Fenomeni di moda Trussardi action
Directed by Dario Argento. assistant: Paolo Zenatello. music: Pino Donaggio.
A fashion show for Nicola Trussardi's Autumn/Winter collection staged on 9 March 1986 at the Piazza del Cannone in Milan (Italy)

Dario Argento complete filmography (part 3)

APPENDIX

3

Video / Laserdisc / DVD details

L'uccello dalle piume di cristallo / The Bird with the Crystal Plumage
Italian video distributor: Creazioni Home Video. Rating: 14. Running time: 103 minutes.
Italian video distributor: Mondadori Video. Running time: 96 minutes. Cat No. MVEC03042.
Danish video distributor: Video International. (released as: Fuglen Med Krystalfjerpragten)
Dutch video distributor: Polygram/Spectrum. Running time: 91 minutes [Full screen]
French DVD distributor: TFI Video. [Letterboxed at 2.35:1, French and Italian language, French subtitles, filmography, Argento interview, photo gallery, screen-saver, Internet link]
German video distributor: Toppic.(released as: Das Geheimnis der Schwarzen Handschuhe)
Greek video distributor: Unknown. [Full screen, English Language, Greek subtitles]
Japanese video distributor: Columbia Video. Running time: 96 minutes 7 seconds. [Letterboxed in English with Japanese subtitles]
Japanese laserdisc distributor: Unknown. [Letterboxed, uncut]
Japanese DVD distributor: Culture Publishers. Running time: 97 minutes. [Letterboxed at 2.00:1, Dolby 2.0 Italian language, optional Japanese subtitles]
Portugese video distributor: Filmitalus.
Spanish video distributor: Manga Films S.L.(released as:el pajaro de las plumas de cristali). Running time: 96 minutes. [Letterboxed at 2.35:1, Spanish language]
UK video distributor: Stablecane Ltd. (released circa 1985). Rating: 18. Running time: 92 minutes 7 seconds [no further BBFC cuts - same as cut UK cinema version]
UK video distributor: Vampix - a Videomedia release (released in May 1983). rating: none. Running time: 92 minutes 10 seconds. catalogue number: HVM 1028
US video distributor: VCI - Video Communications, Inc. (released in July 1989). rating: none. Running time: 98 minutes. catalogue number: 9002.
US laserdisc distributor: Image Entertainment (released in 1990). rating: Cut US PG rated version. [Letterboxed at 2.35:1] catalogue number: ID6593VC.
US laserdisc distributor: Roan Group. Rating: none. [Uncut and letterboxed at 2.35:1]
US DVD distributor: VCI (released on 26 October 1999). Rating: none. Running time: 98 minutes [Uncut, though a portion of one scene has been edited out of sequence. Re-released with corrected print 2001] [2.35:1 / stereo] [extras: theatrical trailer]

Il gatto a nove code / The Cat O'Nine Tails
Italian video distributor: Creazioni Home Video. Rating: 14. Running time: 107 minutes
Italian video distributor: Club Del Video.
Italian video distributor: Mondadori Video. Running time: 111 minutes. [uncut] Cat No. MVEC03043.
French DVD distributor: TFI Video. [2.35:1] [extras: trailer; interview]
Canadian video distributor: Cinema Home Theater. Running time: 112 minutes. [Full screen]
French video distributor: SVP,Cinema Consiel.
Greek video distributor: AV Enterprises.
Hungarian video distributor: Mokep. Running time: 107 minutes. [Letterboxed]

Japanese video distributor: Columbia Video. Running time: 112 minutes. [Letterboxed]
Japanese laserdisc distributor: Sony. Running time: 112 minutes. [Letterboxed]
Japanese laserdisc distributor: Toshiba. Running time: 112 minutes. [Letterboxed]
Japanese DVD distributor: Culture Publishers. Running time: 112 minutes. [Letterboxed at 2.00:1, Dolby 2.0 Italian language, optional Japanese subtitles]
UK video distributor: Warner Home Video (released in September 1996). Rating: 18. Running time: 107 minutes 25 seconds [Full frame, no BBFC cuts]. catalogue number: S 011699
US video distributor: Bingo Video. Running time: cut to less than 90 minutes.
US video distributor: Timeless Video Inc. Running time: 112 minutes. Rating: PG.
US DVD distributor: Anchor Bay. Running time: 112 minutes. [Uncut 2.35:1 anamorphic widescreen, English Dolby 2.0 surround, French and Italian Dolby mono, Exclusive 14 minute interview with Argento, Morricone and Sacchetti, Radio interviews, TV spots, Radio spots, Stills gallery, Talent bios]
Spanish video distributor: Manga Video S.L. Running time: 111 minutes. [Letterboxed at 2.35:1, Spanish language]

4 mosche di velluto grigio / Four Flies on Grey Velvet
Belgian video distributor: Metropole. Running time: 95 minutes. [Letterboxed]
French video distributor: Melisa Video.(released as: Quatre mouches de velours gris). [Letterboxed]
French video distributor: Atlantic.(released as: Quatre mouches de velours gris). [Letterboxed]
Greek video distributor: Sunset Video. [French language with Greek subtitles]
US video distributor: Silver Star. Running time: 93 minutes 27 seconds.

Le cinque giornate
Italian video distributor: Azzurra Home Video. rating: none. Running time: 126 minutes.
French video distributor: Scherzo.

Profondo rosso / Deep Red
Italian video distributor: Domovideo. rating: 14. Running time: 123 minutes. [Letterboxed, end music cuts abruptly] Cat No. 04250
Italian video distributor: Mondadori. Running time: 120 minutes. [Widescreen, Italian language]
Australian video distributor: 7 Keys;Force. Running time: 101 minutes.
Australian video distributor: Cinema Italia. Running time: 121 minutes. [Italian language, English subtitles]
Danish video distributor: Unknown (released as: Mordets Melodi). Running time: 96 minutes. [Letterboxed]
Dutch video distributor: Unknown. [Cut, letterboxed]
Dutch video distributor: Movies Select Video. Running time: 100 minutes 27 seconds. [Widescreen, English language with Dutch subtitles]
European video distributor: Silver Star. Running time: 93 minutes 27 seconds. (NOTE: This is an English language bootleg) [Letterboxed]
French video distributor: VIP 'Genius Collection'. (released as: Les Frissions de

---

This guide to video releases of Dario Argento films, though as comprehensive as possible, is not intended to be a complete summary of all available releases. Note that many of the entries referred to here have been deleted. However, it should prove to be a useful guide to most of the commonly available variants of Argento's films in circulation. Nick Dawe of the Dark Dreams website (www.darkdreams.org) has completely updated this section of the filmography for this latest edition of Art of Darkness.

langoisee). [Full screen, pan & scan]
French video distributor: Jet Video. (released as: Les Frissions de langoisee). [Full screen, pan & scan]
French video distributor: Proserpine Video. (released as: Les Frissions de langoisee). [Full screen, pan & scan]
German video distributor: Unknown. [English language, probably the shorter version]
Japanese video distributor: Columbia Video.(released as: Profondo Rosso).
Japanese laserdisc distributor: Columbia. (released as: Suspiria 2). Running time: 105 minutes. [Letterboxed, English language, Japanese subtitles]
Japanese laserdisc distributor: Beam Entertainment. (released as part of the 'Spectral Collection' in a box set with Suspiria)
Japanese DVD distributor: Culture Publishers. Italian language.
UK video distributor: Redemption Films Ltd. (released in September 1993). Rating: 18. Running time: 121 minutes 9 seconds [BBFC cuts of 11 seconds, a shot of 2 fighting dogs (4s) and a shot of a lizard impaled on a needle (7s). Italian language, full screen, English subtitles] catalogue number: RETN 015
UK video distributor: Techno Film/Fletcher (released in October 1982). rating: none. Running time: 100 minutes 32 seconds. catalogue number: V.188
US video distributor: Thorn EMI. (released as: The Hatchet Murders). [Cut, full screen]
US video distributor: HBO Video Inc. Rating: none. Running time: 100 minutes. catalogue number: TVC 1428
US laserdisc distributor: MCA Home Video (released in 1994). catalogue number: 41941
US DVD distributor: Anchor Bay. Running time: 126 minutes. Rating: none. [Full version, anamorphic widescreen 2.35:1, Dolby 5.1 and 2.0 soundtracks. (Where English language soundtrack is missing, reverts to Italian with subtitles), 25th Anniversary featurette with Argento and members of Goblin, Italian theatrical trailer, U.S. theatrical trailer, biographies]
US DVD distributor: Anchor Bay. (released as part of two disc set with Tenebre comprising of the seperate Anchor Bay releases in different packaging)
Swedish video distributor: Baroness. [Cut, full screen]

Suspiria

Italian video distributor: Ricordi Video. Rating: 14. Running time: 95 minutes.
Italian video distributor: ViViVideo.
Italian video distributor: Columbia Tristar.
Italian video distributor: CDE.
Italian DVD distributor: 20th Century Fox. [Uncut, 2.35:1 anamorphic widescreen transfer supervised by Luciano Tovoli. Dolby 5.1 Italian, Dolby 2.0 English]
Australian video distributor: Thorn EMI. [Uncut]
Bahrain video distributor: Video Dynamic.
Dutch video distributor: Best Video. [Cut, letterboxed at 1.77:1]
French DVD distributor: TFI Video. [2.35:1, French version (stereo) and Italian with French subtitles version (mono), Argento interview, poster gallery, internet link]
French video distributor: SVP.
Greek video distributor: Videosonic. [Cut, letterboxed]
Hungarian video distributor: Mokep.
Japanese laserdisc distributor: Unknown.
Japanese laserdisc distributor: Beam Entertainment. (released as part of the 'Spectral Collection' in a box set with Deep Red)
Japanese DVD distributor: Culture Publishers. [Uncut, widescreen, English

language, Japanese subtitles (selectable), mono, theatrical trailer, 'highlights' reel]
Polish DVD distributor: Imperial. Running time: 93 minutes.
Swedish DVD distributor: Hemvideo. [Cut]
UK video distributor: Thorn EMI. Rating: none. Running time: 94 minutes 0 seconds. (Slightly cut X certificate version). catalogue number: TVB 90 0265 2
UK video distributor: Nouveaux Pictures (released in May 1998). Rating: 18. Running time: 94 minutes 13 seconds [Uncut, letterboxed, stereo]. catalogue number: NP0016
UK DVD distributor: Nouveaux Pictures. Rating: 18. Running time: 94 minutes 13 seconds [Uncut, letterboxed, stereo. Incorrectly states on the packaging that it contains a filmography and stills gallery]
UK video distributor: Entertainment in Video Ltd. (released circa 1990). Rating: 18. Running time: 93 minutes 48 seconds [cut as UK cinema version, i.e. no further cuts for video]
US video distributor: Magnum Entertainment (released in November 1989). Rating: R. Running time: 92 minutes. catalogue number: 3203.
US video distributor: Magnum Entertainment (released in November 1989). Rating: none. Running time: 98 minutes. catalogue number: 3204.
US laserdisc distributor: Image Entertainment (released in 1990). Rating: none. Running time: 97 minutes. [Uncut, widescreen 2.35:1, original 4.0 channel surround, US and European trailers] catalogue number: ID6900MN
US video distributor: Fox Lorber. [Uncut, widescreen]
US video distributor: Quality Video. Running time: Cut to 90 minutes. [Pan & scan, recorded in EP mode]
US DVD distributor: Anchor Bay. Rating: none. Running time: 97 minutes. [Anamorphic widescreen 2.35 :1, THX approved, English DTS ES 6.1, English Dolby EX surround sound, English Dolby 2.0 surround, French Dolby 2.0 surround, Italian Dolby 2.0 surround, theatrical trailers, TV spot, Radio spots, Daemonia music video, Poster and Stills gallery, talent bios]
US DVD distributor: Anchor Bay. Rating: none. Running time: 97 minutes. (released as limited edition 3 disc set). [Anamorphic widescreen 2.35 :1, THX approved, English DTS ES 6.1, English Dolby EX surround sound, English Dolby 2.0 surround, French Dolby 2.0 surround, Italian Dolby 2.0 surround, theatrical trailers, TV spot, Radio spots, Daemonia music video, Poster and Stills gallery, talent bios, 52 minute interview with cast and crew, original soundtrack CD]

Inferno

Italian video distributor: Domovideo - CBS/Fox Video. Rating: 14. Running time: 100 minutes. [Uncut full version] cat no. 0114015
Australian video distributor: Fox Video. Running time: 102 minutes. (cover reports 79 minutes)
Danish video distributor: CBS/Fox Video. (released as: Raedslernes Inferno)
Russian video distributor: Viking Video. Running time: 106 minutes.
UK video distributor: Fox Video Ltd. (released in May 1993). Rating: 18. Running time: 101 minutes 48 seconds (BBFC cuts of 20 seconds). [Letterboxed] catalogue number: WC 1140
UK video distributor: CBS/Fox Video Ltd. (released circa 1987). Rating: 18. Running time: 101 minutes 37 seconds. [BBFC cuts of 28 seconds].
UK video distributor: CBS/Fox Video (released in September 1982). Rating: none. Running time: 102 minutes 8 seconds. catalogue number: 1140-50
US video distributor: CBS/Fox Video [thru Key Video]. Rating: R. Running time: 83 minutes. catalogue number: 1140.
US video distributor: Key Video. Running time: 107 minutes. [Uncut, incorrect running time reported on packaging (89m)]
US DVD distributor: Anchor Bay. Rating: none. Running time: 106 minutes. [Widescreen 1.85:1, Dolby 5.1, Dolby 2.0, trailer, stills gallery, featurette, introduction by Argento]
US DVD distributor: Anchor Bay. Rating: none. Running time: 106 minutes. [Part of two disc set with Phenomena comprising of the separate releases in different packaging]

Tenebrae / Tenebre

Italian video distributor: Creazioni Home Video/Mondadori Video. Running time: 99 minutes.
Italian video distributor: Club Del Video. [Uncut, letterboxed]
Australian video distributor: Palace Explosive. Running time: 96 minutes 49 seconds. [Pan & scan]
Austrian DVD distributor: Sazuma. [1.85:1, uncut, Dolby 5.1, interview with Argento, deleted scenes, trailer]
Bahrain video distributor: Unknown. Running time: 96 minutes 27 seconds. [Letterboxed, English language, Arabic subtitles]
Belgian video distributor: Belga Films. Running time: 96 minutes 44 seconds. [Letterboxed except for the scene showing Peter Neal cycling to the airport. French/Dutch subtitles]
Danish video distributor: Warner/Metronome. (released as: Tenebrae - Terror uden Graenser). [Cut - the arm chopping is shorter, full screen]
Dutch video distributor: Thorn EMI.
French video distributor: SVP. (released as: Tenebres)
French video distributor: Planete Video/Film Office . (released as: Tenebres)
French video distributor: Rene Chateau. (released as: Tenebres) Running time: 95 minutes 12 seconds. [no end credits]
French DVD distributor: TFI Video. [1.85:1, French language, Italian language, or English language with French subtitles (mono), 20 minute interview with Argento, screensaver, internet link]
German video distributor: VPS.
Greek video distributor: Home Video Hellas. Running time: 96 minutes. [Letterboxed]
Greek video distributor: Videosonic. [Uncut, letterboxed]
Japanese laserdisc distributor: Columbia. Running time: 101 minutes 53 seconds. [Letterboxed]
Japanese DVD distributor: Culture Publishers. [Italian language, Japanese subtitles]
Russian video distributor: Viking Video. Running time: 101 minutes.
Spanish video distributor: Manga Video S.L.
Swedish video distributor: Sonet. (released as: Tenebrae - Terror Utan Grns). [Heavily cut, letterboxed]
UK DVD distributor: Nouveaux Pictures. Rating: 18. [cut by 4 seconds and incorrectly framed at 1.66:1]
UK video distributor: Videomedia/Vampix (released in August 1983). Rating: X. Running time: 96 minutes 48 seconds. [Letterboxed at 1.60:1] catalogue number: HVM 1032
UK video distributor: Nouveaux Pictures (released in September 1999). Rating: 18.

Running time: 96 minutes 20 seconds (BBFC cuts of 5 seconds). [Letterboxed] catalogue number: NP 0026
US video distributor: Media Home Entertainment (released in July 1987). Rating: R. Running time: 91 minutes. catalogue number: FR 006
US video distributor: Fox Hills.(released as: Unsane). Running time: Cut to 91 minutes. [Different end credit music (a Kim Wilde track)]
US laserdisc distributor: Roan Group. Running time: 100 minutes 32 seconds. [Some footage is missing due to frame jumps, commentary by Argento and Simonetti, letterboxed, theatrical trailer, remixed into Chace Digital Stereo]
US DVD distributor: Anchor Bay (released as 'Tenebre' on 16 March 1999) Rating: none. Running time: 101 minutes (uncut but with some missing segments due to print damage). [1.85:1, Dolby 5.1, audio commentary with Argento, Claudio Simonetti & Loris Curci, Behind the scenes footage, alternate end credit music, theatrical trailer]
US DVD distributor: Anchor Bay. (released as part of two disc set with Deep Red comprising of the seperate Anchor Bay releases in different packaging)

Phenomena / Creepers
Italian video distributor: Creazioni Home Video/Mondadori Video. Rating: 14. Running time: 110 minutes.
Australian video distributor: Palace Explosive. Running time: 105 minutes 19 seconds. [Full screen]
Danish video distributor: Unknown.
Dutch video distributor: EVC. Running time: 105 minutes 15 seconds. [Slightly letterboxed]
Finnish video distributor: Inferno Video. Running time: Possibly full 116 minute version?. [Letterboxed]
German video distributor: Dragon Entertainment. Running time: 116 minutes. [Two disc set. Disc 1: Uncut 1.85:1 widescreen 'integral' version, Dolby surround, English, German and Italian language, English, German and Dutch subtitles, filmographies, trailers. Disc 2: Interviews with Argento, Claudio Simonetti, Luigi Cozzi, 2 music video's, live Simonetti piano rendition of theme music, behind the scenes featurette, Phenomena and Jennifer Connelly picture galleries]
Japanese laserdisc distributor: ABC. Running time: 116 minutes 08 seconds. [Full screen, Italian language, Japanese subtitles, surround sound, 2 music videos. Termed the 'integral hard' release and includes the Luigi Cozzi documentary 'World of Horror 3']
Japanese DVD distributor: Culture Publishers. 115m [matted widescreen, stereo, Italian language, Japanese subtitles, trailers, music clips]
Russian video distributor: Viking Video. Running time: 111 minutes.
Spanish video distributor: Manga Video S.L.
Swedish video distributor: Prisma Film and Video. Running time:105 minutes 08 seconds. [Slightly cut for violence]
UK video distributor: Palace Video (released circa 1986). Rating: 18. Running time: 79 minutes 31 seconds [BBFC cuts 17 seconds]
UK DVD distributor: Divid 2000. Running time: 111 minutes. [Uncut, widescreen, mono, behind the scenes segment, interviews with Argento and Simonetti. (missing advertised commentary track with Goblin). Taken from French print]
US video distributor: Media Home Entertainment. Rating: R. Running time: 82 minutes. catalogue number: M831
US laserdisc distributor: Roan Group. Running time: 110 minutes. [With commentary by Argento, Sergio Stivaletti and Claudio Simonetti]
US video distributor: EVC. Running time: 117 minutes.
US DVD distributor: Anchor Bay (released on16 March 1999). rating: none. Running time: 109 minutes 47 seconds [1.66:1, 5.1 Dolby Digital soundtrack , audio commentary by Argento, Sergio Stivaletti, Claudio Simonetti & Loris Curci, behind the scenes footage, TV interview with Argento by Joe Franklin, music videos with Simonetti & Bill Wyman, theatrical trailer]
US DVD distributor: Anchor Bay. (released as part of two disc set with Inferno comprising of the separate Anchor Bay releases in different packaging)
West German video distributor: New Vision (released on 17 February 1988). Running time: 83 minutes.

Opera / Terror at the Opera
Italian video distributor: Vivivideo. Rating: 14. Running time: 105 minutes. [Full screen]
Italian DVD distributor: Cecchi Gori. Running time: 103 minutes. [1.85:1, Dolby surround 2.0, Italian language]
Australian video distributor: First Release. Running time: 91 minutes 55 seconds. (dialogue scenes cut by 11 minutes 20 seconds)
Danish video distributor: Unknown.
Dutch video distributor: RCA/Columbia. Running time: 93 minutes. cat No. CVT11559
French video distributor: GCR. (released: Terreur a l'opera).
Japanese video distributor: RCA/Columbia. [Full screen]
Japanese laserdisc distributor: RCA/Columbia. [Full screen]
Russian video distributor: Soyuz Video. Running time: 106 minutes.
UK video distributor: Virgin Vision (released circa 1991). Rating: 18. Running time: 91 minutes 5 seconds [BBFC cuts of 47 seconds]
US video distributor: Southgate Video. Running time: 107 minutes. Rating: none. [HiFi stereo]
US DVD distributor: Anchor Bay. Rating: none. [Anamorphic widescreen 2.35 :1, THX approved, English DTS ES 6.1, English Dolby EX surround sound, theatrical trailers, 36 minute documentary, Daemonia music video, 8 page booklet, talent bios]
US DVD distributor: Anchor Bay. Rating: none. (released as limited edition 2 disc set). [Anamorphic widescreen 2.35 :1, THX approved, English DTS ES 6.1, English Dolby EX surround sound, theatrical trailers, 36 minute documentary, Daemonia music video, 8 page booklet, talent bios, original soundtrack CD]
West German video distributor: RCA/Columbia Video (released on 5 December 1989). Running time: 87 minutes.

Due occhi diabolici / Two Evil Eyes
Italian video distributor: Manzotti Home Video. Rating: 14. Running time: 112 minutes.
Danish video distributor: Unknown. (released as: Chok Pa Chok).
German DVD distributor: Unknown.
Russian video distributor: Viking Video. Running time: 121 minutes.
US video distributor: Media Home Entertainment (thru Fox Video) (released on 23 April 1992). Rating: R. Running time: 105 minutes.
UK video distributor: Medusa Communications Ltd. (released circa 1990). Rating: 18. Running time: 114 minutes 59 seconds [no BBFC cuts]

Trauma
Italian video distributor: Penta Video. Rating: none. Running time: 105 minutes 1 seconds. catalogue number: 1028301
Dutch video distributor: CNR Film & Video.
German video distributor: VPS Film Entertainment. (released as: Aura). Running time: 104 minutes. [Widescreen, mono. All the gore is intact but some incidental footage is missing]
Japanese DVD distributor: Culture Publishers. [Full screen, English language, Dolby 2.0, optional Japanese subtitles]
Russian video distributor: Ekaterinburg Art Home Video. Running time: 102 minutes.
Russian VCD distributor: Unknown. [2 disc VCD set]
UK video distributor: Tartan Video Ltd. (released in September 1999). Rating: 18. Running time: 101 minutes 54 seconds [BBFC cuts of 7 seconds]. catalogue number: TTV 2206
UK video distributor: High Fliers Video Distribution (released on 27 April 1994). Rating 18. Running time: 101 minutes 53 seconds [BBFC cuts of 6 seconds]. catalogue number: HFV 8261
US video distributor: Worldvision Home Video/Republic Pictures (released on 23 March 1994). Rating: unrated & R. Running time: 106 minutes. [EP or SP speed modes]
US laserdisc distributor: World Wide Distribution/Republic Pictures. Running time: 106 minutes. Rating: none. [Full screen]

La sindrome di Stendhal / The Stendhal Syndrome
Italian video distributor: Medusa Video. Rating: 14. Running time: 114 minutes 31 seconds. catalogue number: 1048601
Dutch DVD distributor: Dutch Film Works. Running time: 120 minutes. [Uncut, anamorphic widescreen 1.66:1, English/Dutch Dolby 2.0, 'World of Horror' documentary as an extra]
French DVD distributor: Pioneer. Running time: 120 minutes. [1.85:1, uncut, Dolby surround 2.0, English and French language, trailer]
Japanese video distributor: Columbia Video. [Full screen]
Japanese laserdisc distributor: Unknown. [Uncut, widescreen]
Russian video distributor: Agma/Paradis. Running time: 106 minutes.
Swedish video distributor: Sandrew Metronome. Running time: 112 minutes.
UK video distributor: Marquee Pictures (released in September 1998). Rating: 18. [Letterboxed] catalogue number: MQ 0139
UK video distributor: Fox Guild Home Entertainment (released on 25 February 1997). Rating: 18. Running time: 110 minutes 42 seconds. 2 minutes 47 seconds pre-cut by the distributor. [Full screen] catalogue number: G8891
UK DVD distributor: Marquee Pictures. Rating: 18. [1.33:1, Dolby surround 2.0] 1st issue uncut (black and white label on disc). 2nd issue cut (disc label is printed in colour). catalogue number: DUK 0056
US DVD distributor: Troma (released on 7 March 2000). Rating: none. Running time: 120 minutes [matted full screen print, interviews with Argento & Lloyd Kaufman, theatrical trailer, various Troma stuff]

Il fantasma dell'opera / The Phantom of the Opera
Italian video distributor: Medusa Video. Rating: 14. Running time: 98 minutes 53 seconds.
Italian DVD distributor: Medusa. Running time: 106 minutes. [Uncut, 1.85:1 anamorphic widescreen, Dolby 5.1 Italian and English, behind the scenes featurette, talent bios, trailer]

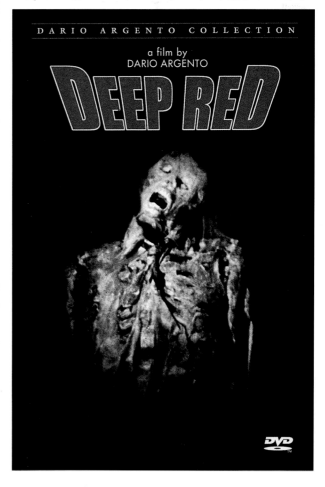

Danish DVD distributor: On Air Video. [Directors cut, widescreen]
French DVD distributor: TFI Video. [Cut, letterboxed, Italian and French language, English subtitles]
Russian video distributor: ORT-Video. Running time: 103 minutes.
Swedish video distributor: Sandrew Metronome. Running time: 100 minutes.
US DVD distributor: A-Pix (released on 30 November 1999). Rating: none. Running time: 103 minutes. [two options: 2.35:1 and 1.33:1, English Dolby 5.1, interview with Julian Sands, behind the scenes footage, article from Fangoria magazine, theatrical trailer]

Nonhosonno / Sleepless
Italian DVD distributor: Medusa. Running time: 113 minutes. [Uncut 1.77:1 anamorphic widescreen, English and Italian Dolby 5.1, Italian DTS, English and Italian subtitles, 15 minute 'making of...' featurette, trailer, talent bios]

Oggi a me... domani a te / Today it's Me... Tomorrow You!
Italian video distributor: Lineafilm. rating: none. Running time: 93 minutes.
UK video distributor: Aktiv (released in November 1995). Running time: 90 minutes 43 seconds.
US video distributor: Commtron. Rating: PG. Running time: 102 minutes. catalogue number: PSM 2872.

Commandos / Sullivan's Marauders
Italian video distributor: Creazoni Home Video. Rating: none. Running time: 112 minutes.
UK video distributor: Guild Home Video Ltd. thru MSD Video Ltd. Rating: 15. Running time: 93 minutes 52 seconds. catalogue number: 93272
UK video distributor: Guild Home Video Ltd. (released in November 1980). Rating: none. Running time: 93 minutes 54 seconds. catalogue number: GH 015
US video distributor: Congress Video Group. Rating: PG. Running time: 89 minutes. catalogue number: 03500
US DVD distributor: D-Vision (released on 10 February 1998). Rating: PG. Running time: 89 minutes. [1.33:1]

C'era una volta il west / Once upon a Time in the West
Italian video distributor: Ricordi Video. Rating: none. Running time: 175 minutes.
UK video distributor (sell-thru): Paramount Home Video (released circa 1995). Rating: 15. Running time: 158 minutes 32 seconds [Letterboxed]
UK video distributor: CIC Video (released circa 1989). Rating: 15. Running time: 158 minutes 27 seconds.
UK video distributor: CIC Video (released in April 1983). Rating: none. Running time: 158 minutes 27 seconds. catalogue number: VHL 2059
US video distributor: Paramount Home Video (released in May 1991). Rating: PG. Running time: 165 minutes.
US laserdisc distributor: Paramount Home Video (released in 1985). Rating: R. Running time: 166 minutes. catalogue number: LV6830

Probabilità zero / Probability Zero
Italian video distributor: Durium. Rating: none. Running time: 90 minutes.
UK video distributor: Xtasy Video (released circa 1987). Rating: 15. Running time: 88 mins 57 seconds (no BBFC cuts).
UK video distributor: Home Video Merchandisers (released in August 1982). Rating: none. Running time: 89 minutes 9 seconds. catalogue number: VMH 023

Una corde, un colt / Cemetery without Crosses
Italian video distributor: Golden Video. Rating: none. Running time: 90 minutes.
UK video distributor: Fletcher Video (released in July 1982). Rating: none. Running time: 86 minutes 56 seconds. catalogue number: V. 165

Metti, una sera a cena
Italian video distributor: Domovideo. Rating: 18. Running time: 121 minutes.

La legione dei dannati / Battle of the Commandos
Italian video distributor: Creazioni Home Video. Rating: none. Running time: 102 minutes.
UK video distributor: VideoForm Pictures (released in November 1982). Rating: none. Running time: 89 minutes 58 seconds. catalogue number: MGS 11

Un esercito di 5 uomini / The Five Man Army
UK video distributor: MGM/UA Home Video (released in June 1984). Rating: 15. Running time: 101 minutes 4 seconds. catalogue number: UMV 10286

Dawn of the Dead / Zombi
Italian video distributor: Playtime. Rating: 14. Running time: 120 minutes.
Dutch DVD distributor: Dutch Film Works. Rating: 16. [two disc set. disc 1: Romero's cut, widescreen. Disc 2: Argento's cut, full screen. Dutch, Swedish, Norwegian, Danish and Finnish subtitles, 'document of the dead' documentary, biographies, filmographies, trailer, gallery]
UK video distributor: Entertainment in Video Ltd. (released circa 1989). Rating: 18. Running time: 120 minutes 8 seconds (BBFC cuts of 12 seconds in addition to original cinema cuts).
UK video distributor: Intervision Video Limited (released in December 1981). Rating: none. Running time: 120 minutes 14 seconds. catalogue number: A-A 0358
US video distributor: HBO Video, Inc. (released in September 1989). Rating: none. Running time: 126 minutes.
US video distributor: Warner Home Video (released in September 1991). Rating: none. Running time: 126 minutes.
US laserdisc distributor: Image Entertainment (released in 1989). catalogue number: ID6683HB
US lasediisc distributor: Republic Pictures Home Video (released in 1993). catalogue number: LV25831
US DVD distributor: Anchor Bay. Running time: 137 minutes. Rating: none. [1.66:1 widescreen, mono, theatrical trailers] cat no: DV10325

Demoni / Demons
Italian video distributor: Creazioni Home Video/Mondadori Video. Rating: 18. Running time: 104 [?] minutes.
German DVD distributor: Dragon Entertainment. Running time: 88 minutes. [1.66:1,

English and German Dolby surround 2.0, German and Dutch subtitles, 2 interview segments with Argento, theatrical trailer, filmographies]
UK video distributor: Caleco Direct Videog (released in August 1996). Rating: 18. Running time: 83 minutes 53 seconds (no further BBFC cuts). catalogue numner: CALD 2
UK video distributor: Avatar Communications Ltd. (released circa 1987). Rating: 18. Running time: 83 minutes 52 seconds (BBFC cuts of 1 minute 5 seconds).
US video distributor: Anchor Bay Entertainment (released in 1992). Rating: none. Running time: 94 minutes.
US video distributor: New World Video (released in March 1988). Rating: R. Running time: 89 minutes.
US laserdisc distributor: Image Entertainment (released in 1988). Rating: R. Running time: 89 minutes. catalogue number: ID5200NW
US DVD distributor: Anchor Bay (released on 16 March 1999). Rating: none. Running time: 88 minutes. [1.66:1, Dolby 5.1, audio commentary by Lamberto Bava, Sergio Stivaletti & Loris Curci, behind the scenes footage, theatrical trailer]

Demoni 2... L'incubo ritorna / Demons 2
Italian video distributor: Creazioni Home Video. Rating: 14. Running time: 88 minutes.
German DVD distributor: Dragon Entertainment. Running time: 88 minutes. [1.85:1, English and German Dolby surround, 2 featurettes, theatrical trailer, filmographies]
UK video distributor: Caleco Direct Video (released in August 1996). Rating: 18. Running time: 87 minutes 27 seconds (no BBFC cuts). catalogue numner: CALD 4
UK video distributor: Avatar Communications Ltd. (released in November 1987). Rating: 18. Running time: 87 minutes 28 seconds (no BBFC cuts).
US video distributor: Best Film & Video Corp. (released in February 1995). Rating: R. Running time: 88 minutes.
US video distributor: Imperial Entertainment (released in April 1988). Rating: R. Running time: 88 minutes.
US laserdisc distributor: Image Entertainment (released in 1994). catalogue number: ID2473IP
US DVD distributor: Anchor Bay (released on 16 March 1999). Rating: none. Running time: 91 minutes. [1.66:1, Dolby 5.1, audio commentary by Lamberto Bava, Sergio Stivaletti & Loris Curci, theatrical trailer]

La chiesa / The Church
Italian video distributors: Vivivideo/Cecchi Gori Home Video. Rating: 18. Running time: 97 minutes.
UK video distributor: First Independent Films Ltd. (released circa 1993). Rating: 18. Running time: 97 minutes 44 seconds (no BBFC cuts).
US video distributor: South Gate Entertainment (released on 30 January 1991). Rating: R. Running time: 110 minutes. catalogue number: 1069

La setta / The Sect / The Devil's Daughter
Italian video distributors: Penta Video / Cecchi Gori Home Video. Rating: 14. Running time: 112 minutes 7 seconds. catalogue number: 1013201
UK video distributor: Genesis Home Video (UK) Ltd. (released circa 1995). Rating: 18. Running time: 111 minutes 49 seconds (no BBFC cuts).
UK video distributor: Marquee Pictures (released in February 1999). Rating: 18. Running time: 111 minutes 49 seconds. catalogue number: MQ 00021
US video distributor: Republic Pictures Home Video (released on 2 January 1992). Rating: R. Running time: 112 minutes. catalogue number: VHS 1012
US laserdisc distributor: Republic Pictures Home Video (released in 1992). Running time: 112 minutes. catalogue number: LV21012

M.D.C. Maschera di cera / The Wax Mask
UK video distributor: Film 2000 (released on 20 October 1997). Rating: 18. Running time: 94 minutes 11 seconds (no BBFC cuts). catalogue number: FM 2003
Dutch DVD distributor: Video Film Express BV. Rating: none. [Letterboxed, Dolby surround 2.0, English and Italian language, Dutch subtitles]

Scarlet Diva
Italian video distributor: Minerva Video. rated: 14. running time: circa 87 minutes. catalogue number: MVB 20025

World of Horror Il meglio di Dario Argento / Dario Argento's World of Horror
Italian video distributor: Edizioni Star Video. Running time: 75 minutes.
UK video distributor: Arthouse Productions Ltd. (released in December 1995). Rating: 18. Running time: 69 minutes 41 seconds (no BBFC cuts). catalogue number: AHF 2003
US video distributor: Trimark Pictures (released in August 1989). Rating: none. Running time: 77 minutes.
US laserdisc distributor: Image Entertainment (released in 1989). Running time: 77 minutes. catalogue number: ID6701VK
US DVD distributor: Synapse (released on 14 July 1998). Rating: none. Running time: 71 minutes [1.33:1, Argento filmography]

Protagonisti del cinema italiano Dario Argento
Italian video distributor: Edizioni Eagle Home Video. Running time: 60 minutes.

Il mondo di Dario Argento 2 / Dario Argento Master of Horror
Italian video distributor: Edizioni Eden Video. Running time: 90 minutes.
UK video distributor: Missing in Action (released in late 1993). Rating: 18. Running time: 80 minutes 8 seconds (BBFC cuts of 39 seconds).

Julian Grainger would like to thank the following people, without whose generosity and patience the various elements of this filmography could not have been drawn together: Bill Connolly, Luigi Cozzi, Roberto Curti, Nick Dawe, Harvey Fenton, Kris Gavin, Mike Lebbing, Adrian Luther-Smith, Alexander Marlow-Mann, Stephen Thrower and Alan Tozer...

and it's about time Mr Marc Morris was awarded a knighthood for services to film...

Bibliography

The following is intended as a guide to some of the texts that have contributed towards to the contents of this volume. While it includes a small selection of entries that relate directly to the films of Dario Argento, the majority of the books and articles referred to below pertain to literary and film theory, a number of which have been referred to directly in the text of *Art of Darkness*. Those wishing to stay abreast of developments in all things related to Dario Argento would be well advised to read *Shivers* magazine (UK), which is usually first with news in print about new Argento movies thanks to its monthly column by Alan Jones. *Fangoria* (USA) and the web site *www.darkdreams.org* are also fine sources.

Abel, Richard: *French Film Theory and Criticism vol.1* (Princeton University Press, Princeton, 1988)
Ahmed, Rollo: *The Black Art* (Senate, London, 1994)
Barthes, Roland: *S/Z* (Jonathan Cope Ltd, London, 1974)
Barthes, Roland: *Image-Music-Text* (Fontana, London, 1982)
Bonitzer, Pascal: *Décadrages* (Cahiers du Cinema/Editions de l'Etoile, Paris, 1987)
Bordwell, David: *Narration in the Fiction Film* (University of Wisconsin Press, USA, 1985)
Bronfen, Elizabeth: *Over Her Dead Body* (Manchester University Press, UK, 1992)
Carroll, Noel: *The Philosophy of Horror* (Routledge, New York and London, 1990)
Clover, Carol: *Men, Women and Chainsaws* (BFI, London, 1991)
Copjec, Joan: *Supposing The Subject* (Verson, London, 1994)
Creed, Barbara: *The Monstrous Feminine* (Routledge, London, 1993)
Dayan, Daniel: 'The Tutor Code Of Classical Cinema', *Film Quarterly*, v.28 n.1, Fall 1974
Dijkstra, Bram: *Idols of Perversity* (Oxford University Press, New York, 1986)
Edmundson, Mark: *Nightmare on Main Street: angels, sadomasochism and the culture of Gothic* (Harvard University Press, USA, 1997)
French, Todd: 'Dario Argento: Myth and Murder' in *The Deep Red Horror Handbook*, edited by Chas Balun (FantaCo Books, New York, 1989)
Freud, Sigmund: *Art and Literature* (Penguin, UK, 1985)
Fulcanelli: *Le Mystere des Cathedrales* (Brotherhood of Life, New Mexico, 1991)
Girard, Rene: *Violence and the Sacred* (Johns Hopkins University Press, Baltimore and London, 1977)
Grant, Barry Keith: *Planks of Reason: Essays on the Horror Film* (Scarecrow, N.J, and London, 1984)
Hardy, Phil: Horror - *The Aurum Film Encyclopedia* (Aurum Press Limited, UK, 1993)
Hunt, Leon: 'A (Sadistic) Night At The Opera: Notes On The Italian Horror Film', *The Velvet Light Trap*, n.30, Fall 1992
Jones, Alan: 'Opera' in *Cinefantastique*, vol .8 n.2-3, March 1988
Jones, Alan: 'Sunday in the Park With Dario' in *Shivers*, n.8, August 1993
Jones, Alan: *Mondo Argento* (Midnight Media, UK, 1996)
Jones, Alan: 'Dario Argento's The Phantom of the Opera' in *Shivers*, n.54, June 1998
Jones, Ernest: *On the Nightmare* (Hogarth, London, 1931)
Kaplan, E. Ann, *Women And Film* (Methuen & Co, London, 1983)
Kaplan, E. Ann: *Psychoanalysis & Cinema* (Routledge, New York and London, 1990)
Kwietniowski, Richard: 'Separations: Chantal Akerman's News From Home and Toute une nuit' in *Movie*, n.34-5, Winter 1990
Magherini, Graziella: *La Sindrome di Stendhal* (Ponte Alle Grazie, Florence, 1995)
Martin, John: *Dario Argento - A Deep Red Opera* (Fantasy Film Memory, France, 1991)
McDonagh, Maitland: *Broken Mirrors, Broken Minds: The Dark Dreams Of Dario Argento* (Sun Tavern Fields, London, 1991)
Mendik, Xavier: 'Upon the Eyelids of Ophelia: The Sexual 'Fragment' of Trauma' in *Necronomicon*, n.7
Moir, Patricia: 'Aesthetics of Ambiguity' in *Cinefantastique*, vol.27 n.8, April 1996
Palmerini, Luca and Mistretta, Gaetano: *Spaghetti Nightmares* (M&P edizioni, Italy, 1996)
Poe, Edgar Allan: *The Unabridged Edgar Allan Poe* (Running Press, USA, 1983)
Rank, Otto: *The Double* (New American Library, New York, 1979)
Rauger, Jean-Francois: 'Dario Argento Decrypté' in *Cahiers du Cinéma*, n.493
Sage, Victor/Lloyd Smith, Allan: *Modern Gothic* (Manchester University Press, Manchester, 1996)
Silverman, Kenneth: *Edgar A. Poe: A Mournful and Never-Ending Remembrance* (Weidenfield and Nicolson, London, 1992)
Stam, Robert: *New Vocabularies in Film Semiotics* (Routledge, London, 1992)
Torok, Jean-Paul: 'Look At The Sea: Peeping Tom', *Powell, Pressburger And The Others*, edited by Ian Christie (British Film Institute, London, 1978)
Vincendeau, Ginette: 'Unsettling Memories' in *Sight & Sound*, vol.5 n.7, July 1995
Williams, Linda Ruth: 'An Eye For An Eye', *Sight & Sound*, v.4 n.4, April 1994
Wollen, Peter, 'Dying For Art', *Sight & Sound*, vol.4 n.2, December 1994
Yates, Frances: *Giordano Bruno and the Hermetic Tradition* (The University of Chicago Press, Chicago, 1991)

Dario and Asia Argento during the filming of **Phenomena**

Index

~ fine ~